D1207494

CONVERTIBLE SECURITIES

A COMPLETE GUIDE TO INVESTMENT AND CORPORATE FINANCING STRATEGIES

Tracy V. Maitland
F. Barry Nelson, CFA
Daniel G. Partlow

NEW YORK CHICAGO SAN FRANCISCO ATHENS LONDON MADRID
MEXICO CITY MILAN NEW DELHI SINGAPORE SYDNEY TORONTO

1 2 3 4 5 6 7 8 9 LCR 27 26 25 24 23 22

ISBN 978-1-260-46290-6
MHID 1-260-46290-0

e-ISBN 1-978-1-260-46291-3
e-MHID 1-260-46291-9

This publication is designed to provide accurate and authoritative information in regard to the subject matter covered. It is sold with the understanding that neither the author nor the publisher is engaged in rendering legal, accounting, securities trading, or other professional services. If legal advice or other expert assistance is required, the services of a competent professional person should be sought.
—*From a Declaration of Principles Jointly Adopted by a Committee of the American Bar Association and a Committee of Publishers and Associations*

Library of Congress Cataloging-in-Publication Data

Names: Maitland, Tracy V., author.
Title: Convertible securities : a complete guide to investment and
    corporate financing strategies / Tracy V. Maitland, F. Barry Nelson, Daniel
    G. Partlow.
Description: 1 Edition. | New York : McGraw Hill, 2022. | Includes
    bibliographical references and index.
Identifiers: LCCN 2021038779 (print) | LCCN 2021038780 (ebook) |
    ISBN 9781260462906 (hardback) | ISBN 9781260462913 (ebook)
Subjects: LCSH: Convertible securities. | Convertible preferred stocks. |
    Convertible bonds. | Portfolio management.
Classification: LCC HG4652 .M35 2022 (print) | LCC HG4652 (ebook) |
    DDC 332.63/2044--dc23/eng/20220104
LC record available at https://lccn.loc.gov/2021038779
LC ebook record available at https://lccn.loc.gov/2021038780

McGraw Hill is committed to making our products accessible to all learners. To learn more about the available support and accommodations we offer, please contact us at accessibility@mheducation.com. We also participate in the Access Text Network (www.accesstext.org), and ATN members may submit requests through ATN.

<Art credits or permissions info or referral to a credits section at the back of the book>

McGraw Hill books are available at special quantity discounts to use as premiums and sales promotions or for use in corporate training programs. To contact a representative, please visit the Contact Us pages at www.mhprofessional.com.

CONTENTS

FOREWORD

Luckily for me, my career as a money manager started off in convertibles. In 1978, when it was time for me to move on after roughly ten years in equity research at First National City Bank, my boss asked me what I wanted to do next. I responded that I was "open to doing anything other than spend the rest of my life choosing between Merck and Lily." I firmly believe that some markets are quite efficient, meaning consensus views – and thus security prices – tend to instantaneously reflect the available information. This makes it hard for investors to regularly identify mispricings and profit from them. To me, the market for large-capitalization stocks was and is such a market, and few people are able to consistently add value there by choosing among those stocks.

In one of the many examples of the good luck from which I've benefitted, my boss answered, "I'd like you to shift to the bond department and run a convertible securities fund." I did so, starting with the princely sum of $16 million (which seemed like a great deal of money at that time). I went from being director of research with a $5 million budget, 75 staff members and membership on the five most senior committees… to working with no budget, no staff and no committee seats . . . and I was thrilled.

The convertibles market was an investing backwater: small and followed by few. Convertibles were and still are little known and little understood. They're hybrid securities with some of the characteristics of debt and some of equities, and for this reason they entail substantial complexity. Because of this hybrid nature, they don't fit easily into most institutional investors' "buckets" – asset allocation categories that have to be filled with securities meeting their definition; thus there are few natural buyers. And because issuing them requires companies to give up features of both debt and equity, they tended 40+ years ago to be issued as a last resort by companies in disrespected industries like conglomerates that had few alternatives.

Most people look at securities with these characteristics and see reasons not to get involved. But for me, the characteristics made convertibles highly attractive. How do investors make superior risk-adjusted big money? In general, by doing things others don't want to do. Companies and securities with obvious merit tend to be thoroughly understood, attractive to all, hotly pursued and thus fully priced. That's not a great description for a place to look for bargains. It's often in areas that are affected by ignorance and prejudice that bargains can best be found, and for me that meant convertibles.

The investment world of 44 years ago was very different from that of today. There were no computerized data bases (and no personal computers through which to search them). There was no reporting of trading in convertibles. There was little performance data. Even the understanding of how to make money with less-than-commensurate risk was fragmentary and not widely possessed.

Warren Buffett talks about having been able to buy dollars for fifty cents. The convertibles market described above presented opportunities for me to do so (albeit not to his extent). There were securities no one knew about and few understood. Thus, there were opportunities to earn high returns without risk, and certainly without commensurate risk. The ability to make money without bearing risk is what we call a "free lunch," and the efficient market hypothesis I studied in graduate school said such opportunities shouldn't exist. But in a little-known backwater like convertibles, they could and they did.

Also fortunately for me, I met Tracy Maitland in my early years as a manager of convertibles, when Merrill Lynch hired him to provide sales coverage to "buy-side" clients like me. We worked together closely and happily, and I felt I could rely fully on the fact that he "got it" and would give me the benefit of his honest opinion. Few people understand convertibles in the depth he does, as he shares through this book. I'm glad to endorse both Tracy and his excellent book.

And, by the way, convertibles remain a relatively unexploited investment backwater. I commend them to your attention.

Howard Marks
January 9, 2022

PREFACE

How would you like to invest your personal money? Convertible securities have provided equity-like total returns for decades with much less risk than outright ownership of common shares of stock. Investing in convertibles is effectively a strategy of winning by not losing because convertibles provide positive asymmetry relative to equities—in many cases capturing the majority of the upside of common stocks while losing far less on the downside. Convertible securities are especially attractive during uncertain times. Undoubtedly, even during times of economic uncertainly, convertible securities have proven to be exceptionally resilient and often outperformed common stocks during volatile periods.

Yet, the opportunities in convertible securities have gone virtually unnoticed by most investment institutions as well as individual investors and financial advisors. Moreover, improvements in the structures of convertibles in recent years appear to have been ignored. Shorter maturities enhance the downside protection of convertibles, improved call protection enhances the likelihood of participation in appreciation of the underlying stocks, and contemporary indentures protect convertible investors from potential losses in the event of changes in control or increases in common dividends.

Convertibles represent a compelling asset class for all investors, and it's time for a comprehensive analysis of convertibles that will clearly explain the advantages and mechanics of convertible securities—from the perspectives of issuing companies as well as investors.

My entire career has emphasized convertible securities. I first gained insights into the attractions of convertibles shortly after I graduated from Columbia University in 1982 and joined Merrill Lynch as a fast-track management trainee. I rotated to departments throughout the firm—including investment banking, sales and trading (which included convertibles, equities, and corporate and municipal bonds), and securities research (where I worked with world-renowned emerging-growth companies analyst Larry Rader). I even worked in the Washington, DC, lobbying office, which focused on securities laws and regulations.

The valuable insights I gained as a trainee inspired me to work in the overlooked convertible securities department. I could not understand why more investors did not invest in convertibles. The concept of capturing a majority of the upside from common stocks while taking only a portion of the downside risk seemed irresistible. I concluded that few investors were aware of the convertible asset class, and as such, I set out to educate investors about convertibles—and I've been doing it ever since. This book is my latest effort.

My success in convertibles took off when Merrill Lynch transferred me to the Detroit institutional office to market convertibles and equity derivatives. I had been mentored by Charles Wright, who was the manager of the New York institutional equity sales office. He recognized the value of convertible securities as an asset class. When Wright was promoted to manage the newly established Great Lakes region of Michigan, Ohio, and Kentucky, he encouraged me to come to Detroit.

The local sales manager in the Detroit office didn't fully appreciate convertibles or equity derivatives. He knew of no major convertible investors in the Great Lakes area; however, I'm not sure that he ever asked the question. And as a result, he suggested that I should have stayed in New York or gone to Boston "where they do those sophisticated strategies." I quickly discovered that one of the largest institutional investors in convertibles was only two floors below the Merrill Lynch office in the Renaissance Center: Lee Munder was a senior portfolio manager at Loomis Sayles. He founded Munder Capital Management in 1985, and his new firm soared to a peak of more than $50 billion in assets under management in 2000.[1]

I saw an opportunity to advise local bank trust departments, insurance companies, asset managers, and corporate and public pension funds on convertibles and equity derivatives. Bank trust departments and insurance companies in many ways were ideal investors in convertible securities. The typical trust clients were high-net-worth individuals who sought income and worthwhile total returns while preserving capital—people who were already wealthy, so generally speaking, they were less inclined to take larger risks, exactly what convertible securities would provide. Despite these facts, I seemed to be the only person marketing convertibles to trust departments. Soon, I had the majority of the institutional market for convertible sales of the trust departments in the Great Lakes territory.

I recognized that the investment needs of insurance companies also could be fulfilled with convertible securities. The insurance companies were conservative and risk averse, and they sought income with rewarding total returns. Insurance companies were soon subjected to risk-based reserve requirements that imposed lower reserves on debt securities than on equities, which made investment in convertibles more capital efficient than investing directly in common stocks—particularly in the context of the long-term total returns from convertibles that were equivalent to the returns from common equities, but with significantly less risk.

As I worked with local trust departments, insurance companies, and other institutions and advised them on the merits of convertible securities as well as equity derivatives, in just a few years the Detroit office generated the second-largest revenues among institutional satellite offices across the Merrill Lynch convertibles platform. Because I had created a market where there had previously been none, Merrill Lynch sent institutional sales personnel from other regions such as the West Coast and Atlanta for me to train.

My progress was in the context of Merrill Lynch becoming the dominant investment bank in convertible securities. Options Marketing Manager Lee Cole proposed a new type of convertible bond in 1983 that evolved into what Merrill Lynch called a Liquid Yield Option Note or LYON.[2] The LYONs were original-issue-discount zero-coupon bonds that provided yields by accretion to par. Exceptionally strong downside protection was provided by multiple interim puts at accreted prices.

The new LYON structure was a breakthrough for investors at a time when many convertibles had maturities as long as 25 to 30 years, which muted the downside protection. The first LYON was issued by Waste Management in April 1985 at a price of $250 with a maturity at $1,000 in 2001 for a yield to maturity of 9.0%. But this was no ordinary 16-year bond. With the first put in three years at $301.87 and with subsequent annual puts accreting toward par, investors in the new LYON had minimal downside risk—and Waste Management was an investment-grade credit. Each bond was convertible into 4.36 shares. With Waste Management shares trading at around $52, the conversion value of 4.36 shares was about $227; that is, investors in the new bond were paying a conversion premium of only 10% more than the market value of the shares into which the bond could be converted. These terms were very attractive to investors.

The LYONs were very attractive to issuing corporations as well—partly because of tax advantages. Although the LYONs had no cash coupons, the accretion to par was annually tax deductible for the issuing companies. Better still for the issuers, if the bonds converted, the non-cash accretion that had been deducted for tax purposes was never paid to the bondholders. This was an especially attractive tax structure at a time when interest rates were high—and the tax savings were a major reason why high-quality tax-paying companies issued LYONs. Of course, taxable investment accounts had to pay cash taxes on the non-cash accretion, but these taxes could easily be deferred by buying the LYONs for individual retirement accounts (IRAs) or other tax-deferred accounts.

Merrill Lynch was regarded as a retail-oriented "wire house" at the time, yet the innovative LYONs quickly attracted institutional investors and enabled Merrill Lynch investment bankers to win entrée to major corporations, including Fortune 400 companies that had traditionally relied on "white shoe" investment banks. Merrill Lynch Capital Markets quickly cultivated and developed new institutional relationships with large corporate banking clients as a result of its dominant position in the convertible market. Indeed, this became a terrific calling card and helped establish Merrill Lynch investment banking as a thought leader in finance.

The LYONs dramatically raised the profile of the Merrill Lynch convertible unit and raised my personal profile high enough to enable access to CEO David Komansky. By the end of 1991, Merrill Lynch had underwritten 43 LYONs that raised $11.7 billion.[3] The success of the LYON structure led to underwritings of other varieties of convertibles and was highly accretive to the firm's entire investment banking business. Soon the Merrill Lynch convertible securities department dominated new issuance and aftermarket trading of convertibles and became one of the firm's most profitable units.

As the increasingly popular LYONs gained share of the new issue market for convertibles, other investment banks began to shorten maturities of new issues of convertibles in an effort to retain their convertible underwriting business in competition with Merrill Lynch. The more LYONs that Merrill Lynch issued, the more the firm became the undisputed leader in convertible investment banking as well as sales and trading of convertibles. Merrill Lynch ultimately had the most resources and infrastructure on Wall Street dedicated to convertibles sales, trading, and research. The firm had 17 marketing representatives globally, the most capital allocated to trading convertibles, and a dedicated publishing research team as well as convertible desk analysts. The firm even created the Merrill Lynch convertible indices, which became the primary standard by which convertible managers were benchmarked.

The indices were sold by Bank of America Merrill Lynch to ICE Data Services in 2017. The firm had not imagined that the indices would become a stand-alone business. The indices had been developed as a methodology for benchmarking managers in this overlooked asset class and perhaps in anticipation of creating an index product. Even today these indices are the most comprehensive and flexible tools to understand and appreciate convertible investment performance.

The ultimate investment consequence of the creation of LYONs was to shorten the maturity schedule of the convertible market and vastly improve the downside protection of convertible securities relative to equities. The convertible asset class earned a stamp of approval in 1987 when Warren Buffett's Berkshire Hathaway negotiated an investment in Salomon Brothers in the form of a private convertible. Then, in 1989, Berkshire invested in USAir via another private convertible. Buffett's fame as an investor gave credibility to the concept of achieving equity-like returns at lower risk from convertibles.

There were approximately 500 people on the Merrill Lynch trading floor in New York in the 1980s, of whom only approximately 30 were on the convertibles desk. Yet, the convertible department commanded almost 70% of the capital allocated to trading—which reflected not only the high profitability of convertibles but also the effectiveness of hedging convertible positions by shorting the underlying stock and overlaying various derivatives.

During this time of dramatic growth for the Merrill Lynch convertibles department, I was transferred back to New York to replace the top convertible marketer, who had joined Michael Milken at his Drexel Burnham office in Beverly Hills, where Milken specialized in convertibles as well as high-yield bonds. In my new role in New York, I was the most senior marketer on the distribution side of the convertibles desk. I also ran the global convertible distribution team for a while, and at the same time, was able to advise major institutional investors throughout the United States as well as in Europe and the Middle East, and developed a broad perspective on the way convertibles were perceived around the world. My global client base helped me understand how different investors used and took advantage of this overlooked and inefficient asset class.

I also gained the advantage of working face-to-face with the head of the convertibles trading desk, Harlan Korenvaes, who was an astute convertible trader and risk arbitrageur. He picked me up every morning at my apartment, and we began our day early on the FDR Drive on the way to Wall Street. Our day ended when he dropped me off in the evening. We spent almost every waking hour evaluating convertibles in our growing franchise. Korenvaes founded HBK Capital Management in 1991, which grew to more than $5 billion in assets under management by the time of his retirement in 2003,[4] after which he established Korenvaes Management and Korenvaes Capital Management, both of which he continues to serve as CEO.[5] Korenvaes remains a successful manager of alternative investments.

I functioned as the major link between institutional investors and the LYONs. As the top producer on the convertibles desk, I was promoted to director in the Capital Markets Division, and in fact, I was one of the top producers in the firm—arguably, I was number one because the marketer who was ahead of me had an entire team working on his production numbers, whereas my number was mine alone.

An important early investor in LYONs was Howard Marks of Trust Company of the West (now called TCW Group), who was a visionary in convertible investing. He helped launch the LYON product. Marks became a major client. In 1995, he founded Oaktree Capital Management, which invests in convertibles as well as securities across the entire capital structure. Oaktree had grown to $148 billion in assets under management as of year-end 2020.[6] When I founded Advent Capital Management, I sought Marks's counsel, and he was instrumental in advising me on the organization and development of the firm.

The opportunities I saw in convertible securities inspired me to found Advent Capital Management in September 1995. I started with less than $50 million under management, and the firm has since grown to become one of the largest money-management firms that emphasizes convertible securities. The firm has approximately $11 billion in assets under management for clients across the United States and around the world as of 2021.

My co-authors and I have long experience in convertibles and other asset classes, and we have successfully navigated through turbulent market cycles. In this book, we endeavor to educate readers on the basics of convertibles as well as the advanced quantitative theories that explain the superior performance of convertible securities—a high-value-added asset class with a unique record of achieving equity-like returns with less risk than outright investment in common stocks. I continue to feel passionate about convertibles—as I have since essentially the beginning of my investment career. Convertibles constitute a rewarding asset class that is understood by few investors.

Tracy V. Maitland
September 30, 2021

ACKNOWLEDGMENTS

The authors enjoyed the support and encouragement of their families during the two years of extracurricular work on this book. We would like to thank Von M. Hughes who encouraged the authors to embark on this project of writing this book on convertibles. We were also enthusiastically aided by our associates, who studied our drafts and contributed many insightful enhancements. These efforts took place while we worked remotely during the COVID-19 pandemic and navigated through record returns from convertibles and record issuance of new convertibles.

Members of our firm who made exceptional contributions include Andrew Rice, Art Richardson, Bob White, Chung Tam, Craig Altshuler, David Hulme, Dave Moore, Dominique Terris, Doug Melancon, Drew Hanson, Ed Delk, Fernando Crespo, Francois Berlioz, Harini Chundu, Ian Mahoney, Kevin Zhao, Madison Brown, Mark Piazza, Michael Miller, Odell Lambroza, Pablo Avila, Paul Latronica, Randi Weitz, Scott Reid, Thomas Cui, and Tony Huang.

Beyond our firm, we were assisted by many insightful denizens of the investment world, including Abigail Adams, Andrew Pratt, Anthony Cichocki, Arthur Ryan, Beat Thoma, Dilip Kotian, Greg Brenneman, Howard Marks, Irina Vilboa, Jack Kawa, Jason Zweig, Jill Baker, Joel Tillinghast, Lawrence Cavanagh, Marty Fridson, Michael Youngworth, Oliver Corlett, Paul Berkman, Paul Robinson, Preston Peacock, Rick Nelson, Roy Brady, Tarun Vanjani, Tatyana Hube, and Venu Krishna.

We three co-authors are proud to have been associated with Advent Capital Management for a combined total of more than 60 years and counting—constantly deepening our knowledge of convertible securities.

ENDNOTES

1. Diya Gullapalli, "A Fund That May Be Forgettable," *Wall Street Journal*, October 3, 2006, https://www.wsj.com/articles/SB115921512811973383.
2. John J. McConnell and Eduardo S. Schwartz, "The Origin of LYONs," *Journal of Applied Corporate Finance* 1992;4(4): 42.
3. *Ibid.*, p. 40.
4. https://www.hbk.com/history.
5. https://www.crowholdings.com/team/harlan-b-korenvaes-bo-d.
6. htts://www.oaktreecapital.com/about.

CHAPTER 1

Introduction to Convertible Securities

Equity-like Returns with Less Risk

[Convertible securities are] the most attractive of all in point of *form*, since they permit the combination of maximum safety with the chance of unlimited appreciation in value.

—*Benjamin Graham et al.*[1]

1.1 CONVERTIBLE SECURITIES

The primary attraction of convertible securities is positive asymmetry: the tendency of a convertible to capture more of the upside than the downside when the underlying common stock appreciates or declines. Over the long-term, convertible returns have been essentially identical with the returns from equities, with less risk than outright investments in common stocks. In this chapter, we explain the favorable asymmetry of convertible bonds. In later chapters, we analyze the sophisticated quantitative models that practitioners use to evaluate convertibles.

1.2 CONVERTIBLE BONDS

It has a kind of "heads I win, tails I don't lose" quality.

—*Railroad Age Gazette*[2]

The most common type of convertible security is the convertible bond. The key feature of a basic convertible bond relative to a non-convertible bond is that the convertible can be converted into a fixed number of common shares in the issuing company. Hence, if the underlying stock appreciates, the bond ultimately must track the stock upward.

Yet, the convertible is a *bond*, so it usually pays interest (albeit at a lower rate than an equivalent non-convertible bond), and it matures at face value (called *par*). A bond is inherently less risky than common stock.

The conversion feature is exercisable at the discretion of the holder, and conversion typically occurs only when the bond reaches maturity or when the issuing company announces a call[3] or other redemption for cash at face value. If the underlying stock has appreciated sufficiently to make converting more valuable than the typical $1,000 face value of the bond, then holders of the convertible will convert. If the conversion value is less than $1,000, then holders will accept the cash redemption. These two outcomes are the basis of positive asymmetry. Most convertibles can be called prior to maturity, but typically call protection lasts for three years or more. Many convertible bonds—especially issues with maturities of five years or less—cannot be called or have *soft* call protection (explained in Section 1.6.3) that prevents a call until the conversion value has risen to perhaps 130% of par.

A simple example would be a convertible bond issued with a maturity of five years, an interest rate of 2%, and a *conversion premium* of 25%. The interest rate is easy to envision: 2% per annum paid at six-month intervals with 1% *coupons*.[4] The conversion premium of 25% in this example means that the $1,000 price of the bond at issuance is 25% higher than the market value of the number of underlying common shares into which the bond is convertible.

We can calculate the conversion value simply by dividing $1,000 by (1 + the conversion premium), or $1,000/1.25 in this example, which gives us a conversion value of $800. If the underlying stock were trading at $40, the $800 conversion value would be achieved by a *conversion ratio* of 20 shares. The *conversion price*—also known as the *exercise price* or *strike price*—of the 20 shares would be $50 (25% above the market price at issuance of the convertible bond).

The conversion price tells us the market value of the stock that will ultimately dictate whether the holders of the bond will accept cash redemption or convert the bond into the underlying common stock because the conversion value—also known as *parity*—will exceed the face value of the bond if the stock price is above the conversion price. With a conversion premium of 25%, the conversion value of this bond—the price of the underlying stock—will have to rise more than 25% to exceed the face value of the bond and thereby make conversion more profitable than cash redemption.

The conversion ratio is an essential measure after a newly issued convertible begins to trade because the price of the underlying stock will fluctuate. Using the conversion ratio, we can readily update the conversion value—or parity—that is, the market value of the shares into which the bond is convertible.

If the stock is trading below the $50 conversion price when our hypothetical convertible bond is due to be redeemed at face value for $1,000 cash, the conversion value of the 20-share conversion ratio will be short of the $1,000 face value of the bond, and the bondholders will accept the cash redemption at $1,000 par rather than convert. At the end of the five-year life of this 2% bond, holders will have received a total of 10 percentage points (or $100) in interest as well as the $1,000 face value of the bond *regardless of how low the stock has dropped*—except in the unlikely event that the issuer has gone bankrupt.

If the underlying stock performs strongly, the conversion feature means that the convertible must participate in the appreciation of the stock. If the stock doubles to $80 a share, the value of the 20 shares into which the bond may be converted will be $1,600; hence, the holders will convert, and the total return over the five years since issuance will be a capital gain of 60% plus 10% in interest. This would equal a total return of 70% versus the 100% return for holders of the common shares. We assume no common dividends. The issuers of convertibles are usually growth companies that pay no dividends. Only 38% of the convertible issuers in the ICE BofA All-Convertibles Index (ticker VXA0) paid common dividends as of year-end 2020.

The minimum 10% simple total return over the five years to maturity of the convertible bond means that the bond will match the return from the stock if the stock appreciates 10%. The combination of interest plus redemption at maturity will *exceed* the return from the stock if the shares are up less than 10%. If the stock rises more than 10%, of course, the convertible will underperform the stock. Yet, there is no limit to how much appreciation can be captured by the convertible because the right to

Table 1.1   Outcomes to Maturity of 5-Year 2% Convertible Issued at a Premium of 25%

Stock Appreciation	Convertible Appreciation	Interest	Convertible Total Return	Convertible Return as % of Stock Return
200%	140%	10%	150%	75%
100%	60%	10%	70%	70%
50%	20%	10%	30%	60%
40%	12%	10%	22%	55%
25%	0%	10%	10%	40%
20%	0%	10%	10%	50%
10%	0%	10%	10%	100%
0%	0%	10%	10%	NMF

NMF No Meaningful Figure
Data: Bloomberg.

convert is independent of the price of the underlying shares. The downside is muted by the interest payments and the guarantee of cash redemption at maturity.

The examples of total returns in Table 1.1 assume that the convertible bond was purchased at issuance and held until maturity. For the sake of simplicity, we have ignored compounding of the semi-annual 1% coupons.

The most rewarding performance from a convertible bond relative to the gains or losses from the stock occurs at the extremes, that is, if the stock does poorly or if the stock does very well. The fact that the stocks of convertible issuers tend to have high volatility (and the issuing companies tend to exhibit high growth) suggests that extreme outcomes are common. Figure 1.1 shows the price dynamics of a convertible bond (but ignores yields). Toward the upper right corner of the chart, the convertible will rise as the stock appreciates. Toward the lower left corner, if the stock drops, the price of the convertible will tend to be supported by its basic *bond value*.

The earliest convertibles—issued by eighteenth-century British and French colonial monopolies such as the East India Company and the Mississippi Company and then by nineteenth-century railroads (see Chapter 3 for US history)—generally were issued by companies with

Figure 1.1 Convertible price dynamics

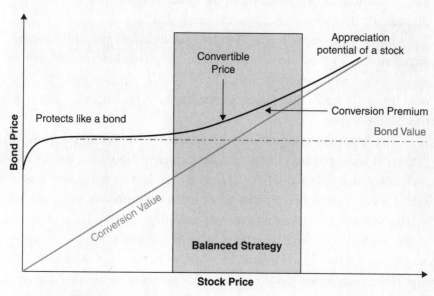

Source: Advent Capital Management, LLC.

explosive growth potential that required capital. This pattern has continued with twenty-first-century US issuers of convertibles enjoying faster
revenue growth than Standard and Poor's 500 (S&P 500) Index companies
as a whole.[5] In today's liquid capital markets, securities are rarely held for
long periods, and investing is dominated by institutions that are judged
by short-term performance, so it's important for institutional investors in
convertibles to project what might occur in the near term. Projecting interim gains and losses from convertible securities is an essential purpose
of quantitative convertible evaluation models.

In an optimistic scenario, a convertible bond will almost never
trade for less than its conversion value because arbitrageurs would lock
in a gain by simultaneously buying the convertible bond and shorting the
shares into which the convertible could be converted. (During market
panics and in some foreign jurisdictions, short selling may be restricted,
in which case convertibles sometimes trade below conversion value, a
bargain for traditional *long-only* investors.) Under normal circumstances,
there is almost never a reason to exercise the conversion right of a convertible
bond prior to cash redemption because an in-the-money convertible will

always participate in the upside of the underlying stock, and a convertible usually provides some downside protection.

Yet, there is no free lunch. The price that investors pay for the conversion feature is a lower interest rate than the capital market would accept on an equivalent non-convertible bond. In 2020–2021, interest rates on some new issues in the United States dropped to zero, and negative rates appeared in Europe.

The lower interest rate is advantageous to the issuing company, of course, as is the prospect of future conversion at a higher stock price than when the convertible was issued. The "free" element for a company that issues a convertible is the volatility of the underlying stock. The convertible market will accept a lower interest rate and a higher conversion premium if the stock is volatile. The sale of volatility costs the issuing company neither cash nor anything else that appears in its financial statements. *All convertible evaluation models confirm that the theoretical value of a convertible is higher with higher volatility.* (See Chapters 8 and 9 for details on quantitative evaluations of convertibles.)

Volatility of the underlying stock is attractive to investors because it suggests greater potential for the stock to surge into the money. Volatility also suggests greater risk that the stock will tumble, but convertibles inherently provide downside protection, and from the perspective of a convertible arbitrageur—typically short the underlying stock—a *decline* in the stock is also a way to make a profit.

In a downside scenario, the market price of a convertible bond may drop below face value if the stock price declines and, hence, the conversion value declines. Yet, in most cases, the bond declines less than the underlying stock. The resulting discount from par value reflects the fact that convertible bonds are issued with interest rates lower than the rates on equivalent *straight* (non-convertible) bonds. Of course, convertible bonds—like non-convertible bonds—eventually are redeemable for cash at face value.

The same negative factors that cause the underlying stock to go down may impair the financial strength of the company, which means that the market will require a wider *credit spread*—that is, a higher yield relative to the yield on US Treasury bonds of similar duration[6]—which can only be obtained by the market price of the convertible declining.

1.3 CONVERTIBLE PREFERRED STOCKS

Convertible preferred stocks were commonplace decades ago when individual investors were more active in trading individual convertibles rather than investing in convertibles via mutual funds and exchange-traded funds (ETFs). The conversion feature of traditional convertible preferreds is identical to that of convertible bonds.

Few convertible preferreds have been issued since the Great Financial Crisis (GFC) of 2008–2009, partly because regulatory changes have caused banks to cease issuing convertible preferreds, which previously boosted regulatory capital. Two very high-yielding bank convertible preferreds were issued before the GFC and play a role in the performance of the $413 billion US convertible securities market (2020)[7] due to their size and high dividend yields: the Bank of America 7.25% convertible preferred and the Wells Fargo 7.5% convertible preferred each have a face value of approximately $4 billion and have appreciated as high as 150% of par ($1,500) as market interest rates declined. The market prices of the Bank of America and Wells Fargo preferreds reflect 130% soft call protection (see Section 1.6.3). Each of these issues made up approximately 1.4% of the US convertible market at year-end 2020. Traditional convertible preferreds (excluding mandatory preferreds—see Section 1.4) constituted only 4% of the US convertible market as of February 2021.[8]

Convertible preferreds are almost always registered with the Securities and Exchange Commission (SEC) and trade on stock exchanges, which makes preferreds readily accessible to individual investors. As with other shares—and unlike most convertible bonds—convertible preferreds usually can be traded electronically.

Preferreds are equities rather than credit obligations, so passing the dividends (unlike missing an interest payment on a bond) does not constitute a default. Passing a preferred dividend usually requires first passing the issuer's common dividend, however, and financial issuers are reluctant to reduce common dividends to zero lest their creditworthiness be in doubt; hence, the dividends on such issuers' preferreds have an implicit degree of safety. (During the GFC, Bank of America cut its quarterly common dividend from 60 cents in 2007 to a token 1 cent in 2009 rather than pass its common dividend, and it maintained the dividends on the 7.25% convertible preferred.) As bonds are debt instruments, they have a higher priority in bankruptcy recovery. Preferreds merely rank in the penultimate position from the bottom of the capital structure, just above common shares. Hence, convertible preferreds pay higher yields than convertible bonds of the same issuer.

Convertible preferreds rarely have a maturity date (with the exception of trust preferreds, which often mature in 30 to 50 years), which means that downside protection from convertible preferreds is weak. Yet, convertible preferreds—like bonds—are callable, so upside potential may be limited by early redemption at the discretion of the issuing company.

Taxable accounts benefit from the Internal Revenue Service (IRS) tax characterization of most US preferred dividends as qualified dividend income (QDI), which is taxed at a rate equivalent to that of capital gains. Most preferred dividends qualify for the dividends received deduction (DRD) for C corporations.[9]

From an issuer's perspective, the advantage of preferreds is equity rather than debt. Preferred dividends, however, are not tax deductible—whereas bond interest usually is tax deductible. Trust preferreds, however, are essentially debt instruments from the tax perspective of both issuers and investors[10] but are similar to traditional (non-trust) preferreds in terms of the risk that the quarterly "dividends" may be passed without inducing bankruptcy. Trust preferreds are given partial equity treatment by credit-rating agencies.[11]

An example of a trust preferred is the New York Community Bank 6%, which has 125% soft call protection. As a trust preferred, which depends on a debt instrument within its structure, the New York Community Bank 6% preferred has a 50-year maturity at $50 face value in 2051.

1.4 MANDATORY CONVERTIBLES

The most common type of convertible preferred in 2021 is the mandatory convertible preferred—invented in 1988—which automatically converts into the underlying common stock, nearly always after three years. Like traditional convertible preferred shares, mandatory preferreds are typically registered with the SEC and are listed on a stock exchange, so all types of investors can easily trade mandatory preferreds. Additionally, mandatory preferreds are treated as equity by credit-rating agencies. Mandatory preferreds differ from both traditional convertible preferreds and from convertible bonds in four key respects: (1) conversion is mandatory, not at the discretion of the investor,[12] (2) there is no cash maturity if the underlying stock fails to perform, (3) the conversion ratio is based on a sliding scale that reduces the ratio to prevent upside price participation during the first 25% or so of appreciation of the underlying stock above its price at issuance of the mandatory, and (4) mandatory convertibles pay the highest yields of any type of convertible securities other than contingent convertibles (see Section 1.7.4).

A new mandatory always yields more than the underlying stock—and mandatory convertibles are almost always issued by large companies that pay common dividends. Mandatory convertibles were an American invention but have gained some popularity in Europe.

The drawback of a typical mandatory is that it suffers full downside price participation—a delta of 100%—if the underlying stock is below the price at issuance at the time of mandatory conversion. Hence, the yield advantage does not promise a positive return over the life of a mandatory, unlike the ultimate positive return from a convertible bond that pays interest and is redeemable in cash at face value at maturity.

The upside price participation of a mandatory is limited by the automatic sliding-scale reduction of the conversion ratio when the stock price is in the *dead zone*, which eliminates participation in appreciation of the underlying common stock until it has risen, usually by 25%, after which the conversion ratio will have been reduced to only 80% of the initial conversion ratio. Once the stock appreciates beyond the dead zone—up more than 25% in our example in Table 1.2—the total return of the mandatory (including the dividend advantage) is typically more than half the total return from the stock.

Mandatory preferreds provide some extra downside price protection if the underlying stock has appreciated into the dead zone because *on the way down* the conversion ratio automatically *rises* to maintain the original issuance conversion value until the stock is below its price at issuance of the mandatory, after which the mandatory is exposed to 100% of further depreciation of the underlying stock. (See total return chart in Figure 1.2.) The downside protection of a mandatory at issuance is provided by the yield advantage over the underlying common stock during the three years until mandatory conversion.

A mandatory convertible is structured in such a way that in the after-market it may exhibit *negative* asymmetry; that is, a mandatory convertible will sometimes suffer a greater percentage of the downside if the underlying stock retreats than it will participate in the upside if the underlying stock continues to appreciate, particularly as the mandatory approaches the mandatory conversion date. From an issuer's perspective, a mandatory convertible is essentially a way to issue common stock in a format that avoids the debt liability of a convertible bond or the longer-term commitment of a traditional convertible preferred while being assured that the convertible will automatically convert into the underlying common stock even if the stock declines. Hence, a mandatory convertible preferred may be an important component of the capital structure of the issuing company. Issuance of a mandatory convertible more closely resembles a secondary offering of common shares than it does the issuance of a convertible bond or a traditional convertible preferred, yet, the issuance of a mandatory is not likely to generate the potentially negative publicity that might result from an offering of common shares.

A typical mandatory convertible preferred might be issued with a 25% conversion premium. If it were priced at $100 with the underlying stock at $50 at issuance, then the initial conversion ratio would be 2.0. The 25% premium would mean that the conversion ratio would be adjusted so that the conversion value of the mandatory would not exceed $100 until the stock had risen more than 25%. That is, the conversion ratio would be reduced to 1.6 as the stock rose 25% to $62.50, so the conversion value would effectively be capped at $100 unless the stock was up more than 25% at the time of mandatory conversion. On the downside, however, the mandatory would convert into the initial conversion ratio of 2.0 shares if the stock was trading at $50 or less at the time of mandatory conversion, after which downside price participation would be 100% of a decline in the price of the underlying stock below $50.

Even in a low-rate environment, most mandatory preferreds have been issued with distribution rates around 5% to 6%, so we feel that it is realistic to assume a yield at issuance of 6% versus a common dividend of 3%. Table 1.2 shows simple three-year total returns (ignoring compounding) under various scenarios for our hypothetical mandatory convertible. The examples of total returns in Table 1.2 assume that the mandatory

Table 1.2 Outcomes over the Three-Year Life of a Mandatory Convertible

Stock Return + 3% Dividends	Convertible Appreciation	Convertible Dividends 6%	Convertible Total Return	Convertible Return as % of Stock Return
100% + 9% = 109%	60%	18%	78%	72%
50% + 9% = 59%	20%	18%	38%	64%
25% + 9% = 34%	0%	18%	18%	53%
10% + 9% = 19%	0%	18%	18%	95%
0% + 9% = 9%	0%	18%	18%	NMF
–10% + 9% = –1%	–10%	18%	8%	NMF
–25% + 9% = –16%	–25%	18%	–7%	28%

NMF No Meaningful Figure
Data: Bloomberg.

convertible was purchased at issuance and held for the three years until mandatory conversion.

Over the three-year life of a typical mandatory—as shown in Table 1.2—the issue will capture most of the upside total return in a strong upward movement of the underlying common stock. If in three years the common stock is below the price at issuance, the mandatory will suffer 100% of the price decline of the stock, but it will lose 9 percentage points less than the stock because of the yield advantage.

Figure 1.2 charts the potential payoffs of our hypothetical mandatory from issuance to the end of its three-year life, that is, a simple return of 18% from the 6% dividend rate if the stock price is unchanged at maturity, bracketed by downside projection on the left and upside on the right.

At issuance, it is reasonable to expect three years of quarterly dividends before the mandatory convertible preferred automatically converts into common stock, and the 12 quarterly dividends typically provide rewarding positive assymetry of total return relative to the total return of the underlying stock (as shown in Figure 1.2). As the remaining life of a mandatory shortens, however, the yield advantage that contributes to positive asymmetry *in the total return* dissipates as the remaining dividends dwindle to the final quarterly dividend just before mandatory conversion; hence, the yield advantage—and the consequent contribution to

Figure 1.2   Total return of a hypothetical mandatory convertible in three years

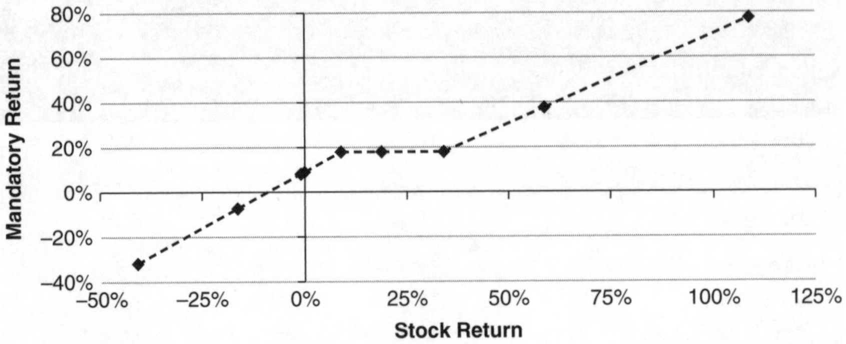

Data: Bloomberg.

asymmetry—favors investing in mandatory convertibles in the first half of the three-year life. Sometimes individual investors and even financial advisors become confused about the yield of mandatory preferreds.

Until recent years, some mandatory preferreds had a fixed conversion ratio with a capped upside. This structure has become rare, if not extinct.

Mandatory convertible preferreds are often called *equity units* because the securities incorporate a note or a preferred share as well as a contract to buy the underlying shares. Mandatory "dividends" are almost always taxed as interest by the IRS (unlike the tax-favored Qualified Divicend Income (QDI) for individuals, and the Dividends Received Deduction (DRD) for corporations, that typify the tax character of traditional convertible preferred dividends). Only 2 of 35 US mandatory convertibles provided QDI as of the end of 2020.[13]

There is a tax advantage for the issuer, however, because the tax character of most distributions from mandatory preferreds is *tax-deductible interest*. Most mandatory preferreds are *units* that, like trust preferreds, incorporate a debt security that collects US tax-deducible interest from the issuing company. Some mandatory preferreds are characterized by the IRS as original issue discount (OID) instruments, in which case the issuing company will be able to deduct a greater amount from taxable income than the amount of the quarterly distributions, and taxable holders of the mandatory will be liable for income taxes on a greater amount than the cash distributions received.

The returns from mandatory convertibles are similar to the returns from a *buy-write transaction*, in which one buys an out-of-the-money call option and simultaneously *writes* (i.e., sells or shorts) an in-the-money call. Because the out-of-the-money call costs a *premium* that is less than the proceeds of the premium from writing the in-the-money call, there is net premium income—which effectively pays for the quarterly distributions in the case of a mandatory convertible. Our example of a typical mandatory convertible issued with a 25% conversion premium would be equivalent to selling a three-year call option at the money and simultaneously buying a call option with a *strike price* (i.e., execution price) that is 25% above the price at issuance.

Although the return profile resembles the proceeds of a buy-write, mandatory preferreds do not run afoul of account restrictions that may prohibit options. Moreover, the quarterly distributions from a mandatory convertible seem more credible than the net premium income earned by a buy-write transaction. Mandatory convertibles are attractive for income-oriented institutional accounts, notably mutual funds, and the total returns—income plus appreciation—over the three years after issuance reflect asymmetry, as illustrated in Table 1.2 and Figure 1.1. A mandatory convertible may incur lower volatility and less downside total return risk than the underlying stock. Mandatory convertibles provide additional industry diversification within a convertible portfolio because they tend to be issued by utilities and other industries that may not typically issue convertible bonds.

1.5 QUANTITATIVE MODELS ARE ESSENTIAL

Over the life of a convertible, opportunities frequently occur in the after-market. Sophisticated quantitative models are especially useful in weighing such opportunities. The analysis of potential returns of mandatory convertibles begs for quantitative evaluation because there are price relationships between a mandatory and the price of its underlying stock at which there may be particularly attractive positive asymmetry—and there may also be price points at which there is undesirable negative asymmetry. Convertible evaluation models project these potential outcomes for mandatory convertibles as well as for convertible bonds. Mandatory convertibles have high sensitivity to the underlying stocks, so hedging with options may be attractive—but it requires modeling. We devote Chapters 8 and 9 to quantitative evaluations.

1.6 UNIQUE AND VALUABLE FEATURES OF CONVERTIBLE SECURITIES

Positive asymmetry is the raison d'être of convertible securities, and downside protection is the key component of positive asymmetry. Convertibles are always evolving. It is a challenge to keep up with the latest enhancements. Institutional investors, of course, have access to sophisticated (and expensive) online quantitative models that quickly evaluate new features. If convertibles seem confusing, recognize that confusion creates investment opportunities for those in the know.

1.6.1 Downside Protection from Shorter Durations

Today, convertible bonds have much shorter maturities than other corporate bonds, which significantly enhances downside protection. This trend is dramatically illustrated in Figure 1.3. Maturity is closely linked to the sensitivity of fluctuations in market interest rates. The longer the maturity, the greater the downside market price risk of a bond if interest rates rise (and the greater the upside potential in the event that rates decline). Hence, maturity provides a quick indication of downside risk.

Duration rather than maturity is the precise quantitative gauge of theoretical bond price sensitivity to changes in interest rates (as explained in Section 12.12.1 and elsewhere), but the trend of maturities parallels the trend of durations—especially in times of low-interest coupons. Duration is the average time to receipt of all cash flows from a bond; hence, a bond with a high interest rate has a shorter duration than a bond of the same maturity that has a low interest rate. Because most convertibles pay interest or dividends, the duration of a convertible is almost always shorter than its time to maturity—except in the case of zero-coupon convertibles, which provide a cash flow only at redemption and therefore have a time to maturity (or time to the next put[14]) that precisely equals the basic duration of these securities. Remembering the duration of a zero-coupon bond is a

Figure 1.3 Average life to maturity of convertible securities—

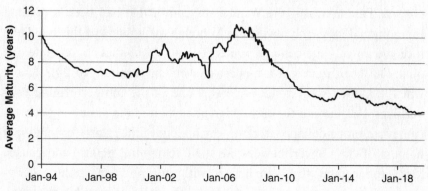

Source: Refinitiv Global Convertible Bond Index.

handy way to remember the *meaning* of duration. Short maturities are a huge protection against declining bond values in the face of increases in market interest rates.

1.6.2 Puts Are Equivalent to Shorter Maturities

A few convertible bonds provide puts, which are an effective defense against rising interest rates as well as weakness in the underlying stock. Puts appeared in the mid-1980s with the invention of zero-coupon original issue discount (OID) convertibles that often had 20-year maturities, and puts have continued to appear in convertible bonds that have long maturities. The Liberty Media 2.75% exchangeable convertible issued in November 2019 has a maturity of 30 years, but the issue features a put just five years from issuance. Such a short put (and, consequently, short duration) means that this bond has little downside risk as the December 2024 put approaches.

1.6.3 Call Protection: Hard and Soft

Hard call protection was introduced in 1980 after a new Wang Laboratories convertible bond was called for cash redemption only 10 months after issuance. The underlying stock had quickly risen, and the conversion value exceeded face value, so the cash call effectively forced holders to convert *after payment of only a single semiannual interest coupon*. Paradoxically, the Wang Labs convertible had been rewarding to traditional long-only investors. Although the holders of this bond had received only 3⅜ percentage points of the 6¾% annual coupon rate, the bond had been issued at a modest conversion premium of 20.3%, and when the stock soared, the issue was one of the top-performing convertibles. Yet, the call for cash redemption caused the remaining conversion premium to collapse to zero, which reduced the return for long-only holders of the convertible despite their remaining gains—and caused *losses* for accounts that were hedged with short positions in the underlying stock (see Chapters 7 and 13 for analyses of convertible hedging). This incident inspired convertible investors to demand call protection, which became a standard feature in essentially all new issues of US convertibles. Hard call protection means that the issuing company cannot call the convertible security for cash redemption for the first three to five years or longer—which provides time for the convertible to be levitated by appreciation of the underlying stock and years of interest income for the convertible holders.

Soft call protection was introduced in 1982. It typically begins after the expiration of hard call protection, and it prevents the issuing company from calling a convertible bond for cash redemption until the conversion value has risen to a specific percentage of the face value of the convertible, typically 125% to 150% of par, usually for 20 of 30 consecutive trading days. Soft call protection ensures that the convertible will remain outstanding until the conversion value becomes significantly greater than par.

A variation of soft call protection is a *make-whole* provision, which permits the issuer to call a convertible for early redemption (prior to the typical hard call protection of three to five years) but requires the issuer to make the holder whole. As explained by Michael Youngworth of BofA Securities, "A 'premium' make-whole compensates the holder for the premium paid at issuance. This premium payment is stepped down over time, deducting dividends/coupons as they are paid. A 'dividend/coupon' make-whole compensates the holder for the forgone future cash flows [the holder] would have received under a hard call scenario. . . . As in the case of a premium make-whole, the payment is reduced over time to reflect coupons received."[15]

1.6.4 Low Risk of Default

Convertibles have historically had default rates that may be lower than implied by their ratings (see Section 2.4.4). A convertible bond is the only debt of many issuers. Another reason for low defaults is that convertible issuers often have ample opportunities to refinance convertible bonds prior to maturity. Even stressed companies may be able to issue a convertible if the terms are sufficiently attractive.

Companies that issue sub-investment-grade convertibles differ from issuers of straight high-yield bonds. Convertible issuers tend to be growth companies. Such companies often are asset light—in contrast to high-yield issuers that usually have physical assets that promise some recovery in the event of bankruptcy. Investors in convertibles usually focus on the appreciation potential from rising earnings and cash flow, whereas high-yield investors often focus on the collateral that protects the principal.

1.6.5 New Features in the Computer Era

Improvements in the structures of convertible securities reflect the market dominance by institutional investors who are armed with online advanced quantitative models that instantly evaluate features such as call protection, dividend protection, and interim puts prior to maturity. Convertible arbitrageurs use leverage and emphasize short-term performance, so deficiencies in the structures of convertibles in the past were particularly detrimental—and arbitrageurs have been strong advocates of enhancements that *benefit all investors in convertibles*.

1.6.6 Protection from Increases in Common Stock Dividends

Today convertible bonds have *dividend protection*, which typically involves an increase in the conversion ratio to compensate for an increase in the common dividend. Such protection is important because otherwise the conversion value would be undermined by increases in the dividend, as such distributions reduce the intrinsic value of the common shares.

Moreover, convertibles are always popular with hedge funds that go long (i.e., *buy*) the convertible and short (i.e., *sell* by borrowing) the underlying stock. Such a long-short hedge would potentially be hurt on both sides without dividend protection because a dividend increase may cause the stock to momentarily spike, while at the same time the short position would require compensating the lenders of the short stock for the higher common dividends. A rising dividend also reduces the volatility of the underlying stock, which reduces the conversion premium.

Dividend protection was introduced in 2003 in response to an incident in which Mandalay Bay initiated a large dividend on its common stock just a few months after issuing a convertible. A year later Mandalay Bay was taken over for cash—and there is zero conversion premium once a convertible becomes convertible into cash. The Mandalay Bay takeover led to protection from cash takeovers.

1.6.7 Protection from Takeovers

Takeover bids always lift the stock price of the target company. Yet, investors in convertibles face disadvantages in the case of *cash* acquisitions. If a convertible becomes convertible into cash rather than the underlying stock, the conversion premium will drop to 0%. Hence, contemporary convertibles almost always include a cash takeover provision that provides for an increase in the conversion ratio to compensate for the loss of conversion premium in the case of a cash takeout. The details of such provisions are generally based on a matrix of prices and dates that are intended to be equivalent to a hypothetical conversion premium that would be lost at the cash takeover price (discussed in Section 8.9). Without such protection, convertible arbitrageurs—who are almost always leveraged—would suffer significant losses in the case of a cash takeover because the classic long-short arbitrage (long the convertible and short the stock) would incur a loss on the convertible losing premium and a loss on the common stock appreciating close to the cash offer. Takeover protections usually expire at the first call date.[16]

If a convertible issuer is acquired by another public company in an exchange of stock, the resulting company is larger and no more indebted, which usually suggests a better credit. Yet, the stock of the acquirer may have less volatility and less growth potential. If an acquisition weakens the credit of the convertible issuer, then the downside protection of the convertible bond is weakened in turn. Many convertibles include a change-in-control put that gives holders of the convertibles the right to put back the convertibles for cash at face value in the event of a change in control. Some convertibles include a provision to increase the conversion ratio in the event of a cash takeover.

1.6.8 Protection from Dilution

Historically, convertibles had protections from dilution caused by extraordinary dividends, rights offerings, spinoffs, stock splits, and so on. In the twenty-teens, investment banks developed new techniques using derivatives that enable issuers to minimize the dilution of earnings per share from new issues of convertibles. Such provisions encourage issuance of convertibles because managements are usually sensitive to reported earnings—as are most investors. Some convertible bonds, on conversion, pay face value of the bond in cash and the excess over par in stock; this *net share settlement* is a way to avoid earnings dilution from the convertible. A few convertibles settle in cash equal to the conversion value (see Section 16.3.1 for further details).

One form of dilution protection is a *call spread* that the issuing company buys from the underwriters simultaneously with the offering of a new convertible bond. This transaction effectively offsets the dilution of earnings from the additional shares underlying the convertible until the stock rises above the hedged conversion premium of the convertible—which can be much higher than the stated conversion premium. The accounting, cash, and taxation implications of call spreads are complicated (see Chapter 16 for further details).

1.6.9 Mitigation of Short Selling by Providing Happy Meals

Issuers of convertible securities dislike the concept that the announcement of a new convertible will inspire immediate short selling of the stock by convertible arbitrageurs, which may pressure the stock price. One way to minimize the downside pressure from short selling is a *happy meal*, which is equivalent to a stock buyback,[17] that is, a new issue of a convertible bond that includes a provision for the issuing company to buy the common shares being shorted by convertible arbitrageurs who are hedging their purchases of the new bond. The twofold nature of the transaction is akin to the McDonald's Happy Meal, which includes a toy as well as food. A happy meal provides an extremely efficient way to buy back stock because it has little effect on the market price of the stock. If the stock performs, of course, the short sellers may ultimately cover their short positions by exercising the right to convert (after the convertible is called for redemption), and this requires the company to issue new shares, which effectively offsets the happy meal stock buyback. Companies often protect against such risk by purchasing derivatives that are intended to mute or prevent dilution if the convertible is ultimately converted into common shares. See Chapters 7 and 13 for further details on convertible arbitrage.

1.7 UNUSUAL TYPES OF CONVERTIBLES

Special structures of convertibles satisfy various issuer and investor needs.

1.7.1 Exchangeable Convertibles

Exchangeable convertibles are issued by a different company from the issuer of the underlying stock. Typically, these convertibles are issued by companies that have large minority holdings in other public companies, and the issuance of an exchangeable is a way to effectively advance sell the underlying interest—without incurring a taxable capital gain (akin to an investor taking a margin loan against a long position). Often the underlying shares are held in a trust to protect the interest of the investors in the exchangeable. An inherent advantage of such convertibles is that the credit of the issuer is *different* from that of the company into which the issue is exchangeable; hence, the creditworthiness of the bond is *uncorrelated with the performance of the stock*, and the asymmetry of the bond is thereby enhanced.

1.7.2 Cross-Currency Convertibles

Cross-currency convertibles are denominated in a different currency from the currency in which the underlying stock is traded. This typically occurs when a foreign company wants to tap the US convertible market. Hence, the principal and interest of the convertible bond are denominated in US dollars, yet, the underlying stock trades in a foreign currency in its home market. In such a situation, the conversion ratio is typically fixed—as in the case of all other convertible bonds. A fixed conversion ratio is established in a cross-currency convertible by fixing the exchange rate into US dollars at issuance.

In essence, US-dollar-denominated cross-currency convertibles provide a "free" currency option that creates an asymmetric relationship with the currency of the underlying stock. The bond is protected from the local currency risk on the downside, yet, the conversion value will benefit if the local currency appreciates and thereby elevates the price of the underlying stock in US dollars. (See Section 13.5 for further discussion of currencies.)

1.7.3 Adjustable Convertibles

These are convertibles with conversion ratios that are adjusted upward to compensate for a decline in the price of the underlying stock below a *trigger* price. The effectiveness of such a feature presupposes that the company remains viable despite a significant decline in the stock price. (This conversion adjustment should not be confused with conversion ratio adjustments on mandatory convertibles, which *reduce* the conversion ratio until the underlying stock has appreciated by more than, say, 25%.)

1.7.4 Contingent Convertibles

Contingent convertibles, or CoCos—also known as *reverse convertibles*— are issued by non-US banks to meet regulatory capital requirements. CoCos have a unique mechanism that causes the bonds to either convert to equity or suffer a principal reduction after a *triggering event*—usually a breach of a capital reserve requirement, but it also can be a discretionary decision from a regulator. CoCo investors are effectively forced to replenish some of the issuer's capital during a crisis. In return, the CoCo investor is compensated by higher coupon rates than prevail on traditional bonds. CoCos provide no upside other than yield—and may entail complete downside price participation if the underlying stock has depreciated by the time of forced conversion or maturity. Hence, reverse convertibles inherently provide negative asymmetry—which calls into question the use of the appellation *convertibles* for these securities.

CoCos were born in Europe in the aftermath of the GFC in 2008–2009 as a way to automatically shore up bank balance sheets in future crises. Basel III[18] in 2010 classified CoCos as either Tier 1 or Tier 2 capital depending on the structure of the CoCo. Following this international recognition, CoCo issuance grew in both Europe and Asia—but not in the United States, where differences in bank regulations preclude the use of CoCos. Basel III required a Tier 1 CoCo to be perpetual, to have a call date within five years of issuance, to have discretionary coupon payments, and to be triggered by regulators on a discretionary basis. These requirements are negative for investors. Consequently, coupon rates have typically been high in order to compensate investors. The first issues typically carried coupon rates of 7% to 9%. Since then, as investors have become more comfortable with the structure and more starved for income, CoCo coupons have fallen sharply.

1.7.5 Synthetic Convertibles

Synthetic convertibles are created by third parties, usually at the request of institutional investors who want a convertible for a specific stock that does not have a convertible. Synthetic convertibles are usually short-term notes. The construction of synthetics typically involves the credit of a bank or another financial institution combined with derivatives. In some cases, a corporation may effectively *rent out* its strong balance sheet by creating a synthetic convertible; the issuer need not be a financial company. The aftermarket for a synthetic is typically confined to the financial institution that issued the security.

Given that the issuers have to provide call options that are effectively sold as part of the structure of the synthetic convertibles, synthetic issues will not model theoretically cheap at issuance. The *manufacturer* of the synthetic must be compensated for the cost of structuring the synthetic.

These issues are primarily for equity-oriented accounts that have strong convictions on specific stocks. Often large institutional investors will request the creation of a synthetic convertible for a company that has a convertible outstanding that has risen deep into the money and has essentially become an equity surrogate. A key advantage of the synthetic structure is that the issuing bank usually has a high credit rating. Synthetic convertibles resemble exchangeables. There is no correlation between the creditworthiness of the issuer and the fortunes of the underlying stock. Banks occasionally issue synthetic convertibles of their own volition, and such issues are sometimes included in convertible indices. Some synthetics are mandatory preferreds, which minimizes the utility of the high credit ratings of the issuers.

1.7.6 Zero-Coupon Original Issue Discount Convertibles

Discount zero-coupon convertibles were introduced by Merrill Lynch as Liquid Yield Option Notes (LYONs) in 1985 and were popular into the early 2000s but have since faded from the new-issue market. The structure of a zero-coupon discount bond evolved into a 20-year maturity interspersed with puts at five-year intervals.

An important legacy of the LYONs is shorter maturities throughout the convertible bond market. There was a huge tax advantage to issuers because these bonds not only paid no cash interest, but they were issued at discounts, and the accretion of the discount to par was a tax-deductible original issue discount (OID) for the issuers under US law. Thus, issuing companies effectively were paid cash in the form of tax deductions, and the companies never had to pay the accretion if the bonds were converted. For taxable investment accounts, of course, the accretion was taxable OID, even though there was no associated cash yield. We presume that many of the OID zero-coupon bonds were used in tax-deferred retirement accounts.

1.8 INVESTORS IN CONVERTIBLES

Convertibles appeal to a broad variety of investors.

1.8.1 Savvy Investors

Decades of experience tell us that savvy investors use convertibles. Our perception is not merely because we are convertible specialists (and it's human nature to regard *ourselves* as savvy). Rather, we have seen world-class investors such as Berkshire Hathaway CEO Warren Buffett invest in multiple privately issued convertibles, each of which was created specifi-cally to facilitate investments by Berkshire Hathaway at times when the issuing companies needed capital (see Chapter 14).

The downside protection that is inherent in convertibles fits nicely with the *loser's game* concept that was advanced by Charles Ellis, who posited that superior investment performance is more likely to be achieved by avoiding losers than by picking winners.[19] Nassim Nicholas Taleb—the famous philosopher and statistician who wrote the *New York Times* best-seller, *The Black Swan* (2007)—includes *convertible* in the *antifragile* column of his 2012 book *Antifragile: Things That Gain from Disorder.*[20] Concepts such as the loser's game and antifragile probably are familiar to savvy investors but are ignored by most investors.

Oaktree Capital Management co-founder Howard Marks recognized the utility of convertible securities early in his career. While still at his first place of employment, Citibank, Marks prevailed on the retail-oriented Value Line Convertibles to introduce an online convertible evaluation ser-vice for institutional investors.[21]

1.8.2 Hedge Funds

For hedge funds, the inherent structural asymmetry of convertibles is es-pecially valuable because the asymmetry makes it a lot easier to hedge in a way that is likely to create profits whether the stock market goes up or down. It doesn't require clairvoyance to be able to project that a convert-ible bond is likely to capture more of the upside from the underlying stock than it will suffer from the downside of the stock.

There is likely to be a positive return from convertible arbitrage—long the convertible and short the underlying stock—if the convertible merely creates its normal asymmetry. Except in cases of severely out-of-the-money and/or credit-distressed convertibles, arbitrageurs usually will bid for a convertible in anticipation of locking in a profit by shorting the underlying common stock. Arbitrageurs also may be willing to offer a con-vertible—that is, short a convertible—in anticipation of locking in a profit by buying the underlying stock. Ownership of the overall convertible market, of course, is usually dominated by long-only investors, for example, endowment funds, insurance companies, pension funds, and mutual funds, which accounted for about 60% of the US market as of February 2021.[22] Convertible arbitrageurs often are a source of liquidity in the convertible market because they are usually quick to trade on the slightest pricing anomaly—and this tendency essentially enables the convertible market to tap the liquidity of the underlying common stocks, which is an advantage relative to non-convertible corporate bonds. See Chapters 7 and 13 for further details on hedging convertibles.

1.8.3 Individual Investors

For individual investors, a simple risk-averse approach to convertible investing is to buy convertible bonds exclusively at par or lower. Convertible bonds rarely default. And if the investor can avoid defaults, holding convertible bonds to maturity (or holding to a put or other cash redemption) that have been purchased at par or lower will ensure a positive return from each position that pays a coupon. It's a lot easier to make credit judgments that will minimize default risk than it is to select common stocks that will always provide positive returns.

It is difficult for individual retail investors to invest directly in convertible bonds because the convertible bond market is dominated by investment institutions that trade on the phone in an over-the-counter *dealer market*. In the retail market, convertible bonds can sometimes be traded online in small lots, but retail transactions generally require speaking with brokers.

Anyone who intends to trade bonds has to be familiar with basic bond terminology, for example, quoting bonds in percentages per each $1,000 par bond (so "100" represents a bond trading at $1,000), and quoted prices *exclude* accrued interest (which is *included* in the cash settlement in every trade of a coupon bond). In contrast, common and preferred shares trade at prices that implicitly *include* accrued dividends. Hence, shares go *ex-dividend*, that is, notch down in price equivalent to a dividend that has just been paid, whereas bonds explicitly exclude accrued interest and therefore do not *visibly* go ex, although the accrued interest drops to zero after a coupon is paid.

Most US convertible bonds are issued under SEC Rule 144A, which technically makes them private placements, and are limited at issuance to qualified institutional buyers (see Chapter 14). Individual investors typically access the convertible market through ETFs and mutual funds, which are allowed to invest in securities issued under Rule 144A. Individuals are generally permitted to trade Rule 144A issues after six months, but brokers often impose permanent bans on unregistered Rule 144A issues in non-QIB accounts. Some Rule 144A issues are subsequently registered. Mandatory convertibles and traditional convertible preferred shares are usually registered and listed, of course, and can be traded easily by individuals.

It is difficult for individual investors to obtain descriptions of convertible securities unless they subscribe to expensive online services that are intended for institutional investors. *Value Line Convertibles* served individual investors but ceased publication in October 2019. See Chapter 16 for further details on convertible investing for individuals.

1.8.4 Institutional Investors

Convertibles typically are held as a separately managed allocation within a pension fund or other institutional investment account (e.g., insurance company investment accounts, endowments, mutual funds). Convertibles are attractive to pension funds because such funds usually assume long-term rates of return that are achievable only from equities or from the equity-like returns of convertibles.

Insurance company investment accounts and endowments are under similar pressure to boost prospective returns in the face of low interest rates. Investments in convertible bonds are a way to potentially capture equity-like returns rather than settle for the low returns that are likely to be generated from non-convertible bonds in a period of low interest rates.

The secondary market for convertibles includes the unique feature that transient investors from other markets—notably fixed-income securities, equities, and hedge funds—occasionally use convertibles in their strategies. This *crossover* trading volume helps to keep the convertible market more liquid than the high-yield market, which is largely confined to specialized high-yield investors. Some institutional portfolio managers opportunistically add convertible bonds to fixed-income accounts that do not have a specific mandate to invest in convertibles but *permit* convertibles. Such investors can use convertibles to enhance their fixed-income returns by capturing equity-like total returns. Equity accounts are sometimes permitted to own convertibles, but not high-yield securities. Transient equity investors may use convertibles to reduce risk. Fixed-income accounts may also want to mitigate the risks of rising market rates of interest by buying convertibles that will be more sensitive to equity price movements. Fixed-income accounts are often permitted to own convertible bonds but not equities.

Bear markets often create opportunities to invest in convertibles that are far out of the money and sometimes temporarily trade at exceptionally high yields when they are being sold by accounts that seek greater equity sensitivity and when some financially leveraged investors are forced to sell by margin calls. Experience shows that it takes anywhere from a few weeks to several months for the market to scoop up such undervalued discount convertibles. Such bonds have the potential to significantly outperform non-convertible bonds when the credit and/or stock markets rally—or the market simply recognizes that an issuing company is creditworthy and the stock is undervalued.

1.9 CONVERTIBLES COMPARED WITH OTHER ASSET CLASSES

Sharpe ratios of convertible indices demonstrate that convertibles provide higher returns relative to volatility when compared with the returns from equities and corporate bonds. The Sharpe ratio ignores the *direction* of volatility; it treats upward and downward price movements identically. So the Sharpe ratio does not recognize asymmetry—which is the biggest advantage of convertible securities. (The Sortino ratio defines risk in terms of the volatility of declining prices while ignoring upside volatility—but the Sharpe ratio dominates.)

The Sharpe ratio of Treasury bonds has usually exceeded that of all other key asset classes during the bull market in Treasury securities that began late in 1981. During this period, Treasury bonds enjoyed capital gains as market rates of interest declined. Should Treasury rates increase, Treasury bonds will be exposed to significant downside risk.

Rising interest rates are less of a threat to convertible bonds than for straight debt for two reasons. First, convertible bonds often are more sensitive to the trend of credit spreads than to the basic risk-free interest yields of Treasury bonds. Second, to the extent that rising Treasury rates reflect improving economic prospects, credit spreads of convertibles are likely to tighten, and convertible securities will also get a boost from strength in the underlying stocks as economic prospects improve.

1.10 SUMMARY AND CONCLUSION

Convertible securities represent a rewarding niche ignored by most investors. Positive asymmetry is key to convertibles: capturing more of the upside of common stocks and suffering less of the downside, thereby achieving equity-like total returns over time—with lower risk. In this introductory chapter, we have focused on the basics, with the in-depth quantitative analysis and modeling to follow in the rest of this book. Our message: develop an understanding of convertible securities and take advantage of convertibles opportunities.

ENDNOTES

1. Benjamin Graham, David L. Dodd, and Sidney Cottle, *Security Analysis* (New York: McGraw-Hill, 1962), p. 601.

2. "The Convertible Railway Bond," *Railroad Age Gazette* 1908; XLV(28):1518.

3. A redemption for cash prior to maturity. For further details, see https://www.investopedia.com/terms/c/callablebond.asp.

4. Before the computer era, interest coupons were clipped from bond certificates at payment dates to obtain the interest.

5. In the five years through September 30, 2020, the median annualized growth rate of sales of the companies in the VXA0 (the ICE BofA All-Convertibles Index) was 8.91% versus 3.55% for the S&P 500 Index.

6. The average time to receipt of all cash flows from the bond, that is, coupons plus redemption at maturity or put; duration measures the interest-rate sensitivity of the market value of a bond—the shorter the duration, the less sensitivity, and the longer the duration, the more sensitivity. See Section 12.12.1 for further details of duration.

7. Refinitiv as of December 31, 2020.

8. Michael Youngworth, *Global Convertibles Primer* (New York: BofA Securities, 2021), p. 33.

9. Taxable corporations as opposed to limited-liability corporations and other tax pass-through structures.

10. Trust preferreds incorporate a note that is funded by US tax-deductible interest payments from the issuing company, and the quarterly distributions from the trust preferreds are taxed as interest by the IRS.

11. Michael Youngworth, *Global Convertibles Primer* (New York: Bank of America Merrill Lynch, 2018), p. 12.

12. Mandatory convertible preferreds often can be converted during the price averaging period just prior to mandatory conversion, and mandatory preferreds usually can be converted prior to the mandatory conversion date in the event of a fundamental change in the issuing company.

13. ICE Data Services.

14. A right for the holder of a convertible to redeem the issue on a specific date without waiting for maturity, that is, a right to *put* the issue back to the company for cash on a *put date* (or dates) prior to maturity.

15. Michael Youngworth, *Global Convertibles Primer* (New York: BofA Securities, 2021), p. 15.

16. *Ibid.*, p. 14.

17. https://www.thestreet.com/opinion/happy-meals-satisfy-firms-hedge-funds-10294031.

18. https://www.bis.org/bcbs/basel3.htm.

19. The concept of the "loser's game" was originally advanced by Charles Ellis in the *Financial Analysts Journal,* Vol. 31, 1975, Issue 4, p. 19, and subsequently in eight editions of his book, *Winning the Loser's Game: Timeless Strategies for Successful Investing* (New York: McGraw-Hill Education) 1998–2021.

20. Nassim Nicholas Taleb, *Antifragile: Things That Gain From Disorder* (New York: Random House, 2012), p. 26.

21. Allan S. Lyons, *Enhanced Convertibles, Investment Secrets of a Top-Performing Money Manager* (Englewood Cliffs, NJ: New York Institute of Finance, 1995), p. 131.

22. Michael Youngworth, *Global Convertibles Primer* (New York: BofA Securities, 2021), p. 21.

CHAPTER 2

Traditional Convertible Strategies

Heads I win, tails I don't lose.

—Anonymous journalist in 1908[1]

2.1 INTRODUCTION: THE GOALS OF INVESTING

All investors seek worthwhile returns, and most seek to minimize risk. Convertible securities are ideally suited to meet these goals.

Institutional investors are almost all benchmarked against relevant indices, and risk is typically measured by the volatility of portfolio returns relative to the volatility of the relevant index. Individual investors presumably take a more basic approach of seeking to minimize downside risk (and often seeking to maximize income). The natural asymmetry of convertible securities fits with the goal of maximizing returns relative to risk—regardless of whether risk is defined as volatility or downside exposure. Convertibles typically provide less volatility than stocks, less downside risk than stocks, and usually more yield than stocks.

Adding convertibles to an equity, bond, or blended portfolio has historically enhanced risk-adjusted returns. We explore the concept of optimal asset allocation in greater depth in Chapter 6, but in this chapter we focus on general principles of selecting convertibles.

2.2 PORTFOLIO DIVERSIFICATION

Convertible diversification is conceptually linked to equity diversification as convertibles are exposed to a portion of both the systemic and idiosyncratic risk of the underlying common stocks—and the inherently lower volatility of convertibles tends to minimize these risks. Defensive equity investors who seek income and low volatility are able to diversify into growth companies with volatile stocks *without violating their mandate* by diversifying into convertible securities.

Investors who seek higher returns are generally more willing to accept higher risk in a quantitative sense, and modern portfolio theory (MPT)—introduced by Harry Markowitz in 1952—and its successor, the capital asset pricing model (CAPM)—introduced by William F. Sharpe and others in the 1960s[2]—each suggest that higher returns are earned by assuming greater risk and that *risk* means higher portfolio volatility. These theories propose that the expected return on a stock is equal to its risk premium plus the risk-free rate. The higher the volatility of the stock, the higher the risk premium and therefore the higher expected return. The arbitrage pricing theory (APT)—introduced by Stephen Ross in 1976— considered many more factors than the MPT and the CAPM.

The fact that convertible indices have generated long-term records of equity-like returns with lower volatility than equities is *not* explained by the MPT, CAPM, or APT, in our opinion. A key tenet of the CAPM is that stocks have sensitivity to the changing values of broad equity indices; this sensitivity is called *systematic risk*, and the measurement of this value is called *beta*. Beta can be expressed as a decimal a stock that is perfectly correlated with the index would have a beta of 1.

Stock movement unexplained by the market index is called *idiosyncratic risk*; it reflects industry or company-specific conditions that are uncorrelated with broad market movements. The lack of correlation among idiosyncratic risks means that some idiosyncratic factors are positive while others are negative, and these idiosyncratic risks partially offset each other within a portfolio, as demonstrated by the fact that the average volatility of the stocks in a broad market index such as the Standard and Poor's 500 Index (S&P 500) is about double (~30% annualized) the volatility of the index itself (~15% annualized).

In other words, about half the volatility of the individual stocks (on average) is systematic risk or market beta, whereas the rest is idiosyncratic and is essentially diversified away when a portfolio is weighted identically to the index—at least under normal conditions. It should be noted that this mix of systematic and idiosyncratic risk is not static. Stocks do become more correlated in *directional markets* when stocks are either retreating or advancing rapidly, which increases the proportion of systematic risk.

Idiosyncratic risk can be minimized by diversification, but systematic risk cannot be avoided.

Convertibles offer ample opportunities for selecting companies with less systematic risk and more idiosyncratic risk. For example, the growth-oriented issuers of convertibles often include biotech companies, which inherently have high idiosyncratic risk and also tend to have highly volatile stocks. The classic example of idiosyncratic risk is that of a biotechnology company developing a single drug. The entire value of the company rests on the success of that drug. Independent of diversification, the convertible structure is ideal to mute such risks.

2.3 CHOOSING THE TYPES OF CONVERTIBLES

A logical approach to investing in convertible securities is to first focus on specific types of convertibles and then seek the most attractive issuers among the types of convertibles that best suit the goals of the investment account. In addition to all the ways that companies can be categorized (i.e., sector, region, credit quality, size, growth versus value profile, etc.), different groups of convertibles have various properties that may give some higher bond content, whereas others are very equity-like, and most represent a blend of bonds and equities.

2.3.1 Convertibles as Equity Alternatives

Most convertible investors favor *balanced convertibles*, which are issues that promise the most positive upside/downside asymmetry. Such issues are sought by most long-only (unhedged) convertible investors. Balanced convertibles are also favored by hedge funds that utilize convertible arbitrage (long the convertible and short the underlying stock) as the greater the asymmetry, the greater the potential profit. The volatility of balanced convertibles is similar to that of the convertible indices.

Investors can also choose *equity surrogate* in-the-money convertibles that have conversion values far above face value and that have risen even farther above the basic investment value that provides downside protection. Such convertibles provide little or no asymmetry. For example, if the conversion value of a bond is, say, $2,000 (or 200 in *bond speak*, i.e.,

200% of the face value of $1,000), the convertible bond will trade at a tiny premium over conversion value (which often reflects a yield advantage as well as the inherent nature of convertible bonds as being higher in the capital structure than equities), and such bonds will essentially move up and down in tandem with fluctuations in the underlying stock (a delta of 100%, to use the most basic Greek descriptor, i.e., the ratio of the change in the price of the convertible to the change in the price of the underlying stock). Barring a large drop in the price of the stock, there will be essentially none of the asymmetric price behavior relative to the price movements of the underlying stock that constitutes the major attraction of convertibles. Equity surrogates provide volatility that is essentially equivalent to the underlying stocks, that is, higher volatility than balanced convertibles.

The most common use of convertibles that trade far-in-the-money reflects a decision to retain convertibles purchased at much lower prices; this is a variation of the equity adage to "let your winners run." The powerful upside potential of equity surrogates also may tempt some bullish fixed-income investors (or convertible accounts, for that matter) to accumulate equity surrogates—and ignore the weak downside protection of such convertibles.

Mandatory convertibles provide higher income while achieving a great deal of equity sensitivity. Mandatory preferreds constitute the only part of the convertible market that is readily accessible to individual investors, because mandatory issues are usually listed on the stock exchange. Although mandatory convertibles have significant sensitivity to price movements in the underlying stocks, the volatility of mandatory preferreds is not especially high, since the higher quality, larger-capitalization stocks that underlie mandatory convertibles are not especially volatile.

2.3.2 Convertibles as Credit Alternatives

Convertible bonds that have fallen to discounts from face value sometimes provide exceptionally attractive yields. The challenge with discount convertible bonds is to evaluate the creditworthiness of the issuer. The reward for the investor is derived by identifying discount convertibles that are *money good*, that is, have low risk of default even though they may be trading at high yields that suggest stress. A focus on cash flow, balance sheets, and earnings quality may identify attractive discount convertibles, especially during market setbacks, when many securities are sold indiscriminately. Discount convertibles that are obligations of companies that will survive at a minimum and preferably enjoy turnarounds are likely to provide high returns. High-yield accounts often include some low-rated or non-rated convertible bonds as a way to capture higher yields from discount convertibles as well as the potential equity upside of convertibles.

Discount convertibles typically provide lower volatility than other convertibles, although such issues will occasionally make rapid positive or negative movements when credit spreads and/or the stock market are volatile. Most discount convertibles that have suffered a decline in bond value—that is, bonds that are trading at wide interest spreads over Treasury bonds—exhibit what we call *phantom delta* and others call a *credit delta*. If the market declines, the bond's credit spreads widen in response to the same negative factors that caused the underlying stock to decline; hence, the convertible drops more sharply than its delta would have suggested. Then, if the stock price starts to recover, the market will reward the bond with narrower credit spreads in response to market recognition of the same improved conditions that are driving the stock back up; hence, the convertible will recover more sharply than its delta would have suggested.

2.3.3 Portfolio Asymmetry

From the perspective of creating a portfolio of convertible securities that promises significant asymmetry, a focus on balanced convertibles is appropriate (see Section 2.7). Portfolio asymmetry also can be maintained in the context of retaining some convertibles that have risen far in the money and have become equity sensitive—provided that the portfolio is balanced by some discount convertibles that are trading near *bond value* (i.e., near the investment value that the convertibles should command if the issues were *straight* non-convertible bonds). Such out-of-the-money issues may provide excellent downside protection, but these issues usually have high conversion premiums (reflecting declines in the prices of the underlying shares) and low deltas and appear to offer little prospect of upside participation unless the underlying stock makes a major recovery.

Mixing in-the-money convertibles with discount convertibles essentially creates a *barbell* portfolio that may behave much like a portfolio of balanced convertibles. Credit research is key to avoiding discount convertibles that are declining because of deteriorating creditworthiness of the issuing company.

2.4 SELECTING CREDITS

The downside protection of convertible bonds is ultimately provided by creditworthiness. Downside protection is essential for convertible arbitrageurs/hedgers (long the convertible, short the stock) as credit deterioration will cause the market price of a convertible bond to drop more sharply than modeled (reflecting a phantom delta on the downside), so hedge ratios (the number of common shares shorted) that assume a stable credit are likely to become unprofitable (i.e., the dollar loss on the convertible is likely to exceed the dollar gain on the short position in the underlying stock). Hedged positions are especially reliant on quantitative models that become less accurate when the creditworthiness of the convertible issuer is in doubt and the credit spread becomes volatile.

Under normal market conditions, the convertible market is much more sensitive to the stock market than it is to the bond market, and practitioners may pay insufficient attention to creditworthiness (which is much more important to convertible valuations than fluctuations in Treasury rates). The most important function of credit analysis is to avoid losses. The capital markets will eventually respond to deterioration in credit, and the response will include not only a decline in the market value of the company's bonds but usually a sharper decline in the market value of the company's common shares; such declines will drive down the market price of any convertibles issued by a company in such difficulty. Yet, a convertible bond will eventually provide significant downside protection if the company merely avoids default—which is usually the case with convertible issuers (see Section 2.4.4). A portfolio that is confined to interest-bearing convertible bonds issued by companies that do not default will earn a positive return from issuance to redemption. (Convertible bonds often decline in weak markets prior to maturity or cash call, but cash redemption is usually independent of market conditions, so market conditions become unimportant as a cash redemption date approaches.)

The second most important function of credit analysis is to identify opportunities in discount bonds that are undervalued. There are numerous elaborate writings that explain credit analysis. The focus of credit analysis is typically limited to bonds, loans, and other debt instruments. It is apparent that stock price performance is correlated with the same fundamental factors that determine credit strength. Co-author Tracy Maitland has always preferred stable to improving credits—and such favorable credit trends are likely to be supportive of the market prices of the underlying stocks as well as convertibles and non-convertible debt. In our view, the importance of credit analysis *across the capital structure* is underappreciated by investors.

Co-author Barry Nelson has managed bond funds and equities as well as convertibles and has heard credit analysts remark that there is no such thing as equity research—there is only credit research. This attitude goes too far. There's substance to the point that the fundamental factors involved in credit research are also important to equity research. Moreover, we feel it is easier to perform credit research that will avoid deteriorating credit situations than it is to perform equity research that will avoid common stocks that may decline in price.

Credit research often exposes changes in trends of cash flow that reflect both negative and positive changes in fundamentals *before* such changes appear in headline measures such as earnings before interest, taxes, depreciation, and amortization (EBITDA) and reported earnings. Deterioration in sales may be temporarily masked by an increase in receivables as customers defer payments or as companies prematurely book future sales—or even hoped-for sales—in an effort to sustain reported earnings. Cash positions may be temporarily maintained by delaying accounts payable. Worst case, there is potential for accounting manipulation that can disguise fraud. Yet, accounting cannot create cash, and cash flow is the ultimate measure of success or failure.

Improvements often appear in credit figures before such improvements are reflected in EBITDA and reported earnings. For example, when receivables begin to be collected, the collections are immediately reflected in cash flow but have no effect on EBITDA or reported earnings—and such changes usually reflect improving business conditions.

Cash outlays that are properly operating expenses are often disguised as capital expenditures in cases of fraud. Regardless of how such uses of cash are characterized, it is our observation that *fraudulent companies always burn cash*—think Enron (2001) and WorldCom (2002).[3]

Overseas, however, more extreme incidents have occurred occasionally. The Italian milk company Parmalat collapsed in 2003 after years of negative cash flow disguised by balance sheets that included more than €3 billion in fake bank accounts that had somehow escaped discovery by international accounting firms.[4] A Chinese forest products company, Sino-Forest, was exposed by a negative research report in 2011.[5] In 2017, the international retail conglomerate Steinhoff International (based in South Africa) began to run short of cash. Steinhoff had claimed to be holding a lot of cash, but nearly €3 billion was "missing."[6]

Fraudulent companies nearly always have complicated capital structures—the better to disguise the truth. Such companies use multiple sources of funds to maintain liquidity in the face of cash burns from operations. Similar characteristics also may be present in companies that are merely inflating their earnings by using aggressive accounting rather than committing outright fraud.

Companies rarely materially violate accounting standards in order to make good earnings appear even better—yet, this apparently happened in the case of Red Hat in 2004.[7] When Red Hat's accounting was exposed, the stock and the company's convertible bonds tumbled—and created a buying opportunity for investors who understood Red Hat's strong cash flow.

2.4.1 Leveraging a Company and a House

An easy way to conceptualize a leveraged company is to consider the company's balance sheet the same way one would consider buying a house with an assumable mortgage. Any company that has a convertible on its balance sheet is financially leveraged—just like a house with a mortgage. Financial leverage enhances earnings of a successful company, but financial leverage becomes dangerous for an unsuccessful company.

Everyone knows that the price of a house is the sum of the down payment plus the mortgage. No buyers of a house with $300,000 down and a $700,000 assumable mortgage would imagine that they had just bought the house for $300,000—but that is exactly the way speculators typically regard common shares. The equity market capitalization of a company is the typical way the market value of a company is represented, which often results in misleading comparisons of the market values of companies that have capital structures with different amounts of debt (net of cash, of course).

Consider the effects of buying a house with a mortgage—with *leverage*. In the preceding example, you paid $300,000 down—the equity equivalent of the common stock in a public company—and took a mortgage of $700,000. If the market value of the house drops 10% to $900,000, then the market value of your equity will drop 33⅓% to $200,000. If the market value rises 10% to $1,100,000, your equity will rise 33⅓% to $400,000. Your equity in the house has higher volatility, more appreciation potential, and greater downside risk than if the house had been bought in an all-cash transaction.

In the case of a company with debt on its balance sheet, the equity market capitalization—that is, the market value of all the company's common shares—is equivalent to the down payment on a house that is purchased with a mortgage. The enterprise value of a financially leveraged company—akin to the value of a house—is the sum of its equity market capitalization plus its net debt.[8] A company's free cash flow as a percentage of its enterprise value is effectively the *yield* one would earn if one bought the whole company at current market price plus debt; this is similar to the rental yield that would be collected on a mortgaged house that was rented out.

Many public companies have large amounts of debt, which cause their stocks to be more volatile—and to return more in a bull market and suffer larger losses in a bear market. Investors should not ignore such basic effects of leverage. All issuers of convertible securities are leveraged by the convertibles, although convertibles that are far in the money—that are highly likely to convert into common shares—may be regarded as equity.

From a credit perspective, if the mortgage on a house is small relative to the market value of the house, then the mortgage is a relatively safe credit even if the borrower is weak—and it should be easy to refinance such a mortgage. A company with a high equity market capitalization relative to its debt has room to refinance its credit obligations, notably by issuing convertible securities—even if its cash flow may be weak or negative (think fast-growing companies that burned cash in early years yet, were able to issued convertible bonds, e.g., Amazon, Apple, and Tesla).

Home ownership is akin to insider ownership of a public company, and it means that there is a large incentive to avoid defaults. One reason home mortgages are usually good credits is because homeowners are motivated to avoid default and consequent foreclosure.

There is a parallel in the investment world in the case of companies that have significant family ownership. Alone among the "Big Three" US auto manufacturers during the Great Financial Crisis (GFC) of 2008–2009, Ford avoided bankruptcy. Ford never defaulted on its 4.25% convertible bond. Ford did suspend the dividends on its 6.5% convertible preferred, but the payout was reinstated including cumulative unpaid dividends in 2010. In our view, the Ford family ownership of millions of Ford shares was a key factor in avoiding bankruptcy.

Most public corporations are led by professional managers whose remuneration and stock options are generous but whose outright ownership of common shares in their companies is trivial. Such managers have incentives to manage aggressively rather than cautiously. In our view, companies with significant family control and/or insider ownership often are underrated as credits because major long-term owners have their wealth at risk.

Studying a company's entire capital structure can be rewarding. Analysts who confine themselves to *silos* within the capital structure are missing opportunities for greater insights into the fundamentals of the companies—as well as opportunities for choosing different securities within the capital structure, for example, substituting a convertible for an equity or a straight bond. Equity analysts often ignore the leverage implications of convertible obligations, in our observation, although they do focus on fully diluted earnings, which are influenced by convertibles. Successful equity investors approach common stocks as investments in *businesses* rather than as speculations in common stocks per se.

2.4.2 Credit-Rating Lags and Leads—in Equities As Well as Bonds

Credit ratings tend to lag fundamental changes in creditworthiness. Cynics may say this is because the rating agencies are typically paid by the companies to rate the companies' securities. Aside from potential conflicts of interest, credit agencies perform elaborate research and must interact with their corporate clients and with their own committees before publicly disclosing that a rating change is possible, and it necessarily takes even longer to actually change a rating. It may be presumed that ratings downgrades—which are more important than upgrades—take longer than upgrades because companies resist downgrades and presumably never object to upgrades. And company managements are naturally persuasive.

The debt markets almost always pressure the market prices of bonds in anticipation of ratings downgrades. Credit research performed by analysts who do *not* work for a credit-rating agency should be freer from constraints and hence, should be timelier. Institutional investment accounts, of course, typically have credit constraints that limit exposure to low-rated securities. It is particularly fruitful to identify bonds that may be downgraded from investment grade (BBB– or higher) to a high-yield (*junk*) rating (BB+ or lower) because there will be weakness in the market prices of such bonds once the issues are placed on watch for a downgrade, and there will be forced selling by accounts that are restricted to investment grade if the issues are actually downgraded to high yield. Moreover, high-yield accounts may be unfamiliar with these *fallen angel* bonds and may be slow to begin bidding to buy these bonds despite attractive yields.

Smaller-capitalization companies within the convertible market tend to have convertible bonds that are either non-rated or have low ratings. Yet, smaller companies that issue convertibles often have no other debt. This greatly simplifies credit analysis, and it suggests a low risk of default, because it is easier to refinance a convertible when it is the only debt. (Note that mandatory convertibles and other convertible preferreds tend to be issued by larger, higher-quality companies, whereas smaller, lower-quality companies are essentially confined to convertible bonds.)

Credit trends tend to lead reported earnings, and when a company has bonds outstanding, the prices of the bonds sometimes move earlier than the market prices of the company's common shares. Hence, credit and cash-flow analysis are rewarding when selecting equities as well as when investing in convertibles.

Selecting equities based on cash flow is a feature of Berkshire Hathaway. An emphasis on cash flow also fits nicely with an emphasis on creditworthiness. As individuals, we all understand the importance of personal cash flow. Yet, cash flow is rarely the focus of investment research and business news commentary.

2.4.3 Recognizing Opportunities in Technology and Biotechnology Convertibles

The convertible market is dominated by technology companies, which have exciting "stories" about growth prospects. Yet, there is evidence that analyzing reported numbers—rather than future prospects—is particularly fruitful in investing in tech stocks. According to Joel Tillinghast in 2017 (manager of the Fidelity Low-Priced Stock Fund since 1989), "Contrary to popular wisdom, picking stocks based on low P/Es [price/earnings ratios] and high free cash flow yields works particularly well with technology stocks."[9]

Some biotechnology managements are skilled at issuing securities when the capital markets are receptive rather than when the companies have to have additional capital. This skill probably reflects the inherent uncertainty of the biotechnology business, which makes such companies appear to be weak credits.[10]

We recall a biotech company that was planning to issue a new convertible bond while it had an existing discount convertible bond outstanding, which traded at a high yield that obviously reflected market doubts about the ability of the company to redeem the bond at maturity. Yet, the company was aggressively promoting a new convertible. When the CFO visited us, we did not reveal that we were primarily interested in the current discount convertible bond, which promised a rewarding yield to maturity if it avoided default.

We lambasted the company for its failures to develop successful products and for its consequently chronic cash burn. The CFO was unperturbed. We concluded that the new convertible was essentially an advance re-funding of the existing convertible. We inferred that the CFO was opportunistically issuing a new convertible in a strong market—so, from a credit perspective, it didn't matter if the company's revenues were inadequate to redeem the existing convertible; there was going to be plenty of capital from the new convertible, therefore the existing convertible provided an attractive yield to maturity with little default risk.

2.4.4 Low Default Rates

Convertible securities tend to have low default rates, perhaps lower than expected relative to the credit ratings of the individual securities. One reason may be that convertible issuers often are modern, asset-light companies that frequently have strong cash flow. Asset values provide cushions for workouts in bankruptcy and sometimes enable interim survival as portions of distressed companies are sold off. But cash flow sustains companies, and it is usually relatively easy to refinance a convertible if the convertible is the only debt on the balance sheet. (See default rates in Figure 2.1.) Volatility is associated with weaker credits, yet, volatility enhances the value of the conversion privilege; hence, volatility may favor issuing convertibles to refinance.

Indeed, the structure of convertibles issued by companies in financial difficulty sometimes resembles a bankruptcy; that is, a new convertible bond may be sold with a relatively high coupon and a relatively low conversion premium. Such a structure dilutes the common shares, but it may provide cash to keep the company alive long enough to recover. Moreover, it may be possible for convertible arbitrageurs to hedge such structures in a way that virtually guarantees them a profit—even if the company goes under.

In recent decades, convertible defaults have been driven by unusual market developments. The 1990s saw dot-com companies with little or no cash flow, and the early 2000s saw fraudulent companies. In our view, credit and cash-flow analysis could have exposed the shortcomings of such

Figure 2.1   Annual default rates of convertibles, high-yield bonds, and leveraged loans

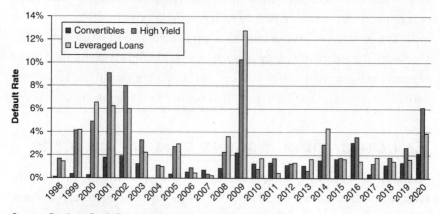

Sources: Barclays, Credit Suisse, and BofA Securities.

companies—and some managers were able to avoid these deteriorating situations using the techniques discussed in this chapter, which did not identify fraud but exposed fundamental weaknesses of companies pretending to be growing and profitable.

2.5 CONVERTIBLE MARKET FEATURES GROWTH

The most common characteristic of corporations that issue convertibles is the promise of growth. Convertible issuers tend to grow rapidly, as can be demonstrated statistically using revenue figures.[11] Growth is reflected in the industries that dominate the US convertible market, that is, technology and healthcare. Investors in convertibles have a choice of securities limited to the several hundred convertible securities in the world.[12] Growth prospects—and disappointments—probably are reflected in the high volatility of the underlying stocks of convertible issuers. In February 2021, Bloomberg reported that the 162-week average volatility of the stocks of issuers in the ICE BofA All-Convertibles Index (VXA0) was 56.96%, whereas the average volatility of the stocks in the S&P 500 was only 37.65%. Volatility per se drives quantitative models of convertible securities; that is, the higher the volatility of the underlying stock, the higher the theoretical value of the convertible. In order to ultimately obtain appreciation from the conversion privilege, the underlying stock has to appreciate—and volatility is usually (although not necessarily) a side effect of appreciation. Moreover, if a convertible bond is a good credit and it promises strong positive asymmetry, high volatility of the underlying stock should be a plus because such a bond is much more likely to capture upside volatility than to suffer on the downside.

The prospect of growth is an ideal investment feature of convertible issuers, and the record of convertible indices essentially matching the returns of equity indices over decades may partly reflect the superior growth of convertible issuers relative to the growth of companies found in equity indices.

2.6 CONVERTIBLE ISSUERS COME IN ALL SIZES

Some of the largest US companies have issued convertibles. Tesla issued five convertible bonds in 2013–2019. Mid-cap and small-cap companies often issue convertibles. Startup companies that are not yet, public

Table 2.1 VXA0 Issuer Characteristics (as of December 31, 2020)

	5-Year Revenue CAGR	Market Cap	162-Week Volatility
Median	10.96	$3.42 billion	53.35
Average	17.64	$15.30 billion	56.67

Sources: VXA0, Bloomberg.

frequently issue privately placed convertibles. Hence, the overall convertible market is all cap. The sizes of the equity market capitalizations of US issuers of convertibles are 77% large capitalization (>$5 billion), 19% midcapitalization ($1 billion–$5 billion), and 4% small capitalization (<$1 billion) as of year-end 2020 according to the VXA0 (see Table 2.1). Many investors feel more comfortable with large companies that typically are high-quality credits and have stocks with lower volatility.

2.7 BALANCED CONVERTIBLES PORTFOLIO STRATEGIES

The goal of equity-like returns with lower risk is likely to be achieved by employing a *balanced* convertible strategy that emphasizes positive asymmetry, that is, a portfolio that holds convertibles that are likely to participate much more in the appreciation than the downside risk of the underlying stocks. (The concept of balanced does not imply low risk in the sense of low volatility, although a balanced convertible bond is likely to have lower volatility than the underlying stock.)

A balanced portfolio typically would be confined to convertible bonds that trade in a range of, say, 85 to 135 at purchase and portend high upside/downside asymmetry. The usual sell discipline is twofold: (1) harvest capital gains when the bonds trade so high above face value that they no longer provide significant downside protection, and (2) sell bonds that have lost upside participation as the underlying stocks have declined and the conversion premiums have risen. (Such issues have typically provided some downside protection relative to the underlying stock.) In each case, the portfolio manager would swap into more balanced issues.

There is no limit to the appreciation potential of a convertible bond. If the underlying stock soars, the conversion value also will soar, and a convertible bond can appreciate to 200, 300, or higher. In 2020, Tesla convertibles traded above 1,000. At such prices, the bond will trade essentially in lockstep with the stock, that is, with a delta of 100% and little downside protection. The volatility of such a bond will be as high as the volatility of the underlying stock. Such a bond is still a convertible, but the key advantages of convertible investing—downside protection, lower volatility, and even yield—have faded to insignificance.

The quantitative method to determine whether a convertible is balanced is to measure its delta, its gamma, and the resulting projected upside/downside relative to the price action of the underlying stock. A delta of between 60% and 70% probably would be an ideal balanced portfolio holding in a statistical sense. Beyond delta, of course, a portfolio manager should consider gamma, that is, the *rate* of change in delta. The higher the gamma, the greater the upside/downside asymmetry; high-gamma convertibles are ideal for balanced convertible strategies.

Credit analysis is critical to achieving the goal of realizing balanced returns. If the financial strength of the issuing company is deteriorating, then the downside risk of the convertible bond will be increasing regardless of what a model concludes. It is important to analyze the credits and to apply appropriate credit spreads to whatever convertible evaluation model one is using. Otherwise, the concept of downside protection may be an illusion.

2.8 DEFENSIVE CONVERTIBLES PORTFOLIO STRATEGIES

Lower-delta convertibles are generally referred to as *defensive* because in a period of equity market decline, their reduced sensitivity to stock prices helps them to resist price declines, whereas higher-delta, more in-the-money convertibles suffer greater price setbacks.

2.8.1 Defensive Portfolio Tactics

Traditional long-only convertible strategies can be achieved by constructing portfolios with appropriate weighted averages of deltas, gammas, and premiums over bond value. It is simpler, however, to construct such portfolios exclusively with convertibles that conform to the strategy. Moreover, such disciplined portfolios are more likely to achieve their goals than undisciplined portfolios that permit portfolio managers to express bullish or bearish views that may turn out to be incorrect.

The basic method to construct a defensive portfolio is to confine investments to convertible bonds that are trading at low premiums over investment value, that is, at low premiums over the estimated market value of these convertible bonds if they were *not* convertible. Low premiums over bond value suggest less downside risk as well as lower volatility than more equity-sensitive convertibles. The next step is to look for issues that promise significant upside participation as well as downside protection, that is, convertibles with high gammas. Yield advantage over the underlying common stock is also important—and the yields on discount convertibles may be high. (*Discount* convertibles are defined as issues that have declined to significant discounts from par and are typically trading at low premiums over bond value and at high premiums over conversion value—with relatively high yields to maturity.)

Convertible bonds trading at discounts are attractive, but the fundamentals of the issuing companies must be carefully analyzed to confirm that the issuers of discount convertibles are creditworthy—and that any weakness in fundamentals is likely to be temporary. Obviously, the credit obligations of companies in danger of going bankrupt will almost always trade at deep discounts from par. The rare instances of fraudulent companies usually turn out to be situations where some market participants have identified the dangers before most market participants—much less the credit-rating agencies—and became aware of the credit risk. Hence, discount convertible bonds that appear to be undervalued require deep research because the market may be right, and the apparent bargains may be too good to be true.

Defensive strategies may include convertible preferreds to the extent that an investment value equivalent of *bond value* can be estimated for preferreds. The defensive character of convertible preferreds is inherently deficient in two respects: First, the dividends can be passed without creating an act of default. (The only safeguard against passing the dividend is a provision that the common dividend will have to be passed before the preferred dividend can be passed; this is a meaningful constraint on banking companies that generally maintain common dividends under any conditions short of collapse.) Second, convertible preferreds rarely have a maturity. An exception is convertible trust preferreds where the maturities may be decades in the future, so this future redemption provides almost no downside protection until it becomes imminent.

The attraction of convertible preferreds is the relatively high yield. And traditional convertible preferreds (not trust preferreds) typically are registered and listed, so they can be traded easily by individual investors, and their dividends usually are tax-favored qualified dividend income (QDI). (The distributions on trust preferreds are paid quarterly—like dividends—but the distributions are fully taxed interest.)

Mandatory preferreds are rarely appropriate for defensive convertible strategies because of the ultimate absence of downside price protection; that is, after three years, mandatory convertibles automatically convert into the underlying stock, whether the stock is up, sideways, or down. And the last is the potential killer of the total return. A favorable exception occurs when a mandatory is trading at or slightly above the upper range of its dead zone—it will provide some defensive downside price protection because the conversion ratio will automatically *increase* once the underlying stock falls into the dead zone.

One defensive convertible investor who was also a military historian once observed that the strategy works in much the same way as the Duke of Wellington's reverse-slope defense in the battle of Waterloo, where he defeated Napoleon. For a complete review of this colorful analogy, please visit www.AdventCap.com/Book/SupplementaryMaterial.

Defensive convertibles capture less of the upside of the underlying stocks than balanced convertibles—but there are advantages. Accounts that emphasize quantitative measures will appreciate lower volatility and a potentially higher Sharpe ratio. Accounts that focus on the magnitude of drawdowns will appreciate the superior downside protection of defensive convertibles. A further reason to choose a defensive strategy (see Chapter 5) is that lower volatility and muted drawdowns are easier to handle emotionally. That is, it should be easier to stick with a defensive strategy than to stick with a balanced strategy.

2.9 DISTRESSED CONVERTIBLES

Distressed convertible bonds are rare under most economic and market conditions, so distressed convertibles per se cannot be an ongoing strategy. Yet, when panic strikes the capital markets—particularly when there is a *credit* panic, as in 2008—marginal credits in the convertible market suddenly begin to *trade* distressed, and some of these convertibles that are trading distressed are in fact *money good*. As we explained in Section 2.4.4, convertibles rarely default.

At first, when a company's prospects are regarded as deteriorating, the price of a convertible bond will tend to hold up better than the price of the underlying stock—in keeping with the expected asymmetry. As the market begins to doubt the credit, however, the credit spread of the convertible will widen sharply, and the market price of the convertible will start to catch up with the stock on the downside. The bond may even drop *more* than the stock (in percentage terms). Consider what would occur if a company that had issued a convertible bond was declining to an enterprise value of *zero*; the concept of credit spread would disappear, and both the convertible bond and the stock would drop to zero. Ultimately, the delta of the convertible bond would rise to 100% or higher *as the price of the bond declined*, so a convertible bond trading at less than 50 may have a delta that is as high as if the bond were trading at 150.

The realized delta of a distressed convertible may be 100% or higher even though the premium may be extremely high because the price of a distressed convertible bond reflects bankruptcy recovery value rather than conversion value. As recovery value moves to the forefront, all the usual metrics of evaluating convertibles—conversion premium, premium over bond value, yield, maturity—become less relevant. Multiple bonds of the same issuer often will converge on similar prices regardless of differences in maturities and coupons. As quantitative modeling becomes less relevant, hedging such convertible bonds becomes guesswork—and arbitrageurs who depend on quantitative evaluations have an imperative to sell.

The confusion surrounding convertible bonds trading at distressed levels creates opportunities. If in-depth research can conclude that a convertible that is trading distressed is in fact going to survive at least and prosper at best, then there are potentially large profits for buyers. Distressed convertibles often are acquired by distressed bond specialists who normally avoid convertibles. When such an opportunity develops in a convertible, it usually takes some time for the issue to begin to be accumulated by high-yield and distressed investors, and this period of depressed market prices is the opportune time to accumulate distressed convertibles. Once market participants recognize the creditworthiness of a stressed or distressed convertible bond, the bond may rise as fast as the price of the common stock for a time as the credit spread tightens dramatically. Inevitably, the realized delta will decline from 100% as the price of the bond recovers from distressed levels.

2.10 INVESTMENT GRADE

The attraction of an exclusively investment-grade convertible strategy is driven primarily by regulations. Most insurance companies have strict regulations on their investment accounts (see Section 5.6.4). States and municipal jurisdictions often impose detailed restrictions on their pension accounts. In the United States, the investment-grade portion of the convertible market is small, but most of the issues are large, and the issuers are large-cap companies that also have liquid common stocks. A portfolio of exclusively high-quality credits typically provides lower volatility, less downside risk, and greater liquidity than the convertible market as a whole; hence, there is less need for diversification.

A danger in the investment-grade range of the convertible bond market is that the need for investment-grade issues in certain institutional portfolios sometimes causes high-quality issues to become overvalued (as can easily be confirmed with quantitative models or even on the proverbial back of the envelope). As described in Chapter 3, Berkshire Hathaway once issued an AAA-rated convertible bond with an effective yield of −0.75%. It appeared that the market placed a high value on the triple-A rating. Despite a yield that was lower than the zero yield on Berkshire Hathaway common stock, the convertible bond did provide a rewarding return as the underlying stock appreciated. (Of course, it is always advantageous to convertible investors when the underlying stock pays no dividend and instead appreciates in response to the internal compounding of retained earnings, which raises the intrinsic value of the stock—and Berkshire Hathaway is an unusual example of an old successful company that lacks a common dividend.)

Investment-grade convertible bonds tend to have low coupons, but most mandatory convertible preferreds are investment grade and provide the highest current yield in the new-issues market. If mandatory securities are permitted in an investment-grade account, the addition is a good way

Table 2.2   Convertible Ratings by Region (as of December 31, 2020)

	Europe	US
Investment grade	25.76%	11.31%
High yield	3.50%	10.96%
Unrated	70.74%	77.73%

Data: Refinitiv Europe and US Convertible Indices.

to increase the portfolio yield while also providing significant equity sensitivity. As we explained in Chapter 1, mandatory convertibles at issue usually provide significant positive asymmetry if held to mandatory conversion three years later. And sometimes mandatory preferreds provide excellent positive asymmetry in the aftermarket as well, particularly when the underlying common stock is trading near the upper end of the dead zone, because the conversion ratio adjustment will provide significant downside protection when such a price relationship prevails.

In Europe, the proportion of convertible bonds considered investment grade is higher than in the United States see Table 2.2. European markets lack the highly developed high-yield bond market that has prevailed in the United States since the 1980s (see Table 2.2).

A complication arises because investment-grade companies in Europe often forgo paying to have their bonds rated, apparently because directors and managements of high-quality European companies feel that their credit strengths are obvious to market participants. This is the reverse of US practice, where investment-grade issues usually have ratings, sometimes provided gratis by rating agencies—whereas non-rated (NR) issues in the United States typically are low quality. Hence, US investors generally *assume* that an NR security is below investment grade, and this assumption may inhibit the use of high-quality European convertible bonds in US-based investment-grade accounts.

Given the availability of investment-grade convertible bonds in Europe and in a few other countries outside the United States, it is easier to create a diversified global investment-grade portfolio than a domestic US investment-grade portfolio. (Mandatory preferreds are most prevalent in the United States, however, and if permitted, they are useful in a US investment-grade strategy.)

2.11 GLOBAL BALANCED AND GLOBAL DEFENSIVE STRATEGIES

These global strategies essentially mirror domestic balanced and domestic defensive convertible strategies but with global investments rather than exclusively US issues. The convertible market is dominated by issuance in certain areas, notably the United States, Europe (including Britain despite Brexit), and Asia. Different regions come and go in the convertible market. Japan was a dominant issuer in the 1980s, but regulatory changes led to a decline in issuance that has persisted for decades. Non-Japan Asia issuance is dominated by companies that are essentially Chinese, although incorporations and listings may be in Hong Kong, offshore, or even in the United States or United Kingdom. Latin America has had a pocket of convertible issuance in Brazil. At one time, a few large Argentine, Brazilian, Chilean, and Mexican companies issued US dollar–denominated convertible bonds, but such issues are now extinct.

When comparing global and domestic investments, it is important to weigh the effects of currency exchange-rate risk and hedging. Hedging against currency risk requires the use of foreign exchange (FX) forward contracts to lock in a rate at which the future value of the bond can be exchanged back into its local currency. Engaging in this sort of hedge has either a cost or a positive return depending on the relative risk-free interest rates between the local and foreign currencies.

From the beginning of 2012 until 2020, the cost of hedging a US dollar (USD) investment for a Euro zone investor became increasingly expensive, reaching nearly 4% per year. For a US investor, the opposite was true, because a euro (EUR) forward hedge generated a positive yield of nearly 4%; therefore, the total return on euro-denominated convertibles was significantly higher net of a hedge. Global indices include hypothetical FX hedging effects when publishing index returns on either a USD- or EUR-hedged basis.

Some investors choose to leave FX exposures unhedged because there is often a built-in economic hedge given that equity markets tend to appreciate when their local currency depreciates and vice versa—a phenomenon likely to be especially prevalent in the prices of shares of global, multinational, and export-oriented companies. However, this effect is complicated and is difficult to anticipate.

2.12 CONCLUSION

Convertibles represent a niche asset class that is ignored or misunderstood by most investors. We feel that a combination of credit research and equity research—which reflects the hybrid nature of convertible securities—is the ideal way to select the most attractive convertible securities and to avoid deteriorating situations. Successful companies generate cash, just as successful investors generate positive returns.

Traditional convertible strategies can be as simple or as complicated as an investor chooses. The long-term record of long-only convertible indices essentially matching equity returns with less risk suggests that a basic approach to convertibles is highly rewarding, although more complicated approaches may also enhance returns and/or reduce risk.

ENDNOTES

1. "The Convertible Railway Bond," *Railroad Age Gazette* 1908; XLV(28): 1518.
2. https://en.wikipedia.org/wiki/Capital_asset_pricing_model.
3. Adam Hayes, "WorldCom," Investopedia, October 6, 2020, https://www.investopedia.com/terms/w/worldcom.asp.
4. https://www.econcrises.org/2016/11/29/parmalat/.
5. https://en.wikipedia.org/wiki/Sino-Forest_Corporation.
6. https://ftalphaville.ft.com/2018/03/01/1519909775000/Steinhoff-International--cash-is-missing/.
7. https://www.cnet.com/news/red-hat-stock-dives-on-earnings-restatement/.
8. For simplicity, ignoring cash on a company's balance sheet.
9. Joel Tillinghast, *Big Money Thinks Small: Biases, Blind Spots, and Smarter Investing* (New York: Columbia Business School Publishing, 2017), p. 188.
10. Bill Feingold, *Beating the Indexes Investing in Convertible Bonds to Improve Performance and Reduce Risk* (Upper Saddle River, NJ: FT Press, 2012), p. 88.

11. The average revenue growth for US convertible issuers over the last five years through 2020 was 18.95%.

12. CONV, the ICE BofA Global Convertible Index, had 667 individual issuers at year-end 2020.

CHAPTER 3

Convertible History

Steam Railways to the Internet Highways

It was a common practice to finance with convertible bonds.

—*John Moody, 1924*[1]

3.1 FUNDING DISRUPTION, INNOVATION, AND GROWTH

The US convertible market has funded disruption, innovation, and growth since the early nineteenth century. Historical anecdotes provide timeless examples of using ever-evolving convertible securities in pursuit of new opportunities.

The first American convertible bond apparently was issued by the New York & Erie Railroad in 1843—at a time when steam locomotion was the most disruptive technology and railroads were innovative growth companies. Steam railroads were much faster than horses and canals. In a precursor to globalization, railroads enhanced trade patterns and migration. Canal companies were driven out of business—except for the Delaware & Hudson, which was the only canal carrier with the foresight to build a railroad (which still exists as part of Canadian Pacific).

Convertible bonds became "the favored way to finance railroads."[2] US railroads sometimes issued convertibles in London at a time when the United States was an emerging market and often adopted the British appellation *railway*. The Erie changed its name from railroad to railway in 1861[3] and issued another convertible in 1868.[4]

Railroad construction required large amounts of capital—and promised future growth. Hence, railroads were ideal issuers of convertible bonds—foreshadowing the success of Amazon, Spotify, and Tesla, which together issued 10 convertibles between 1999 and 2021. The theme of technology and growth among convertible issuers persists nearly two centuries after the first Erie Railroad convertible.

The post–Civil War era marked the golden age of US railroad expansion from 35,000 miles in 1865 to a peak of 254,000 miles in 1916.[5] The Morris & Essex Rail Road (M&E) in New Jersey issued a $3 million convertible bond in 1869 with a 7% coupon—and a restriction that it was convertible for only five years, which would have forced the bondholders to convert if the stock was above the conversion price on the fifth anniversary of issuance. In 2011, Bank of America issued a private preferred security to Berkshire Hathaway that was usable to exercise warrants that expired in 10 years (see Section 14.5)—which created the same imperative to convert as the time limit on the M&E convertible 142 years earlier. The structures of the M&E and Bank of America convertibles are manifestations of the ongoing evolution of convertible structures—while the basic concept of asymmetric returns has been a constant.

The magnitude of convertible issues in the golden age of railroad growth is exemplified by the 1874 issuance of a $10 million convertible bond (equal to about $2 billion in 2021 dollars, matching the $2 billion issues in 2021 by Airbnb and Ford) by the Rome, Watertown & Ogdensburgh Rail Road (RW&O). The 7% RW&O bond paid *quarterly* coupons, although semiannual coupons were already prevalent, as confirmed by an 1853 railroad convertible that paid semiannually.[6] The RW&O bond was convertible for only five years. In the years following issuance of the large RW&O bond, the convertible market saw "hundreds more railroad bonds."[7]

Convertible issuance by railroads virtually disappeared after 1880 but resumed in 1901 with issues from the Baltimore & Ohio (B&O) and the Union Pacific (UP).[8] The B&O was the first railroad in North America in 1827.[9] The UP is the largest US railroad in 2021. Downside protection was evident during the Panic of 1907 when UP shares "fell to . . . 75% below the conversion price of the bonds." Yet, the convertible "at no time fell below 78¼."[10] *Railroad Age Gazette* reported in 1908 that "[t]he . . . convertible bond is coming more and more into use as a form of railway finance."[11]

Convertible bonds often were issued at yields that approximated the yields on the underlying stocks. So an increase in the common dividend might represent an *increase* in income for the convertible holders if they converted into the underlying stock. The conversion premium often was zero, so from the perspective of investors, choosing a convertible rather than the underlying stock was a way to lock in the current yield of the stock and avoid the risk that the common dividend might be cut—while retaining the option to capture 100% of the dividend increases and appreciation of the underlying stock by converting the bonds. Issuing companies defended against the prospect of conversions that would require the companies to pay *more* in cash dividends than the interest on the convertibles by sometimes including a provision for delayed conversion; a newly issued convertible bond might not be convertible for 10 to 12 years or more.[12] Delayed conversion eventually disappeared.

The popularity of railroad convertibles in 1910 had "not yet, begun to wane," and the face value of convertibles outstanding was "the rather startling total of over $1.5 billion,"[13] which equates to about $40.8 billion in 2021 dollars.

Some investors in convertibles were ill-informed, as in 1910, when a 7% Chicago, Milwaukee & St Paul Railroad bond matured with a conversion value of $1,700, but "many . . . turned in their bonds for redemption at par" for $1,000.[14] The comprehensive annual guide to railroad bonds, *Moody's Steam Railroads*, peaked at over 2,000 pages in the 1930s. Yet, US rail mileage had peaked in 1916, after which the need for capital declined. Because railroads were no longer growth companies, railroad convertibles offered less potential for appreciation. Yet, railroads continued to issue convertibles until the dawn of the Great Depression in the 1930s.

Moody's Steam Railroads survived through the 1940s, which was near the end of the steam locomotion era that lasted more than a century in the United States. In the post–World War II period, competition from motor vehicles and airlines led to a decline in profits of US railroads despite huge cost reductions from the substitution of diesel locomotives for steam. US railroading reached a nadir in 1970 with the bankruptcy of Penn Central Transportation—which was the largest US railroad at the time and which also constituted the largest bankruptcy in US history at the time. US railroads began a long recovery after the 1976 government-funded consolidation of Penn Central (PC) and other northeastern lines that had followed the PC into bankruptcy.

Issuance of railroad convertibles briefly resumed in the 1990s. Canadian National and Union Pacific issued convertible preferreds that provided high yields and rewarding total returns during the era of dot-com boom and bust, when the concept of investing in an old industry like railroads was subject to ridicule. More than a century after railroad construction essentially ceased in North America, railroads were being built in China, and the China Railway Construction Corporation issued $500 million of convertible bonds in 2016.[15]

3.2 INDUSTRIAL ISSUANCE IN THE TWENTIETH CENTURY

Issuance of convertibles by industrial companies advanced in the early twentieth century and has persisted into the twenty-first century. Industrial convertible bonds were discussed by investing author Montgomery Rollins in 1910,[16] including American Telephone & Telegraph Company, which was a technology company at the time—in keeping with the seemingly endless tendency of convertible bonds to fund new technologies. Beat Thoma, CIO of Fisch Asset Management in Zurich, cites several household names that had convertible bonds outstanding in the early 1900s, including General Electric, International Paper, Western Union, and Westinghouse,[17] three of which were essentially technology companies.

Convertible issuance resurged after World War II,[18] but railroads were losing traffic and were no longer prominent among convertible issuers. In keeping with the convertible tradition of innovation and growth, convertibles were issued by aerospace companies, airlines, and some of the faster-growing industrial companies.

Convertible bonds were of lower quality in the post–World War II period. Economist Otto H. Poensgen[19] concluded that the conversion feature was necessary to make "an otherwise unpalatable instrument acceptable to the investor." Poensgen observed that "subordinated bonds are usually convertible." He cited an article entitled, "Subordinated Debentures: The Debt That Serves as Equity."[20]

The 1960s were a period of strong convertible issuance, with retail investors able to participate through traditional convertible preferreds that often were issued in exchange for common shares in acquisitions. In 1960–1967, 85% of convertible preferreds were issued in conjunction with mergers.[21] There were 315 "actively trading" preferreds among a total of "above 850" convertibles in 1968 per Sidney Fried in *Investing and Speculating with Convertibles*.[22] Fried counted 45 convertible preferreds that were issued in the first half of 1968 as part of mergers.[23]

Fried's book includes numerous examples of convertibles that chronically traded at essentially zero conversion premiums once the underlying common stocks had risen high enough to push the conversion value above par. Low premiums were a consequence of the lack of call protection; the convertibles could be cash called at any time. If the premiums were low enough and the yields were high enough, simple arithmatic would enable an investor to calculate that such issues would tend to outperform the underlying stocks up, down, or sideways. Such opportunities apparently reflected the ignorance of convertibles that has commonly prevailed.

Poensgen observed in 1965 that "corporations issuing convertible bonds had a significantly better past growth record."[24] Convertible issuers have continued to achieve superior growth. The median sales growth rate of US convertible issuers was 8.91% versus 3.55% for the S&P 500 in the five years through September 30, 2020.[25] Fried's book lists a dozen convertible issuers regarded as fast growing "Nifty Fifty"[26] growth companies with "One Decision" stocks in the first couple of years of the 1970s.

Most convertible preferreds in the early 1970s were a legacy of the merger and acquisition activity of the 1960s.[27] Some acquisitive issuers, for example, International Telephone & Telegraph (ITT), were members of the Nifty Fifty.

The target companies of acquisitions sometimes had common stocks that yielded more than the shares of the acquiring company, so paying the target shareholders with a higher-yielding preferred was attractive to the target shareholders. Moreover, the exchange of common stock for preferred shares of the acquirer was not a taxable event—unlike a cash takeover. The convertible preferreds were convertible into the underlying shares at a premium, which was an advantage to the issuing companies. The passing of the merger mania plus changes in accounting and other factors led to declining issuance of convertible preferreds, although the use of convertible bonds in deals persisted—notably in the case of the gigantic Kohlberg Kravis Roberts & Co. leveraged buyout of RJR Nabisco in 1988, which included a $2.3 billion convertible bond as part of the $24.8 billion consideration paid to RJR shareholders.[28]

3.3 EVALUATING CONVERTIBLES

We can only guess how convertibles were evaluated in times when sophisticated calculations were made with slide rules. Some clues appeared in the *Railroad Age Gazette* in 1908: "If the bond has a considerable time to run . . . it is apt to fall below the ratio of value to the stock based upon the presumptive value of the stock at the time of convertibility. . . . The shrewd broker addresses the old conservative holder of the stock . . . that by selling his stock, buying its equivalent in [convertible] bonds . . . he can enjoy a return better secured by the bond and equivalent to the uncertain [common] dividend, and can also pocket, when convertibility comes, a handsome profit besides." At the time, common dividends represented high payouts of earnings that carried the risk of dividend cuts. And high dividends inhibited the appreciation potential of common stocks. Safety of income was a bigger attraction of convertibles than in eras when payout ratios were lower and appreciation potential was consequently greater.

The first convertible valuation models were developed in 1935.[29] *Value Line Convertibles* introduced quantitative convertible evaluations by 1972.[30] The *Value Line Convertibles* model was empirical, based on observations of how the convertible market behaved. The Value Line model probably was inspired by William Schwartz,[31] who published *The Warrant-Convertible Compass* prior to 1967,[32] and his associate, Julius Spellman, with whom Schwartz had written *Guide to Convertible Securities* (1968).[33] Schwartz and Spellman may have used semi-log-scale graph paper to plot convertible price movements relative to underlying stocks.[34] Schwartz was "a creator and editor of the *Value Line Convertibles* Securities Service" along with "the late Julius Spellman—also a contributing editor until his untimely death [in 1970]."[35] The *Value Line Convertibles* model was also influenced by the econometrically derived warrants model developed by Sheen T. Kassouf in 1965.[36] The *Value Line Convertibles* model was programmed by Bob Brown at Value Line.[37]

Value Line Convertibles provided the public with comprehensive information about essentially all the hundreds of publicly traded convertible securities—at a modest subscription price that attracted thousands of individual investors and essentially all the institutions that were active in convertibles at the time. In 1972–1979, prior to the widespread use of personal computers and the availability of online data, "for most users, [*Value Line*

Convertibles] was the only available source of information and analysis of convertibles.[38]

The *Value Line Convertibles* model projected the upside-downside asymmetry of individual convertibles relative to price movements of the underlying stocks. The model predated the 1973 publication of the now-famous Black-Scholes-Merton (BSM) equation, which eventually became the basis of essentially all evaluations of convertibles, options, and other derivatives. We can infer that the BSM equation quantified market relationships between derivative securities and their underlying interests that were captured by the empirical calculations of the *Value Line Convertibles* model.

Computer technology seems to have had little effect on the convertible market until after the development of inexpensive minicomputers in the 1960s. The personal computer and the internet came into widespread use in the 1980s and ultimately put convertible models on the desks of essentially all convertible professionals.

The analyses of convertibles at Value Line inspired convertibles research at investment banks. *Value Line Convertibles* senior analyst Paul Berkman was recruited by Merrill Lynch in 1979 to initiate what probably was the first convertibles research at an investment bank. Two years later, convertibles analyst Richard Nelson left Value Line for Thomson McKinnon Securities, where he introduced a quantitative model and published convertibles research that linked equities research to specific convertible securities. Subsequently, Rick Nelson expanded his convertible analysis at four other investment banks (Kidder, Peabody & Co., Lehman Brothers, Furman Selz, and J. Giordano Securities) as convertibles research spread to numerous banks into the 1990s. But convertible research at investment banks waned in the early twenty-first century as online convertible evaluation models became common and data sources such as Bloomberg instantly provided information that previously had been difficult to obtain and compile.

3.4 INDIVIDUAL INVESTORS IN THE CONVERTIBLE MARKET

Historically, individual investors accounted for much more of the trading volume than institutions in the US capital markets. Convertible preferred shares were much more common in the first three decades after World War

II, when individuals still dominated the stock market. Preferred shares are always much easier for individuals to trade than corporate bonds, even though corporate bonds were listed on exchanges through the 1960s. In 1969, there were 264 convertible preferred shares listed on the New York Stock Exchange, with a market value of $17.8 billion,[39] and there were 176 new issues of convertible bonds with a face value of $3.0 billion.[40]

Early in 1969, the broad stock market peaked (as reflected in the Value Line 1700 Index) after a euphoric bull market that had seen many electronic technology startups go public and had included heavy issuance of convertibles among smaller companies as well as large and acquisitive companies, including some of the Nifty Fifty. The bear market that started with smaller-capitalization stocks in 1969 finally enveloped larger-capitalization stocks and even the Nifty Fifty in 1973 and bottomed in November 1974—with a consequent reduction in the issuance of convertibles.

In the early 1970s, perhaps more than half the value of the US convertible market was in convertible preferreds. Convertible preferreds typically were issued by larger companies and were of larger size than the convertible bonds of the day, some of which were only in the few tens of millions of dollars. The transition toward institutional investing began in the 1960s. *Institutional Investor* magazine began publication in 1967.[41] The institutionally dominated era grew with the long bull market that began in late 1974. In the late 1970s, the convertible market resumed its growth; there were more issues, larger issues, and growing interest among institutional investors.[42]

Investor interest in mutual funds began to resume in the 1980s (after having faded during the 1969–1974 bear market and its immediate aftermath), and some open-end convertible funds were established, including three no-load funds in 1985: two Noddings-Calamos convertible funds (one oriented toward growth, the other toward income) and the Value Line Convertible Fund.[43] More and larger mutual funds followed, including some closed-end funds.

It is difficult today for most individual investors to purchase convertible bonds because the preponderance of new convertible bonds are issued as private placements under Securities and Exchange Commission (SEC) Rule 144A, which avoids registration requirements and confines sales at issuance (and for six months afterwards) to investment institutions that meet SEC standards as qualified institutional buyers (QIBs). See Chapter 14 for further details on Rule 144A convertibles.

Registration aside, bonds are inherently more difficult to trade than shares—especially for individual investors. (See details on executing orders for convertibles in Section 16.6.) Few retail brokers are sophisticated enough to execute corporate bond orders. It is difficult to trade bonds electronically, although there are glimmers of hope for easier retail participation in the future via electronic trading. For most retail investors, it is most practical to choose an exchange-traded fund (ETF) or a mutual fund. Retail investors who are sophisticated and who have very large portfolios may want to trade individual convertible bonds.

Two convertible bonds totaling $3.3 billion in January 2002 were structured as New York Stock Exchange–listed *baby bonds*, which traded exactly like listed convertible preferreds. Unlike all other US convertible bonds at the time, these two General Motors (GM) issues—underwritten by Morgan Stanley—were the only convertible bonds issued at $25 each rather than the usual $1,000 par.

Baby bonds may have existed in the convertible market in the past. At the time, the GM bonds were often mistaken for preferred shares because the nature of their pricing and distributions required them to be input in databases as preferreds. This led to multiple data services erroneously characterizing the two GM bonds as preferreds—which raised red flags for accounts prohibited from holding preferreds. Perhaps this is the reason why this structure has not been repeated. After GM filed for bankruptcy in June 2009, the old GM was renamed Motors Liquidation Company, which published a list of frequently asked questions and answers that included "Q. What will happen to my 'preferred shares'? A. Motors Liquidation Company does not have any preferred stock, although many investors mistakenly use that term to refer to several series of convertible debentures."[44]

GM shares had long been regarded as a traditional *widows and orphans* stock, and there was alarm among individual shareholders as the fundamentals of the company deteriorated in the years leading up to the bankruptcy. A few holders of GM common stock realized their capital losses and swapped into the GM convertible bonds in the hope that GM would recover. It was our understanding that the IRS regarded the convertible bonds as materially different from the common stock; hence, such a swap created a tax loss on the common shares and did not trigger a wash sale when the GM convertible bonds were purchased. Ultimately, GM stock went to zero while the convertible bonds presumably obtained some equity in the reorganized General Motors.

3.5 THE 1980S WERE BIG FOR CONVERTIBLES

The 1980s saw a resumption of convertible bonds being issued by household names, notably IBM, with the flotation of a $1.25 billion convertible bond in 1985, when IBM still had an AAA credit rating. Other prominent companies with convertibles outstanding in 1985 included Bell & Howell, Digital Equipment Corp., Johnson Controls, and United Telecom.[45] Growth companies were also a theme of 1980s convertible issuance—as usual—and included The Home Depot and Wendy's.[46]

The zero-coupon original-issue-discount (OID) convertible was invented in 1983 by the late Lee R. Cole of Merrill Lynch. The new type of convertible was called a Liquid Yield Options Note, or LYON. The first LYON was issued in April 1985 by Waste Management; it had a put at accreted value in just over three years, followed by annual puts. Over the next seven years, 67 LYONs were issued, and Merrill Lynch dominated convertible securities underwriting and trading. Co-author Tracy Maitland had joined Merrill Lynch in 1982 and became the firm's top marketer of convertible securities. He founded Advent Capital Management in 1995. (See further details of his career at Merrill Lynch in the Preface.)

Zero-coupon OID convertibles provided excellent downside protection because of interim puts, which eventually evolved into relatively standard 5-year intervals for a 20-year bond. While the downside protection of LYONs was superior, the appreciation potential was muted because the conversion ratio was fixed; as a LYON accreted toward 100 over time, the conversion price increased at the rate of accretion; that is, if a holder wanted to convert, the holder would be converting a bond with an ever higher par value as the bond accreted to its puts and maturity, while the conversion ratio was fixed.

The concept of a conversion price that effectively rose appears to be a throwback to structures of interest-bearing convertible bonds that were issued in the two decades following World War II. Otto H. Poensgen noted in 1965 that

"40% of a sample of 165 postwar [convertible] bonds . . . [have] a conversion price that changes . . . usually in five-year intervals, invariably increasing."[47] Over time, as market interest rates declined, issuance of zero-coupon OID convertibles faded, but the LYON's structure left a legacy of shorter maturities. At the same time, convertible preferred shares—which typically had neither maturities nor puts—also faded from the convertible market.

It is difficult to track the size of the convertible market historically. As recently as 1989, the US convertible market was only $50 billion.[48] As of year-end 2021, the US market had grown to $406 billion, with the total global convertible market $659 billion.[49]

For decades after the Great Depression, most *straight* (non-convertible) *high-yield* or *junk* bonds were *fallen angels*, that is, former investment-grade bonds that had been downgraded. But underwritings of high-yield bonds picked up in 1976 with nine new issues, the largest of which was a 9% bond of then-prominent City Investing, underwritten by Blyth Eastman Dillon in December 1976. Drexel Burnham Lambert underwrote its first high-yield bond in 1977 and quickly gained market share by underwriting 19 of the 73 high-yield issues in the two years 1977–1978.[50] Michael Milken's high-yield department aggressively pursued underwriting and trading of high-yield bonds[51] as well as below-investment-grade convertible bonds and gained a significant share of the convertible market in underwritings and aftermarket trading in the 1980s,[52] prior to regulatory and legal actions that led to the bankruptcy of Drexel Burnham Lambert in February 1990.[53]

Before the 1980s, both individual and institutional investors often made a practice of holding bonds until maturity. By the early 1980s, bond trading in general was accelerating—partly in response to a bear market in fixed-income instruments that had lasted three decades until the 30-year Treasury bond yield peaked at a record high of 15.2% in late 1981. There was a general view among demoralized fixed-income investors that bonds had become inherently volatile, that interest rates would continue to rise indefinitely (and thereby drive bond prices lower), and that bonds—including Treasury bonds—were merely trading instruments, no longer investments despite record high yields. Convertibles proved an excellent alternative to non-convertible bonds in the face of inflation and rising interest rates because convertibles captured upside from the underlying stocks regardless of the direction of interest rates.[54]

Maturities of convertible bonds shortened after the 1970s, when issues with 20- to 30-year maturities were still common, and convertible preferreds had usually been perpetual. By the 1990s, maturities of most new issues ranged from about 4 years to 10 years, whereas OID zero-coupon convertibles with nominal maturities of as long as 20 years had puts in as little as 1 or 3 years from issuance.[55] The convertible market grew substantially in the 1990s and became dominated by institutions—including hedge funds—that traded much more actively than the individual investors who had previously dominated the market.

Convertible hedge funds effectively constitute a liquidity-enhancing multiplication of the number of dealers that make markets in convertibles. The ability to hedge long (or short) positions in convertibles by going short (or long) the underlying stock (see Chapter 7) means that convertibles reflect the liquidity of the underlying stocks—unlike straight non-convertible bonds, which are difficult to hedge. And the liquidity of equities is also much greater than in the past.

The institutional accounts that came to dominate investing in the 1980s invariably had contractual restraints that may contribute to anomalous opportunities in the convertible market. Institutional equity accounts typically are prevented from investing in fixed-income securities—including convertibles—even though convertibles often are superior substitutes for outright investments in equities. Similarly, fixed-income accounts usually prohibit equities—which may prohibit convertible preferreds that are essentially fixed-income instruments. Yet, some fixed-income accounts do not differentiate between straight bonds and convertible bonds, and this enables such accounts to allocate a portion of their portfolios to convertibles in order to participate in the typically higher returns of the equity market.

The new issue market in convertibles has become relatively continuous since the 1980s. Except for momentary panic conditions in the market, there has been a relatively constant stream of new issues.

3.6 CONVERTIBLE ARBITRAGE HAS ITS OWN HISTORY

The basic principle of convertible arbitrage—being long a convertible bond and short some of the underlying common shares—was a strategy used by sophisticated investors more than a century before it became a stand-alone strategy (see Section 7.3.1). A few investors were practicing arbitrage in the early 1970s—including pioneering securities analyst Benjamin Graham.[56] In 1971–1973, a prestigious bank used a convertible arbitrage strategy as part of its internally managed pension fund. The strategy produced positive returns almost every month, but it was abandoned partly because management of the bank was uncomfortable with the concept of being long convertible bonds while simultaneously being short the common shares of the same company.[57] Moreover, some of the convertibles used in the strategy were below investment grade—and investing in high-yield bonds was still taboo among conservative institutions in the early 1970s.

Computer-based convertible models have encouraged convertible arbitrageurs. The widespread use of evaluation models has made the convertible market more efficient and more liquid.

Hedge funds that specialize in convertible arbitrage began to appear in the 1980s.[58] By the early 2000s, both hedge funds and convertible arbitrage had grown dramatically. *Forbes* magazine proclaimed in 2002 that "seven out of ten convertible buyers are cash-laden hedge funds."[59] The year 2003 probably marked a peak for hedge fund investments in convertibles as a percentage of the convertible market as a whole. After the difficulties that faced convertible arbitrage in late 2008, the strategy fell into disfavor and has averaged about 33% of the US convertible market in the following years, although it had grown to 36% by 2021 as performance picked up.[60]

3.7 IRRATIONAL EXUBERANCE AND THE RESUMPTION OF GROWTH

The Airline Deregulation Act of 1978 was followed by more than a decade of aggressive expansion and heavy competition. Pan American World Airways had a convertible bond with a double-digit coupon. By the mid-1990s, airlines were prospering. In the words of Dean Witter transportation analyst Jack Kawa in late 1995, "People are flying as never before. This is more than a cyclical recovery."[61]

A well-timed airline success story was JetBlue, founded in 1988, which issued a convertible bond when it was expanding and was not yet, cash-flow positive. Following the Great Financial Crisis (GFC) of 2008–2009, however, each of the old established but heavily indebted *legacy carriers* that survived deregulation filed for bankruptcy by 2011.

A period in the mid-1990s saw a rash of *roll-up companies* that made multiple acquisitions of smaller private companies in what appeared to be antidilutive deals that increased the earnings per share of the acquiring companies. The roll-up companies often issued convertible bonds as a way to raise cash for acquisitions.

The highlight of 1990s convertible issuance was the dramatic increase in technology issues in the latter half of the decade—driven by enthusiasm for the internet and the dot-com companies of the "new economy." In the two years through November 2000, 34 convertible bonds raised $13 billion for internet-related companies.[62] Amazon and Apple tapped the market, and some say that these companies were rescued by the timely issuance of convertibles.

Technology issues were objects of market euphoria in 1999—especially dot-com companies. At the time, we calculated that year-to-date through April 1, 1999, if one had purchased every new dot-com convertible at issuance, the total return would have been 100%. This period marked the peak of the "irrational exuberance" that had been observed by Federal Reserve Chair Alan Greenspan in a speech in December 1996.[63] The sharp market correction following the dot-com boom primarily affected the securities of technology companies and other high flyers.

Amazon is one of the most successful companies in history, yet, its early years were marked by cash burning. The need for capital inspired Amazon to issue three convertible bonds. The first was a $325 million zero-coupon discount convertible bond in May 1998. Amazon planned to issue a $500 million 4.75% convertible bond in January 1999, but demand for the issue was so great that the offering was more than doubled to $1.25 billion.[64] Amazon quickly followed the $1.25 billion convertible with a €690 million 6⅞% convertible bond in February 2000. Amazon shares peaked at over $100 a share in 1999 and then plunged to under $6 by 2002 after the dot-com bust but the 4.75% convertible never defaulted (see Figure 3.1).The stock subsequently enjoyed an incredible long-term advance to more than $3,000 in 2021.

Berkshire Hathaway issued a convertible bond that essentially entailed an unprecedented *negative interest* rate in May 2002. The concept apparently was the brainchild of CEO Warren Buffett, who prevailed on

Figure 3.1   Price of Amazon 4.75% 2009 convertible bond

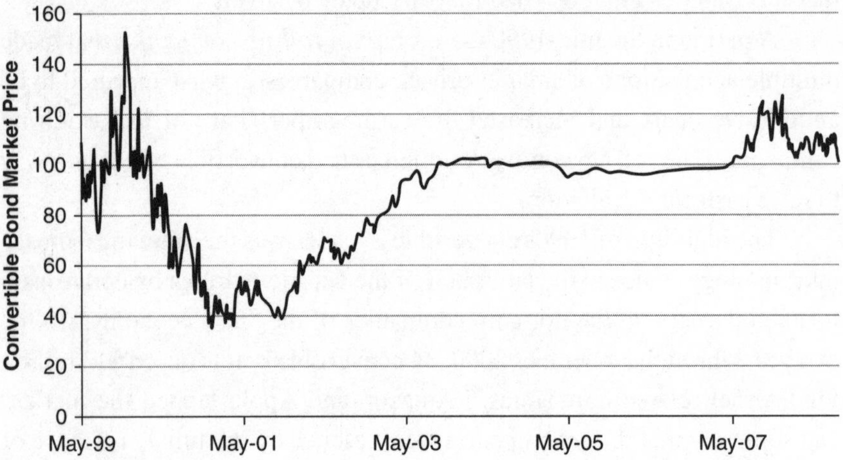

Source: Bloomberg.

Goldman Sachs to design the new convertible. As we understand the structure, it was a usable bond with a non-detachable warrant—essentially a
plain vanilla convertible bond in which the bond can be converted into
the underlying shares. The conversion premium (based on face value of
$10,000 per bond) was a modest 15%. The bond paid a nominal 3% inter-
est—but the interest payments were not distributed to the bondholders;
rather, the 3% interest was the price to Berkshire to maintain the attached
warrants. Moreover, the $10,000 par bonds were sold for $10,340 for each
$10,000 bond, with the extra $340 enabling Berkshire to purchase zero-
coupon Treasury bonds with a yield to maturity of 0.75%—which was the
remaining consideration for the warrants. The new convertible bonds had
an effective yield to maturity of −0.75%. On the plus side, the bonds had
annual puts at face value of $10,000, so the downside risk was minimal.
Demand for the singular convertible bond was so strong that the planned
$250 million offering was increased to $400 million.

Berkshire shares appreciated more than 40% in the ensuing five
years, so the convertible bond did provide a rewarding return: Effectively,
buyers at issuance had paid $10,340 for an ultimate conversion value of
about $14,120. Berkshire's AAA credit rating and the long record of ap-
preciation of the stock—combined with the superb downside protection—
must have been the motivation for investors.

Berkshire Hathaway has also negotiated the purchase of six multi-billion-dollar private convertible securities in order to make low-risk investments in major public companies that needed capital and that offered a combination of high yields on the new convertibles and significant price recovery potential (see Chapter 14).

3.8 EVOLVING VARIETIES AND FEATURES

The late twentieth century saw a variety of new types of convertibles. After the 1970s, convertibles were no longer just plain vanilla convertible bonds and convertible preferreds. Mandatory convertible preferreds—invented in 1988—automatically convert into the underlying stock at the end of three years. Such issues are usually registered and can be readily traded by individual investors, but valuation of mandatory preferreds requires sophisticated quantitative analysis. Mandatory convertibles are highly equity sensitive and lack significant downside protection. Such issues do provide positive asymmetry under certain conditions—as explained in Section 1.4 and discussed further in Chapter 2.

Convertible trust preferreds followed the introduction of non-convertible trust preferreds in 1993. These issues create tax-deductible interest expense for the issuing company but pay quarterly distributions like other preferreds (although the "dividends" on trust preferreds are taxed as interest income). Trust preferreds were almost exclusively issued by bank holding companies and insurance companies because the trust preferreds counted as capital for regulatory purposes. Issuance of convertible trust preferreds essentially ceased after the Dodd-Frank Act of 2010 prohibited most banking companies from counting trust preferreds as capital. At least one convertible trust preferred—the New York Community Bank 6%—remains outstanding as of this writing.

The first CoCo convertibles had contingent conversion ratios that enabled the issuing companies to avoid counting the conversion feature in fully diluted earnings until the stock had risen approximately 30% above conversion (because the bonds were not convertible until conversion value had risen to the contingent conversion price). These issues were popular in the 1990s as a way to minimize reported dilution from the issuance of convertibles.

The original CoCos are not to be confused with the CoCo *bail-in bonds* that prevailed since first issued by European banks as a capital safeguard in the wake of the Great Financial Crisis (GFC) of 2008–2009. Effectively, these bank CoCos reverse the nature of traditional convertibles because conversion occurs if the issuing bank's capital declines below a predetermined level. If the bank is in trouble, its capital will automatically be increased by elimination of the CoCo debt, which will be converted into common shares. Hence, holders of these bank CoCos have no upside beyond the yield—and have unlimited downside if converted into the common stock of a bank that is short of capital. Investors in these CoCos are compensated—they hope—by relatively high yields.

Zero-coupon OID convertibles (issuance of which has ceased) pay no cash interest but have a yield to maturity based on accretion to par at maturity—usually 20 years—and have interim puts at accreted value, usually at 5-year intervals. The issuing corporation was able to tax effect the accretion despite the absence of cash interest payments, and taxable accounts that owned zeroes had to pay taxes on the non-cash imputed interest.

Synthetic convertibles typically are created by investment banks at the behest of institutional investors who want a convertible security for a company that does not have a convertible outstanding. These structures usually are short-term notes (credit obligations of the issuing banks) and sometimes mandatory preferreds. Given that the issuer has to make a profit from a structure that involves hedging with options or other derivatives, synthetic convertibles are rarely, if ever, theoretically undervalued. Moreover, the issuing bank usually is the only entity that would buy such issues if the institutional investors wanted to sell, so liquidity is uncertain. Other types of synthetic convertibles exist; given the widespread availability of options, it is possible to create convertible-like structures.

Call protection has been standard on convertibles since the early 1980s, with a three-year period being prevalent. In the 1970s, convertible bonds lacked call protection. Issues without call protection that traded in the money were subject to a cash redemption call by the issuers in order to force conversion. In 1981, Wang Laboratories called a convertible before its second semi-annual coupon was paid, which prompted criticism in *Forbes* magazine that apparently inspired convertible arbitrageurs and other convertible investors to demand call protection. Yet, Wang common stock had surged, and the unhedged long-only convertible holders had made a big gain during the brief life of the issue.

Call protection was particularly important for convertible arbitrageurs, whose leveraged positions could suffer large losses if an issue with a substantial conversion premium was forced to convert by a call for redemption—which would mean that the price of the convertible would instantly drop to conversion value, eliminating the conversion premium.

Call protection makes it easier to project the upside participation of the convertible, makes it easier to value the right to convert, and provides time for the underlying stock to advance. (Conversion is not a taxable event, but converting into the common stock obviously eliminates the yield advantage and asymmetry of the convertible.)

Dividend protection became essentially standard in the early twenty-first century. This structure adjusts the conversion ratio to compensate for initiation of common dividends, increases in common dividends, or extraordinary dividend distributions. In a sense, this is a throwback to the *participating* feature of certain bonds and preferreds that had existed in the twentieth century at least until the 1960s.[65] Participating securities simply participated in future dividend increases. The spread of dividend protection was dramatic from 6% of issuance in 2001 to 94% in 2005.[66]

Exchangeable bonds were developed in Europe in the 1980s, with some issued in the United States. These issues convert into shares of a completely different company than the original issuer. This is a way for a company to monetize its ownership in another company, typically by issuing a convertible with a conversion feature into shares that are owned by the issuing company. Often these shares are placed in a trust. The sale of such a bond is not a taxable event for the issuing company; it's akin to a margin loan against shares. Sometimes such exchangeables are issued in cases of companies that were privatized. The government of Italy issued a $1.1 billion exchangeable into the major insurance company INA in 1996.

Private convertible issues grew dramatically in the late twentieth century and early twenty-first century. These issues often were convertible preferreds. Such convertibles are often issued by private startup companies and are rarely disclosed to the public (see Chapter 14).

3.9 GREAT FINANCIAL CRISIS (GFC) AND ITS AFTERMATH

The credit panic that followed the September 2008 collapse of Lehman Brothers was a challenging period for convertible securities. Many convertibles were held by over-leveraged hedge funds susceptible to shareholder redemptions and margin calls, so convertible securities often were dumped at low prices by desperate hedge funds. For a time, no securities performed well except US Treasury bonds. No such credit panic had been seen in the United States since perhaps 1931. It was also the first time in the history of the world's largest mortgage market that home mortgages were regarded as risky.

Fortunately, the recovery was quick—and convertibles performed well on the rebound (see Figure 3.2). As the Federal Reserve injected liquidity, instruments ranging from leveraged bank loans to high-yield bonds and lower-rated convertibles began to recover in November 2008. Other than GM, few convertible issuers defaulted—and huge recoveries and/or gains were made by investors who held/bought at very high yields near the bottom. In March 2009, equities had a strong rally, and a long bull market supported convertible returns as market rates of interest declined (see Figure 3.3).

Figure 3.2   S&P 500 versus convertibles total return 2008–2009

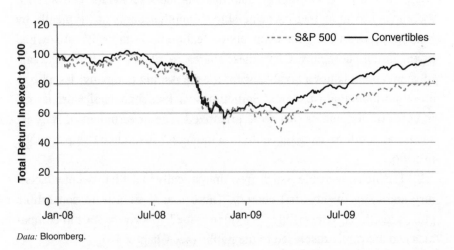

Data: Bloomberg.

Figure 3.3   S&P 500 versus convertibles total return 2008–2020

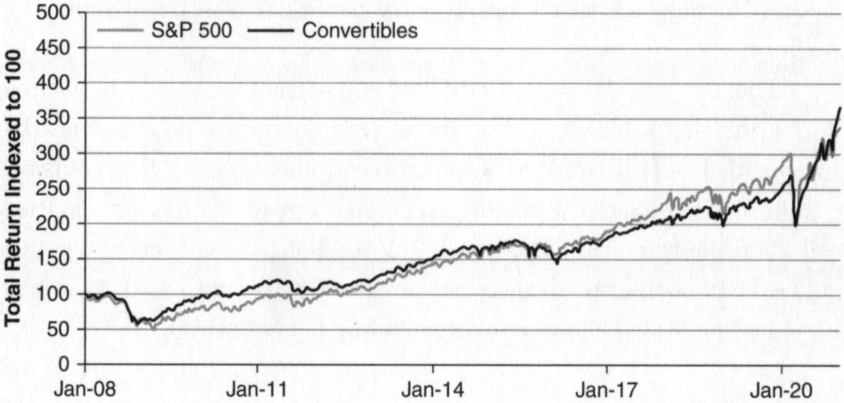

Data: Bloomberg.

Issuance of new convertibles was quick to resume in 2009. Numerous new issues recapitalized companies that had suffered during the GFC. Over the next several years, however, convertible issuance returned to its historic growth orientation, which primarily meant in the technology sector. By 2018, a *Wall Street Journal* headline stated, "Bull Market in Tech-Company Convertible Debt Rages On."[67] *Value Line Convertibles* ceased publication in October 2019, and now retail investors no longer have any inexpensive way to track convertible securities.

3.10 PANDEMIC PANIC

The onset of the COVID-19 pandemic in 2020 sparked a short but steep market panic, followed by a strong return of convertible issuance. Some of the new issues constituted turnaround financing to provide capital to keep the issuers liquid despite the impaired revenues during the pandemic.

Amid a global shutdown of the cruise industry in April 2020, Carnival Corp. (ticker CCL) issued a three-year $1.95 billion non-callable BBB rated 5.75% convertible. Each $1,000 bond convertible is convertible into 100 shares of CCL. At the time of issuance of the convertible, CCL stock price had plunged to $8, down from over $50 only three months earlier. It was obvious that the new Carnival convertible had tremendous upside potential if the stock recovered. After the Carnival issue, convertible bonds were also issued by other companies that were hard hit by the pandemic, including American Eagle Outfitters, Booking Holdings, Dick's Sporting Goods, Norwegian Cruise Lines, Royal Caribbean Cruises, and Southwest Airlines.

The convertible market provided significant downside protection during the sharp market decline in the first quarter of 2020 as COVID-19 spread. The ICE BofA All-Convertibles Index (ticker VXA0) was off −13.62% in the quarter, while the S&P 500 dropped −19.6% and the Russell 2000 plunged −30.62%. In 2020 as a whole, the convertible market enjoyed a phenomenal advance that saw the VXA0 return 46.22%, which bested all major US equity indices including the NASDAQ.

3.11 CONCLUSION: TECH AND GROWTH

The history of the US convertible market has been primarily characterized by issuance from cutting-edge companies with very strong future growth prospects. Often such companies have been in stages of heavy capital investment and negative cash flow, for example, the Erie Railroad in 1843 and Tesla in the twenty-teens. Convertibles have also been repeatedly issued as turnaround financing for companies that were beset by temporary difficulties, for example, Apple in 1996[68] and the aforementioned airlines, cruise lines, and traditional retailers during the pandemic in 2020.

Structures of convertible securities have continually evolved, with radically different trends of yields, conversion premiums, maturities, and features. Perhaps the only genuinely new type of convertible is the mandatory convertible preferred that was invented in 1988.

Throughout the history of convertible securities, the key to favorable returns has been the inherent asymmetry of convertible bonds that provide downside protection yet, also enable investors to participate significantly in the upside of the underlying stock. Another constant is that no matter how large the convertible market becomes, convertibles always seem to remain a niche asset class. While many individual or institutional investors are aware of convertibles, many are not or may have not closely focused on convertibles as an asset class. As a result, significant inefficiencies and opportunities persist for both investors and issuers.

ENDNOTES

1. John Moody, *Moody's Steam Railroads* (New York: Moody's Investor Services, 1924).

2. Jeremy Josse, *Dinosaur Derivatives and Other Trades* (Hoboken, NJ: Wiley, 2015), pp. 61–63.

3. *Ibid.*, p. 60.

4. Montgomery Rollins, "Convertible Bonds and Stocks," *Annals of the American Academy of Political and Social Science* 35(3), Stocks and the Stock Market (May 1910): pp. 99–100.

5. "Chronology of Railroading in America," Association of American Railroads, Washington, DC, June 2018, p. 2.

6. "Convertible Structures," Deutsche Bank, London, March 2002 (front cover photo).

7. Beat Thoma, "Convertible Bonds: Key Lessons from 150 Years of Issuance," *Investment & Pensions Europe*, April 2015, https://www.ipe.com/convertible-bonds-key-lessons-from-150-years-of-issuance-/10007311.article.

8. John P. Calamos, *Convertible Securities: The Latest Instruments, Portfolio Strategies, and Valuation Analysis* (New York: McGraw-Hill, 1998), p. 7.

9. "Chronology of Railroading in America," Association of American Railroads, Washington, DC, June 2018, p. 1.

10. Montgomery Rollins, "Convertible Bonds and Stocks," *Annals of the American Academy of Political and Social Science* 35(3), Stocks and the Stock Market (May 1910): p. 103.

11. "The Convertible Railway Bond," *Railroad Age Gazette* 1908;XLV(28): p. 1518.

12. Montgomery Rollins, "Convertible Bonds and Stocks," *Annals of the American Academy of Political and Social Science* 35(3), Stocks and the Stock Market (May 1910): p. 104.

13. *Ibid.*, pp. 97–98.

14. *Ibid.*, p. 101.

15. Nia Tam, "China Railway Construction Issues $500m Convertible Bond," *Infrastructure Investor*, January 25, 2016.

16. Montgomery Rollins, "Convertible Bonds and Stocks," *Annals of the American Academy of Political and Social Science* 35(3), Stocks and the Stock Market (May 1910): pp. 104–108.

17. Beat Thoma, "Convertible Bonds: Key Lessons from 150 Years of Issuance," *Investment & Pensions Europe*, April 2015, https://www.ipe.com/convertible-bonds-key-lessons-from-150-years-of-issuance-/10007311.article.

18. Benjamin Graham, David L. Dodd, and Sidney Cottle, *Security Analysis* (New York: McGraw-Hill 1962), p. 602.

19. Otto H. Poensgen, "The Valuation of Convertible Bonds," Massachusetts Institute of Technology, Cambridge, MA, 1965, p. 1.

20. R. Johnson, *Journal of Finance* 1955; 10(1): p. 16.

21. Robert M. Soldofsky, *Financial Analysts Journal* 1971; March–April: p. 63.

22. *Investing & Speculating with Convertibles* (Wilmington, DE: RHM Associates of Delaware, 1968), p. 76.

23. *Ibid.*, p. 73.

24. Otto H. Poensgen, "The Valuation of Convertible Bonds," Massachusetts Institute of Technology, Cambridge, MA, 1965, p. 25.

25. Convertibles represented by the issuing companies in the ICE BofA All-Convertibles Index (VXA0); data source: Bloomberg.

26. Jason Zweig, *The Devil's Financial Dictionary* (New York: Public Affairs Books, Member of the Perseus Books Group, 2015), p. 143.

27. Robert M. Soldofsky, *Financial Analysts Journal* 1971; March–April: p. 63.

28. https://apnews.com/article/ ca3da235bb74a4ee08c8a693236c66bc.

29. Beat Thoma, "Convertible Bonds: Key Lessons from 150 Years of Issuance," *Investment & Pensions Europe*, April 2015. https://www.ipe.com/convertible-bonds-key-lessons-from-150-yearsof-issuance-/10007311.article.

30. Recollections of Paul Berkman, *Value Line Convertibles* analyst 1972–1979.

31. *Ibid*.

32. "Convertibles Get Realistic Image," Willilam Schwartz, CPA, *Financial Analysts Journal*, July-August 1967, p. 55.

33. New York: Convertible Securities Press, 1968.

34. Recollection of Paul Berkman, Value Line Convertibles analyst 1972–1979.

35. *Finance* 1971; 89: p. 7.

36. Recollections of Lawrence Cavanagh, *Value Line Convertibles* analyst 1991–2011.

37. Recollection of Paul Berkman, *Value Line Convertibles* analyst 1972–1979.

38. Paul Berkman, "Convertible Research," J Giordano Securities Group, New York, July 21, 2006, p. 1.

39. Robert M. Soldofsky, "Convertible Preferred Stock: Renewed Life in an Old Form," *Business Lawyer* 1969; July: p. 1392.

40. Robert M. Soldofsky, *Financial Analysts Journal* 1971; March–April: p. 62.

41. https://en.wikipedia.org/wiki/Institutional_Investor_(magazine).

42. Paul Berkman, "Convertible Research," J Giordano Securities Group, New York, July 21, 2006, p. 1.

43. Thomas Watterson, "Convertible Bonds Are a Bit Racier but Relatively Safe," *Christian Science Monitor*, October 16, 1985.

44. http://graphics8.nytimes.com/packages/pdf/gmliquidation.pdf (accessed October 6, 2020).

45. Thomas Watterson, "Convertible Bonds Are a Bit Racier but Relatively Safe," *Christian Science Monitor*, October 16, 1985.

46. John P. Calamos, *Convertible Securities: The Latest Instruments, Portfolio Strategies, and Valuation Analysis* (New York: McGraw-Hill, 1998), p. 8.

47. Otto H. Poensgen, "The Valuation of Convertible Bonds," Massachusetts Institute of Technology, Cambridge, MA, 1965, p. 2.

48. Per Merrill Lynch Convertible Research.

49. Per Refinitiv indices.

50. Recollections of noted high-yield analyst Martin Fridson, formerly of Blyth Eastman Dillon and Merrill Lynch.

51. https://www.encyclopedia.com/social-sciences-and-law/economics-business-and-labor/money-banking-and-investment/junk-bonds.

52. Recollections of Oliver Corlett, analyst in Michael Milken's office of Drexel Burnham Lambert in 1987–1989.

53. https://en.wikipedia.org/wiki/Drexel_Burnham_Lambert.

54. Daniel Partlow, "Convertibles and Inflation Cycles," Advent Capital Management, New York, June 2021, https://www.adventcap.com/insights/convertibles-and-inflation-cycles/.

55. Venu Krishna et al., "The Return of Zeros," Barclays Equity Research, New York, March 18, 2021, p. 3.

56. Benjamin Graham, *The Intelligent Investor: A Book of Practical Counsel* (New York: Harper and Row, 1973), p. 205.

57. As related by one of the portfolio managers, who requests anonymity.

58. Paul Berkman, "Convertible Research," J Giordano Securities Group, New York, July 21, 2006, p. 2.

59. "Closing Up the Convertibles," *Forbes*, May 9, 2002, https://www.forbes.com/2002/05/09/0509convertibles .html?sh=638876e457d4

60. Michael Youngworth, "Convertible Arbitrage Primer," BofA Securities, New York, September 27, 2021, p.1.

61. Recollection of coauthor Barry Nelson, who was then lead manager of the Value Line Convertible Fund, which was a client of Dean Witter.

62. Hilary Rosenberg, "Steep Climb for Convertibles," *Banking & Capital Markets*, December 1, 2000.

63. https://en.wikipedia.org/wiki/Irrational_exuberance.

64. Gregory Zuckerman and George Anders, "Amazon.com Launches Convertible-Bond Issue," *Wall Street Journal*, January 29, 1999.

65. Benjamin Graham, David L. Dodd, and Sidney Cottle, *Security Analysis* (New York: McGraw-Hill, 1962), p. 601.

66. *KYNEX Bulletin*, March 2006.

67. Maureen Farrell, "Bull Market in Tech-Company Convertible Debt Rages On," *Wall Street Journal*, May 25, 2018.

68. https://www.institutionalinvestor.com/article/ b14zbbkwhmfj5t/2013-deals-of-the-year-apple-bond-issue- makes-history.

CHAPTER 4

Global Convertibles by Sector

Funding Technology, Growth, Turnarounds

> Here's to the crazy ones . . . who see things differently. . . . They push the human race forward, and while some may see them as the crazy ones, we see genius, because the ones who are crazy enough to think that they can change the world are the ones who do.
>
> —*Steve Jobs*[1]

4.1 INTRODUCTION

Today *tech* is practically synonymous with electronics. Today's electronics-savvy youths, some of whom were raised on *Thomas the Tank Engine*, probably have no idea that steam locomotion was an exciting new technology only two centuries ago. Electronics are so ubiquitous in modern railroading that locomotive engineers gripe about imperfect software.[2]

Innovators who have brought the most revolutionary technologies to market have often issued convertibles. Convertible investors value the potential growth that new technologies promise—even though the outcomes are uncertain. Convertible bonds provide downside protection because a convertible bond has a *bond floor*, that is, a basic value as a fixed-income instrument that is independent of its conversion feature. Beyond convertible bonds, essentially all contemporary convertibles, including mandatory preferreds and traditional convertible preferreds, yield more than the underlying stocks. Straight (non-convertible) debt investors are more wary of unproven technologies because they do not benefit from the upside of risky ventures.

We explored some key historical examples of technology in the convertible market in the nineteenth and twentieth centuries in Chapter 3. In this chapter we will include twenty-first-century technology and biotechnology companies that issued convertibles. In a sense, any company that issues a convertible is innovative because convertibles constitute a financing vehicle that most companies overlook.

4.2 TECHNOLOGY-INTENSIVE INDUSTRIES

Information technology (IT) convertibles had grown to nearly $143 billion market value as of year-end 2020, which was 22% of the global convertibles market, and US IT companies were 28% of the US convertible market at $118 billion.[3]

4.2.1 Technology Has Been Dominated by Electronics

Decades ago, computers were an innovative subset of the electronics industry that began by serving the military, large corporations, and universities. Until the late 1960s, computers were huge machines that were housed in glass-walled *computer rooms* with their own climate control. Then computers began to shrink: there were minicomputers, then kit-built personal computers for enthusiasts, the first Apple computer, and the IBM personal computer—and the internet.

The spread of what can broadly be termed *computers* required myriad components that spawned distinct industries. Tiny devices with more power than the computers of yesteryear have become ubiquitous in airplanes, cell phones, entertainment systems, vehicles, and so on. Technology constitutes the largest segment of the US convertible market, including industries with nicknames like *biotech*, *medtech*, *health-tech*, and *fintech*.

Nowadays the appellation *technology* often applies to companies that *use* electronic technology rather than solely to companies that *provide* electronic technology. As Bill Gates observed, "Information technology and business are becoming inextricably interwoven."[4] Tesla is an example of an automotive company that resembles a technology company.

4.2.2 Computer Manufacturers

Apple, Dell, Hewlett-Packard, and IBM have issued convertibles. IBM marked a milestone in the convertible market in 1985 when it issued a $1.25 billion AAA-rated 7.875% convertible bond in exchange for the 77% of Rolm Corp. shares that it did not already own. IBM dominated the computer industry, but electronic technology did not yet, dominate the convertible market.

Apple became one of the most successful companies in the world. Yet, in 1996, Apple was burning cash after operating for 11 years without the benefit of cofounder Steve Jobs, who had quit in 1985. The company issued a $661 million convertible bond in 1996 "when Apple got into a little bit of trouble and needed capital," in the words of Goldman Sachs CEO David Solomon, speaking on CNBC's *Squawk Box* 24 years later.[5] Apple was obviously a weak credit. The bond had to be issued on excellent investment terms: a high 6% coupon and a low conversion premium of 18%. This convertible subsequently provided a huge payoff to investors while arguably enabling Apple to survive its financial straits and sail on to spectacular success—a remarkable denouement that exemplifies the rewards of convertibles for both investors and issuers.

At the end of 1996, Jobs sold NeXT (the company he had launched when he left Apple) to Apple. This transaction brought Jobs back to Apple. In July 1997, Jobs was named interim CEO. Just a month later, Jobs negotiated an armistice with Microsoft that included selling a $150 million private convertible preferred to Microsoft. With fresh capital from two convertibles and with Jobs back at the helm, Apple sailed from victory to victory, and Jobs retained command until shortly before his untimely demise in 2011.

4.2.3 Semiconductor Manufacturers

Advanced Micro Devices (AMD), Intel, Lam Research, NVIDIA, and ON Semiconductor have issued convertibles. AMD has had extreme ups and downs. Its market is cyclical, and it has historically jockeyed with Intel for market share. The growth potential of its business and the high volatility of its stock have enabled AMD to repeatedly raise capital by issuing convertibles. AMD's most recent convertible was a 2.125% bond issued in 2016. In 2007, AMD had issued a $2 billion 6% convertible bond. Volatility is a key to attracting convertible investors, and AMD stock traded as low as $1.625 in 2015 and as high as over $140 in 2021.

Lam Research makes equipment that is used by semiconductor companies to *manfacture* semiconductors. Lam issued a 1.25% convertible bond in 2011 with a 32.5% conversion premium (see Figure 4.1) to fund a stock buyback, and its stock price *rose* on the date of the convertible issuance—unlike the momentary stock price setbacks that often occur when a new convertible is issued. Following issuance of the convertible, Lam achieved market share gains that paid off tremendously, especially after Lam bought competitor Novellus Systems (which also had issued a convertible) in 2012.

Semiconductor Manufacturing International Corporation (SMIC) is the largest semiconductor company in China, with offices around the world. It is incorporated in the Cayman Islands—an offshore structure that

Figure 4.1   Lam Research 1.25% 2018

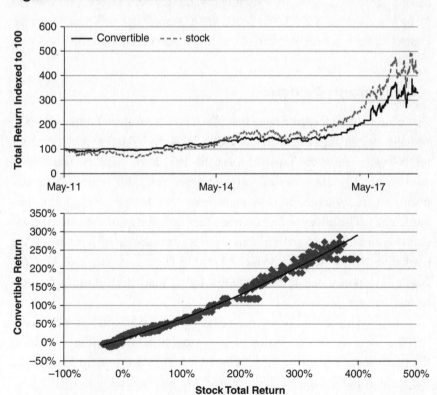

Source: Bloomberg.

is common among Chinese companies that issue securities in the United States and other foreign countries. SMIC is a state-owned enterprise (SOE), which is a type of corporation that is prominent in Asia. SOEs resemble US government–sponsored enterprises such as Fannie Mae and Freddy Mac. About 40% of SMIC shares are owned by three state-owned organizations.

China introduced the *National IC Development Guideline* in 2014 and the Made in China 2025 initiatives in 2015, jumpstarting a wave of development of advanced technologies. Semiconductors play a key role in the Made in China 2025 strategy. As the leading semiconductor foundry in China, SMIC is a direct beneficiary of government support programs.

In 2016, SMIC issued a 0% convertible bond with a July 2022 maturity to fund additional capacity. The convertible had a 34% conversion premium. The company subsequently announced its growth target of 20% revenue compound annual growth rate over the next five years with gross margins around 25%. Within six months, the convertible bond had surged to 140 (see Figure 4.2). Since 2019, SMIC's ability to sell product in the United States has been restricted, and sales growth has slowed.[6]

4.2.4 Storage Devices

One of the older storage device manufacturers is Western Digital (WDC), which entered data storage in the 1980s. Western Digital and its competitor, Seagate, constitute most of the hard disk drive industry. Hard disks are traditionally used by desktop computers and data centers. Both applications are switching to solid-state drives (SSDs), which are faster than hard drives. The advent of SSDs and other new forms of data storage, together with the transition to mobile devices, has caused the hard disk drive market to decay—at the expense of Western Digital and Seagate. Western Digital's response was to buy SanDisk for its market position in the new technologies in 2016 for $19 billion.

In January 2018, Western Digital issued a $1.1 billion 1.5% convertible bond and a $2.3 billion 4.75% straight bond in order to redeem the much more expensive 7.375% bond it had issued to help finance the purchase of SanDisk. The 1.5% convertible was floated with a 40% conversion premium and a February 2024 maturity.

Figure 4.2   SMIC 0% 2022

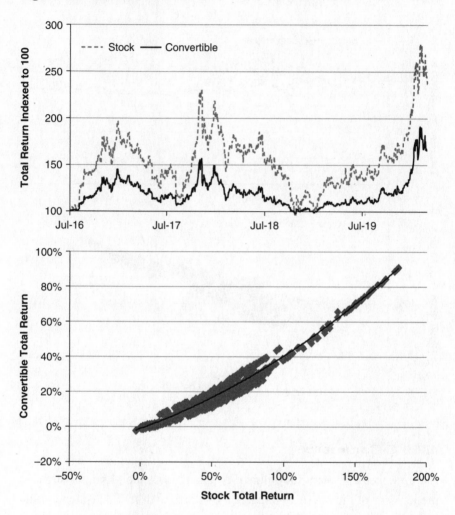

Source: Bloomberg.

Data storage is highly cyclical; hence, Western Digital's earnings (and its share price) are prone to sharp peaks and troughs. Western Digital timed the convertible issuance well because early 2018 saw a peak in the stock price at more than $100. But the convertible cushioned the subsequent downside suffered by shareholders (see Figure 4.3). The company's credit was helped by passing the common dividend in mid-2020.

Figure 4.3   Western Digital 1.5% 2024

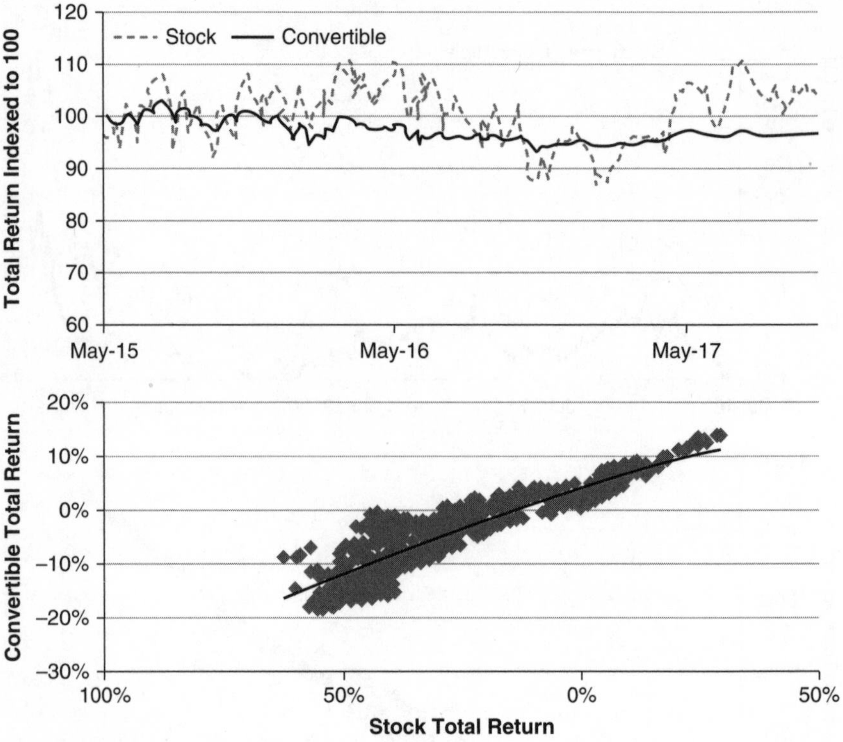

Source: Bloomberg.

4.2.5 E-Commerce

The first formal system for online e-commerce was the Minitel system—a predecessor of the internet—launched by the French PTT telephone utility in 1981. Although the United States was destined to eventually dominate online transactions, it was not until 1994 that the *New York Times* heralded "what was apparently the first retail transaction on the internet"[7] in the United States. A year later, Amazon introduced its online book-selling service and went on to fund its expansion with three convertibles (see Section 3.7).

4.2.6 Software and Services

Software and service companies such as Microsoft, Oracle, and Zoom have all issued convertibles. Microsoft relied on equity financing to fund its early growth. By 2010, Microsoft was able to issue debt at 0%

by structuring a new bond as a convertible with a short three-year maturity. Microsoft's AAA rating was a big attraction to accounts that needed investment-grade securities, for example, insurance companies. While the short three-year maturity provided excellent downside protection, it also meant that the value of the conversion feature would decay quickly. The zero-coupon bond yielded less than the underlying stock because the stock pays dividends. The stock was modestly valued, however; including net debt, the enterprise value of Microsoft was only 6.5 × earnings before interest, taxes, depreciation, and amortization (EBITDA), which reflected market perception that Microsoft was no longer a growth company, with sales having advanced only 7% in fiscal year 2010 after having declined in fiscal year 2009 after the recession. The company was also struggling to adapt to the increasing prominence of mobile computing.

The convertible spent its entire life trading between 98 and 110 with a final run during the 2013 bull market taking parity to around 107. The concerns about the rapid decay of the embedded call option were proved valid because each subsequent spike in Microsoft's share price was met with decreased price participation by the convertible (see Figure 4.4).

4.2.7 Cloud Computing

Nearly every cloud computing company has issued convertibles, including Workday, Salesforce, ServiceNow, and VMware. The term *cloud computing* gained currency in the late 2000s and spawned an industry in the 2010s, but the practice of shared storage and computation is much older. Today the leaders on the cloud are Amazon, Microsoft, Google, and Salesforce, followed by IBM and Oracle—each of which except Google has issued one or more convertibles.

4.2.8 Social Media

Many social media companies, including LinkedIn, Twitter, Snap, Yandex, and IAC, have issued convertibles. Social media was once synonymous with Facebook, but the roots of online social media go back to online discussion forums such as Usenet, dating services such as Match, personal web pages such as MySpace, and mail services such as AOL, Yahoo, and Rocketmail. Operation Match was introduced in 1965. Although the

Figure 4.4   Microsoft 0% 2013

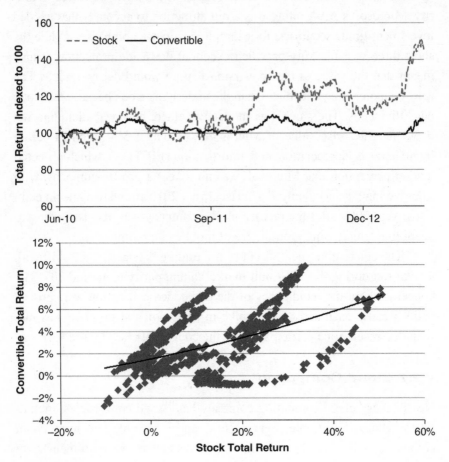

Source: Bloomberg.

matches were identified by a mainframe computer, the *interface* was via snail mail. The concept was still hot in 2021 when Bumble went public and its shares surged 63% on the first day.

Many of the corporate innovators of social media have used the convertible market to help launch and build their services, including Twitter, LinkedIn, Snap, Yandex, and IAC (the parent company of the latter-day Match Group). IAC had three business lines: Match Group, ANGI Homeservices, and "other," where the primary source of value is driven by the incubator pipeline. Match owns a portfolio of online dating sites that generate revenue by offering membership and/or paid features to customers seeking matchmaking services.

Figure 4.5 IAC 0.875% 2022

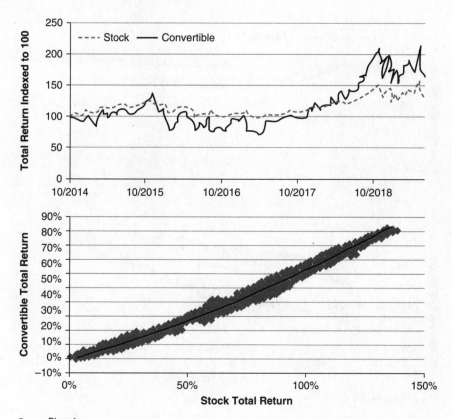

Source: Bloomberg.

IAC issued a 0.875% convertible bond with a 32.5% conversion premium in 2017 in order to fund the growth of nascent business concepts (see Figure 4.5). IAC's valuation was largely driven by Match (minority share initial public offering [IPO], same with ANGI). Match grew rapidly. In July 2020, Match was fully spun off from IAC along with much of IAC's debt. The IAC convertible became convertible into Match common shares.

Most of Twitter's revenues nowadays come from three levels of promoted real estate inserted among a user's timeline (or compilation of posts): Promoted Tweets, Promoted Accounts, and Promoted Trends (some of which generate revenues per click-through). Twitter has rapidly gained usage as it has grown from its early days as a social media apparatus into a general communications mechanism for business, journalism, politicians, and any institution that wants to reach its constituents in real time. Twitter

Figure 4.6   Twitter 0.25% 2019

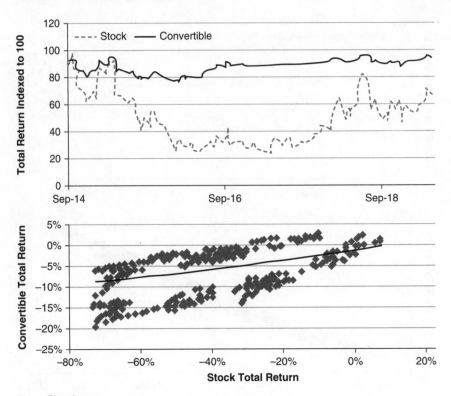

Source: Bloomberg.

entered the convertible market with the issuance of *two* convertible bonds simultaneously in September 2014: a $935 million 0.25% bond due 2019 (Figure 4.6) and a $954 million 1.0% bond due 2021, each with a 47.5% conversion premium, which boosted Twitter's large cash balances from its IPO and its $1.0 billion undrawn revolver. Twitter again accessed the convertible market in June 2018 by issuing a $1.150 billion 0.25% convertible bond with proceeds used to refinance its initial five-year convertible that was maturing in 2019.

4.2.9 Network Security

Many network security companies, including FireEye, Cisco, and Palo Alto Networks, have issued convertibles. The hit movie *War Games* in 1983 captured the imagination of a generation of young programmers with a dramatization of how computer hacking could result in a nuclear war.

Since then, an industry has developed to protect individuals, businesses, and government agencies from the threat of e-thieves and surreptitious hostile foreign governments. The industry now includes everything from products to maintain passwords, to message encryption, to network firewalls, to virus scanners, to biosecure hardware that scans fingerprints and retinas, and to consulting services helping businesses and other organizations to design and maintain secure infrastructures.

Palo Alto Networks is a leader in global cybersecurity. Despite a history of acquisitions, Palo Alto's balance sheet is only modestly leveraged, and the bonds it has outstanding are exclusively convertible. In 2018, Palo Alto issued a five-year convertible bond with a 0.75% coupon and a 27.5% premium that exemplified the volatility that often characterizes technology stocks (Figure 4.7).

Figure 4.7   Palo Alto Networks 0.75% 2023

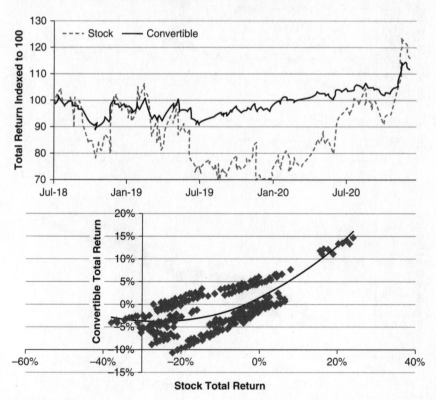

Source: Bloomberg.

4.2.10 Online Entertainment

Online entertainment companies such as Netflix, iQIYI, and Take-Two Interactive have issued convertibles. iQIYI is a Chinese entertainment platform that was launched in April 2010 as a video streaming service. The platform features highly popular original content, as well as a comprehensive selection of professionally produced and partner-generated content (~80% of the cost of iQIYI's content is currently for outside content).

In 2018, iQIYI issued a 3.75% 2023 convertible bond with a 40% premium (see Figure 4.8) in order to fund its content costs. At the time, iQIYI stock was speculative, with the primary downside protection being structural; that is, iQIYI was founded by Baidu, which retains a large stake in iQIYI. As an independent entity, iQIYI had significant cash

Figure 4.8   iQIYI 3.75% 2023

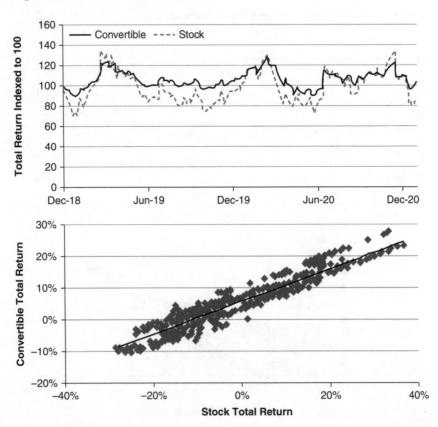

Source: Bloomberg.

burn. The iQIYI convertible provided a way to participate in the China/ emerging-market momentum at modest risk given the support of Baidu, a well-capitalized e-commerce company. A second convertible—a huge $2 billion issue—was floated in December 2020.

4.3 HEALTHCARE CONVERTIBLES

The healthcare sector was the third largest convertible issuer after technology and consumer discretionary at the end of 2020, with a more than $60 billion market value in the United States and only $14 billion in the rest of the world, according to Refinitiv.[8] There are several subsectors within healthcare, including health maintenance organizations (HMOs), hospitals, biotechnology, major and specialty pharma, agricultural, and medtech per ICE BofA classifications.

4.3.1 Biotechnology

I'm an investor in a number of biotech companies, partly because of my incredible enthusiasm for the great innovations they will bring.

—Bill Gates[9]

Many biotech firms, including Genentech, Incyte, Amgen, and Gilead, have issued convertibles. In 2010, Gilead issued a 1.625% convertible bond with a 2016 maturity and a 36% conversion premium (see Figure 4.9) in order to finance a share-buyback program—a rare use of proceeds in an industry that is chronically in need of funding for research and development, acquisitions, and other growth initiatives. The credit profile was strong, the business outlook was very stable, management had a good track record of mergers and acquisitions, and the stock appeared undervalued. Subsequently, in 2011, Gilead acquired Pharmasset, which turned out to be a successful acquisition.

Illumina is the leading provider of gene sequencing machines in the world and a serial issuer of convertibles. In 2014, Illumina issued a 0% 2019 convertible bond with a 55% conversion premium (see Figure 4.10) for potential acquisitions and other purposes. The Illumina investment thesis has been based on the gene sequencing utility expanding from research

Figure 4.9   Gilead 1.625% 2016

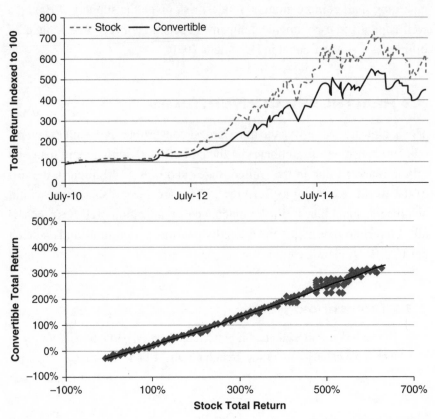

Source: Bloomberg.

purposes to routine clinical tests for various diseases including cancer. As the cost of gene sequencing has fallen, this trend has strengthened.

4.3.2 Medtech

Many medtech firms such as Medtronic, Becton Dickinson, Abbott Laboratories, and Hologic have issued convertibles. Hologic develops and produces diagnostic and imaging products. The company has a heavy focus on women's health, with mammography being the company's single largest source of revenue and a strong source of revenue growth.

In 2010, Hologic issued a convertible bond to refinance a portion of an existing convertible. The new convertible bond was issued with a 45% premium and a somewhat unusual coupon structure. The bond was

Figure 4.10 Illumina 0% 2019

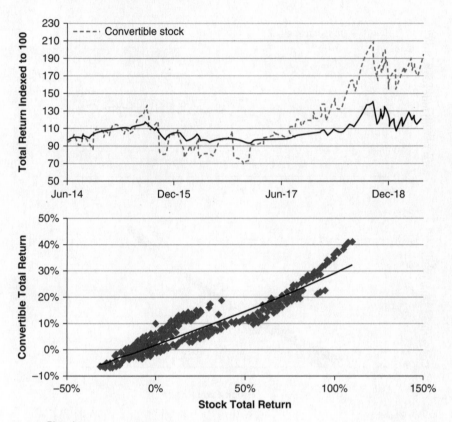

Source: Bloomberg.

issued with a 2% cash coupon, but, according to the prospectus, after December 15, 2016, the cash coupon payments would cease, and instead the principal would accrete at 2% per year. In addition, if the trading price of the convertible exceeded 120% of the accreted principal, the bond would make an additional contingent interest payment of 0.4% of its current trading price.

The initial performance of the Hologic convertible bond was modest for the first few years (although with the bond trading in the midteens by the end of 2012, bondholders had not suffered). Performance improved beginning in November 2013 when activist investor Carl Icahn announced a 12.5% position in the stock and plans for improvements at the company. These announcements, followed by improved profitability, led to strong appreciation for both the stock and the convertible (see Figure 4.11).

Figure 4.11   Hologic 2% 2015

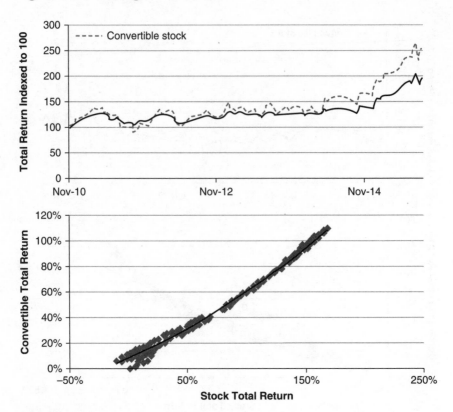

Source: Bloomberg.

4.3.3 Other Healthcare Including Pharmaceuticals, Hospitals, HMOs, Telehealth

Teva is one of the largest manufacturers of generic drugs and was once the crown jewel of the Israeli stock market. For a long time, the investment thesis for Teva was that the company would continue to grow its global presence in generics, while its multiple sclerosis drug Copaxone would continue to grow and fend off patent challenges, and additional acquisitions would be accretive. The thesis seemed valid until Teva acquired the generics unit of Allergan for nearly $40 billion in 2016—just before the US government began investigations into the pricing of generic drugs. The combination of negative news and additional debt weakened the price of the stock, but the credit remained relatively strong, and the convertible began to hold up, partly as a consequence of the par put in February 2021, which extinguished the issue (see Figure 4.12).

Figure 4.12   Teva .25% 2026 (puttable February 1, 2021)

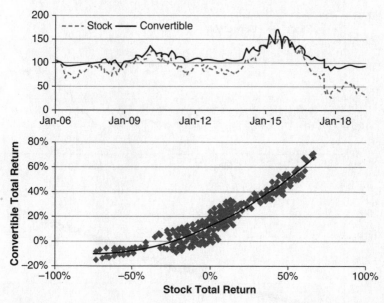

Source: Bloomberg.

4.4 FINANCIAL SERVICES

Financial services represent the fourth most significant issuer of convertibles with more than $27 billion outstanding in the United States and nearly $28 billion in the rest of the world as of year-end 2020.[10] Subsectors within financial services include banks, brokers, insurers, mortgage real estate investment trusts, and financial technology.

4.4.1 Fintech

Many fintech companies have issued convertibles, including MSCI, Square, PayPal, SoFi, and Cardtronics. Square is a payment processor and merchant acquirer that allows businesses to connect to the global financial payments systems. Known for its terminal hardware, the company has since added cash payments, retail/restaurant operations software, financing, and payroll to its product set. Square has issued multiple convertibles. The 0.5% issue in Figure 4.13 is the second of three convertibles issued by Square. It has a five-year maturity. It was issued to finance the acquisition of Weebly in mid-2018. However, Square has always had a large cash balance, similar to CEO Jack Dorsey's first public company, Twitter, and the

Figure 4.13   Square 0.5% 2023

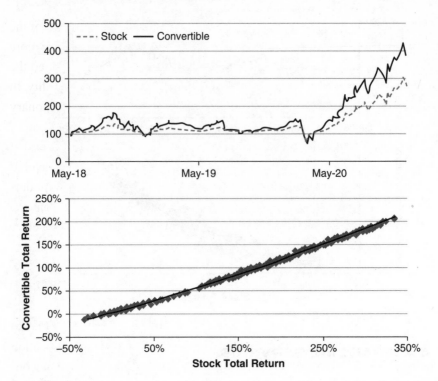

Source: Bloomberg.

issue raised far more than the cash portion of the Weebly acquisition. In all three convertible issuance cases, Square spent over 15% of the proceeds on call spreads to raise the effective conversion premium from the initial 42.5% to more than 100%, suggesting that the company was not in need of the cash and was more concerned with eventual dilution. The decision to float excess cash reserves could have been motivated by the company's entrance into businesses such as financing (Square Capital) that could require more capital.

The 0.5% issue is the second of three convertibles issued by Square. At issuance of the 0.5% convertible, we concluded that Square had developed a strong brand name across global commerce that would allow it to rapidly gain payment market share and enable it to upsell more products to its customer base. Square shares traded in a broad range until the COVID-19 pandemic. After the initial setback, Square shares have had very strong performance, and the convertible captured most of the appreciation.

4.5 CONSUMER DISCRETIONARY

The consumer discretionary sector grew to the second largest sector of the US convertible market in 2020 as it became a source of significantly more issuance by retailers, travel, and entertainment businesses that tapped the convertible market as a way of financing a bridge to future profitability. In the United States, there was nearly $79 billion of consumer discretionary convertibles, more than $20 billion in Europe, and nearly $12 billion in the rest of the world as of year-end 2020.[11] Performance of consumer discretionary convertibles was spectacular, partly because the market favored turnaround situations that issued new convertibles to restore liquidity during the pandemic and most importantly because three large Tesla convertible bonds each surged to more than 10 times par in 2020—and together constituted about 9.15% of the VXA0 at year-end.

4.5.1 Retail

In June 2015, Restoration Hardware (RH) issued a convertible bond to fund share repurchases while supporting an aggressive capital allocation policy. (The CEO owns roughly 30% of the outstanding shares.) The convertible was priced as a zero-coupon bond with a conversion premium of 25% and a five-year term. After the convertible bond was issued, problems with RH's logistics network and inventory management depressed earnings, and the share price dropped. Subsequently, rationalization of the company's logistics network enabled meaningful expansion in margins, and both the stock and the convertible performed well after the first quarter of 2017 (see Figure 4.14).

4.5.2 Automotive

Tesla Motors (TSLA) was founded in 2003, went public in 2010, and issued its first convertible bond in May 2013, when it raised $525 million to repay a Department of Energy loan and to fund expansion of its manufacturing facilities via a convertible bond with a 1.5% coupon and a 35% conversion premium. Tesla subsequently funded its growth with four more convertible bonds, which eventually soared along with the underlying stock and made Tesla the largest issuer in the convertible market in 2020

Figure 4.14   RH 0% 2020

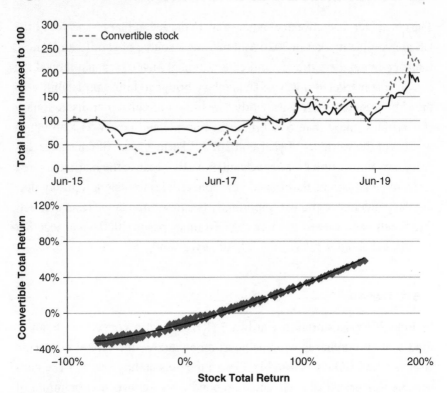

Source: Bloomberg.

(based on the market value of its three outstanding convertibles of 9.15% of the ICE BofA All-Convertibles Index).

A notable example of a convertible bond that demonstrated asymmetry is the $327.5 million (par) Tesla 2.375% of 2022, which was issued in March 2017. Each bond is convertible into 3.0534 shares of Tesla. Tesla stock is always volatile, and by June 2019, holders of Tesla common shares from the day of issuance of the 2.375% convertible were down –28.6%, whereas holders of the convertible had lost only –4.6% (including interest; see Figure 4.15).

When the convertible and the stock bottomed, the convertible was trading in the high 80s with fewer than three years to maturity—which provided a significant yield to maturity. Then Tesla shares soared. By the interim peak in January 2020, Tesla shares were up 253.9% during the period since the 2.375% convertible had been issued, and the convertible had

**Figure 4.15   Performance of 2.375% Tesla convertible issued
March 2017–January 2020**

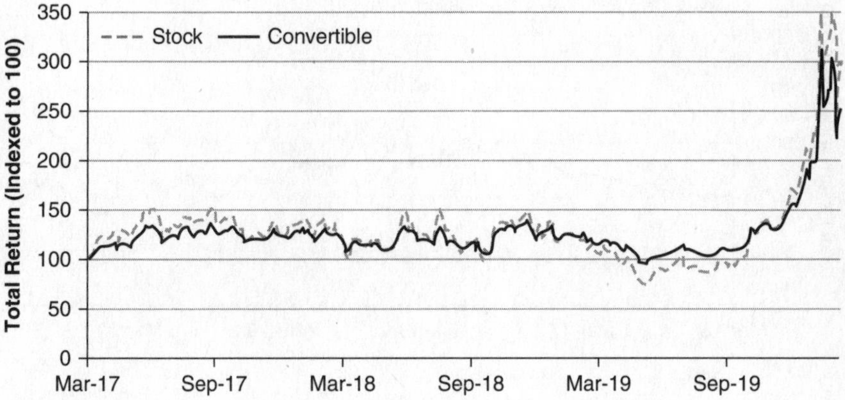

Source: Bloomberg.

returned 216.6%—capturing 85% of the return of the underlying stock. After the market setback when the pandemic worsened in the first quarter of 2020, Tesla stock resumed its spectacular rise, and the Tesla 2.375% convertible rocketed to 1,000 by year-end. We have not extended the chart to the end of 2020 in Figure 4.15 because it would be difficult to fit in this book—and the convertible had become an equity surrogate with little asymmetry.

Suzuki Motor is a Japanese automaker the sells cars primarily in India and Japan. Suzuki was pioneer in India, where its 56.2% owned subsidiary Maruti Suzuki commands the largest share of the market. In its home market, Japan, Suzuki Motor is the number two producer of light vehicles. Because of its large market share in India, Suzuki can be regarded as an indirect way to invest in the Indian auto market, which has historically enjoyed double-digit growth per annum.

In 2016, Suzuki Motor issued two convertible bonds to fund a ₹185 billion ($2.8 billion translated from rupees) factory in India's western Gujarat state (₹160 billion in capital expenditures and ₹25 billion in research and development) and a ¥15 billion expansion of its sales network in Japan.

The two bonds were issued March 7, 2016, and each raised ¥100 billion. The first was a zero-coupon bond with a 44% conversion premium that matured in March 2021. The second bond was another zero-coupon

Figure 4.16   Suzuki 0% 2023

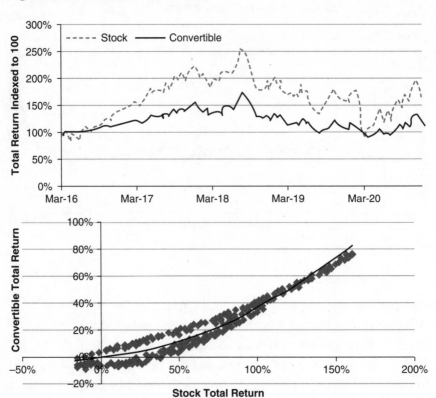

Source: Bloomberg.

bond issue with a 44% conversion premium, but maturity was two years later in 2023 (see Figure 4.16).

At the time of issuance, Suzuki Motor had a 46% market share in India and prospects for double-digit growth in Maruti Suzuki's India sales in 2017. Moreover, the central government was planning to increase public servants' wages starting in April 2016, and similar wage increases in the past had stimulated automotive demand. New models are also an important driver of growth in the Indian auto market, and Suzuki began increasing its market share in India in 2014, mainly as a result of launching new models. The stock and the convertibles got off to a strong start, with the 0% 2023 bonds trading above 150 in November 2017 (see Figure 4.16).

The Suzuki convertibles demonstrate the potential rewards from investing in companies with strong market positions in fast-growing emerging markets. In 2017, Indian auto sales grew by more than 8.5%, well above auto sales growth in developed economies. This rate of growth was not maintained, however, and in 2019, Indian auto sales fell, following more than a year of weak performance by both the stock and the convertibles.

4.5.3 Travel: Travel Agencies, Airlines, Airports, Cruise Lines, Hotels

In the wake of pandemic-related cancellations, air and cruise lines sought financing to bridge the liquidity gap. The new financing in the convertible market was followed by a quick bounce in the stock prices. Carnival (CCL) stock rebounded 36% in the first five days after issuance (Figure 4.17), and the convertible participated in nearly 80% of the upside (see Figure 4.17).

Figure 4.17   Carnival 5.75% 2023

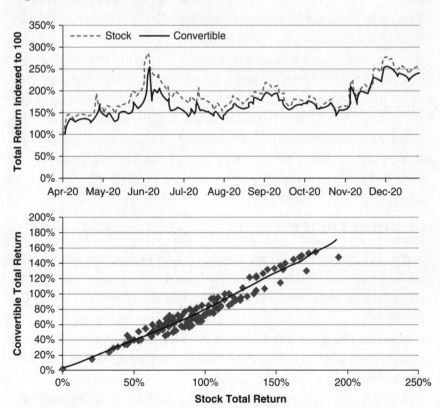

Source: Bloomberg.

4.6 CONSUMER STAPLES

The consumer staples sector has historically been a less significant issuer of convertibles, with less than $2 billion in the United States but more than $3.5 billion in Europe and nearly $3 billion in the rest of the world as of year-end 2020.[12] Herbalife is a convertible issuer that is classified as a consumer staples company. Most of its products are targeted at weight management, with the remainder being nutrition (particularly vitamins and supplements). Herbalife (HLF) uses multilevel marketing (MLM) to sell and distribute *wellness* products. The company is geographically diversified with approximately 80% of sales more or less split equally among Europe, Middle East, and Africa and Asia Pacific, North America, and China.

At the end of 2012, William Ackman, CEO of Pershing Square Capital Management, characterized Herbalife as a pyramid scheme, and he maintained an aggressive short campaign for years. In 2014, Herbalife issued a five-year convertible bond to raise capital during this period in which its business model was under question. The convertible bond had a 2% coupon and a 25% conversion premium.

The company has a flexible cost structure yielding an attractive free-cash-flow profile. The stock trades at a discount to the S&P 500 Consumer Staples Index. After the pyramid allegation failed to produce any major legal or regulatory action, Herbalife shares staged a strong recovery. But weakness resumed, apparently in response to Chinese investigations into MLM practices, a Foreign Corrupt Practices Act investigation, and the COVID-19 pandemic (see Figure 4.18).

4.7 INDUSTRIALS

Industrials have been significant issuers of convertibles, with a nearly $22 billion market value outstanding in the United States, more than $14 billion in Europe, more than $12 billion in Asia excluding Japan, and less than $8 billion elsewhere at year-end 2020,[13] according to Refinitiv's broad definition of industrials, which includes air, marine, rail, and road carriers. Some of the key issuers include ArcelorMittal, International Flavors & Fragrances, KUKA, and Sika.

KUKA is a German robotics company that focuses on industrial automation. At the time of issuance of its convertible, KUKA was the second

Figure 4.18   Herbalife 2% 2019

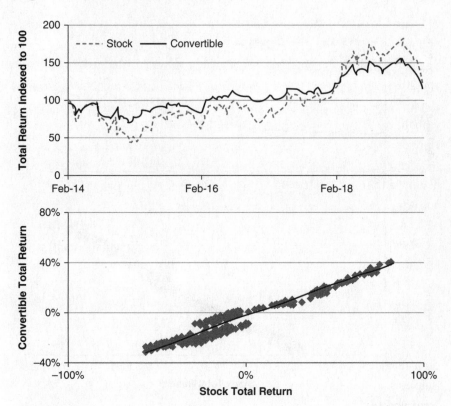

Source: Bloomberg.

largest manufacturer of automotive robots worldwide, which reflected the utility of its products as well as the strong installed base of its equipment in Germany. Despite the company's importance in industrial automation, its equity market capitalization was modest at €1 billion with its stock at €29 when it issued its convertible; in retrospect, the market was undervaluing the company.

In 2013, KUKA issued a small €60 million convertible bond to finance its growth and to develop advanced robots that can cooperate together to complete a task. The convertible bond had a 2% coupon, a five-year term, and three years of call protection, and the conversion premium was 26%.

At the time of issuance of the convertible, KUKA had a leading market share in a growing industry, and it had no major shareholder that

Figure 4.19   KUKA 2% 2018

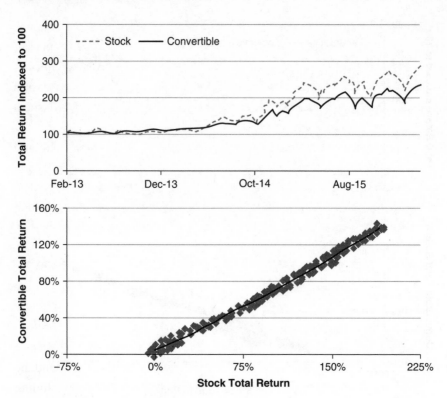

Source: Bloomberg.

might have been in a position to block a takeover bid. There was also the potential attraction of KUKA's plan to separate its Systems Division (automated warehousing), which would make the company a pure robotics investment.

The bond performed well after issuance (see Figure 4.19), and KUKA eventually was acquired. The Chinese appliance manufacturer Midea took a 5% stake in KUKA in late 2015 and then raised its holding to 10% early in 2016. KUKA called the bond and thereby forced conversion in February 2016 after the stock had more than doubled to €85 since issuance of the convertible. Subsequently, Midea made an offer for the rest of KUKA at €115 per share in June 2016, to the benefit of the admittedly small number of convertible bondholders who had continued to hold the stock after being forced to convert by the call.

4.8 TELECOMMUNICATIONS

The telecommunications sector has been a source of convertible issuance primarily in the United States and Europe, with a nearly $59 billion market value of telecommunications and other communications services convertibles outstanding in the United States, nearly $18 billion in Europe, and less than $5 billion in the rest of the world at year-end 2020.[14] Issuers include Vodafone, Telecom Italia, Cellnex, KDDI, and ATT.

KDDI is a telecommunication company in Japan, with mobile and fixed-line communications businesses. It issued a ¥200 billion zero-coupon convertible bond in November 2011 with a December 2015 maturity. The convertible was priced at a very attractive 10% conversion premium, which appeared to compensate for the short two years of hard call protection followed by soft call protection at only 120% of the conversion price. Unlike effectively all US convertibles, the KDDI convertible bond did not provide full dividend protection. Instead, KDDI convertible investors were only compensated for dividends in excess of 120% of the estimated ¥15,000 2012 dividend, rising by 20% per year. The bond provided change-of-control protection via a matrix that depended on both the timing and price of the relevant event. KDDI said that proceeds would be used to help fund the repurchase of up to a maximum of ¥250 billion worth of shares, including 357,541 shares sold at ¥521 per share by TEPCO.

Prior to the convertible, the Tokyo Electric Power Company (TEPCO, 9501 JP) owned 7.9% of KDDI's shares. Following the accident at its Fukushima nuclear plant in March 2011, TEPCO was forced to sell assets in order to finance compensation programs for the victims. TEPCO wanted to avoid selling its KDDI shares at a discount in the open market, and KDDI wanted the buyer of TEPCO's stake to be an entity that was acceptable to KDDI. Eventually, KDDI satisfied both goals at once by issuing a convertible bond and using the proceeds to buy TEPCO's KDDI position directly from TEPCO.

The new convertible bond removed an overhang on KDDI shares by eliminating the risk of TEPCO selling its KDDI stake on the open market. Fundamentally, KDDI equity was undervalued versus the Japanese and global industry averages, apparently because of KDDI's weak subscriber growth and declining average revenue per user. At that time, sales of iPhones in Japan were licensed only to KDDI's competitor, Softbank, which gained market share from KDDI as a result. But KDDI negotiated a

Figure 4.20   KDDI 0% 2014

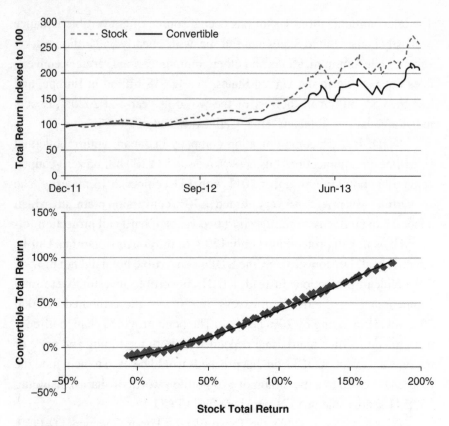

Source: Bloomberg.

license from Apple to sell iPhones, thus removing a competitive disadvantage. KDDI shares performed very well after issuance of the convertible, and the bond was called in two years (see Figure 4.20).

4.9 ENERGY

The energy sector has been a source of convertible issuance primarily in the United States and Europe, with a nearly $10 billion market value of convertibles outstanding in the United States and nearly $11 billion in the rest of the world as of year-end 2020.[15] Issuers include exploration and production companies such as Pioneer Natural Resources, oil field services companies such as Nabors, and natural gas distributors such as Cheniere and have included solar companies such as Solar City.

Cheniere Energy operates two large liquefied natural gas (LNG) facilities on the US Gulf Coast that liquefy domestically produced natural gas by chilling it to −260°F. The liquefaction process reduces the natural gas volume by 600 times, increasing the energy density and making exports to Asia and Europe economically viable using special LNG transport ships.

Liquefaction facilities are massive investments. To finance its capital investment needs, Cheniere has issued large amounts of debt and equity both through its holding company and through the operating subsidiary. Cheniere has issued convertible instruments through the holding company in order to diversify its funding sources, minimize its interest burden, and manage its maturity schedule.

In 2015, Cheniere issued a 4.25% convertible bond with a significant 70% conversion premium. The high interest rate and high conversion premium reflected the company's concerns about dilution. The convertible also had an unusually long maturity of 30 years.

Cheniere's credit is supported by long-term take-or-pay agreements with a large, diverse set of investment-grade counterparties and by its operational track record. These contracts provide Cheniere with reliable cash flow regardless of fluctuations in energy prices due to a guaranteed payment schedule. Cheniere has enjoyed increasing free cash flow and debt reduction because distribution has been enhanced by additional LNG railroad trains, and management's goal is to maintain its operating entities as investment-grade credits while keeping the intermediate and holding company entities as BB credits (see Figure 4.21).

Sinopec demonstrates the importance of understanding the regulatory environment of the country/industry of a convertible issuer. Sinopec is China's largest producer and marketer of oil products (gasoline, diesel, and jet fuel), the number one supplier of major petrochemical products (synthetic resin, synthetic fiber, synthetic rubber, and fertilizer), and the second largest crude oil producer in China. Critically, the Chinese government indirectly owns 55.06% of Sinopec, making the company an SOE.

In April 2007, Sinopec issued a $1.5 billion convertible bond for general corporate use. The issue was a zero-coupon bond due April 2014 with a conversion premium of 50%. At the time, Sinopec was rated A+ by S&P and Fitch.

Figure 4.21   Cheniere 4.25% 2045

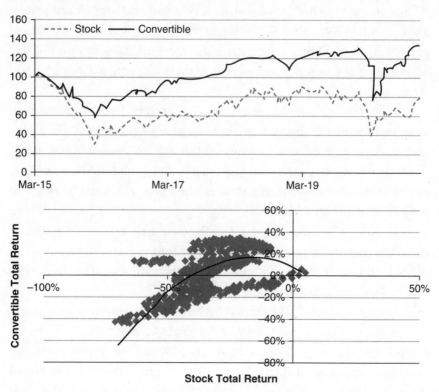

Source: Bloomberg.

When the convertible was issued, Sinopec stock had underperformed its peer, CNOOC, because of weakness in Sinopec's refining business caused by a rise in the price of crude oil. Refining uses crude oil as a raw material, meaning that an increase in oil prices raises Sinopec's costs and squeezes profit margins. Sinopec's margin squeeze was aggravated because the Chinese government did not allow a hike in regulated-product (gasoline/diesel) prices.

At the time of issuance of the new convertibles, the margin problem appeared to have been discounted by the reduced share price. Moreover, declining inflation in China suggested that the government could soon relax the price controls on refined products. The new convertible bond had surged to 130 in October 2007, but it subsequently suffered as global markets retreated during the Great Financial Crisis that began in 2008.

Figure 4.22 Sinopec 0% 2014

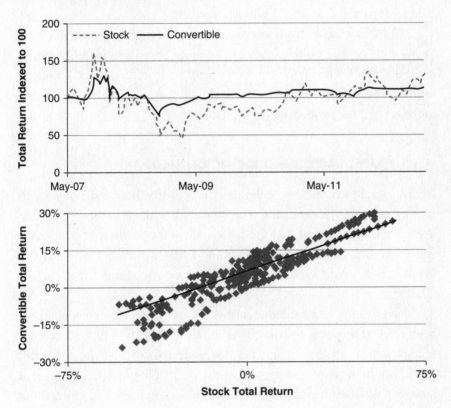

Source: Bloomberg.

Sinopec is an example of the advantage that can be gained from understanding the regulatory and industrial environment of foreign issuers. Country-specific knowledge is essential to exploit opportunities in foreign countries (see Figure 4.22).

4.10 MATERIALS AND UTILITIES

The materials sector has been a minor source of issuance for the convertible market. Key issuers include cement producers such as Cemex and Asia Cement, gold producers such as Newmont, and commodity traders such as Glencore. As of year-end 2020, there was a more than $12 billion market value of materials convertibles in Europe, nearly $6 billion in the

United States, more than $3 billion in Japan, nearly $3 billion in Asia excluding Japan, and nearly $3 billion elsewhere.[16]

Utilities have been a source of issuance, primarily in the United States with electric utilities such as Dominion, NextEra, PG&E, Sempra, and Southern Company. There was a nearly $30 billion market value of utility convertibles outstanding in the United States and nearly $11 billion in the rest of the world as of year-end 2020.[17]

4.11 SUMMARY AND CONCLUSION

Recent decades have seen technology companies repeatedly funded by issuing convertible securities. The convertible market has always been associated with growth, but the period since the 1990s marks an especially exciting association with cutting-edge technologies—which led the ICE BofA All-Convertibles Index to a return of more than 46% in 2020.

Investing in convertible securities of promising tech companies has been a rewarding way to participate in the appreciation of volatile technology shares while avoiding the downside risk of outright ownership of the common shares. Sectors other than technology cannot be ignored, however. We have included numerous non-tech examples in this chapter, although some of the non-tech companies do seem like tech companies—most notably Tesla. Convertibles have often been used by capital-intensive industries to raise capital at lower interest rates.

Considering global and US sector returns in the convertible and equity asset classes since sector-level record keeping began (December 31, 1997), it is clear that convertibles deliver equity-like returns with less risk, as illustrated in Table 4.1.

Table 4.1   Return and Sharpe Ratio by Sector 1997-2020

	Equity Indices		Convertible Indices			
Return	Global	US	Global	US	Europe	Asia
C. discretionary	**8.72%**	**10.60%**	8.28%	10.24%	6.96%	8.19%
C. staples	**7.93%**	**7.85%**	6.87%	4.80%	*10.53%*	*8.02%*
Energy	**4.71%**	**4.46%**	2.13%	-0.55%	3.27%	*7.28%*
Healthcare	**8.60%**	**9.16%**	5.63%	6.06%	4.83%	8.59%
Financials	4.42%	4.53%	**9.86%**	**11.42%**	6.15%	5.44%
Industrials	**7.23%**	**7.86%**	5.94%	6.70%	5.12%	7.48%
Materials	**7.89%**	**7.55%**	5.75%	5.25%	8.89%	8.99%
Media	7.59%	7.86%	**9.33%**	**8.32%**	*6.80%*	2.82%
Tech	**10.42%**	11.05%	9.53%	**11.70%**	10.09%	10.24%
Telecom	**5.17%**	4.57%	4.29%	**10.60%**	6.00%	*5.43%*
Utilities	6.44%	7.39%	**6.64%**	**7.76%**	8.28%	6.08%
Sharpe Ratio	Global	US	Global	US	Europe	Asia
C. discretionary	0.38	**0.46**	**0.46**	0.37	0.50	0.46
C. staples	0.50	**0.47**	0.49	0.22	*0.80*	*0.48*
Energy	0.12	**0.11**	0.01	(0.13)	0.10	*0.39*
Healthcare	0.51	**0.49**	0.34	0.33	0.34	0.60
Financials	0.12	0.11	**0.84**	**0.71**	0.49	0.30
Industrials	0.30	0.32	**0.46**	**0.35**	0.30	0.44
Materials	0.27	**0.26**	**0.30**	0.15	0.49	0.39
Media	0.28	0.28	**0.63**	**0.45**	*0.36*	0.05
Tech	0.35	0.36	**0.58**	**0.56**	0.51	0.64
Telecom	0.18	0.13	**0.20**	**0.47**	0.39	*0.34*
Utilities	0.34	**0.35**	**0.54**	0.35	0.58	0.46

Note: *Italicized values represent subindices that had zero weight for part of the 23-year period.*
Bold values represent the higher value comparing equity and convertible performance.

Source: ICE BofA, Bloomberg.

ENDNOTES

1. https://en.wikiquote.org/wiki/Apple_Inc.
2. Joseph D. Santucci, "Technological Wonders and Why They Make Us Wonder (and Swear)," *Bridge Line Historical Society Bulletin*, May 2020, p. 31.
3. As of December 31, 2020, per Refinitiv.
4. https://www.brainyquote.com/quotes/bill_gates_173262 Bill Gates.
5. Malcolm Owen, "Goldman Sachs CEO Happy with Apple Relationship Dating Back to Steve Jobs' Return," *AppleInsider*, January 23, 2020, https://appleinsider.com/articles/20/01/23/goldman-sachs-ceo-happy-with-apple-relationship-dating-back-to-steve-jobs-return.
6. https://www.wsj.com/articles/chinas-smic-says-its-missing-out-on-the-chip-boom-due-to-u-s-restrictions-11612526175?page=1.
7. Peter H. Lewis, "Attention Shoppers: Internet Is Open," *New York Times*, August 12, 1994, p. D1.
8. As of December 31, 2020, per Refinitiv.
9. https://www.brainyquote.com/quotes/bill_gates_626063.
10. As of December 31, 2020, per Refinitiv.

11. *Ibid.*

12. *Ibid.*

13. *Ibid.*

14. *Ibid.*

15. *Ibid.*

16. *Ibid.*

17. *Ibid.*

CHAPTER 5

Behavior and Risk Aversion in the Context of Convertibles

We simply attempt to be fearful when others are greedy and to be greedy when others are fearful.

—Warren Buffett[1]

5.1 FEAR VERSUS GREED

Emotions are our enemy in investing. Investors who reduce volatility and downside risk by choosing convertibles in lieu of common stocks are likely to face fewer emotional challenges. Being cautious in strong markets and taking advantage of undervalued securities in weak markets are easier said than done—and raise a number of practical questions.

How much does the market have to decline for one to recognize that investors are fearful? The S&P 500 has had 20% setbacks 11 times in the last 75 years into 2020, 10% corrections 49 times, and 5% declines 220 times. Following 5% declines, 133 times the market advanced in the following two weeks. Similarly, with 10% corrections, 29 times the market advanced in the following two weeks. Finally, in the case of 20% setbacks, 7 of 11 times the market advanced in the following two weeks.

Clearly, there is neither a magnitude of decline nor a time horizon in which past performance reliably predicts the near-term direction of the market. On *average*, both a 5% decline and a 10% correction are completely recouped by the market within one year, and a 20% setback is recouped within a year 90% of the time.

The stock market tends to increase year over year. This upward bias, combined with the random nature of stock movements over the short-term, constitutes what mathematicians call a *submartingale process*—which is ever advancing in the long-term and should help investors sleep at night.

Yet, when markets plunge, many investors have a natural tendency to try to protect what they have left by selling even when the market is in freefall.

Fear is an emotion that causes investors to make poor decisions. When markets are advancing, *fear of missing out*—FOMO—is nearly as strong as the fear of loss during declining markets. The performance of most professional portfolio managers is graded relative to a market index; hence, such managers have an incentive to be fully invested, because they may underperform if they are less than fully invested during a market advance.

Professional managers who lose money in a bear market will have plenty of company, so their careers are not likely to be jeopardized for going down *with* their benchmark—whereas such managers may be in trouble when they deviate from the benchmark *if such deviations cause them to lag the benchmark*. Except for a tiny minority of exceptionally talented investors, investing is usually a *loser's game* in which avoiding losses is a more important determinant of total returns than the extremely challenging game of identifying winning stocks before such stocks have been levitated by a sophisticated, institutionally dominated market.[2]

5.2 PSYCHOLOGY OF INVESTING

If you're emotional about investment, you're not going to do well.

—*Warren Buffett*[3]

We feel that investment in convertible securities is a reassuring way to pursue equity-like returns without the emotional stress that is caused by the more extreme market gyrations of common stocks compared with the lower volatility and reduced downside risk of convertible securities.

5.2.1 Fear Not Convertibles

The real charm of the convertible . . . strikes deeper into the psychology and sentiment of investment. It has a kind of "heads I win, tails I don't lose" quality.

—Journalist in 1908[4]

Table 5.1   Returns of US Convertible Indices VXAO[i] and VOAO[ii] Versus US Equity Indices, December 31, 1987–December 31, 2020

	Return	Volatility	Sharpe Ratio	Sortino Ratio	Median Upside Capture vs SPX	Median Downside Capture vs SPX	Upside/ Downside
VXAO	10.43%	12.07%	0.60	0.73	79.1%	68.2%	1.16
VOAO	10.79%	12.10%	0.62	0.78	78.6%	63.5%	1.24
SPX	10.99%	14.51%	0.55	0.58	100.0%	100.0%	1.00
Russell 2000	10.00%	19.08%	0.39	0.71	116.9%	130.2%	0.90
NASDAQ	12.51%	21.26%	0.44	0.60	127.8%	126.9%	1.01

(i) ICE BofA All US All Convertible Index
(ii) ICE BofA All US Convertible Index excluding mandatory convertibles
Data: Bloomberg data, Advent Capital Management calculations.

It should be emotionally easier to achieve equity-like returns over time by holding convertible securities rather than by investing directly in common stocks. Why? Because our fear of losses tends to be greater than our pleasure from gains,[5] and convertibles entail lower volatility and less downside risk than common stocks while providing equity-like returns over time—as demonstrated in Table 5.1, which tracks median upside/ downside returns of the two major US convertible indices relative to the S&P 500. (Our use of medians rather than averages is to avoid distortions caused by outlying convertibles that exaggerate the upside participation of convertibles.)

The late Benjamin Graham acknowledged the psychology of investing on the first page of the Preface to the 1962 edition of his seminal work, *Security Analysis*: "What's needed is a sound intellectual framework for making decisions and the ability to keep emotions from corroding that framework."[6] Books on behavioral investing generally assume equity investments while ignoring other asset classes. A doyen of behavioral investing, James Montier, wrote a remarkably insightful and comprehensive 706-page opus, *Behavioural Investing*,[7] which he followed with his condensed *Little Book of Behavioral Investing*.[8] Co-author Barry Nelson has a BA in psychology and has studied Montier's research since Montier was a global strategist for investment banks in London from 2000 to 2009. Nelson feels that Montier's insights apply to convertibles.

If we accept that the returns of convertibles are likely to be indistinguishable from the returns of common stocks over time—as has been the case over the long-term—then it will be emotionally easier to invest in convertibles and avoid underperforming the stock market indices over the long-term. The emotional dangers of investing are the human tendencies to become more confident as bull markets persist and to become more fearful as bear markets unfold. It's easy to say "buy low, sell high," but few investors have the fortitude to adhere to such logic—particularly when stock prices are plunging or surging. As Warren Buffett has observed, "Investing is simple, but not easy."[9]

A common theory of why investors sell into bear markets is the *fight or flight syndrome*; that is, we humans have survived because of an automatic neural reaction to danger that encourages an instant decision to either fight or run away. Yet, in investing, a declining market usually presents opportunities, whereas our automatic emotional reaction is to run away— to sell in fear that stock prices will go lower—and to be afraid to buy. In a bear market, if convertibles drop less than equities, the emotional pressure to sell should be reduced.

5.2.2 How Will You Feel . . .

How will you feel after the stock market has dropped 10% to 20% in a bear market? Will you be able to hold on or—better yet—accumulate equities at attractively low prices in the face of a stream of bad news from the media and presumably from your family, friends, and associates? As James Montier puts it, "Fear causes people to ignore bargains . . . especially if they have previously suffered a loss."[10]

Now ponder how you will feel if you have invested in convertible securities and your portfolio is down less than common stocks—maybe down 5% to 10% in our scenario. Moreover, when a bear market causes convertible bonds to sink to significant discounts from par, it is easy to anticipate high returns from such convertible bonds merely by recognizing the returns to maturity that ensue when bonds trade at large discounts. Holders of discount obligations of creditworthy issuers may be confident that their convertible bonds are going to pay interest and be redeemed at par regardless of how low the stock market might sink. When a bond is redeemed for cash at maturity, it doesn't matter if the stock market is down.

If your fear is slight, you could realize the muted losses in your convertible bonds and use the proceeds of such sales to swap into other convertibles that are more equity sensitive—or even swap into outright positions in equities that will provide maximum upside when the stock market rebounds. Convertibles also may be emotionally calming in a bull market. It's difficult to express euphoria by investing in convertibles. We concede that investors who are susceptible to FOMO during a euphoric market may regard convertibles as insufficiently aggressive, even though the downside protection that is inherent in convertibles would objectively be especially attractive in a euphoric market that is prone to overvaluation.

5.2.3 Mutual Fund and Exchange-Traded Fund "Gaps" in Returns

> If you think a plunge in the value of your investments won't bother you, you are either wrong or abnormal.
>
> —Jason Zweig[11]

Volatile investments and volatile markets widen the *negative-return gap*, that is, the shortfalls between the returns that investors as a group *realize* from mutual funds and exchange-traded funds (ETFs) versus the actual returns of the funds and ETFs. Morningstar's biennial report, *Mind the Gap 2019*,[12] analyzed the gaps through 2018 and concluded that across all asset class categories globally, the gaps were "the worst where returns are most volatile."[13] Moreover, "the gap widens around dramatic market reversals such as those seen in 2008 and 2009 because some investors panic . . . thus missing out on a dramatic rebound."[14] Something similar almost certainly occurred during the V-shaped market collapse and advance in 2020. Convertible securities are less volatile and less prone to losses than common stocks; hence, we posit that investors in convertibles would be less likely to suffer a return gap.

5.3 THE DISCIPLINE OF PROCESS

A key to overcoming emotions in investing is to adhere to a process.

5.3.1 Setting the Right Goals

Buffett's fear–greed dichotomy essentially reflects two sides of the same coin. Jim Cramer, host of the *Mad Money* TV show, says that his "Rule No. 1" is "Bulls make money, bears make money, pigs get slaughtered."[15] If you are positioned defensively (e.g., by investing in convertibles), you will outperform in down markets and might lag in up markets, yet, over the long run you should do well. But if you are too aggressive, you run the risk of frighteningly large losses during market setbacks that will emotionally inhibit you from rationally anticipating a market rebound.

5.3.2 Convertible Investment Process

> Predicting rain doesn't count. Building arks does.
>
> —Warren Buffett[16]

Convertible securities fit well with process given the typical utilization of convertibles as a way to provide positive asymmetry. The selection of individual convertible bonds ideally uses credit research. Evaluating the creditworthiness of a corporate issuer and its bonds—that is, assessing the risk of default and potential losses—is a lot easier than estimating the potential upside and downside of common stocks.

James Montier advises, "Prepare—Don't predict,"[17] and we regard this advice as being consistent with choosing to invest in convertibles as a substitute for equities. A convertible bond purchased around par usually provides downside protection in the event of weakness in the underlying stock while also participating in the upside if the underlying stock appreciates.

The trend toward *closet indexing* (a tactic pursued by some managers of actively managed funds that minimizes significant deviations from the benchmark) is less of a problem in the convertible market than in other asset classes. Most convertible managers have a stated *process* that typically precludes investment in convertibles that lack upside/downside asymmetry (the basic rationale for investing in convertibles). Examples of convertibles that would be avoided by typical *balanced* convertible strategies are twofold.

First, deeply discounted convertibles that are far out of the money and have low deltas because the underlying stocks have collapsed do not fit the balanced profile. Such issues have effectively become bond-like and often are distressed. Calculating deltas for such issues is fraught with uncertainty because fluctuations in the price of the underlying stock reflect changes in the market perception of creditworthiness, so the bond price and the stock price are correlated in a way that is difficult to model.

Second, are convertibles that reflect the underlying stock soaring—and have such high deltas that the issues are also incompatible with typical balanced convertible strategies. Tesla convertible bonds that surged to multiples of par in 2020 were examples of equity-like convertibles with deltas of 100%.

5.3.3 Trading and Selling

There is academic evidence that active trading of equities hurts performance. Trading convertibles on a whim is difficult. Convertible bonds do not trade electronically except in tiny retail lots; almost all trading of convertible bonds is done by telephone or by Bloomberg messaging—and trading is primarily among institutional investors. There are no unified markets for corporate bonds; trading ensues when buyers and sellers are matched. Moreover, trading bonds entails higher frictional costs than trading equities because the bid–ask spreads on bonds are much wider than on equities (see Section 16.6).

The common convertible discipline of selling convertible bonds that have risen far in the money—and therefore entail volatility and downside risk that is akin to ownership of the underlying stocks—is helpful for determining when to sell, which often is a huge challenge to investors in common stocks. Some investors resist selling their winners even when such stocks have become dangerously overvalued. On the downside, many investors resist realizing losses even though they would probably be unwilling to buy the disappointing stocks that they continue to hold. Because a convertible bond ultimately will be redeemed at par unless the issuer defaults, the magnitude of the losses suffered by convertible investors who fail to cut their losses is minimized.

5.3.4 Individual Investors Versus Institutional Investors

Individual investors rarely have access to sophisticated quantitative models or to convertible trading desks, yet, individuals do have some advantages. They have no institutional constraints. They are free to mix convertibles with stocks. They are not bound to benchmarks. They will not lose clients or their jobs if they underperform. So they should be less fearful. Individuals should be able to take advantage of Benjamin's Graham's fictional "Mr. Market,"[18] who has schizophrenic tendencies to sometimes sell his securities for less than they are worth and at other times to buy securities for more than they are worth.

Institutional investors have superior access to information and to quantitative models, but they face an imperative to *do something*. Clients do not want to pay fees to their managers for doing nothing. Institutional investors have instant online information from electronic sources, so any good or bad market-moving or breaking news is instantly seen and heard. Institutional investors who are exposed to instant news flow are like soldiers going into battle with panic-inducing enemy propaganda blaring in their earbuds. There's a risk of overtrading and other mistakes.

Today, retail investors can enter orders for common stocks on computers and even on smartphones. Brokerage commissions are low or even zero. The ease of contemporary retail trading of stocks creates temptations to overtrade, which will reduce returns over time. It is much more difficult for individuals to trade convertible bonds as opposed to trading common stocks, which may be an advantage of investing in convertible bonds. The only effective ways for most individuals to make short-term trades in the convertible market is via mutual funds and ETFs.

5.4 RISKY BEHAVIOR: NEUTRAL, AVERSE, AND LOVING

It is useful to determine the utility of positive returns relative to the risk of loss. This paradigm, called the *expected utility of money*, descends from the utilitarian economics of John Stuart Mill and Jeremy Bentham in the early 1800s and from Nicolas Bernoulli's 1713 letter describing the St. Petersburg paradox. Bernoulli discovered a certain game of chance that theoretically has an infinite expected value to the gambler; the statistical weighted-average payoff is infinite. Therefore, one would expect a gambler to pay a high price for the opportunity. However, despite the statistical value, the amount almost any gambler is willing to pay for the chance to play is minimal. Bernoulli reasoned that even though the expected value of the opportunity is high, because the risk of loss is also high, the game does not seem like a bargain.

Bernoulli's cousin, Daniel Bernoulli, who published the St. Petersburg paradox, wrote, "The determination of the value of an item must not be based on the price, but rather on the utility it yields. . . . There is no doubt that a gain of one thousand ducats is more significant to the pauper than to a rich man though both gain the same amount."[19]

Application of the risk-aversion theory to *investment* risk was described in a pair of papers by Kenneth Arrow[20] and John Pratt[21] in the mid-1960s that featured a paradigm that envisions three relationships between return and risk and provides a pair of continuous measurement metrics called the *coefficient of absolute risk aversion* and the *coefficient of relative risk aversion*.

In the first relationship, which is called *risk neutral*, the first dollar of return has the same utility as the last (*n*th) dollar of return. There is no premium for risk. In other words, the risk or standard deviation of outcomes is inconsequential. The only thing that matters is the expected (probability-weighted) return.

In the second relationship, which is called *risk averse*, the first dollar of return is of greater utility than the last (*n*th) dollar of return. A premium must be paid for risk. In other words, the higher the risk or standard deviation of outcomes, the greater the expected return must be.

In the third relationship, which is called *risk loving*, the first dollar of return is of less utility than the last (*n*th) dollar of return. There is a discount for risk. In other words, the lower the risk or standard deviation of outcomes, the greater the expected return must be.

Because this book is dedicated to investing rather than gambling, our focus is on risk-neutral and risk-averse investment decisions.

5.4.1 Risk Neutral: Indifferent to Risk

In a risk-neutral world, everyone maximizes expected absolute return regardless of the potential downside. Consider two investment possibilities, A and B.

Investment A has a 75% chance of making 100% and a 25% chance of losing 100%. The expected return is

$$0.75 \times 100\% + 0.25 \times -100\% = 50\%$$

Investment B has a 60% chance of making 60% and a 40% chance of making 20%. The expected return is

$$0.6 \times 60\% + 0.4 \times 20\% = 44\%$$

Because the expected 50% return of A is greater than the expected 44% return of B, in a risk-neutral world, everyone would choose investment A.

5.4.1.1 Using Convertibles to Increase Utility for a Risk-Neutral Investor

Let's consider a risk-neutral investor who has an opportunity to invest in a hypothetical stock with a standard deviation of 30%, an equity risk premium of 8%, and zero dividend yield or a hypothetical three-year convertible on the same underlying stock with a conversion premium of 20%, a 2% coupon, and a presumed recovery rate in a bankruptcy settlement of 50%. The risk-free rate is 1%.

For the sake of simplicity, let us consider only four states: bankruptcy, a poor outcome (1 standard deviation below the expectation), an expected outcome, and a strong outcome (1 standard deviation above the expectation), assigning a 1% chance of bankruptcy and a 33% chance to each of the other three possibilities.

The equity risk premium combined with the risk-free rate suggests that the stock should return 29.50% over the next three years $[(0.08 + 0.01 + 1)^3 - 1 = 0.2950]$. The standard deviation indicates a band of ±51.96% above and below the expected return over the next three years $(\sqrt{3} \times 0.30)$. Therefore, the strong and weak stock returns are 81.46% and −22.46%, respectively. Table 5.2 shows the relative performance of the stock and the convertible and the expected value *given our hypothetical assumptions*.

In the strong and base cases, the convertible participates in the return of the stock above the conversion premium and also receives the coupon. In the poor case, the convertible is redeemed at par and receives its coupon, whereas the stock falls. In the case of bankruptcy, the stock becomes

Table 5.2   Probabilities of Outcomes Under Various Hypothetical Scenarios

Outcome	Probability	Stock Return	Convertible Return
Strong	33%	81.46%	67.46%
Base case	33%	29.50%	15.50%
Poor	33%	−22.46%	6.00%
Bankrupt	1%	−100.00%	−44.00%
Expected value		28.21%	28.92%

Source: Advent Capital Management.

worthless, and the convertible receives its recovery rate plus the coupons paid prior to bankruptcy. So the expected value of the convertible, weighing the probability of all four cases, is higher than the expected value of the stock, and therefore, a risk-neutral investor would invest in the convertible rather than the stock.

5.4.2 Risk Averse

Investors require compensation for taking greater risk. A younger investor might be only slightly risk averse. Someone approaching retirement might be unwilling to expose a significant portion of life savings to the risk of loss. There is a continuum of risk aversion.

In their quest to apply risk-aversion theory to investing, economists Kenneth Arrow and John W. Pratt proposed a *risk-aversion coefficient*, which is a value that quantifies the amount of return premium that is required to compensate for additional risk *for a particular investor*.[22] In the example of investment A, a 25% possibility of losing 100% of an investment, if it is of a significant amount, is a staggeringly high risk that few investors are willing to take. Although the expected return of investment A is 6 percentage points greater than the expected return from investment B, 6 percentage points may be insufficient compensation for the risks taken—at least for many investors.

The Arrow-Pratt measure of risk aversion describes *absolute risk aversion* (ARA) as the second derivative of the utility function divided by the first derivative times negative one:

$$A(w) = -\frac{u''(w)}{u'(w)}$$

In risk aversion theory, A is defined relative to a change in return necessary to accept a marginal increase in standard deviation according to the following formula:

$$\text{Utility} = \text{excess return} - (\text{standard deviation})^2 \times 0.5A$$

$$\text{Marginal utility} = \text{change in expected return} -$$

$$(\text{change in standard deviation})^2 \times 0.5A$$

Comparing the stock and the convertible, we will also consider a 50:50 blend of the two. The standard deviation of the stock is 44.14%, the convertible is 27.86%, and the 50:50 blend is 35.43% (see Table 5.3).

Calculating the marginal utility for multiple levels of risk aversion (3, 5, 7), we find that the marginal utility of the convertible is higher than the marginal utility of either the stock or the 50:50 blend at every level of risk aversion (A). Consider a slightly different convertible. If the convertible had been issued with a conversion premium of 35% rather than 20%, in the strong outcome, the convertible return would have been 15 percentage points lower. Also, in the base case, the stock would have failed to reach the conversion premium, so the return would simply be the coupon, as in the poor outcome. These outcomes would result in a lower expected value for the convertible. Hence, when $A = 0$, the risk-neutral case, the

Table 5.3 Probabilities with Marginal Utility at 20% Conversion Premium

Outcome	Probability	Stock	Convertible	50:50 Blend
Strong	33%	81.46%	67.46%	74.46%
Base case	33%	29.50%	15.50%	22.50%
Poor	33%	−22.46%	6.00%	−8.23%
Bankrupt	1%	−100.00%	−44.00%	−72.00%
Expected value		28.21%	28.92%	28.56%
Standard deviation		44.14%	27.86%	35.43%
Marginal utility $A = 0$ (risk neutral)		28.21%	28.92%	28.56%
Marginal utility $A = 3$		−1.02%	17.28%	9.73%
Marginal utility $A = 5$		−20.50%	9.52%	−2.82%
Marginal utility $A = 7$		−39.98%	1.75%	−15.37%

Source: Advent Capital Management.

Table 5.4   Probabilities with Marginal Utility at 35% Conversion Premium

Risk-Free Rate 1%, Premium 35%				
Outcome	Probability	Stock Return	Convertible Return	50:50 Blend
Strong	33%	81.46%	52.46%	66.96%
Base case	33%	29.50%	6.00%	17.75%
Poor	33%	−22.46%	6.00%	−8.23%
Bankrupt	1%	−100.00%	−44.00%	−72.00%
Expected value		28.21%	20.83%	24.52%
Standard deviation		44.14%	22.74%	32.51%
Marginal utility A = 0 (risk neutral)		27.21%	19.83%	23.52%
Marginal utility A = 0.5		22.34%	18.54%	20.88%
Marginal utility A = 1		17.47%	17.25%	18.24%
Marginal utility A = 2		7.73%	14.66%	12.95%

Source: Advent Capital Management.

marginal utility of the stock would be highest. Similarly, for an investor who is only very slightly risk averse ($A = 0.5$), the stock would have the highest utility. We note that for a slightly risk-averse investor ($A = 1$), the highest utility is actually the 50:50 blend of stock and convertible, but for investors with higher risk aversion ($A = 2$ and above), the convertible still has the highest utility (see Table 5.4).

While investment decisions are made on an ex ante (forward-looking) basis, it is useful to consider the marginal utility of various asset classes on an ex post basis. The lines plotted in Figure 5.1 represent returns relative to risk-free Treasury bills, where marginal utility is constant for investors of a particular risk-aversion level. These lines are called *indifference curves* because investors should be indifferent to any investment that lies along the indifference curve line.

While equities (S&P 500, NASDAQ, Russell 2000) and convertibles delivered higher returns than the fixed-income asset classes (Treasury bills, Bloomberg Barclays US Aggregate, loans, high yield), equities and convertibles had higher volatility. Although the Russell 2000 returned almost 10%, only the risk-neutral investor would derive more utility from it than from Treasury bills, which returned only 0.63% over that time. A slightly risk-averse and a moderately risk-averse investor would derive

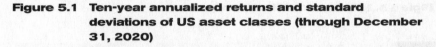

Figure 5.1   Ten-year annualized returns and standard deviations of US asset classes (through December 31, 2020)

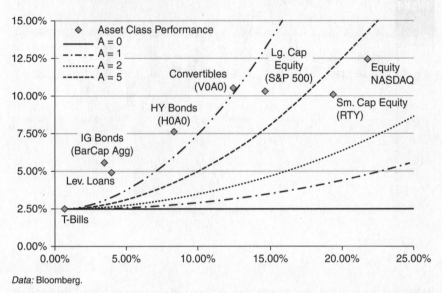

Data: Bloomberg.

utility from owning the S&P 500 or the NASDAQ but not a highly risk-averse investor ($A = 15$). An investment "above" an indifference curve has positive marginal utility. Figure 5.2 shows the marginal utility of the asset classes for investors of varying risk aversion levels.

The bar chart in Figure 5.2 shows that convertibles, as well as the NASDAQ and S&P 500, had high marginal utility for slightly risk-averse investors ($A = 2$). For moderately risk-averse investors, convertibles delivered the highest utility, followed by high yield (HY) and the S&P 500. For highly risk-averse investors, convertibles, as well as the Bloomberg Barclays US Aggregate, loans, and high yields delivered the highest utility. Across all three groups—slightly, moderately, and very risk-averse investors—convertibles delivered the highest average marginal utility.

5.4.3 Risk Loving: The Gambler

In gambling casinos, both high and low rollers participate in games of chance for the thrill to satisfy their addictions. However, the odds of every wager favor the house, so there is a negative expected return on every game (with the exception of *card counters* and other gamblers with exceptional

Figure 5.2 Marginal utility by risk aversion

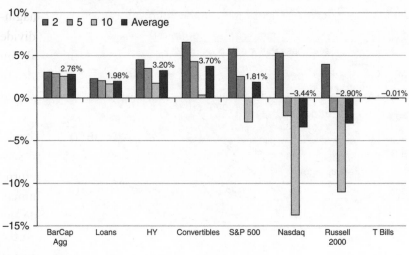

Data: Bloomberg.

talents who may be able to overcome the odds—as confirmed by casinos that ban such persons).

But to the gambler, the money at risk is the cost of satisfying a craving; risk is not neutral or averse but loved. (Apologies to compulsive gamblers, for whom gambling is a costly financial disability.) The risk lover will have an Arrow-Pratt risk-aversion coefficient of less than zero (negative). We will devote no further consideration to risk lovers because our focus is on investing rather than gambling. Moreover, no risk lover would love convertible securities.

5.5 RISK-AVOIDANCE CALCULATIONS

Although risk can be defined in many ways, the most common definition is the possibility of loss or the worst case. A second definition—which is often overlooked—is the risk of missing an opportunity for gain or *fear of missing out* (FOMO). One way to build confidence in your investment strategy and to overcome adverse emotions is to apply rules that either minimize the downside of bear markets or minimize poor relative performance under multiple scenarios (to the upside as well as the downside).

5.5.1 The Minimax Process

Minimax[23] is a decision theory that can be simply exemplified by imagining two possible investments with two potential outcomes. You can divide your portfolio in any percentage between the two investments, and you want the *max*imum possible return while *mini*mizing your downside. In other words, downside protection takes absolute precedence over expected return.

In our example in Table 5.5, we provide strong, base, poor, and bankruptcy case returns. Because the bankruptcy case is the worst-case scenario, the minimax process eliminates all but the worst possible returns in the worst-case scenario, which leaves nothing for the stock. Minimax then selects the investment that has the best expected return. While the stock, which is partially hedged with a put, has a downside equal to the worst-case return of the convertible, the stock has an expected value that is far below that of the convertible. Therefore, the convertible is the natural choice in a minimax framework.

5.5.2 Balancing Left-Tail Risk with FOMO: Minimizing Regret

Consider the scenarios that could cause regret, and consider charting the course of your portfolio using convertibles to minimize expected regret. According to decision theory, if information about the best course of action

Table 5.5 Returns with a Put

Put Cost: 27.88%				
Outcome	Probability	Stock Return	Convertible Return	Stock + 0.7765 Put
Strong	33%	81.46%	67.46%	59.81%
Base case	33%	29.50%	15.50%	7.85%
Poor	33%	−22.46%	6.00%	−30.63%
Bankrupt	1%	−100.00%	−44.00%	−44.00%
Expected value		28.21%	28.92%	11.78%

Source: Advent Capital Management.

arrives *after* making a decision, the human emotional response of regret is often suffered and can be measured as the difference in value between a made decision and the optimal decision.

Co-author Dan Partlow was fortunate to have been employed early in his career by Ron Dembo, founder of Algorithmics, who used the imagery of a tree in which each branch is a potential future return as a way to illustrate the process of minimizing regret. Risk management is therefore the process of pruning the branches of the tree of potential outcomes that could cause the greatest regret, and prudent investing involves selecting between trees (investments) that have more good-outcome branches than bad-outcome branches.

Dembo defined *regret* as the underperformance of a portfolio relative to some benchmark and *expected regret* as the probability-weighted average of the relative return in multiple future scenarios. Table 5.6 has an additional third option for comparison, which is a 50:50 blend.

Expected regret is found by taking the sum product of the probability of each outcome and the amount of regret in that outcome. The convertible has the lowest expected regret, making it the best investment in the regret-minimization paradigm. Alternatively, you could take a minimax approach

Table 5.6   Stock and Convertible Expected Value and Regret

Outcome	Probability	Stock Return	Convertible Return	50:50 Blend
Strong	33%	81.46%	67.46%	74.46%
Base case	33%	29.50%	15.50%	22.50%
Poor	33%	−22.46%	6.00%	−8.23%
Bankrupt	1%	−100.00%	−44.00%	−72.00%
Expected value		28.21%	28.92%	28.56%
Regret	Probability	Owning Stock	Owning Convertible	Owning 50:50
Strong	33%	0.00%	14.00%	7.00%
Base case	33%	0.00%	14.00%	7.00%
Poor	33%	28.46%	0.00%	14.23%
Bankrupt	1%	56.00%	0.00%	28.00%
Expected regret		9.95%	9.24%	9.60%

Source: Advent Capital Management.

to minimizing regret. In this approach, maximum potential regret is minimized rather than expected regret. We can use our stock and convertible expected-value table once more to show how this works.

Using minimax, the convertible remains the optimal investment because it has the lowest maximum regret of 14% compared with 28% and 56% for the 50:50 mix and stock, respectively. Minimax is clearly a less sophisticated process than expected value, but it does have one key advantage, namely that it does not require the user to predict the probability of each event occurring. For example, let's say that we decided that the strong and base case each had a 40% chance of occurring. With those probabilities, stocks become the optimal choice.

Note that for values that represent the best outcome in a given case, the regret is zero (see Table 5.7). In the strong and base cases, this is the stock, and in the poor and bankrupt cases, this is the convertible. The other values represent the difference between the return of the position and the maximum return for that case. The convertible underperforms the stock in the strong and base cases by 14 percentage points, which is its regret in those two cases. Because the stock underperforms the convertible in the poor and bankrupt cases by 28.46 and 56.00 percentage points, respectively, that is its regret in those two cases. Because the 50:50 blend

Table 5.7   Maximum Regret of Investment Alternatives

Outcome	Probability	Stock Return	Convertible Return	50:50 Blend
Strong	33%	81.46%	67.46%	74.46%
Base case	33%	29.50%	15.50%	22.50%
Poor	33%	–22.46%	6.00%	–8.23%
Bankrupt	1%	–100.00%	–44.00%	–72.00%
Expected value		28.21%	28.92%	28.56%
Regret	**Probability**	**Owning Stock**	**Owning Convertible**	**Owning 50:50**
Strong	33%	0.00%	**14.00%**	7.00%
Base case	33%	0.00%	**14.00%**	7.00%
Poor	33%	28.46%	0.00%	14.23%
Bankrupt	1%	**56.00%**	0.00%	**28.00%**
Maximum regret		56.00%	14.00%	28.00%

Source: Advent Capital Management.

always underperforms either the stock or the convertible, it has positive regret in all cases equal to the best return less the blended return under an expected-regret process. The result of the minimax process remains the same because maximum regret is independent of probability. As long as returns can be projected accurately, a minimax process can be used; this is a useful distinction when probability is difficult or impossible to predict.

5.6 INVESTOR TYPES AND THEIR INVESTMENT GOALS

Convertibles have broad appeal.

5.6.1 Individual Investors

The traditional asset-allocation recommendation to individual investors is to have a well-diversified portfolio, taking more risk when the savings are not needed for decades and reducing the amount of risk as the time to pay college tuition or support retirement approaches. Wealth builders—young to middle-aged earners with a 30 to 40 year horizon—are encouraged to take more risk in their investment portfolios with a goal of maximizing return because risk is likely to be rewarded over time, and they have no immediate need to tap their investment accounts. This type of investor is likely to use convertibles as a defensive tool to boost growth equity allocations.

Wealth preservers are typically those who are retired or nearing retirement with a 10 to 30 year horizon. The major consideration for these investors is that if they were to lose a substantial portion of their wealth, they might not have enough time to earn it back. Hence, they tend to be more risk averse.

A common investment joke goes that after a sharp sell-off, equity-heavy retirement accounts fall from being a 401(k) to a 201(k). This is not a laughing matter to someone on the verge of retirement whose account contracts sharply because it has too much risk. The person's goal should be to earn the best return possible with minimum downside risk. A typical asset-allocation range for this group is 20% to 30% equity, 50% to 70% fixed income, and 10% to 20% cash or money-market assets. The purpose of low-risk assets is to ensure sufficient funds for future non-investment purposes.

However, new retirees in 2021 are facing historically low bond yields that provide little income to live off. Worse, the long-term declining interest-rate cycle that has boosted straight bond prices threatens to undermine bond prices if rates rise. Retirees can use convertibles as a reduced-risk equity allocation or as a reduced-duration (interest-rate risk) fixed-income allocation with better prospects for capital appreciation.

Target-date funds were a convenient innovation for individual investors saving for retirement that became popular in the early 2000s. The manager plans a transition from a high equity allocation to a low equity allocation by the approximate retirement date of the investor. Given the fact that traditional fixed income provides such low yields, retirement savers would be wise to consider using convertibles instead of target-date funds.

5.6.2 Active Investment Fund Managers

Active investment fund managers typically have shorter time horizons. Their performance and compensation are evaluated primarily on the last 12 months or possibly 3 to 5 year returns relative to a benchmark. US fixed-income managers are typically compared to the Bloomberg Barclays US Aggregate Bond Index or some subindex based on the asset class they manage. They are expected to achieve superior returns without increased volatility. Historically, this has been achieved with extra duration and extra credit spread. However, neither of these strategies is likely to work as well in the future as it did during the great bond bull market that began late in 1981, given the much lower yields and tighter credit spreads as of 2021. Convertibles offer the possibility of equity-like returns with lower duration risk and minimal additional credit risk relative to bonds.

5.6.3 Pension Fund Managers

Pension fund managers generally fall into two categories; the smaller of the two are those within strong *funded ratios* that have sufficient assets to meet projected obligations. The larger group represents those with lower funded ratios. Each has an actuarial hurdle rate to meet, but the latter group has a more urgent need for capital appreciation to improve the portfolio funded ratio. In such cases convertibles are used in anticipation of enhanced returns in the fixed-income portion of the pension fund, whereas higher-funded-ratio pension plans may use convertibles as defensive "equities" to safeguard the prospect of achieving satisfactory returns.

5.6.4 Insurance Companies

Insurance companies are a special case among institutional investors because insurers maintain investment accounts that are a key source of income. Traditionally, these accounts have been invested in high-quality non-convertible bonds. In an environment of persistently low interest rates, however, there is an obvious need for higher returns—and convertibles provide potentially equity-like returns for insurers' investment accounts without taking equity-like risk.

In the United States, state insurance regulators require insurers to have sufficient capital to cover future policy claims, and having too much risk in the investment portfolio can put policyholders at risk. In the early 1990s, the National Association of Insurance Commissioners (NAIC) developed uniform risk-based capital standards that require insurers to maintain minimum capital according to the credit risk of individual investment securities. Given that these standards evaluate convertible bonds as credits (the ultimate source of downside protection, in our view), increased allocations to convertibles offer a capital-efficient way for insurance companies to potentially achieve equity-like returns while maintaining a defensive fixed-income structure that requires little extra capital.

From a convertible perspective, the most important aspect of the NAIC requirements is that convertible bonds require the same risk-based capital as non-convertible bonds with identical NAIC credit ratings. In order to assess the necessary risk-based capital for each security, the NAIC has developed a 1–6 rating system that equates to a Standard & Poor's credit-rating range of AAA-A⁻ for NAIC rating 1 down to CC-D for 6. (The NAIC uses agency ratings for most bonds but performs its own credit research and assigns its own ratings for non-rated bonds. Most convertible bonds are unrated by the credit agencies.) The necessary risk-based capital factors range from less than 1% for bonds rated 1 up to 30% for bonds rated 6. The same hefty 30% capital is required for common stock as for the lowest-rated bonds.

Bonds in a range of BBB to B (NAIC 2–4)—which encompasses most convertible bonds—require capital ranging from less than 2% in category 2 up to 10% for category 4 for life insurers and 4.5% for property and casualty and health insurers.[24] Hence, convertible bonds incur much lower capital requirements than common stocks, yet, convertibles historically have returned approximately as much as common stocks over the long-term.

The NAIC is planning to introduce more granular ratings effective 2022. There will be 20 definitive ratings instead of 6, and each of the 20 ratings will require specific risk-based capital. The new ratings will more closely reflect the 21 credit ratings provided by Moody's and the 22 credit ratings from Standard & Poor's. The risk-based capital for the 20 NAIC ratings will continue to range from less than 1% for bonds rated 1 to 30% for bonds rated 20 (and 30% for common stocks). The capital advantage of investing in convertible bonds rather than common stocks will remain. We consulted the NAIC in developing this information.

Insurers in the European Union must adhere to regulatory rules of individual countries that are typically based on an international framework called *Solvency II*,[25] which was developed by the European Insurance and Occupational Pensions Authority in 2016. Solvency II provides regulatory capital guidance for investments in convertible bonds within the context of the solvency capital requirement (SCR) test.[26] Co-author Dan Partlow prepared a paper in 2017 that concludes that there is comparative efficiency of convertible bond strategies with the SCR framework.[27]

5.6.5 Sovereign Wealth Funds

Sovereign wealth funds are a feature of countries that are heavily dependent on oil and other commodity exports. According to the Sovereign Wealth Fund Institute, the objectives of sovereign wealth funds include diversifying away from non-renewable commodity export income, earning higher returns than income from foreign currency reserves, helping the monetary authority invest excess liquidity, and achieving sustainable long-term capital growth. Convertibles can help achieve all these objectives because very little of the asset class is exposed to commodity risk, and returns are significantly better than sovereign debt that makes up the largest part of foreign currency reserves.

5.6.6 Alternative Investors

Hedge funds and other alternative investments typically seek high returns that are uncorrelated with equity markets or other risk assets. Again, convertibles provide an excellent vehicle for uncorrelated total returns when structured as a convertible arbitrage strategy (see Chapter 7) or through bespoke private transactions with both public and private companies (see Chapter 14).

5.7 SUMMARY AND CONCLUSION

President Franklin D. Roosevelt counseled in his Inaugural Address in 1933, "The only thing we have to fear is fear itself—nameless, unreasoning, unjustified, terror *which paralyzes needed efforts to convert retreat into advance* [italics added]." Our brains are hardwired to automatically favor bold action in order to avoid a threat. In the words of investment columnist and author Jason Zweig, "Emotional circuits deep in our brains make us instinctively crave whatever feels likely to be rewarding—and shun whatever seems liable to be risky."[28] But we should *not* flee weak markets; rather, we should either hold on or we should buy securities "on sale." And in strong markets, we should become more cautious—not more enthusiastic. These simple but difficult principles are the basics of behavioral investing and are key ingredients of successful investing. Active management of convertible securities usually follows disciplines that help achieve investment goals despite the inevitable emotions of investing. Martin Luther King Jr. once said, "We must build dikes of courage to hold back the flood of fear."[29]

Convertible securities constitute an asset class that has provided equity-like returns over time while entailing lower volatility and less downside risk than equities—hence, convertibles are less prone to arouse our emotions, convertibles provide dikes of courage, and we are less likely to make the mistakes that reflect the human tendency to buy high and sell low. Convertibles are less frightening than common stocks. The fact that convertibles are less prone to euphoria also may be helpful from an emotional perspective. It should be much easier for convertible investors to keep their emotions under control than it is for equity investors.

ENDNOTES

1. https://www.berkshirehathaway.com/letters/1986.html. p. 15.
2. See Charles D. Ellis, *Winning the Loser's Game* (New York: McGraw-Hill Education, 2017).
3. http://quotation.cloud/warren-buffett-emotional-about-investing/.
4. "The Convertible Railway Bond," *Railroad Age Gazette* 1908;XLV(28):1518.
5. https://www.behavioraleconomics.com/resources/mini-encyclopedia-of-be/loss-aversion/.
6. Benjamin Graham, David L. Dodd, and Sidney Cottle, *Security Analysis* (New York: McGraw-Hill, 1962), p. vii.
7. James Montier, *Behavioural Investing: A Practitioner's Guide to Applying Behavioural Finance* (West Sussex, UK: Wiley, 2007).
8. James Montier, *The Little Book of Behavioral Investing: How Not to Be Your Own Worst Enemy* (Hoboken, NJ: Wiley, 2010).
9. https://quotefancy.com/quote/931531/Warren-Buffett-Investing-is-simple-but-not-easy.
10. James Montier, *The Little Book of Behavioral Investing: How Not to Be Your Own Worst Enemy* (Hoboken, NJ: Wiley, 2010), p. 23.

11. Jason Zweig, *Your Money and Your Brain* (New York: Simon & Schuster 2007), p. 151.

12. https://www.morningstar.com/articles/942396/mind-the-gap-2019.

13. *Ibid.*, p. 1.

14. *Ibid.*, p. 2.

15. https://www.thestreet.com/video/25-commandments-cramer-says-pigs-get-slaughtered-1460826114608261.

16. https://observer.com/2015/08/warren-buffett-on-wobbly-market-predicting-rain-doesnt-count-building-arks-does/.

17. James Montier, *The Little Book of Behavioral Investing: How Not to Be Your Own Worst Enemy* (Hoboken, NJ: Wiley, 2010), p. 57.

18. https://www.investopedia.com/terms/m/mr-market.asp.

19. Daniel Bernoulli, "Exposition of a New Theory on the Measurement of Risk," *Econometrica* 1954;22(1): 23–36.

20. K. J. Arrow, "Aspects of Risk Aversion," in *The Theory of Risk Aversion* (Helsinki: Yrjo Jahnssonin Saatio, 1965).

21. John W. Pratt, "Risk Aversion in the Small and in the Large," *Econometrica* 1964;32(1–2):122–136.

22. K. J. Arrow "Aspects of the Theory of Risk Bearing", in *The Theory of Risk Aversion*, (Helsinki: Yrjo Jahnssonin Saatio, 1965). Reprinted in: *Essays in the Theory of Risk Bearing* (Chicago: Markham Publ. Co., 1971), 90–109.

23. https://en.wikipedia.org/wiki/Minimax.

24. https://content.naic.org/sites/default/files/inline-files/Master%20NAIC%20Designation%20and%20Category%20grid%20-%202020.pdf.

25. https://www.eiopa.europa.eu/browse/solvency-2_en.

26. https://www.investopedia.com/terms/s/solvency-capital-requirement.asp.

27. Daniel G. Partlow, *Why Convertible Bond Strategies Make Sense Given Solvency II and Other Regulatory Market Stress Tests*, Advent Capital Management, New York, July 2017.

28. Jason Zweig, *Your Money and Your Brain* (New York: Simon & Schuster 2007), p. 3.

29. https://www.brainyquote.com/quotes/martin_luther_king_jr_297514, from Martin Luther King Jr., *A Gift of Love: Sermons from Strength to Love and Other Preachings* (Boston: Beacon Press, 2012), p. 120.

CHAPTER 6

Convertible Indices, Performance, and Asset Allocation

What is wanted, consequently, is a work which shall embody within convenient compass a statement of... the condition of all our companies, and at the same time present a history... from year to year... to compare similar enterprises that might be made the subject of investigation and inquiry. Such a history is now given...

> — Henry Varnum Poor (Namesake "Poor" in "Standard and Poor's") anticipating the need for broad market indices for the sake of performance comparisons.[1]

6.1 INTRODUCTION TO INDICES

Indices are essential for tracking markets and making comparisons. Today, capitalization-weighted indices dominate. The weight of each constituent is determined by its market value, which matches movements in the index to movements in the market. Relative to managed portfolios—as opposed to index products—such indices become unbalanced if a few large-capitalization companies begin to dominate. Some index managers impose restrictions to more closely match diversified portfolios. Refinitiv's convertible indices cap individual issuer weights at 2% to 4%; this policy causes Refinitiv's indices to differ from the underlying markets, yet, the restrictions make the indices more reflective of managed portfolios. In contrast with the exposure limit in the aforementioned Refinitiv indices, three Tesla convertibles together constituted 9.15% of the ICE BofA All-Convertibles Index (VXA0) at the end of 2020; few institutional portfolios would tolerate such high exposure to a single company. Historically, US professional managers and institutional clients have capped portfolio exposures to individual issuers at 5% or less.

There are two key purposes of indices: (1) they track the performance of an asset class or segment of the market, and (2) they serve as a benchmark for portfolios. These goals are difficult to satisfy simultaneously.

Unrestricted indices expose managers who adhere to diversification restrictions to randomly lag or lead such indices. Another challenge for convertible index construction is whether small and illiquid convertibles should be included. It is logical to include such issues when considering convertible performance as an asset class. Yet, convertible managers may avoid small issues because of illiquidity, and it is inappropriate to compare a manager's performance against an index that includes convertibles that are impermissible for the manager's strategy. Refinitiv's convertible indices address these issues by imposing liquidity and size requirements.

6.2 CONVERTIBLE INDICES AND METHODOLOGIES

The two oldest families of convertible indices are managed by Refinitiv and ICE Data. The ICE Data family of indices is less restrictive in size and liquidity requirements. ICE Data indices lack limits on position weights and may become dominated by large issuers, but they have the advantage of providing a more complete record of convertible performance. The ICE Data indices include a broad array of subindices that slice the convertible market into many different pieces. Some of these subindices are questionable as benchmarks, but they clarify the sources of the overall performance of the broader convertible indices.

We can see the consequences of the differences in methodology of the ICE Data and Refinitiv index families by comparing the characteristics and performance of the basic US convertible indices of the two providers. As of year-end 2020, the ICE BofA All-Convertibles Index (ticker VXA0) tracked 479 convertibles from 358 issuers, whereas the Refinitiv US Convertibles Index contained only 261 convertibles from just 206 issuers and was capped at 3% weight per issuer. The difference in the number of convertibles is largely due to the VXA0 including many convertibles that are too small for the Refinitiv index. As of July 2020, the smallest convertible in the Refinitiv index was roughly $180 million outstanding, whereas the VXA0 included all issues above $50 million.

Both indices are capitalization weighted, so a small convertible issue will have a small effect on the return of the broader index—hence the differences in construction of the two indices do not materially change the performance of the two indices *over the short-term*. Yet, the performance gap between the two indices is significant *over the long-term*. In the course of 30+ years, the Refinitiv US Convertibles Index outperformed the VXA0 by about 30 basis points per annum, which compounded to a total outperformance of 85.71 percentage points through June 30, 2020. Small convertibles underperformed for many years prior to 2021; hence, the VXA0's inclusion of small convertible issues apparently reduced performance.

6.3 US CONVERTIBLES PERFORMANCE

Positive alpha is the return of an asset class above what would be expected given a move in a broad equity index and the long-term sensitivity of the asset class to the index. For convertibles, it could be expressed as follows:

$$\text{Average return of convertibles}$$
$$-\left(\text{beta of convertibles} \times \text{average return of index}\right)$$
$$= \text{alpha of convertibles}$$

Populating these values using long-term returns (1973–2020), we have:

$$12.20\% - (0.7467 \times 12.12\%) = 3.15\% \text{ alpha of convertibles}$$

Using annualized compounded returns rather than average returns gives a similar result:

$$11.01\% - (0.7467 \times 10.65\%) = 3.05\%$$

It is beyond dispute that convertibles have provided long-term structural alpha for nearly 50 years and probably longer because there is anecdotal evidence suggesting that growth companies have dominated the convertible market historically.

While the long-term average beta is 0.75, it is higher in up years and lower in down years (Figure 6.1). In up years, convertibles captured more than 90% of the return of the S&P 500. Yet, in all but one down year (2008), convertibles muted the downside. Including 2008, convertibles participated

Figure 6.1   Convertibles provided 3.15% alpha versus the S&P 500 with 0.75 beta, 1973–2020

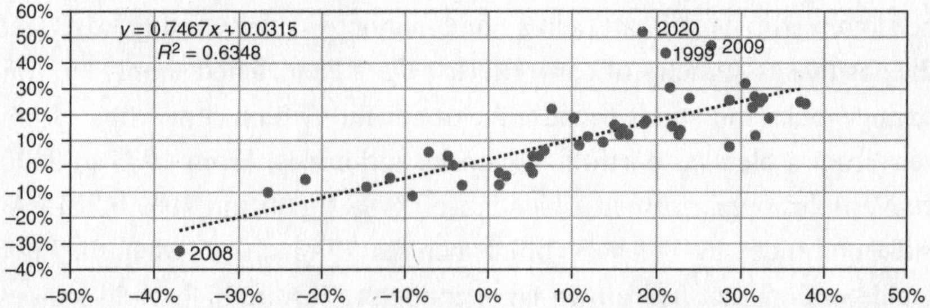

Sources: Ibbotson Associates prior to June 1992, ICE BofA All-Convertibles ex-Mandatory Index (V0A0) thereafter.

in less than 49% of the downside of the S&P 500; while excluding the singular conditions in 2008, the downside participation was only 34%.

Under normal circumstances, when equity prices declined, convertible returns approached a bond floor, and prices tended to level out. In 2008, the bond values fell as credit spreads spiked. Worse, 2008 was a time of excess leverage among hedge funds that held convertibles—as well as the leverage of Lehman Brothers, which was a major prime broker in London—and convertible yields rose through straight bond yields. This situation quickly reversed, and there has been significantly less leverage in the convertibles market ever since partly because prime brokers no longer permit such high leverage.

By excluding both the collapse in 2008 and the dramatic credit rally in 2009, we get a better feel for the "normal" relationship between convertibles and the S&P 500 over the 48 years through 2020. During this period, convertibles delivered a low beta of 0.68 and a high alpha of 3.65% per year. Some of this alpha was due to the nonlinearity of convertibles, and when adding an x-squared factor (S&P 500 returns squared), the regression shows a coefficient of positive 0.11 reflecting increased upside and diminished downside participation. This is because gamma returns and vega returns are nonlinear and asymmetric and reduce the correlation with the S&P 500, which is both linear and symmetric; therefore, gamma and vega reduce the portion of convertible returns that is counted as beta to the S&P 500. Whatever return is removed from beta returns gets counted as alpha in the expression Return of convertibles = beta × return of the S&P 500 + alpha.

6.3.1 Outperformance Versus Blended Benchmarks

Some investors have ignored convertibles with the rationale, "Why do I need convertibles if I can own a combination of stocks and bonds?" Yet, the positive asymmetry of convertibles cannot be matched simply by combining stocks and bonds because the optionality within convertibles is absent from a blended portfolio of stocks and bonds. From 1973 to 2020, convertibles outperformed a blend of 60% S&P 500 and 40% ICE B0A0 All-Bond Index by 143 basis points per year. From 1981, when the high-yield bond market had grown large enough to inspire high-yield indices, convertibles outperformed a 50:50 blend of the S&P 500 and high-yield bonds by 59 basis points per year.

If we take monthly data since the beginning of the Great Financial Crisis (GFC) and regress the returns of the V0A0 to the S&P 500 and the Bloomberg Barclays Aggregate Index as well as the ICE High-Yield Corporate Bond Index, we can demonstrate the contribution to return from beta to those three indices. Using the betas to create a blended portfolio, the return of that portfolio falls far short of the return of convertibles, as shown in Figures 6.2 and 6.3.

6.3.2 Equity-like Returns with Less Volatility

The most important US index is the S&P 500 Index, which is a capitalization-weighted index of the stocks of approximately 500 large companies. No equity index is perfect for comparison with convertible returns. The S&P 500 is imperfect because a criterion for inclusion is equity market

Figure 6.2 Convertibles outperform equities, fixed income, and blends, December 31, 2007–December 31, 2020

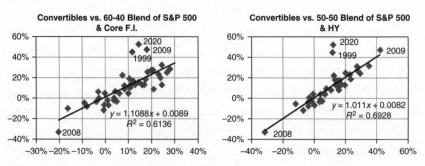

Sources: Bloomberg, ICE Data, Advent Capital Management.

Figure 6.3   Convertibles exhibit significant idiosyncratic outperformance, December 31, 2007–December 31, 2020

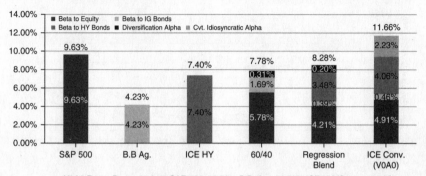

V0A0 Factor Beats: 50.94% S&P 500, 10.79% B.B. Ag., 54.89% ICE HY (Sum = 116.6%)
Regression Blend = 43.68% S&P 500, 9.25% B.B. Ag., 47.07% ICE HY (Sum = 100%)

Sources: ICE Data, Bloomberg.

capitalization of at least \$9.8 billion.[2] Most US convertible issuers are large-capitalization to mid-capitalization companies, yet, fewer than 30% of year-end 2020 VXA0 issuers were large enough to qualify for the S&P 500. The Russell 1000 Index could be considered a better index for comparison with convertible performance because it includes most midcapitalization companies as well as the large-capitalization companies; the Russell 2000 includes 2,000 companies smaller than the top 1,000 and is regarded as the small-cap index.

The NASDAQ Composite Index of 2,700 stocks[3] parallels the *character* of convertible issuers by overweighting technology and growth. The NASDAQ Index has a single criterion for inclusion: all NASDAQ-listed stocks. Yet, Figure 6.4 shows that the NASDAQ has a tendency toward dramatic spikes and sharp corrections that convertibles rarely reflect. Convertible total returns have closely tracked the total returns of the aforementioned equity indices over time, as shown in Figure 6.4.

The performance of US convertibles from December 31, 1987, through December 31, 2020, was strong. The VXA0 had an annualized rate of return of only 0.56 percentage point behind the S&P 500 and 2.08 percentage points less than the NASDAQ while being significantly less volatile than these equity indices. The VXA0 has approximated the return of the Russell 1000 and has slightly outperformed the Russell 2000.

We measure return per unit of risk with the Sharpe and Sortino ratios. The *Sharpe ratio* is the return on the asset class minus the risk-free rate

Figure 6.4   US All-Convertibles Index versus US equity indices cumulative and year by year

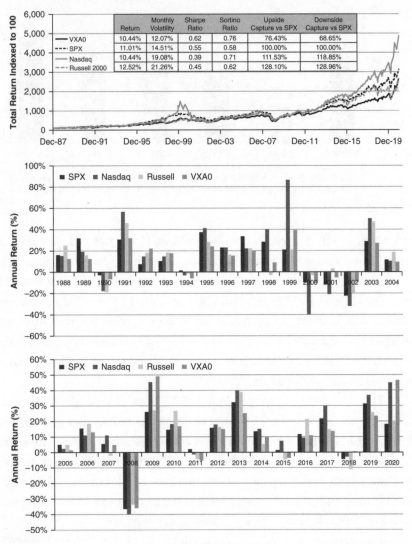

	Return	Monthly Volatility	Sharpe Ratio	Sortino Ratio	Upside Capture vs SPX	Downside Capture vs SPX
VXA0	10.44%	12.07%	0.62	0.76	76.43%	68.65%
SPX	11.01%	14.51%	0.55	0.58	100.00%	100.00%
Nasdaq	10.44%	19.08%	0.39	0.71	111.53%	118.85%
Russell 2000	12.52%	21.26%	0.45	0.62	128.10%	128.96%

Data: Bloomberg.

divided by the volatility. The *Sortino ratio* is similar to the Sharpe ratio with one critical improvement: the Sortino ratio uses only *downside volatility*. The logic behind the Sortino ratio is that while volatility is often used as a proxy for risk, investors are concerned primarily with the risk of their investment going *down*. Investors needn't fear the volatility "risk" that their portfolio will spike *upward* except in the context of missing opportunities.

The VXA0 has a higher Sharpe ratio than any of the three equity indices in Table 6.1 and also has the highest Sortino ratio. We can also look at upside and downside capture for the different indices in order to calculate the extent to which convertibles participate in upward and downward movements of a reference index.

We used the S&P 500 (SPX) as the reference index and compared the upside and downside captures of two equity indices—the Russell 2000 and the NASDAQ—as well as the VXA0. Each of the two equity indices suffered disproportionate downside capture, while the VXA0 had higher upside capture than downside capture relative to the SPX (see Figure 6.4).

The bar charts in Figure 6.4 show the year-by-year breakdown of the performance of the four indices. Based on these figures, convertibles broadly follow the performance of US equities; for example, it's rare for convertibles to be down when stocks are up and vice versa. We can also see that the VXA0 is closely correlated with the NASDAQ Index. The four best years for convertibles returns were 2020, 2009, 1999, and 1991. During these years, the NASDAQ strongly outperformed other US equity indices, and convertibles enjoyed strong performance relative to the other equity indices. In 2020, the VXA0 outperformed the NASDAQ return of 43% with a total return of more than 46%.

6.3.3 Subindices by Valuation, Size, and Equity Sensitivity

ICE Data slices the VXA0 into subindices using objective measures that rebalance the subindices every month. These subindices highlight differences in performance among different varieties of convertibles. The convertible market is an all-capitalization market, ranging from small-cap companies up to large-cap issuers like Tesla. If there's a theme among convertible issuers, it's growth.

One of the starker comparisons within the convertibles market is the performance chasm between growth convertibles and value convertibles, which are tracked by the Vanguard Growth Exchange-Traded Fund (ETF) Portfolio (VGRO) and the Vanguard Global Value Factor UCITS ETF (VVAL) subindices, respectively. The two indices are constructed by splitting the VXA0 based on price/earnings (P/E) and price/book ratios—essentially inferring the growth or value characteristics from these objective measures.

Convertibles of the issuers of more highly valued stocks are categorized as *growth* convertibles, whereas convertibles from issuers with lower-valued stocks are *value* convertibles. P/E ratio is the determining factor except in cases of very low earnings (or losses) that make the P/E ratio concept meaningless. In such cases, the price/book ratio becomes more important.

Figure 6.5 shows that growth convertibles have sharply outperformed value convertibles, as defined by the ICE Data indices. The VVAL has generated a meager return since inception and has *negative* Sharpe and Sortino ratios. In contrast, the VGRO has provided exceptionally high returns with a favorable Sharpe ratio and an exceptionally high Sortino ratio.

The bar charts in Figure 6.5 show that the VGRO has outperformed the VVAL every year since 1998. In 1997, however—a year when technology lagged—the VVAL was up 21.27% versus 18.05% for the VGRO. The VGRO has outperformed the VVAL even more strongly in *down* markets. From the start of 2008 to the end of 2009, the VVAL was down −23.25% (whereas the S&P 500 was down −20.32%), but the VGRO was *up* 18.87%. A similar story

Figure 6.5 Performance of value versus growth convertibles cumulative and year by year

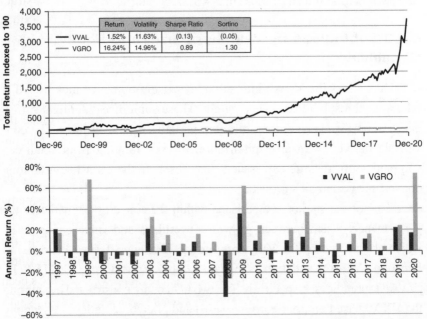

Data: ICE VVAL, VGRO, Bloomberg.

emerged during the COVID-19 pandemic in 2020. Through June 2020, the VVAL was down just under −8% for the year, but the VGRO was *up* 15.84%.

There are several explanations for such a wide performance gap. As we noted earlier, the VVAL and the VGRO are built by separating the VXA0 into high-P/E and low-P/E (and/or low price/book) issuers, but the constituents of the two indices are not static. There is a process for reevaluating the VXA0 monthly based on changes in the price ratios of the underlying stocks. This creates a dynamic where a VVAL issuer can "graduate" from the VVAL if its stock price grows faster than its earnings or book value (implying that the market anticipates faster growth). And a convertible can be dropped from the VGRO into the VVAL if its P/E and/ or P/B ratio declines (implying that the market anticipates slower growth). This effectively means that the VGRO has a bias toward issuers that are gaining market favor and that the VVAL has a bias toward issuers that are downgraded to the VVAL as they fall into disfavor in the market; *this is essentially a bias toward price momentum.*

Another cause of the gap between the VVAL and the VGRO is that the convertible structure mechanically favors growth issuers. Growth stocks are more volatile and have more upside potential, so growth stocks are inherently more likely to satisfy the asymmetric upside return structure of convertibles. For example, if an investor had to choose which stock would be more likely to rise above a 30% conversion premium in the five-year life of a typical convertible, the investor would be much more likely to choose a fast-growing technology stock rather than a stable utility stock. Consequently, lower-growth companies must structure convertibles with lower conversion premiums so that investors have some chance that the stock exceeds the conversion price at expiration. Furthermore, as the underlying stock rises, the delta of the convertible increases, so the convertible captures more and more of the appreciation until the delta reaches its ultimate limit of 100%, after which the price of the convertible essentially moves in tandem with the price of the underlying stock.

The VGRO outperformance is part of a much larger trend. In the twenty-first century into 2021, growth in general has outperformed value. As Figure 6.4 shows, the best-performing US equity index by far has been the technology-heavy NASDAQ. If the stocks of growth companies outperform, so will the many convertible obligations of growth companies.

Assume that a VGRO company grows rapidly and its underlying stock appreciates 75% in five years. With a 30% premium, the initial conversion value is 76.92 bond points. Multiply by 1.75, and the conversion value rises to 134.6, which would cause the convertible to be up 34.6% at maturity; add the 5 percentage points of interest, and the total return would be just shy of 40%—nearly eight times higher than the 5% return from the VVAL convertible with an underlying stock that failed to overcome its conversion premium.

Given the differing performances of growth and value convertibles, we will compare the performances of value and growth convertibles with the S&P 500 and Russell 2000 value and growth subindices.

Both value stock indices have greatly outperformed the VVAL. The cumulative returns chart in Figure 6.6 illustrates the huge VVAL performance lag that has accumulated over the long-term, whereas the annual returns bar chart shows that much of the VVAL's underperformance can be traced to five consecutive years—1998–2002—when the VVAL was down

Figure 6.6 VVAL cumulative returns versus value stocks, December 31, 1996–December 31, 2020, cumulative and year by year

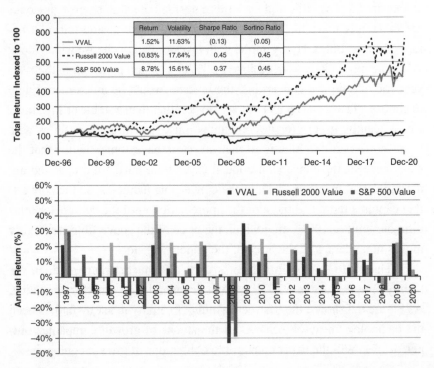

	Return	Volatility	Sharpe Ratio	Sortino Ratio
VVAL	1.52%	11.63%	(0.13)	(0.05)
Russell 2000 Value	10.83%	17.64%	0.45	0.45
S&P 500 Value	8.78%	15.61%	0.37	0.45

Data: Bloomberg.

Figure 6.7　VGRO performance versus growth stocks cumulative and year by year

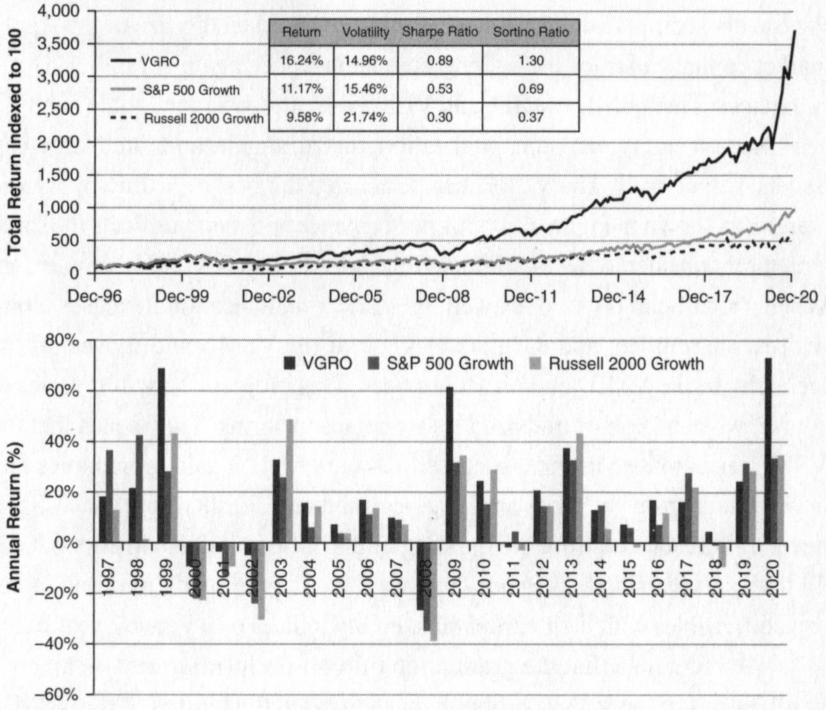

	Return	Volatility	Sharpe Ratio	Sortino Ratio
VGRO	16.24%	14.96%	0.89	1.30
S&P 500 Growth	11.17%	15.46%	0.53	0.69
Russell 2000 Growth	9.58%	21.74%	0.30	0.37

Data: Bloomberg.

every year. More recently, in 2016–2020, value convertibles have returned 11.03% annually, while the Russell 2000 value and S&P 500 value have returned 4.71% and 8.85%, respectively.

The VGRO has sharply outperformed the growth stock indices in both total returns and risk-adjusted returns. The VGRO has provided an impressive 16.24% annual rate of return for 1996–2020 with only 14.96% volatility. This has given the VGRO Sharpe and Sortino ratios nearly double those for the S&P 500 growth. The annual return bar chart in Figure 6.7 shows that some of the VGRO's strength has come from downside protection during market corrections. In 2008, the VGRO went down less than both equity indices (as one would expect given the protection of the bond floor) but then soared in 2009. A similar phenomenon occurred when the dot-com bubble burst in 2000 and during the COVID-19 pandemic in 2020–2021. These results demonstrate the boost that the convertible market derives from its natural overweight in growth companies.

6.3.4 Comparisons with US Equity Market Capitalization Indices

We can also compare convertible performance based on the size of the equity market capitalization of the issuing companies, once again using ICE BofA subindices. The VSML, VMID, and VLRG are three US convertible subindices based on equity market capitalization, that is, small-, mid-, and large-cap issuers, respectively. The VLRG has performed the best over time by a large margin, as shown in Figure 6.8. This performance apparently reflects the same structural considerations that affected the VVAL versus VGRO comparison. When a small-cap issuer does well, its market capitalization increases along with its share price, and it "graduates" from the VSML and moves up the hierarchy to the VMID and VLRG indices. This progression will reverse, of course, when a large or midsized issuer begins to shrink. This means that the VSML tends to lose its most successful issuers while it gains companies that have shrunk from the mid- and large-cap indices. Furthermore, the VSML never truly recovered from the bursting of the dot-com bubble in 2000–2002. To limit survivorship bias in our data, we can compare small, mid, and large-cap convertibles with their comparable equity indices on a year-by-year basis.

We recognize that the graduation of high-performing small-cap convertibles out of the VSML probably has inhibited the returns of the VSML, yet, small-cap convertibles do appear to be a weak segment of the convertibles market. Through 2002, the VSML was down for five consecutive years. The poor performance of the VSML was similar to that of the VVAL (see Figure 6.6).

The mid-cap VMID convertible index has performed better than the VSML, although its 6.56% annualized return since inception significantly lagged the 11.12% return of the S&P 400 midcap index. Midcap convertibles over this period had volatility of 13.20% versus 18.20% for the S&P 400 mid-cap index. The lower volatility of the VMID was insufficient to prevent its Sharpe and Sortino ratios from being lower than the ratios of the S&P 400. There were some years of outperformance by the VMID. In 2009, the VMID rebounded more than 15 percentage points above the S&P 400. It beat the S&P 400 by nearly the same 15 percentage point margin in 2020. In all other in-between years except one, however, the VMID has underperformed the S&P 400 in both up and down years, which widened the lag behind the performance of mid-cap equities.

Figure 6.8 Performance of convertibles based on equity market capitalization, 1997–2020

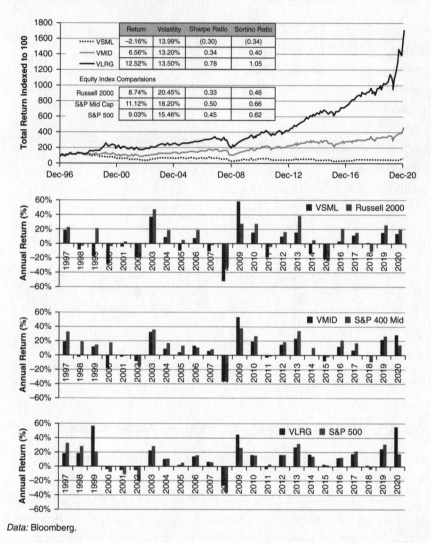

Data: Bloomberg.

The VLRG large-cap index has comfortably outperformed the S&P 500. The VLRG has had an average return of 12.52% versus 9.03% for the S&P 500 while having a volatility of only 13.5%. This is reflected in the VLRG having Sharpe and Sortino ratios of 0.78 and 1.05, respectively (well above the 0.45 and 0.636 of the S&P 500). The VLRG provided downside protection relative to the S&P 500 in every down year (although in 2011 the VLRG was *down* a bit, whereas the S&P 500 was *up* a hair).

Figure 6.9   Performance of ICE Data convertible indices by delta, cumulative and year by year

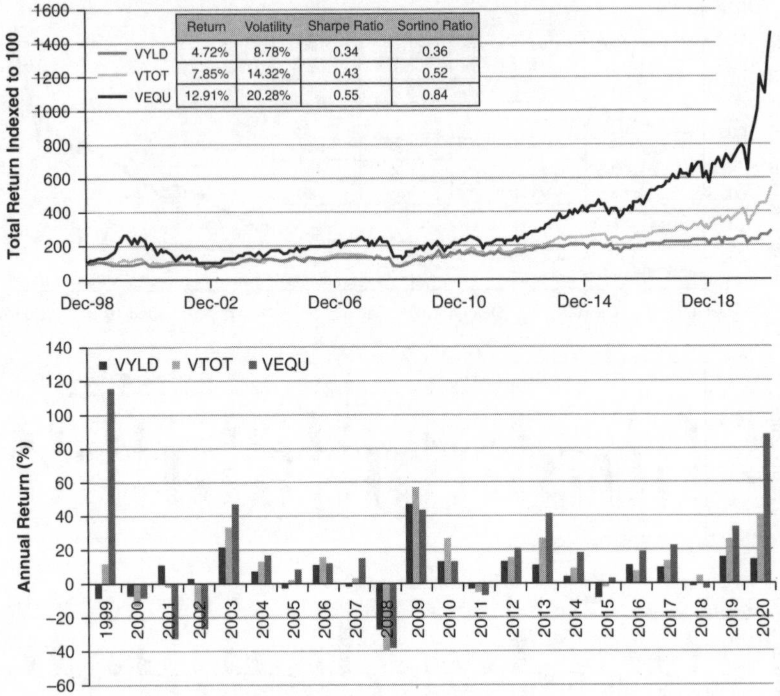

	Return	Volatility	Sharpe Ratio	Sortino Ratio
VYLD	4.72%	8.78%	0.34	0.36
VTOT	7.85%	14.32%	0.43	0.52
VEQU	12.91%	20.28%	0.55	0.84

Data: Bloomberg.

6.3.5 Convertible Equity Sensitivity Subindices

One final way to segment the US convertible market is to separate convertibles by delta. We will explain delta in detail in Chapter 11, but for now it is sufficient to understand that delta is the degree to which the convertible price moves when the price of the underlying stock changes. A convertible with a high delta is equity sensitive, whereas a convertible with a very low delta is not directly affected by movements in the underlying stock price and is presumed to be *bondlike*. ICE Data offers three subindices that slice the VXAO into low, mid, and high-delta indices (the VYLD, VTOT, and VEQU, respectively). We can use these indices to see what role delta has played in performance (see Figure 6.9).

The high-delta VEQU has provided the highest returns for 1999–2020 with an annualized rate of 12.91% compared with 7.85% for the mid-delta

VTOT and 4.72% for the low-delta VYLD. The VEQU also has the highest volatility by far at 20.28%, but its high returns result in the highest Sharpe and Sortino ratios of the three indices, 0.55 and 0.76, respectively. The high-risk, high-reward nature of the VEQU is logical because it is the most equity sensitive of the three indices and the many years after 1998 reflect an overall bull market. Moreover, there seems to be a component of momentum in the three classifications because the deltas of convertible securities tend to rise and fall as the underlying stocks rise and fall.

It is also useful to compare these three indices with other non-convertible asset classes.

Comparison of the VYLD with traditional fixed-income asset classes has been unfavorable for low-delta convertibles over time. The VYLD had the lowest rate of return at 4.72% and was slightly more volatile than high-yield bonds, so the VYLD has the lowest Sharpe and Sortino ratios of the four indices. Looking at the year-by-year data in Figure 6.10, there is generally weak performance, which seems to highlight the inherent unattractiveness of low-delta convertibles as a whole.

A low-delta convertible is a convertible where the stock price of the underlying shares is well below the conversion price. A convertible of this nature is essentially a corporate bond with an unusually low coupon. Yet, this does not mean that all low-delta convertibles are bad investments. There are many examples of individual convertibles with low deltas where the underlying shares were able to stage a major recovery and/or the credit spread on the convertible tightened after a temporary problem was resolved. The high return of the VYLD in 2009 (see bar chart in Figure 6.10) exemplifies a sharp rebound after the extreme widening of credit spreads in 2008. When a convertible bond trades distressed, it effectively trades as though it has a *high* delta (which we have nicknamed the *phantom delta*) because the market prices of both the distressed bond and the stock will respond in tandem to market anticipation of bankruptcy or survival. Careful credit research and fundamental analysis should be used when investing in low-delta convertibles given their weak performance in aggregate.

The comparisons of the returns of the VTOT in Figure 6.11 use a *balanced portfolio* that is a 60:40 split of the S&P 500 and the Bloomberg Barclays Aggregate. It also should be noted that the VYLD, VEQU, and VTOT indices start in 2000. This starting year marks the beginning of a

Figure 6.10 Performance of the VYLD, high yield, leveraged loans, and corporate bonds, cumulative and year by year

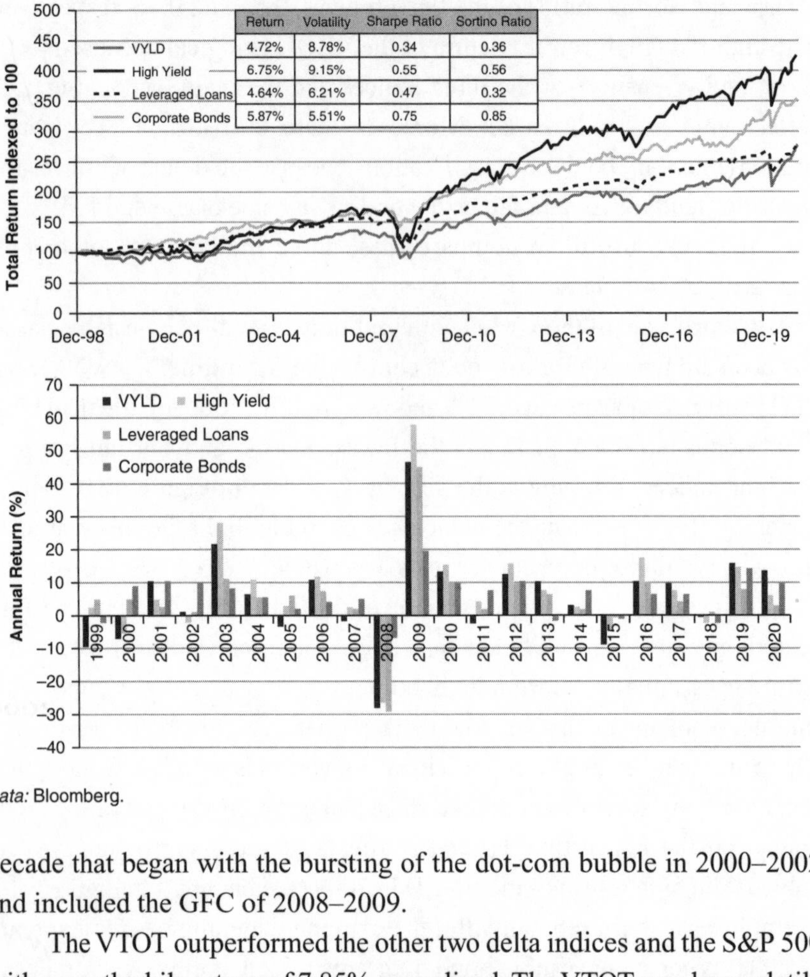

	Return	Volatility	Sharpe Ratio	Sortino Ratio
VYLD	4.72%	8.78%	0.34	0.36
High Yield	6.75%	9.15%	0.55	0.56
Leveraged Loans	4.64%	6.21%	0.47	0.32
Corporate Bonds	5.87%	5.51%	0.75	0.85

Data: Bloomberg.

decade that began with the bursting of the dot-com bubble in 2000–2002 and included the GFC of 2008–2009.

The VTOT outperformed the other two delta indices and the S&P 500 with a worthwhile return of 7.85% annualized. The VTOT was less volatile than the S&P 500, but the VTOT was more volatile than the high-yield or balanced portfolio, so it had lower Sharpe and Sortino ratios despite its outperformance. The VTOT represents the most balanced of the three convertible indices and probably is typical of managed convertible portfolios.

The VEQU is composed of the most equity-sensitive convertible issues in the VXA0. By its nature, the VEQU has the most upside capture of the three indices but is the most exposed to equity volatility and downside. The numbers in Figure 6.12 make it clear that the VEQU is the turbocharged convertible index. Since 1999, the VEQU has returned 12.91%

Figure 6.11   Performance of the VTOT, high yield, S&P 500, balanced portfolio, 1998–2020

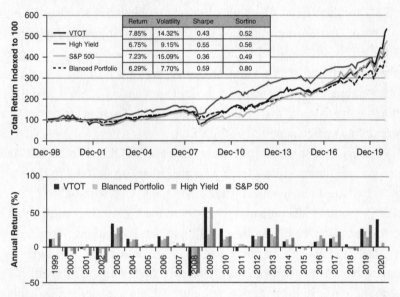

	Return	Volatility	Sharpe	Sortino
VTOT	7.85%	14.32%	0.43	0.52
High Yield	6.75%	9.15%	0.55	0.56
S&P 500	7.23%	15.09%	0.36	0.49
Blanced Portfolio	6.29%	7.70%	0.59	0.80

Data: Bloomberg.

Figure 6.12   Performance of the VEQU, S&P 500, Russell 2000, and NASDAQ, cumulative and year by year

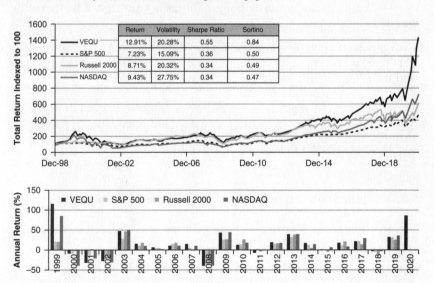

	Return	Volatility	Sharpe Ratio	Sortino
VEQU	12.91%	20.28%	0.55	0.84
S&P 500	7.23%	15.09%	0.36	0.50
Russell 2000	8.71%	20.32%	0.34	0.49
NASDAQ	9.43%	27.75%	0.34	0.47

Data: Bloomberg.

versus 7.23% from the S&P 500. Even the NASDAQ does not surpass the VEQU return despite having a volatility of 22.75% compared with 20.28% for the VEQU. The high-delta convertible index also has the highest Sharpe and Sortino ratios of the four indices shown in Figure 6.12. However, before investors become too excited about buying the highest-delta convertibles, they should recognize that much of the VEQU's superior cumulative performance was derived from its 115.6% and 87.4% returns in its *first and last years*, 1999 and 2020. These years demonstrate the extreme upside potential of the VEQU.

Investors also should recognize that the VEQU—like all ICE indices—has no limits on how large a single issuer can become in the index. The VEQU is a much smaller index than the VXA0 with only 127 issues as of year-end 2020 compared with 499 in the VXA0. This means that its performance can be driven by a small number of positions in the index if they are large enough. In particular, as of December 31, 2020 *three Tesla convertible bonds constituted 21% of the VEQU index*. Tesla will play a meaningful role in index performance until the two remaining Tesla bonds are extinguished in 2022 and 2024. Yet, Tesla alone does not explain the VEQU's remarkable 87% return in 2020. The VEQU return potential may be as strong as the potential from key equity indices because of the growth nature of convertible issuers.

Convertibles are typically bought for the asymmetry of their returns, and the modest performance of the VYLD supports that preference (with the disclaimer that good credit and fundamental research can identify huge recovery potential among discount convertibles, particularly during market panics). On the opposite end of the spectrum of convertible deltas, the performance of high-delta VEQU convertibles has been compelling, assuming that investors are willing to tolerate the volatility and downside risks that are inherent in high-delta convertibles.

6.3.6 Convertibles Versus Straight Bond Indices

We can compare convertible returns with the performance of traditional non-convertible bond indices. The Bloomberg Barclays US Aggregate Bond Index is the go-to benchmark for measuring the performance of the investment-grade US fixed-income market; it includes corporate debt,

Treasury bonds, mortgage-backed securities, and asset-backed securities. An investment-grade rating is the only requirement for inclusion. This rating distinction differs from US convertible issues, few of which are rated investment grade. The aggregate's average maturity of about eight years is almost twice as long as the maturities of most convertible bonds.

Government and asset-backed bonds are too different from convertibles to make useful comparisons. Yet, there is utility in comparing the performance of different types of credit-sensitive debt because such debt usually will be correlated with equity prices. The equity correlation of credit-sensitive nonconvertible bonds partially replicates the equity sensitivity of convertible bonds.

We will use the ICE BofA US High Yield Master II Index (H0A0) and the ICE BofA US Corporate Index (C0A0). These two indices track US high-yield and investment-grade corporate bonds, respectively. We will also examine leveraged loans—which are sometimes regarded as an alternative to convertibles—by using the Credit Suisse Leveraged Loan Index.

Figure 6.13 shows that convertibles trade differently from other types of fixed-income securities. Although convertibles provide much of the risk-reduction characteristics of traditional fixed income, the equity sensitivity of convertibles dominates the pattern of the VXA0. Convertibles do somewhat track high-yield bonds because the credit exposure of high yield creates a correlation with the stock market. The sensitivity of high yield to equities is particularly noticeable during major market corrections; the negative effects of the GFC of 2008 and the COVID-19 pandemic of 2020 are visible in Figure 6.13.

Fixed income performance from 1991 to 2020 requires an important caveat. Since late 1981, Treasury rates in the United States have declined sharply. In the past, 5% was often used by economists as the long-term risk-free interest rate in the United States. However, the three-month Treasury rate has not been that high since 2006. Decreasing interest rates have provided long-duration debt portfolios with a strong tailwind.

While the long downtrend in interest rates has undoubtedly boosted convertible performance, the low rho and short maturities of convertibles have minimized the gains from decreasing interest rates relative to the uplifting effects on long-maturity straight bonds. On the positive side, the prospective total returns from convertibles are not as impaired by the low

Figure 6.13   US convertible versus fixed-income classes, cumulative and year by year

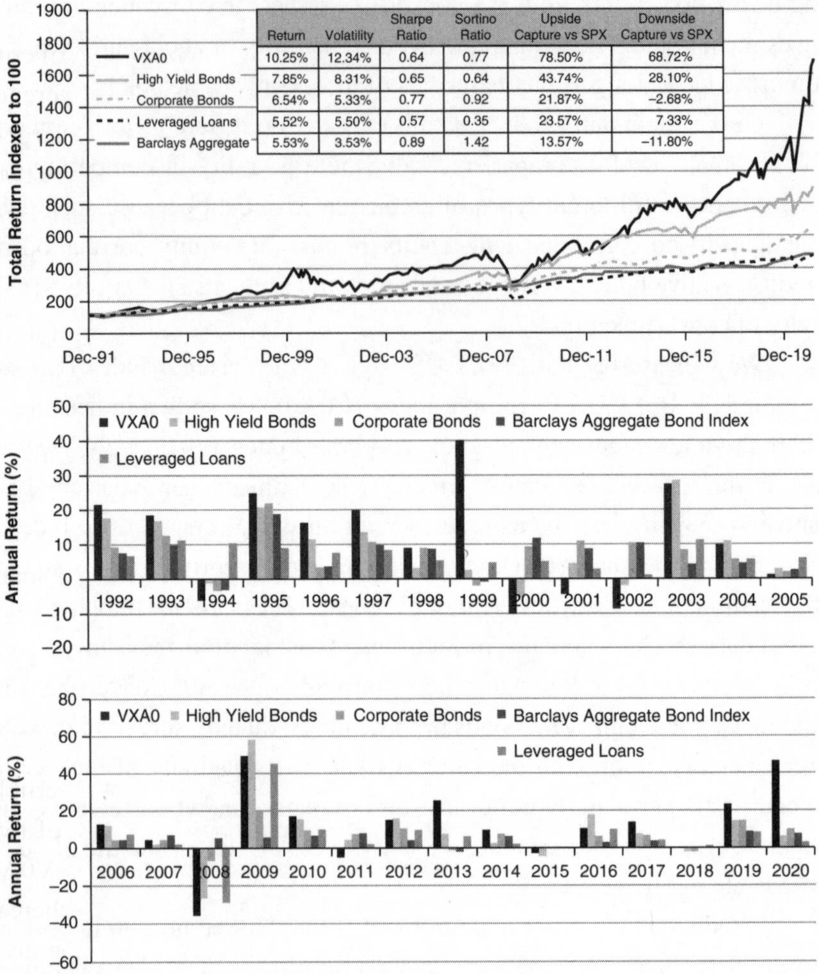

	Return	Volatility	Sharpe Ratio	Sortino Ratio	Upside Capture vs SPX	Downside Capture vs SPX
VXA0	10.25%	12.34%	0.64	0.77	78.50%	68.72%
High Yield Bonds	7.85%	8.31%	0.65	0.64	43.74%	28.10%
Corporate Bonds	6.54%	5.33%	0.77	0.92	21.87%	−2.68%
Leveraged Loans	5.52%	5.50%	0.57	0.35	23.57%	7.33%
Barclays Aggregate	5.53%	3.53%	0.89	1.42	13.57%	−11.80%

Data: VXA0, H0A0, C0A0 and Bloomberg.

rate environment as are the returns from nonconvertible bonds because convertibles will participate in equity appreciation independent of low-interest coupons.

Convertibles have generated higher returns than any other part of the bond market. Convertibles are also more volatile than other segments of the bond market. Sharpe and Sortino ratios show that convertible volatility is similar to the volatility of high-yield bonds and is higher than the volatility of leveraged loans. Corporate bonds and the Bloomberg Barclays

Aggregate have the best volatility ratios, but these bond categories have benefited the most from declining rates yet, have lagged the absolute returns of convertibles and high-yield bonds.

We have also calculated the upside/downside capture ratios of convertibles and these bond segments versus the S&P 500 as the reference index. These calculations show that most types of bonds are largely uncorrelated with movements in the S&P 500. The exceptions are two: (1) convertibles because of their equity sensitivity, and (2) high-yield bonds because of their credit sensitivity, which is correlated with equity prices.

Figure 6.13 shows that convertibles did not decline meaningfully more than high yield or leveraged loans in the GFC of 2008 or during the increase in interest rates in 1994. The most obvious deviation between convertibles and the more credit-sensitive debt sectors (high yield and leveraged loans) was during the internet bubble and subsequent bust. This is because the technology bias of convertibles placed them front and center for both the rise and the fall of the internet bubble, while leveraged loans and high-yield bonds had little exposure.

6.3.7 Credit Quality Subindices

Next, we will consider how credit risk is rewarded in the convertible market. We can do this by looking at the historical performance of two indices offered by ICE Data: (1) the V0A1 and (2) the V0A2. The V0A1 is composed of all investment-grade convertibles in the VXA0, whereas the V0A2 is all the high-yield convertibles in the VXA0. Unlike the division of the VXA0 into the VGRO and the VVAL, the V0A1 plus the V0A2 does *not* equal the VXA0. This is because the definitions of V0A1 and V0A2 reflect credit ratings, and more than two-thirds of the VXA0 issues are nonrated. When looking at the performance of the V0A1 and the V0A2, we will compare them to traditional investment-grade and high-yield bonds, once again using the ICE C0A0 and H0A0 indices. We will also include the Credit Suisse Western European Leveraged Loan Index as an alternative form of credit-sensitive debt.

Convertibles with high-yield ratings have generated higher returns than investment-grade convertibles with the annual return of the V0A2 being 2.15 percentage points higher than the historical return on the V0A1. However, this excess return comes at disproportionately higher volatility (17.00% for the V0A2 versus 9.11% for the V0A1). As a result, investment-grade convertibles have higher Sharpe and Sortino ratios than their more speculative cousins. Despite having lower returns than sub-investment-grade convertibles, the V0A1 has outperformed high-yield bonds, corporate bonds, and leveraged loans. Because the V0A1 is an investment-grade index, it is logical to compare it with corporate bonds and compare the V0A2 with high-yield bond and leveraged-loan indices.

The investment-grade convertible index V0A1 has generated higher returns than the investment-grade corporate bond index (8.52% versus 6.54%). Yet, the V0A1 has lower Sharpe and Sortino ratios than the corporate bond index. Both ratios are lower for the V0A1 than for corporate bonds. Because the Sortino ratio weighs downside volatility instead of overall volatility, the Sortino ratio for the V0A1 reflects the extreme V0A1 decline of 35.7% during the GFC in 2008, which presumably reflected forced selling from hedge funds and other leveraged accounts. The GFC saw corporate bonds drop only 6.8% in 2008 (see Figure 6.14). Although both indices are investment grade, the returns of the V0A1 and corporate bonds deviate from each other on a regular basis, as shown in the figure. Measured by monthly returns, the V0A1 is only 47.0% correlated with investment-grade corporate bond returns, although this correlation is higher than that of high-yield convertibles (V0A2), which is only 38.7%. Indeed, the V0A1 is more tightly correlated with high-yield bond returns at 70.0%. Hence, inclusion of investment-grade convertibles in investment-grade fixed-income portfolios appears to provide significant diversification. We will compare the high-yield rated V0A2 with other types of credit-sensitive debt, namely non-convertible high-yield bonds and leveraged loans.

Even without knowing that the volatility of the V0A2 was 17%, it is obvious from Figure 6.14 that high-yield convertibles are more volatile; indeed, the volatility of the V0A2 is close to that of S&P 500 equities (see Figure 6.12) and far higher than the volatility of high-yield bonds and leveraged loans (which have volatilities of 8.31% and 5.50%, respectively; see Figure 6.14).

A major portion of the historical volatility of the V0A2 reflects the extreme price fluctuations of high-yield convertibles during the dot.com bubble. The V0A2 was up more than 57% in the final year of the bubble

Figure 6.14 Performance of the VOA1 and the VOA2 versus high yield and corporate bonds and leveraged loans, cumulative and year by year

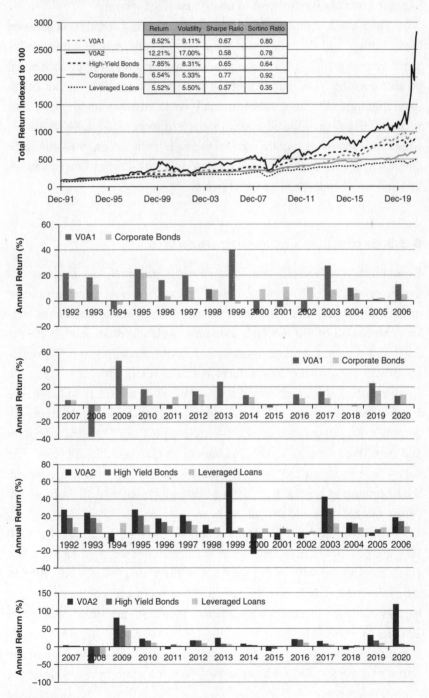

Data: Bloomberg.

before declining three years in a row. Then, once the recovery started, the index returned more than 40% in 2003. These fluctuations of the VOA2 increased its volatility relative to traditional fixed income.

The historical returns demonstrate that there is a connection between credit ratings and the risk/return trade-offs of convertibles. More credit-sensitive convertibles on average generate higher rates of return but entail greater volatility. The fact that credit is an important determinant of returns highlights the importance of credit research when investing in convertibles. Because of the absence of ratings of most convertible securities, convertible investors require internal credit research in order to minimize credit risk and volatility—and in order to take advantage of opportunities that appear when there is a market panic.

6.3.8 Economic Cycle Comparisons

Economic cycles reflect periods of strength and weakness in gross domestic product (GDP) growth, higher or lower interest rates, advancing or declining equity markets, and strengthening or weakening credit markets. Across all of the last five economic cycles through June 2020, the S&P 500 returned 11.7%, whereas convertibles returned 11.3%, delivering over 96% of the total return, but with about 20% less volatility. Convertibles also outperformed a 60:40 blend of the S&P 500 and core fixed income by about 116 basis points per year. Table 6.1 contains the cumulative return of four asset class indices plus a 60:40 blend of equity and core fixed income across 5 economic cycles and 20 subcycles. The subcycles are identified by GDP transitions from negative to positive, the beginning of central bank interest-rate increases, and the subsequent equity market peak and trough.

As shown in Table 6.1, in the economic cycle of the 2010's, the S&P 500 returned 14% annualized, whereas convertibles returned 12.5%. Convertibles captured 90% of the S&P 500 with about 19% less volatility. In the cycle of the early 2000s, the S&P 500 lost about 1.5% on an annualized basis, whereas convertibles were up more than 2.5% and did so with about 22% less volatility. In the cycle of the 1990s, the S&P 500 returned 13% annualized, whereas convertibles returned 11.7%, delivering 90% of the return of the S&P 500 with about 11% less volatility. In the cycle of the

Table 6.1 Asset Class Performance and Volatility through Economic Cycles

Economic Cycle & Asset Class	Beg. of Growth to 1st Rate Hike	1st Rate Hike to Equity Peak	Equity Peak to Equity Trough	Equity Trough to End of Rec.	Cycle Return (an)	Volatility	Sharpe Ratio	Sortino Ratio
1. 2009-2020	7/1/2009 12/13/2016	12/14/2016 2/19/2020	2/19/2020 3/19/2020	3/20/2020 6/30/2020				
1. S&P 500	186.3%	59.4%	-28.7%	29.4%	14.0%	13.4%	1.01	1.33
2. HY	103.1%	20.5%	-13.1%	8.1%	7.9%	7.1%	1.09	1.38
3. Convertibles	133.5%	56.2%	-24.6%	33.0%	12.5%	10.9%	1.11	1.47
4. BarCap Ag	32.1%	14.6%	1.5%	2.6%	4.2%	2.9%	1.29	1.80
5. 60/40	115.9%	40.6%	-17.2%	18.5%	10.4%	7.5%	1.36	1.69
2. Early 2000s Cycle	1/1/2002 6/30/2004	7/1/2004 10/9/2007	10/10/2007 3/4/2009	3/5/2009 6/30/2009				
1. S&P 500	3.7%	45.7%	-52.8%	24.9%	-1.5%	15.5%	-0.22	-0.28
2. HY	25.9%	29.0%	-28.8%	30.6%	5.7%	11.7%	0.31	0.40
3. Convertibles	23.2%	29.4%	-38.8%	23.0%	2.5%	12.2%	0.03	0.03
4. BarCap Ag	15.0%	15.4%	7.1%	3.9%	5.3%	3.9%	0.72	1.18
5. 60/40	9.6%	33.5%	-32.7%	16.6%	1.9%	9.4%	-0.01	-0.10
3. 1990s Cycle	4/1/1991 2/3/1994	2/4/1994 8/31/2000	9/1/2000 9/21/2001	9/22/2000 12/31/2001				
1. S&P 500	34.9%	259.1%	-35.7%	19.34%	13.0%	14.1%	0.59	0.66
2. HY	63.1%	55.5%	-3.3%	4.37%	9.1%	5.9%	0.73	0.78

(Continued)

Table 6.1 Asset Class Performance and Volatility through Economic Cycles (Cont.)

Economic Cycle & Asset Class	Beg. of Growth to 1st Rate Hike	1st Rate Hike to Equity Peak	Equity Peak to Equity Trough	Equity Trough to End of Rec.	Cycle Return (an)	Volatility	Sharpe Ratio	Sortino Ratio
3. Convertibles	64.4%	151.0%	−27.0%	8.62%	11.7%	12.5%	0.57	0.65
4. BarCapAg	33.0%	50.5%	11.7%	0.68%	7.8%	3.8%	0.82	1.15
5. 60/40	34.6%	158.6%	−19.2%	11.6%	11.2%	8.9%	0.72	0.98
4. Mid-Late 80s Cycle	1/1/1983	4/1/1988	6/29/1990	2/1/1991				
	3/31/1988	6/28/1990	1/31/1991	3/31/1991				
1. S&P 500	112.6%	50.7%	−14.7%	31.0%	16.7%	11.8%	0.76	1.11
2. HY	95.8%	9.8%	−6.7%	24.0%	11.7%	7.6%	0.51	0.88
3.Convertibles	84.9%	20.5%	−15.8%	32.2%	11.6%	10.5%	0.32	0.50
4. BarCap Ag	90.8%	21.2%	3.8%	8.4%	12.3%	8.4%	0.57	0.93
5. 60/40	107.9%	38.6%	−7.6%	21.6%	15.3%	9.49%	0.81	1.27
5. Late 70s-Early 80s Annual data	12/31/1974	12/31/1977	12/31/1979	12/31/1981				
	12/31/1977	12/31/1979	12/31/1981	12/31/1982				
1. S&P 500	57.9%	26.4%	26.0%	21.6%	15.0%	15.4%	0.40	0.54
2. HY	na	na	na	na	na	na	na	na
3. Convertibles	68.5%	24.1%	31.7%	30.9%	17.4%	10.4%	0.83	1.16
4. BarCap Ag/B0A0	38.3%	−4.3%	−3.6%	43.8%	7.9%	15.3%	−0.07	−0.12
5. 60/40	46.6%	7.6%	8.6%	34.9%	11.0%	12.6%	0.17	0.27

Source: ICE Data, Bloomberg data, Advent Capital Management.

middle to late 1980s, the S&P 500 returned 16.7%, whereas convertibles returned 11.6%, delivering 70% of the return of the S&P 500 with about 11% less volatility. In the cycle of the late 1970s to early 1980s, the S&P 500 returned 15%, whereas convertibles returned 17.4%, delivering 116% of the return of the S&P 500 with about 33% less volatility. The last two columns of Table 6.1 show that convertibles have always had a more favorable Sortino ratio than Sharpe ratio, which reflects the downside protection of convertibles.

Over the last four cycles, high yield has returned 8.6% annualized versus 10.0% for convertibles. The outperformance of convertibles relative to high yield has increased over time partly due to declining yields of high-yield bonds and also because of higher appreciation of convertibles. In the cycle of the 2010s, convertibles outperformed high yield by 466 basis points per year. Convertibles outperformed the 60:40 blend by 209 basis points per year in the cycle of the 2010s because of the lower yields earned on core fixed income. Because duration-related capital gains delivered a substantial portion of the total returns of both investment-grade and high-yield straight bonds, and rates remain low as we go to press in 2021, convertibles are likely to continue to outperform straight debt.

6.3.8.1 Convertible Performance Across Economic Subcycles

It is exceptionally difficult to recognize, much less anticipate, the economic cycle. GDP is announced after the end of a quarter, and therefore, recessions are declared after they started. Even in the midst of a growth cycle, markets can correct in excess of 10% multiple times.

Over the last four economic cycles, the first subcycle has lasted about 18 quarters. After the first interest-rate hike, the equity market peak has taken about 15 quarters. Equity markets anticipate a coming recession by between two and six months, although the COVID-19-induced recession was a no table exception. From peak to trough is about three quarters on average, with 2020 providing the exception when the market trough came only one month after the prior market peak. Once the market begins to recover, economic growth typically recovers within one quarter.

During the first subcycle, convertibles have outperformed all other asset classes, including stocks, returning 305 basis points per quarter. In the second sub-cycle, stocks have tended to outperform, and strength in equities has helped convertibles to outperform high yield. These first two subcycles represent about 90% of the time of an economic cycle. During the market declines from peak to trough, convertibles have outperformed equities but trailed other fixed-income assets, but in the rebound from the market trough, convertibles have performed nearly as well as or better than the S&P 500. On average, convertibles returned 23% per quarter, whereas the S&P 500 returned 25% in what is sometimes called the *junk rally*.

In 2020, convertibles beat the S&P 500 by 360 basis points from the market trough to the end of the recessionary second quarter. From the market peak on February 19, 2020, until the end of the second quarter, stocks had declined 7%, high yield had declined 6%, yet, convertibles had already surpassed their previous highs (see Table 6.2).

From an asset-allocation perspective, it is worth comparing the traditional 60:40 blend versus a blend that contains 10% convertibles and one that contains 10% high yield. During the economic cycle of the 2010s, the blend with 10% convertibles outperformed the 60:40 blend by 31 basis points per year. It also outperformed the blend with 10% high yield by 42 basis points per year (see Table 6.3).

Table 6.2   Convertible Performance by Position in the Economic Cycle

Last 4 Cycles – Avg Qtrly Return	Beg. of Growth to 1st Rate Hike	1st Rate Hike to Equity Peak	Equity Peak to Equity Trough	Equity Trough to End of Rec.
Average # Qtrs.	18	15	3	1
1. S&P 500	3.01%	4.23%	−12.65%	25.16%
2. HY	2.95%	1.61%	−4.56%	15.71%
3. Convertibles	3.05%	3.01%	−9.59%	22.98%
4. BarCap Ag	1.89%	1.45%	1.87%	3.75%
5. 60/40	2.66%	3.17%	−6.79%	16.44%

Source: Advent Capital Management.

Table 6.3   Portfolio Performance by Position in the Economic Cycle

Asset Allocation	Beg. of Growth to 1st Rate Hike	1st Rate Hike to Equity Peak	Equity Peak to Equity Trough	Equity Trough to End of Rec.	Cycle Return (an)
60:40	115.94%	40.58%	−17.24%	18.50%	10.43%
55:35:10Conv	119.38%	42.57%	−18.29%	20.17%	10.74%
55:35:10HY	116.68%	39.01%	−17.05%	17.84%	10.32%

Source: Advent Capital Management.

6.3.9 Convertible Performance When Treasury Rates Rise

Because of their relatively low interest-rate rho, relatively short effective duration, and relatively high interest-rate convexity, convertibles are the best-performing fixed-income asset class during periods of rising Treasury rates (as shown in Figure 6.15). From 1990 through 2020, there were 10 periods when the 10-year Treasury yield rose by more than 100 basis points (from month end to month end). In the 137 months when the 10-year Treasury yield rose more than 100 basis points, convertibles returned 750%, compared with −59% for 10-year Treasurys, 0.2% for municipal bonds, 5% for investment-grade corporate bonds, 6% for mortgage-backed securities, 32% for preferred stock, 133% for bank loans, and 228% for high-yield bonds. For additional information about the performance of convertibles during periods of rising interest rates and during periods of rising or high inflation, visit www.AdventCap.com/SupplementaryMaterials.

6.4 GLOBAL CONVERTIBLE MARKETS

Between 1980 and 2005 the world embraced the free market policies of Milton Friedman. A new age of globalization ushered in economic integration of trade flows, capital flows, and migration at an accelerated pace. Living standards rose sharply, while life expectancy, infant mortality, educational attainment, and democracy improved, and absolute poverty declined. These were not coincidences.

—Prof. Richard Wong, University of Hong Kong[4]

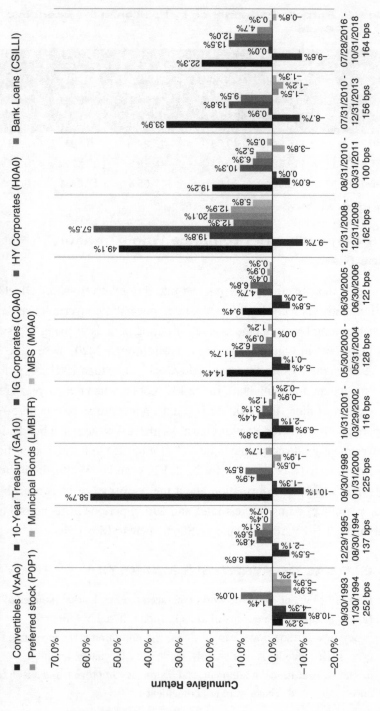

Figure 6.15 Convertibles outperform in periods of rising interest rates

■ Convertibles (VxAo) ■ 10-Year Treasury (GA10) ■ IG Corporates (C0A0) ■ HY Corporates (H0A0) ■ Bank Loans (CSILLI)
■ Preferred stock (P0P1) ■ Municipal Bonds (LMBITR) ■ MBS (M0A0)

Source: Bloomberg, ICE Data.

US companies are the largest issuers of convertibles in dollar terms. Yet, there are nearly twice as many convertible issuers outside the United States. As Professor Wong asserted, globalization has been a source of economic advancement for the world. If Professor Wong is correct, then the ability to freely invest globally is a cornerstone of financial health. International convertibles should be considered in order to expand the number of opportunities and to build an even more diversified portfolio.

The Refinitiv Qualified Global Convertible Index is intentionally managed to track the global convertible market in a manner that reflects the way most professionally managed convertible portfolios are constructed. No individual issuer can represent more than 2% of the index, and there are stringent issue size requirements. US convertible issues need to be $300 million in order to be included in the index at issuance (in 2020, this rule excluded around 18% of the VXA0's face value). These requirements dilute the ability of the Refinitiv Qualified Global Convertible Index to reflect the performance of global convertibles as a whole, but these boundaries create a benchmark for a global convertible strategy that is aligned with the kind of portfolio a convertible manager actually would construct.

During the 1990s and early 2000s, convertibles grew rapidly to a peak of $700 billion in 2007 as stock markets set new highs prior to the global financial crisis (GFC). After this peak, the global convertible market contracted for a few years and then began a recovery that became pronounced in early 2020 as US issuance and the size of the US convertible market set records into 2021. The global decline after the GFC had been driven primarily by reductions in issuance overseas, particularly in Japan and Europe. In early 2020, the COVID-19 pandemic saw stocks and convertibles tumble and then recover, and the subsequent powerful advance in technology stocks was a major catalyst for convertible issuance and convertible performance, especially in the United States. At year-end 2020, the global convertible market was $645 billion according to Refinitiv.

The average *current*[5] yield of global convertibles declined steadily from more than 4% in 2008 to less than 2% in 2018–2021, as shown in Figure 6.16. Indeed, the decline in interest rates on convertible bonds pushed yields to maturity below zero among some new issues in Europe that were floated at premiums over par. Of course, a negative yield to maturity does not eliminate the inherent asymmetry of convertibles—particularly in the case of investment-grade issues that are highly likely to pay

Figure 6.16   Average running (current) yield of the Refinitiv Qualified Global Convertible Index and other global indices

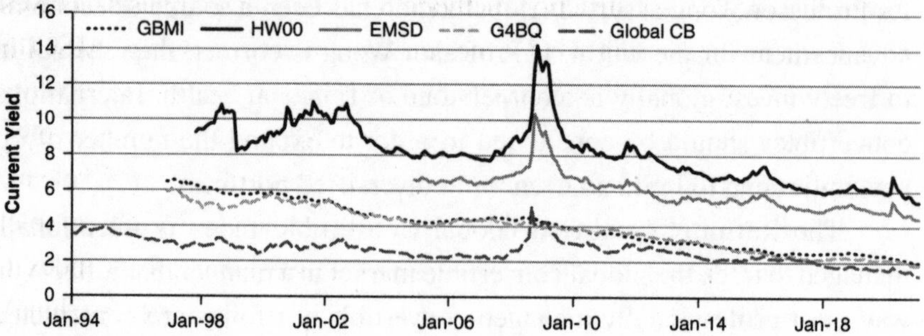

Data: Refinitiv, ICE Data.

off at maturity regardless of potential weakness in the underlying shares. (One reason for market acceptance of negative yields to maturity in Europe may be the generous takeover provisions provided by most European convertibles, which can easily result in substantial appreciation.) A negative yield to maturity is potentially irresistible to issuers. Yet, the basis-point declines in yields of convertibles have been significantly less than the declines in yields on nonconvertible bonds because the lower interest coupons on convertibles provided less room to fall.

A notable deviation from the multi-decade downtrend in yields occurred during the GFC as leveraged and/or panicked investors—especially hedge funds that were hit with redemption requests from their investors as well as margin calls from their prime brokers—became forced sellers of securities. Much wider credit spreads were required to attract buyers.

6.5 GLOBAL CONVERTIBLE MARKETS, INDICES, AND PERFORMANCE

When comparing the performance of the Refinitiv Qualified Global Convertible Index with global equities, we will use the Morgan Stanley Capital International (MSCI) World Index, which is the most commonly used global equity index. The MSCI World Index includes stocks from 23 countries but excludes emerging or frontier markets. China is the most notable exclusion from the MSCI World Index given the large size of its economy and its capital markets. China is still classified as an emerging market and is therefore included in the MSCI Emerging Markets Index.

Like Refinitiv's convertible bond indices, MSCI's equity indices are intentionally designed to be used as benchmarks for portfolio managers. This means that MSCI's construction methodologies have an emphasis on investability when determining what issues qualify for inclusion (e.g., MSCI indices have float-adjusted market capitalization and liquidity requirements). MSCI has specific guidelines for how its indices are constructed, but it sometimes overrides the guidelines in order to fulfill the intended role as a benchmark. An example of an override has been the slow and incomplete inclusion of Chinese A shares in the MSCI Emerging Markets Index (*A shares* are shares of Chinese stocks that are traded domestically in China).

MSCI has been hesitant to include domestically traded shares of Chinese companies because of the difficulties of trading these shares by non-Chinese investors and also because Chinese companies would represent a large percentage of the index if fully included. MSCI has adopted a compromise solution that includes A shares at only 20% of the mathematical weight (up from 5% prior to 2019), and MSCI began including mid-cap A shares in 2019.[6]

China is likely to become a much larger component of the global bond market, however, and Chinese convertibles will also be a much larger part of global convertible indices. UBS observed in September 2020 that "US-China tension has not deterred China's ambition to open its financial market."[7] Mainland Chinese corporations issued about $55 billion of convertibles in 2019, "equal to the previous two years combined," according to Bloomberg Opinion.[8] The similar index philosophies of Refinitiv and MSCI make their indices suitable for global comparison purposes. We use the ICE BofA VXA0 to compare the US the convertible market.

Figure 6.17 shows that global convertibles have outperformed the MSCI World Equity Index by 0.7% annually over the last 23 years. This return is especially attractive because global convertibles were less volatile than global equities during the 23 years. Table 6.4 shows that the VXA0 had a higher overall return than the global convertible index. But the VXA0 incurred higher volatility. Figure 6.17 shows that the higher return from the VXA0 is the result of recent strength rather than long-term superiority. The VXA0 trailed global convertibles until late 2016, after which it increased its lead through 2020. US technology growth stocks made a major contribution given the technology bias in US convertibles.

The global convertible index and the VXA0 have similar Sharpe and Sortino ratios despite the differing returns of the two indices. Both indices have better ratios than the MSCI World Index. The favorable risk/reward profiles of the convertible indices is confirmed by the upside and downside capture ratios. Remarkably, global convertibles provide both a higher return and lower volatility than global equities.

ICE Data provides indices that track the performance of both the global bond market in aggregate and global high-yield bonds. These indices are the ICE Global Broad Market Index (ticker GBMI) and the ICE Global High Yield Index (ticker HW00), respectively. We can use these indices to contrast the performance and risk of convertibles with traditional nonconvertible fixed income.

Figure 6.18 shows that global convertible bonds have generated higher absolute returns than both global high-yield bonds (HW00) and

Figure 6.17   Global convertibles versus global equity

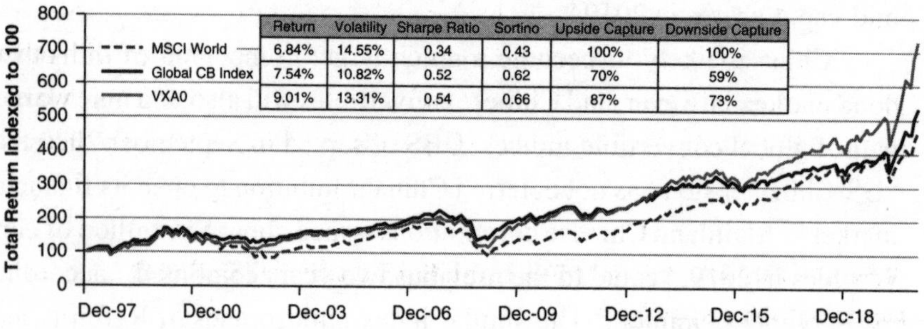

	Return	Volatility	Sharpe Ratio	Sortino	Upside Capture	Downside Capture
MSCI World	6.84%	14.55%	0.34	0.43	100%	100%
Global CB Index	7.54%	10.82%	0.52	0.62	70%	59%
VXA0	9.01%	13.31%	0.54	0.66	87%	73%

Data: Bloomberg, Refinitiv.

Figure 6.18   Global convertibles versus global bonds

	Return	Volatility	Sharpe Ratio	Sortino	Upside Capture	Downside Capture
HW00	6.74%	9.73%	0.50	0.53	50%	36%
GBMI	4.81%	5.32%	0.55	0.93	12%	−10%
Global CB Index	7.54%	10.82%	0.52	0.62	70%	59%

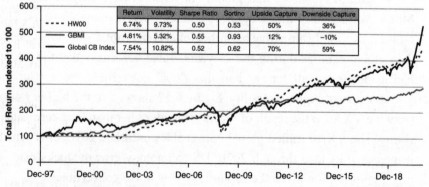

Data: Bloomberg, ICE Data, Refinitiv.

global investment-grade bonds (GBMI), and global convertibles also were more volatile than both bond indices. As a result of the higher volatility, convertibles have a slightly lower Sharpe ratio and a much lower Sortino ratio than high-yield bonds and significantly lower ratios than the global bond aggregate.

The apparently favorable returns from bonds relative to volatility may be a manifestation of the standard warning that past performance is not a guarantee of future returns, because the most significant trend supporting the total return from bonds since the early 1980s has been the severe decline in interest rates, which provided a strong tailwind for bonds with long durations. Both convertibles and high-yield bonds tend to have shorter durations than high-quality straight bonds and consequently less appreciation potential in response to declining market rates of interest. The GBMI has the longest duration of the three indices, which makes it a key beneficiary of falling interest rates. With interest rates negative in many countries and barely above zero in the United States, it is unlikely that global bonds will generate high returns over the next 23 years.

So far we have been comparing the global convertible index with other global indices. We repeat that global indices include US assets, and we estimate that US convertible issues constitute about 70% of global indices.

6.6 GLOBAL CONVERTIBLE ISSUANCE AND PERFORMANCE

The United States is the largest convertible market, followed by Europe, Asia ex-Japan, and then Japan. While Europe is the second largest market for convertibles, the amount of outstanding convertibles has been declining since a high point in the early 2000s, when there was more than $200 billion of European convertibles. The Continental European market had grown in the 1990s as local equity markets became more sophisticated and offered an alternative to bank financing and as some government-owned companies and cross-holdings were spun off by the expedient of exchangeable convertible bonds. The European convertible market had shrunk to less than $100 billion by 2020 (see Figure 6.19).

The convertible market in Asia ex-Japan is much larger than it was at the turn of the millennium, having risen to about $70 billion in 2007,

Figure 6.19 Convertible market size

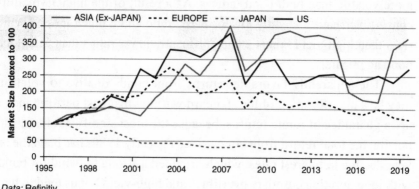

Data: Refinitiv.

then dipped in 2016–2017, and recovered to around $70 billion at year-end 2020. This trend suggests that Asia will surpass Europe and become the second largest convertible market.

The wild card in Asia ex-Japan is China. Currently Chinese domestic convertibles are restricted to certain "qualified foreign institutional investors,"[9] which limits access to the onshore convertible market and causes domestic Chinese convertibles to be excluded from major international convertible indices. However, demand for cheap financing in China, as well as Chinese regulations that restrict the issuance of new equity (which convertible issuance sidesteps), has led to a large increase in the number of convertibles issued in China.[10] As China opens its bond market, the giant country will likely become a key component of the global convertible market—just as China has become a key component of global trade.

Foreigners are able to trade domestic RMB-denominated Chinese bonds on the Hong Kong Stock Exchange via Bond Connect.[11] According to UBS, "Bond Connect could benefit from foreign investors' higher appetite for China's onshore bonds, likely driven by a widening interest rate gap, index inclusions . . . and expansion of global rating agencies in China."[12] We expect Bond Connect to enable foreign access to onshore Chinese convertible bonds (see Tables 6.4 and 6.5).

In 1995, the amount of Japanese convertibles outstanding was more than 10 times the amount of all other Asian nations combined ($208 billion versus $20 billion). However, various internal factors in Japan subsequently led to low issuance, and in July 2020, there was only $22 billion in Japanese

Table 6.4   China Onshore (A Share) New Issues of Convertible Bonds by Year

Year	Rmb (billion)	US$ (billion)	# New Issues	Avg Size per Issue (million US$)
2018	107.1	15.8	77	204
2019	269.5	39.6	151	262
2020	266.7	41	195	210
Total	643.3	96.4	423	228

Data: http://data.eastmoney.com/kzz/default.html, Advent Capital Management calculations.

Table 6.5   China Onshore Convertible Bond Issuance Year to Date August 2020 Is the Second Largest after the United States

Country	$ Billion
USA	86
Asia	36.1
China onshore (A-share)	26.1
Asia (including China Offshore)	9
Japan	1
Europe	21
Total	143.1

Data: http://data.eastmoney.com/kzz/default.html, Advent Capital Management calculations.

convertibles outstanding. In 2019, only $1.2 billion worth of new convertibles were issued in Japan compared with $109.6 billion issued globally.[13]

There are a couple of explanations for the decline of Japanese convertible issuance, and both are the result of the economic situation in the country. Since the Japanese asset bubble collapsed in 1991, Japan has experienced persistent low growth and deflationary pressure. While originally given the moniker the *Lost Decade*, the economic challenges have persisted for multiple decades. In order to reignite growth and fight deflation, Japan has engaged in some of the most aggressive monetary stimulus in the world.

The combination of low growth and monetary stimulus has kept Japanese interest rates near zero persistently; hence, the savings in interest from the lower rates on convertibles is small. The lower the absolute rate on a nonconvertible bond, the less is the saving in interest from issuing a convertible bond. Convertible issuance and growth go hand in hand. The structure of convertibles makes them more attractive for both investors and issuers when the underlying shares have the potential to grow. There are simply fewer growth companies in Japan that would inspire issuance of convertibles. Japan lacks a high-yield market, so there's no trade-off in favor of issuing a convertible instead of a nonconvertible high-yield bond.

6.6.1 European Convertibles Performance

European convertibles have a more even sector distribution without the strong bias toward technology and healthcare that is generally a feature of the US convertible market. European convertibles are also more likely to be investment grade than convertibles from any other region. Based on broad index characteristics alone, we would expect the European convertible index to have a lower rate of return but less risk than US convertibles.

We will compare the performance of European convertibles, US convertibles (using the VXA0), European high-yield bonds (HE00), and the MSCI Europe equity index. Figure 6.20 shows the long-term performance of the aforementioned five indices indexed to 100. The Refinitiv Europe index had a higher long-term return than the MSCI Europe Index or either European bond index. The outperformance of the Refinitiv Europe con-

Figure 6.20   European convertible performance

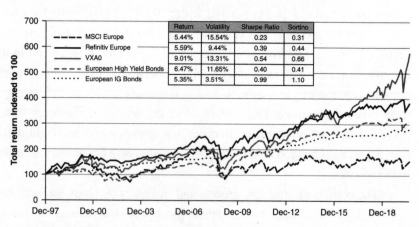

	Return	Volatility	Sharpe Ratio	Sortino
MSCI Europe	5.44%	15.54%	0.23	0.31
Refinitiv Europe	5.59%	9.44%	0.39	0.44
VXA0	9.01%	13.31%	0.54	0.66
European High Yield Bonds	6.47%	11.65%	0.40	0.41
European IG Bonds	5.35%	3.51%	0.99	1.10

Data: Bloomberg, Refinitiv.

vertible index relative to the MSCI Europe Equity Index is particularly impressive given that the Refinitiv European convertible index has less than two-thirds the volatility of the equity index. The performance of high-yield bonds is higher than that of convertibles. The high-yield index is also more volatile than the convertible index. The Sharpe and Sortino ratios of convertibles and high yield are similar. European investment-grade bonds performed surprisingly well and have the highest Sharpe and Sortino ratios, presumably reflecting the positive effects of the long decline in market rates of interest. However, with interest rates historically low in Europe, it is likely that investment-grade bonds will struggle to replicate their performance. (At the end of August 2020, the European investment-grade convertible index had a yield to maturity of just 0.13%.)[14] European convertibles have lagged US convertibles and have slightly lower risk-adjusted ratios.

European convertibles have been a bright spot in a region where investment performance has been disappointing. Convertibles have outperformed equities in the region both on an absolute basis and on a risk-adjusted basis. One potential cause for weakness in European equity performance is meager economic growth.

European convertibles are skewed toward core countries that have prospered. Moreover, the biggest corporate problems in Europe in recent years have afflicted European banking and financial companies that rarely issue convertibles. And many of the larger European convertible issuers are global growth companies that are hurt less by the slow growth in Europe. Superior takeover provisions among some European convertibles have also contributed to favorable returns relative to equity.

6.6.2 Performance of Asia ex-Japan Convertibles

The MSCI Asia Pacific ex-Japan Index was established in 1987 and is a widely used index that has been imitated by other data providers. Currently, Asia ex-Japan is the third largest region for convertible issuance (although if *domestic* Chinese convertibles were included, Asia ex-Japan probably would surpass Europe as the second largest region for convertibles). The Japanese convertible market is typically tracked separately from the rest of Asia. This is a longstanding practice that goes back to the period when Japan had the largest convertible market in the world—as recently as 1996.

Figure 6.21   Asian convertible performance December 1993 to December 2020

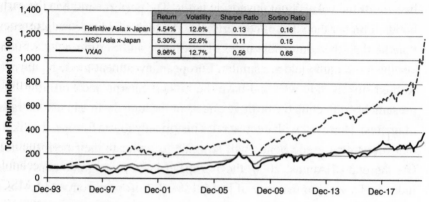

	Return	Volatility	Sharpe Ratio	Sortino Ratio
Refinitive Asia x-Japan	4.54%	12.6%	0.13	0.16
MSCI Asia x-Japan	5.30%	22.6%	0.11	0.15
VXA0	9.96%	12.7%	0.56	0.68

Data: Bloomberg, Refinitiv.

We will compare the Asia Refinitiv convertible index with American convertibles by using the VXA0, and we will approximate the returns of the underlying Asian stocks by using the MSCI Asia ex-Japan Index. The Refinitiv Asia convertible index has returned more than the MSCI Asia ex-Japan Index (5.30% versus 4.33%) with less than half the volatility (12.6% versus 22.6%) (see Figure 6.21).

Asian convertibles have a higher Sharpe ratio than the MSCI Index (0.52 versus 0.43; In contrast, Asian convertibles have lagged American convertibles. The VXA0 has generated an average annual return that is nearly 3.5 percentage points higher than the Refinitiv Asia convertible index. The Sharpe ratio of the VXA0 is higher than that of the Asia index (0.68 versus 0.52, respectively) (see Table 6.6).

Asian convertibles have trailed US and European convertibles since the early 1990s when the indices were created. Two factors have con[1]

Table 6.6   Asian Convertible Performance and Volatility, September 30, 2004–December 31, 2020

	MSCI Asia	Asia Refinitiv Index	VXA0
Return	10.08%	6.57%	9.93%
Volatility	20.48%	10.27%	12.74%
Sharpe ratio	0.43	0.52	0.68
Sortino ratio	0.59	0.49	0.78

Data: Bloomberg, Refinitiv.

tributed to the underperformance. First, corporate governance has been an issue for some convertible bond issuers in China and India. There have been multiple fraudulent convertible issuers in China. In India in the early 2000s, some issuers were able to call the convertibles in local currency rather, which reduced returns in hard currency terms. Additionally, some Indian convertibles had low coupons offset by premium puts/redemptions, however many issuers were unable to honor the premium feature, particularly during the 2008-2009 financial crisis. These problems inhibited the performance of Asian convertibles relative to other regions.

Currently, Asia's market composition is in a state of transformation. China's role in the market has grown rapidly, as has the weight of technology stocks. As of year-end 2020, China represented 40% of the MSCI Asia Pacific ex-Japan Index (MSCI APxJ), double it's weight (20%) in 2015, and the internet sector alone had grown to 22% of the equity index, up from just 5% in 2015. Asian convertibles trailed equity markets in this transition because only 10% of Asian convertibles were in the outperforming technology sector. Nevertheless, Asian convertibles have performed favorably relative to Asian equities on a risk adjusted basis, particularly in periods of volatility when markets correct.

6.6.3 Performance of Japanese Convertibles

When evaluating the performance of Japanese convertibles, we will compare the convertible returns versus the Nikkei 225 Index, which tracks the stock prices of 225 large public companies and is a classic *price-weighted index* (like the venerable Dow Jones indices). When discussing Japanese equities, it is important to recognize that the central bank—as part of its monetary stimulus efforts—has become a major purchaser of equity ETFs, thereby supporting the Japanese stock market since 2013. The Bank of Japan may own 75% of the Japanese ETF market and 8% of the Japanese stock market[15] (see Figure 6.22).

The biggest attraction of the Japanese convertible market is the much lower volatility than that of Japanese equities. Going back all the way to 1993, Japanese convertibles have outperformed the return of Japanese equities with little more than half the volatility. Japanese convertibles have a Sharpe ratio that is lower than that of US or European convertibles but higher than that of Asia ex-Japan convertibles (0.31 versus 0.13). These

Figure 6.22 Japanese convertible performance, November 1993–June 2020

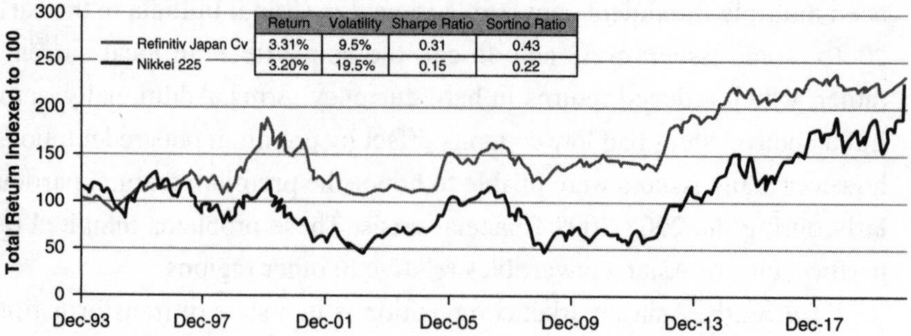

	Return	Volatility	Sharpe Ratio	Sortino Ratio
Refinitiv Japan Cv	3.31%	9.5%	0.31	0.43
Nikkei 225	3.20%	19.5%	0.15	0.22

Data: Refinitiv.

figures demonstrate that convertible bonds have been particularly strong versus equities when growth was weak—as has also occurred in Europe.

While both Japanese Equity and Japanese Convertible returns from 1993 through 2020 were low (just over 3% per year), there were periods of stronger performance. For example, when the Bank of Japan increased its program of buying domestic ETFs in 2013, equities soared. In the three years through mid-2015, the Nikkei 225 returned over 100% and Japanese convertibles responded well, with a return of over 40%. However, by the fourth quarter of 2018, average convertible delta had fallen into the defensive range. With even lower deltas from December 2018 to December 2021, convertibles participated in only 16% of the return of the Nikkei during that period (see figure 6.23).

6.6.4 Performance by Economic Sector

The US convertible market bias toward technology issuers is unique. The sector distribution of convertibles varies from one region to another. Figure 6.24 shows the percentage of outstanding convertibles by region and economic sector as of year-end 2020. The figure shows that the technology bias of convertibles is driven entirely by the United States. In the 23 years 1998-2020, the top performing sector in both Global and US equity indices was technology, according to MSCI and S&P indices. Moreover, US technology convertibles actually outperformed US technology equities by 65 basis points per year, and global technology convertibles captured 91% of the return of global technology equities. Similarly, European and Asian technology convertibles returned 97% and 98% of the global technology

Figure 6.23 Japanese convertible performance, December 2012 to December 2021

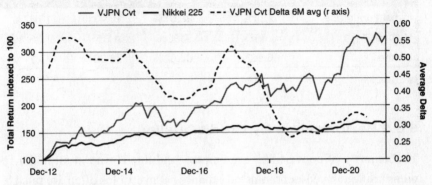

Data: Bloomberg, Refinitiv.

equity index, respectively. This strong performance, combined with the lower volatility of convertibles, gave convertible technology indices nearly double the Sharpe ratio of technology equities (0.51 to 0.64 vs. 0.35 to 0.36). In fact, eight out of eleven global convertible sector indices had Sharpe ratios in excess of comparable global equity indices. Even some of the weakest performing sectors, such as telecom, financial, and utility convertibles had strong relative performance (see Section 4.11, Table 4.1).

Figure 6.24 Sector Distribution by Region July 2020

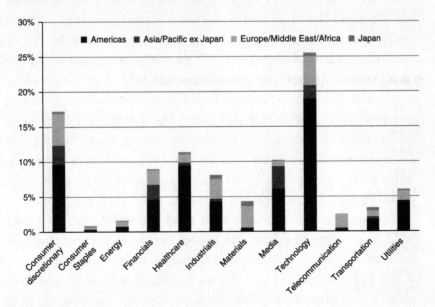

Data: Refinitiv.

Table 6.7   Ratings by Fitch, Moody's, and S&P

	Asia ex-Japan	Europe	Japan	US
Investment grade	3.29%	28.07%	12.43%	10.37%
High yield	0.15%	4.33%	1.35%	16.53%
Unrated	96.56%	67.60%	86.22%	73.11%

Data: Refinitiv.

6.6.5 Performance by Credit Quality

The majority of convertibles are unrated, and this is true in all major regions (although yen-denominated Japanese convertibles often are rated by the Japan Credit Rating Agency [JCR]). Yet, there are noticeable differences in credit quality from one region to another (see Table 6.7).

The most extreme example of nonrated convertibles is in Asia ex-Japan, where only 3.44% of convertibles are rated by the largest US rating agencies (Fitch, Moody's, and S&P). In Japan, only 13.78% are rated by the top three US rating agencies, but the Japanese convertible market is dominated by investment-grade issues. Japanese issuers pay for the US credit ratings only in instances of convertibles that are intended for foreign buyers and are denominated in euros or US dollars. The domestic Japanese market relies on the JCR ratings, which are accepted by Japanese investors, although JCR ratings tend to be a notch or two higher than equivalent ratings from the US agencies, in our opinion. A convertible data service from Jefferies International Limited[16] in London in September 2020 included data on 63 Japanese convertibles, and only 16 of the issues had an estimated credit spread of more than 100 basis points over the London Inter-Bank Offered Rate (LIBOR). Japan has a deep asset swap market for convertible securities in which local banks effectively buy the bond and separately sell the option; such swaps require tight credit spreads that confirm high credit quality. In our observation, Japanese convertibles tend to provide good downside protection even in unfavorable circumstances.

Outside the United States, most rated convertibles are investment grade. The European convertible market has the largest percentage of convertibles rated investment grade by the US credit-rating agencies: as of July 2020, 28.07% of convertibles in Europe were rated investment grade. This is more than double the percentage with such ratings in the

United States and Japan. Moreover, anecdotal evidence suggests that perhaps a fifth of the nonrated convertible bonds in Europe are obligations of investment-grade companies, which would mean that the European convertible market is about 40% investment grade. (European issuers sometimes have investment-grade credit ratings on their *straight* debt, which makes it a simple matter to calculate *implied* investment-grade credit ratings on the convertible obligations of such issuers by adjusting for the different maturities, subordination, etc. of the convertibles.)

In the United States, few nonrated issues are obligations of high-quality companies. The US convertible market is singular in that there are more convertibles *rated* high yield than there are convertibles rated investment grade. US issuers of lower credit quality apparently are more comfortable applying for ratings, just as US investors are more willing to invest in convertibles that are below investment grade, presumably in recognition that convertible bonds are always structurally safer than the underlying stocks regardless of credit quality. Self-selection bias in the decision to be rated is much stronger overseas than it is in the United States.

6.7 ASSET-ALLOCATION OPTIMIZATION

Asset allocation is the process of allocating investment dollars to various investment strategies and ultimately to specific investments and/or investment managers. Asset allocation is intended to maximize returns with the least risk. The task involves defining the investment goals and the time frame involved and developing an optimal mix of investments—often at the asset class level—that will best achieve one's investment goals. The task is often led by financial advisors for individual investors and by consultants for institutional accounts.

6.7.1 Two-Asset Optimization

A two-asset optimization tracks the records of two investments or indices and blends them into a series of hypothetical two-asset portfolios—varying the percentage of each asset. Figure 6.25 shows a blend of the V0A0 together with the S&P 500 Low Volatility Index, which was one of the strongest performing equity indices in the 2010s, bucking the theory that lower-volatility stocks should have lower returns. The chart shows how

Figure 6.25 Blend of convertibles and low-volatility equity (trailing 10 year and trailing 30 year)

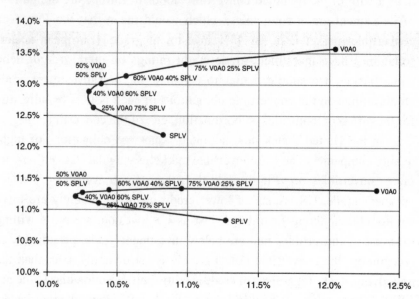

Sources: Bloomberg, ICE Data.

convertibles have had even higher returns and less volatility during both the last 10 years and the last 30 years. Depending on the risk aversion of the investor (which is discussed in depth in Chapter 5), the optimal blend during these decades would have been in the vicinity of 20% to 40% global low volatility and 60% to 80% global convertibles. The returns assume monthly rebalancing to the target weights.

6.7.2 Markowitz Mean-Variance Optimization of Asset Allocation (Ex Post)

Another approach to optimization is a process named after Nobel laureate Harry Markowitz, who used average returns and covariance matrices to determine optimal blends. Table 6.8 shows the average returns and the covariance matrix of four bond indices, two convertible indices, and two equity indices. We then use an optimization process to calculate the blend of those indices that provides the maximum return given a target standard deviation. Figure 6.26 illustrates the optimal index weight by target

**Table 6.8   Covariance Matrix and Average Returns of Asset
Class Indices, December 31, 1987–December 31,
2020**

	B0A0	C0A0	H0A0	GA10	V0A0	VXA0	SPXT	RTY	Avg. Ret
B0A0	1.47	1.63	0.66	2.27	0.48	0.51	0.51	(0.09)	0.519
C0A0	1.63	2.31	2.03	2.02	2.14	2.21	2.15	2.04	0.59
H0A0	0.66	2.03	5.61	(0.33)	6.04	6.15	6.20	8.38	0.69
GA10	2.27	2.02	(0.33)	4.12	(0.88)	(0.86)	(0.87)	(2.30)	0.52
V0A0	0.48	2.14	6.04	(0.88)	12.16	12.06	11.91	16.77	0.93
VXA0	0.51	2.21	6.15	(0.86)	12.06	12.08	12.23	16.74	0.90
SPXT	0.51	2.15	6.20	(0.87)	11.91	12.23	17.47	18.86	0.96
RTY	(0.09)	2.04	8.38	(2.30)	16.77	16.74	18.86	30.24	0.99

Sources: Bloomberg, ICE Data.

**Figure 6.26   Optimal portfolio weightings by target volatility,
December 31, 1987-December 31, 2020**

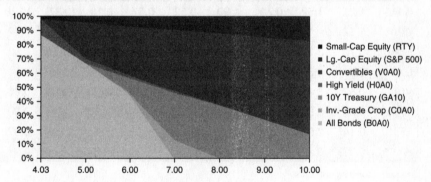

Source: Bloomberg Data, ICE Data, Advent Capital Management.

volatility in a range of target volatilities from 4% up to 10% per year. Figure 6.27 illustrates the performance. Convertibles (the V0A0) make up a substantial part of the optimal portfolio for all target volatilities from 5% and above. Optimizing on Sharpe ratio, we can determine the optimal portfolio mix from a risk/reward perspective. Convertibles comprised 18% of the optimal portfolio. The optimizer selected the V0A0 rather than the VXA0 because of its higher return at a similar level of volatility (see Table 6.9 and Figure 6.28). The V0A0 excludes mandatory convertibles.

Figure 6.27   Performance by asset class index and target volatility, December 31, 1987–December 31, 2020

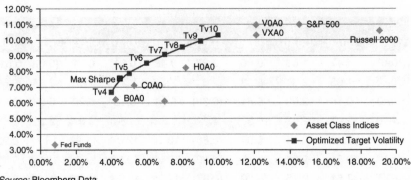

Source: Bloomberg Data.

Table 6.9   Covariance Matrix and Average Returns, December 31, 2005–December 31, 2020

	B0A0	C0A0	H0A0	GA10	V0A0	VXA0	SPXT	RTY	Avg. Ret
B0A0	1.25	1.52	0.70	1.90	0.52	0.57	0.14	(0.37)	0.378
C0A0	1.52	2.81	3.14	1.34	3.43	3.56	2.98	3.25	0.47
H0A0	0.70	3.14	7.76	(1.34)	8.65	8.86	8.96	11.66	0.63
GA10	1.90	1.34	(1.34)	4.01	(2.17)	(2.17)	(2.83)	(4.52)	0.40
V0A0	0.52	3.43	8.65	(2.17)	13.87	13.96	14.23	19.03	0.96
VXA0	0.57	3.56	8.86	(2.17)	13.96	14.14	14.52	19.15	0.90
SPXT	0.14	2.98	8.96	(2.83)	14.23	14.52	18.85	23.04	0.87
RTY	(0.37)	3.25	11.66	(4.52)	19.03	19.15	23.04	34.19	0.91

Sources: Bloomberg, ICE Data.

Given the changes in market conditions since 1987 and the reduced yields in all asset classes, it is logical to consider the optimal allocation over a shorter time period that is more similar to conditions in 2021. Table 6.9 shows the covariance matrix and average returns since 2005 through 2020. Convertible returns have been substantially higher than either the large- or small-cap equity indices; hence, the optimizer assigns a significant weight to convertibles and almost no weight to equities. Longer-duration bonds are the primary diversifier chosen by the optimizer

Figure 6.28   Optimal portfolio weightings by target volatility, December 31, 2005–December 31, 2020

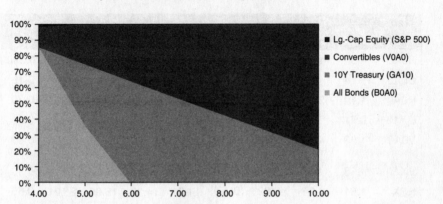

Source: Bloomberg Data, ICE Data, Advent Capital Management.

because of the negative covariance with the more volatile asset classes. Using Sharpe ratio as the value to maximize, the optimizer includes a 38% allocation to convertibles.

6.7.3 Optimizing for Future Performance in US Markets

It is interesting to learn what the optimal portfolio weightings would have been in prior periods, yet, most investors want to know the optimal weighting *at present*. There are multiple ways of calculating optimization. The Markowitz model requires a covariance matrix and average returns. An ex ante Markowitz analysis therefore uses expected future covariances and average returns. A defining issue of 2021 is the 40-year trend of gradually declining interest rates, which will ultimately reverse. Therefore, we have constructed a covariance matrix based on the 15 years through 2020—*but only when 10-year Treasury rates were flat to higher*. We have then used estimates of monthly returns consistent with rising interest rates, and we have also adjusted the variance of the bond indices up to a level consistent with rising interest rates. The portfolio optimized on Sharpe ratio calls for a 52% weighting to convertibles. As depicted in Table 6.10, the GA10 index, which represents 10-year US Treasury bonds, has the lowest

Table 6.10   Covariance Matrix and Average Monthly Returns by Asset Class Index Ex Ante Estimate

	B0A0	C0A0	H0A0	GA10	V0A0	VXA0	SPXT	RTY	Avg. Ret
B0A0	4.50	1.14	1.19	0.71	1.53	1.58	1.61	1.57	0.080
C0A0	1.14	4.00	3.59	0.57	4.35	4.53	4.36	4.70	0.15
H0A0	1.19	3.59	8.00	(0.42)	8.60	8.90	8.82	10.51	0.30
GA10	0.71	0.57	(0.42)	5.00	(0.26)	(0.30)	(0.10)	(0.63)	0.06
V0A0	1.53	4.35	8.60	(0.26)	14.07	14.20	14.01	17.90	0.50
VXA0	1.58	4.53	8.90	(0.30)	14.20	14.43	14.32	18.05	0.50
SPXT	1.61	4.36	8.82	(0.10)	14.01	14.32	18.05	21.21	0.55
RTY	1.57	4.70	10.51	(0.63)	17.90	18.05	21.21	31.16	0.60

Sources: Bloomberg, ICE Data.

covariance to convertibles and other higher risk asset class indices, making it a strong diversifier.

Figure 6.29 depicts the optimal asset class weighting at target levels of volatility from 4% to 10%. Figure 6.30 depicts the risk and return profile of optimal portfolios at target volatility from 4% to 10%.

Figure 6.29   Optimal portfolio weightings by target volatility ex ante estimate

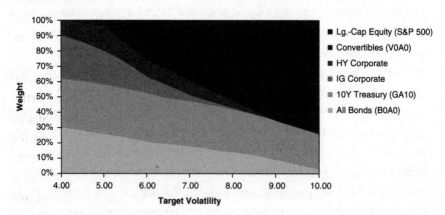

Sources: Bloomberg Data, ICE Data, Advent Capital Management.

Figure 6.30 Return and risk performance by asset class index and target volatility ex ante estimate

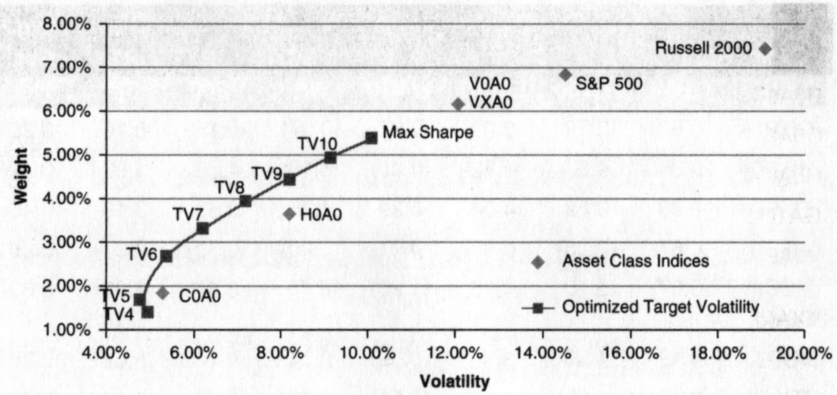

Sources: Bloomberg, ICE Data.

6.7.4 Mean-Variance Optimization in Global Markets

The Markowitz mean-variance process was run using the indices for global investment-grade bonds (GBMI), global high-yield corporate bonds (HW00), emerging market (EMSD), global duration (W4G0), global equity (MSCI World), global convertibles (VG00), and balanced global convertibles (Refinitiv Global Focus) since 2012. While global equity had the highest return, averaging 80 basis points per month, global convertibles average return was nearly as high, averaging 75 basis points and with less than half the variance of equities. Duration has a negative correlation with these asset classes and is the best *diversifier*, as noted in Section 6.7.2. Table 6.11 depicts the covariance matrix between asset class indices. Of the indices listed, the W4G0, which represents global duration, has the lowest covariance to convertibles.

In fact, the optimizer selected global convertibles and global duration as the only two members that appear in each of the optimal portfolios with target volatility of up to 8%, including the maximum Sharpe portfolio, which is 29% global convertibles. Above 8% volatility, duration is replaced by equity, yet, convertibles are still the highest weight in the optimal portfolio. Figure 6.31 depicts the optimal asset class weighting at target levels of volatility from 4% to 10%. Figure 6.32 depicts the risk and return profile of optimal portfolios at target volatility from 4% to 10%.

Table 6.11   Asset Class Index Covariance Matrix and Average Monthly Returns

	GBMI	HW00	EMSD	W4G0	MSCI Wor	VG00	Glo. Focus CB	Avg. Ret
GBMI	0.62	0.39	0.69	0.67	(0.07)	0.18	0.15	0.26
HW00	0.39	4.33	3.82	(0.25)	6.10	4.36	3.80	0.47
EMSD	0.69	3.82	4.04	0.20	4.76	3.58	3.16	0.40
W4G0	0.67	(0.25)	0.20	0.91	(1.20)	(0.59)	(0.51)	0.26
MSCI World	(0.07)	6.10	4.76	(1.20)	13.55	8.31	7.03	0.80
VG00	0.18	4.36	3.58	(0.59)	8.31	6.14	5.02	0.75
Global Focus	0.15	3.80	3.16	(0.51)	7.03	5.02	4.44	0.47

Sources: Bloomberg, Advent Capital Management.

Figure 6.31   Markowitz mean-variance-optimized blended portfolio weights

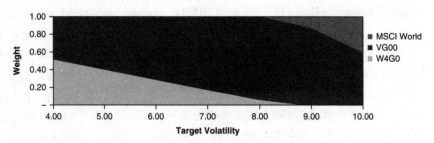

Sources: Bloomberg Data, ICE Data, Advent Capital Management.

Figure 6.32   Asset class and Markowitz mean-variance-optimized blended portfolio performance

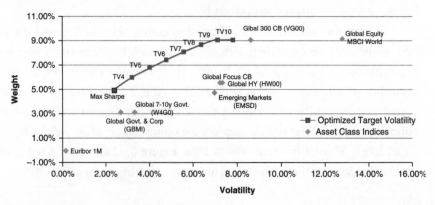

Sources: Bloomberg, Advent Capital Management.

6.8 ADVANCED ASSET CLASS MODELING: MONTE CARLO OPTIMIZATION

A Monte Carlo optimization first uses a Monte Carlo process to generate a large number of future return series for various asset classes. Then it uses an optimization process to determine the optimal portfolio asset class weightings. The Monte Carlo process recognizes that asset class returns— or at least the *drivers* of returns—are correlated. It also considers the asymmetry of asset class returns relative to various drivers of return, such as the positive asymmetry convertibles have to equity prices or the positive asymmetry convertibles have to interest rates. Monte Carlo simulations can be built in any spreadsheet application. Please visit www.AdventCap. com/SupplementaryMaterials for details on the use of Monte Carlo modeling in asset class allocation. Other asset-allocation model studies, including those conducted in a Black-Litterman framework, are also available at www.AdventCap.com/SupplementaryMaterials.

6.9 CONCLUSION

The historical returns of the convertible market can be accurately analyzed using data sources that are readily available to institutional investors. We can learn precisely what indices and subindices returned and how these indices were correlated. If the past is at all prelude, this information should be useful for asset allocation in anticipation of favorable future returns relative to risk. Global investing is in a constant state of flux. Various social and political conflicts may impair global capital flows, yet, new opportunities will appear—and convertibles are a safer way to participate in foreign markets.

ENDNOTES

1. Henry Varnum Poor, History of the Railroads and Canals of the United States of America (New York: J.H. Schultz & Company, 1860), p. 5.

2. https://www.prnewswire.com/news-releases/sp-dow-jones-indices-announces-update-to-sp-composite-1500-market-cap-guidelines-301187806.html.

3. https://indexes.nasdaqomx.com/Index/Weighting/COMP.

4. Richard Wong, "Changing of An Era," *South China Morning Post*, October 19, 2016, http://wangyujian.hku .hk/?p=7329&lang=en.

5. Current yield, as explained at https://www.investopedia.com/ terms/r/runningyield.asp.

6. Morgan Stanley, *The Prospects for RMB Assets in a Multipolar World* (New York: Morgan Stanley, 2020), p. 54.

7. UBS Global Research, *Will Opening of a Potential US$35trn China Bond Market Support Growth in Global Financials?* (New York: USB, September 7, 2020), p. 1.

8. Bloomberg Opinion, Shuli Ren, "In China, a 67% Return Will Make a Lot of Converts," Bloomberg, New York, January 7, 2020, p. 2.

9. https://www.investopedia.com/terms/q/qualified-foreign-institutional-investor-qfii.asp.

10. Samuel Shen and Andrew Galbraith, "RPT-Virus-Driven Surge in China Convertible Bonds Raises Crackdown Risk," Reuters, New York, April 15, 2020.

11. https://www.chinabondconnect.com/en/About-Us/Company-Introduction.html.

12. UBS Securities Asia Limited, Global Research, *Hong Kong Exchanges and Clearing* (Hong Kong: UBS, September 7, 2020), p. 1.

13. Data provided by Refinitiv.

14. ICE BofA EUMO, September 16, 2020.

15. "ETF Insight: Tackling the Bank of Japan's ETF Dilemma," https://www.etfstream.com/features/etf-insight-tackling-the-bank-of-japans-etf-dilemma/.

16. *CBDataReport*, September 15, 2020, jefferiesintlconvertibles@jefferies.com.

CHAPTER 7

Hedged Convertibles

Basics and Performance

Kites rise highest against the wind, not with it.

—*Winston S. Churchill*[1]

7.1 INTRODUCTION

Convertibles are a natural for hedging for two reasons: (1) because of the inherent asymmetry of convertible price behavior relative to the price of the underlying common stock, and (2) because of the tendency of convertibles to trade cheaply relative to theoretical value. Hedged convertibles generate yield plus capital gains. The yield comes in three forms: income from the convertibles, rebates earned from shorting the underlying stock, and a *volatility yield* from the natural volatility of the equity and the dynamic hedging process (which creates multiple trading gains). Capital gains are also derived from the richening of cheap implied volatility and the richening of cheap credit spreads of individual convertibles or when a *take-out table* is triggered by a corporate takeover. Hedged convertibles are generally equity neutral (*delta neutral*) and long volatility, which theoretically provides gains whether the stock market is up or down—which makes hedged convertibles a popular hedge fund or alternative investment strategy.

7.2 WHY HEDGE CONVERTIBLES?

While there are many variations on hedged convertibles, the simplest and most common form is delta hedging; the basic position consists of owning the convertible bond and shorting the underlying shares. The equity sensitivity of the convertible is hedged by the stock short, and what remains is a position typically called *delta neutral, creating a position that should*

200

be profitable regardless of the direction of small movements in the price of the underlying shares. Because the hedged position is low risk, it can safely use a moderate amount of leverage. This concentrates the position on residual properties—the most desirable being asymmetry.

Gamma measures the asymmetry of a convertible. Gamma (as we explain in detail in Chapter 11) combines with equity price movement (i.e., volatility) to create an *asymmetry yield*. Volatility is the dispersion of returns from the trend or average. The more volatility, the greater is the profit from a hedged convertible because of the convertible bond's asymmetry. Hence, the value of the convertible is greater if the underlying stock is volatile.

A hedged convertible position is said to be *long volatility*; volatility has essentially been isolated, and when volatility increases, it increases the value of the convertible. Vega measures the increase in value of the convertible for a one-volatility-point increase in implied volatility (see Chapter 11). Volatility also generates a positive return through the rehedging process. The use of leverage is intended to enhance the return.

Volatility of convertible bonds is usually negatively correlated with declines in equity and credit markets, except during severe market setbacks, such as in late 2008 and early 2020. Implied volatility is the expected future volatility that is *priced into* the market value of a convertible. Implied volatility is sensitive to expected volatility in yields and to changes in the shape of the yield curve as well as equity market volatility. Therefore, a strategy that is long volatility is a particularly useful diversifier in an investment portfolio. Modern portfolio theory explains that idiosyncratic risk is significantly reduced in a well-diversified portfolio. Systemic risk, which is correlated with the broad equity market, remains. The long-volatility hedged convertible strategy is a unique systemic risk reducer that also has attractive long-term expected returns.

7.2.1 How Does Convertible Hedging Work?

In Chapter 11 we explain how to calculate gamma and the way it enhances convertible returns both on the downside (by reducing exposure to equity prices as they decline) and on the upside (by increasing participation in equity prices as they rise). For now, assume that the return from gamma in a *long-only* convertible position is simply the change in equity sensitivity (delta) times the change in the equity price divided by two.

In a delta-neutral hedged convertible position, the gamma return differs in four ways: (1) it is primarily a function of stock volatility, (2) it is a function of its leverage (hedge fund positions are almost always levered), (3) the upward-drift component of equity price change is less relevant than in long-only accounts, and (4) increased volatility makes it more likely that theoretical cheapness can be extracted.

Consider two scenarios. First, if a stock appreciates every trading day by exactly 10 basis points, the stock price will rise 28.64% over the course of a 252-trading-day year $(1.001^{252} - 1)$. But the volatility will be zero because each day's return equals the average return. Second, if a stock that returned zero every day until the last trading day of the year jumps 28.64% on the last trading day, it will have the same total return as in the first scenario, but its volatility will be 28.64%.

A long-only convertible bond position will have the same gamma return in each of the two aforementioned scenarios. Expected gamma return of a *long-only* convertible bond is the total price change of the convertible times the gamma divided by two. If gamma is 0.5, then the gamma return will be 2.05 percentage points. This is distinct from delta return, which would be delta times the equity price change. If delta is 0.5, then the delta return will be 14.32% in our example, for a combined delta and gamma return of 16.37%. However, it should be noted that the higher the gamma, the more rapid the return profile of a convertible changes given a change in the underlying stock price.

Gamma measures the asymmetry in the return of a convertible relative to the stock price. Gamma exists because as the stock price increases toward and past the conversion price, the odds increase that the convertible will be converted into the underlying stock. When the stock price declines, it becomes increasingly likely that the convertible will be redeemed for par value rather than converted. As long as the investment value of the convertible holds, the value of a convertible becomes less sensitive to the price of its underlying stock as the stock price declines.

A *hedged* convertible position with a short stock position equal to the long delta of the convertible will have a different return in the two aforementioned scenarios. Expected unlevered gamma return of a delta-neutral position is the volatility squared times gamma divided by two.

In the first scenario, the gamma return will be near zero because volatility is zero. In the second scenario, the unlevered gamma return will be 2.05%.

There are techniques for capturing some of the upward drift in a hedged convertible strategy that will be explored later in this chapter. These are departures from the standard fully stock hedged delta-neutral strategy. If leverage is three times, then the total gamma return will be 6.15% excluding the cost of leverage. The actual path of the equity price matters little. For example, a stock that advances 11.8% in the first quarter, falls back to the starting price in the second, falls 11.8% in the third quarter, and rises back to the original price in the fourth quarter will have the same annualized volatility as the second scenario. A stock that increases 1.82% one day, falls back to the original price the next day, and continues this pattern for the whole year will also have the same annualized volatility, or a stock that is flat all year but falls 28.64% on the last day. In all three of these cases, the expected unlevered gamma return with 0.5 gamma will be 2.05%, or 6.15% with three times leverage.

7.2.2 Hedged Convertibles Run like Clockwork

The hedged convertible strategy works this way because the process of adjusting the hedge requires buying back stock as the equity price falls (covering the short) and selling stock short as the equity price appreciates—a natural buy-low, sell-high discipline. The more movement in the stock, the more hedge adjustment activity there is, and the more gamma returns are generated. Adjusting hedges is analogous to a grandfather clock that is driven by a pendulum swinging back and forth driven by the force of gravity. The hands will stop if the pendulum stops, but a mechanical ratchet prevents the hands from moving backward. A hedged convertible works similarly to the clockwork gears—converting the oscillating movement of stocks into continuously positive returns.

7.2.3 A Clock with Many Moving Parts

A convertible has multiple components. Besides the sensitivity to equity prices, it is also exposed to credit spreads, equity volatility, interest rates, and call or put provisions and takeover features—each of which has value and therefore can be under or overvalued relative to other securities in a company's capital structure or relative to derivatives on the various securities. Convertible arbitrage involves the isolation of the part of the convertible that is *cheap* relative to its theoretical or comparative value, eliminating or at least mitigating unwanted exposures to extract the theoretical cheapness.

If the implied volatility of a convertible is less than the expected stock volatility or the implied volatility of long-dated equity options, a vega or long-volatility position can profit from the mispricing. If the credit spread is narrower than that of another bond in the capital structure, or if it is expected to contract or outperform similarly rated bonds in the event of credit market weakness, then a credit strategy can isolate the credit mispricing. If a manager has confidence in the performance of the underlying equity relative to its industry peers or the broad market, a light equity hedge can be applied to isolate stock alpha from equity market beta, and if the value of a potential event such as takeover or refinancing is not fully reflected in the price of a convertible given features such as calls or takeover ratchets, an event strategy can be applied. Each of these tactics can produce uncorrelated returns.

For hedged convertibles to create a profit, the portfolio manager does not have to accurately predict that one asset will outperform a similar asset; rather, the manager merely has to select convertibles that deliver positive asymmetry. The natural advantage of hedged convertibles is the pronounced tendency of convertible bonds to capture more of the upside of the underlying stock if the stock appreciates while suffering less of the downside if the underlying stock declines. The yield advantage of the convertible is also a factor in providing positive returns from hedged convertibles.

The quantitative analysis of the position is crucial because of the many factors that influence price behavior of convertibles relative to the underlying common stocks. The rise in the use of hedged convertibles (and the rise of hedge funds in general) has paralleled the spread of quantitative analysis since the 1980s. Yet, managers of hedged convertibles who rely on quantitative analysis and market intuition sometimes give short shrift to credit research. Hence, some convertible hedge funds have a tendency to overhedge convertibles trading out of the money (i.e., discount convertibles trading near bond value after the underlying stocks dropped and the conversion premiums expanded). Heavy hedging—shorting stock in excess of what is necessary to be delta neutral—will be profitable if the underlying shares continue to plunge. Conversely, the hedge will lose money if the shares recover. A heavy or light ratio can be chosen to reduce or enhance the equity and/or credit exposure. Opportunities for reduced hedges on money-good convertible bonds should be considered to exploit opportunities to earn high yields and enjoy significant price recovery in discount convertible bonds.

7.3 HISTORICAL PERFORMANCE OF THE CONVERTIBLE ARBITRAGE STRATEGY

Historically, convertible arbitrage has been very profitable and relatively low risk for those who have employed the strategy judiciously.

7.3.1 Examples in the 1800s

"How Jacob Little Manipulated Matters Years Ago" read the headline in the *New York Times* on February 23, 1882. Raiload magnate Jay Gould[2] had replicated a convertible hedge that famed short-seller Jacob Little had used with spectacular success 27 years earlier. The article demonstrates that an investor who accurately forecasts a jump in stock volatility can profit handsomely with little downside risk by using hedged convertibles. Jacob Little capitalized on a short squeeze by using hedged convertibles. The article continues:

> Mr. Jay Gould's little scheme for advancing his interests in the Central Railroad of New Jersey by the sudden conversion of bonds into stock has attracted much attention. But . . . the idea was old. . . . The big man in the stock market 25 or 30 years ago was Jacob Little . . . It was in 1855. Little was on top of Erie . . . flooding the Street with the stock, selling options. . . . In the midst of this bear campaign . . . an attack on Little was planned. Nelson Robinson . . . Abraham B. Baylis and Robert L. Cutting comprised the "Happy Family." . . . Nearly the entire capital stock of the Erie Company was soon under their control,

the greater portion being at command on buyers' options. Options in those days gave the privilege of calling for the delivery through six months or a year. . . .

Nelson Robinson and his confreres . . . issued the necessary one day's notice on sellers, demanding delivery. . . . Robinson . . . began to make offers for cash stock. . . . There was not a share of cash Erie in the market. But Jacob Little . . . cheerily declared a desire to make further sales of options. . . . Delivery was due on the day following. Stocks were . . . then . . . required to be made by formal transfer. . . .

"Give me that transfer-book," said Little. . . . "Well, boys, what do you want?" he demanded. . . . "Ah! You're after 2,000 shares. . . . Here you are. And you want 1,000, take it; here is 5,000 for you; here's 2,500 for you," and so he kept up his writing, passing out the demanded stock quite as fast as his tongue and pen could move.

"Where does all this stock come from?" ejaculated the amazed representative of the "Happy Family."

"Never mind where it comes from—here it is. Does anybody else back here want to call on me?" . . . Nobody else did want to call. Upon the contrary, there was a sudden stampede for the street, and dealers upon the curbstone saw prices slip away from them like so many eels. The break was overwhelming. Little was ahead to the amount of hundreds of thousands of dollars;[3] the "Happy Family" had learned too late that Jacob all through their bull campaign had been in possession of a big block of . . . bonds with a convertible clause . . . which he had exchanged for stock.

The Treasurer of the Erie, Daniel Drew, performed a similar feat 11 years later. The Erie being commonly short of cash, in 1866 Drew advanced it $3,500,000, taking 28,000 shares of unissued stock and three millions of convertible bonds. Simultaneously he went short on Erie . . . 58,000 shares. When the stock sank from 95 to 50 he took enormous profits.[4]

7.3.2 Performance of the Convertible Arbitrage Strategy in Modern Times

The goal of the convertible arbitrage strategy is to provide a strong and consistent rate of return with low volatility and little exposure to underlying equity markets. Hedge Fund Research, Inc. (HFRI), began tracking the performance of various hedge fund strategies in 1989.

As illustrated in Figures 7.1 and 7.2, convertible arbitrage has returned 7.80% per year from 1989 to 2020 with annualized volatility of 6.16%. As shown in Figure 7.2, this is about 80% of the return of the S&P 500, but with only 40% of the volatility. Convertible arbitrage also had 3.5 times the excess return of US government and agency bonds, but with only 47% of the volatility. Consequently, convertible arbitrage had a Sharpe ratio of 0.82, which exceeded all major asset classes including large-cap stocks (0.51), government and agency debt (0.70), investment-grade corporate debt (0.79), high-yield debt (0.66), and even unhedged convertibles (0.64). Since 2008, the comparison is even more striking, with hedged convertibles achieving a Sharpe ratio of 1.39 versus large-cap equity (0.97), government and agency debt (0.65), investment-grade corporate debt (1.26), high-yield debt (1.24), and even unhedged convertibles (1.31).

As illustrated in Table 7.1, convertible arbitrage had the best Sharpe ratio in the late 1990s (2.63) and the best Sortino ratio in the early 2000s (4.62). While massive deleveraging in every asset class during the Great Financial Crisis (GFC) suppressed the performance of convertible arbitrage in 2008, in the following years, convertible arbitrage has had the best risk-adjusted returns, as measured by both the Sharpe (1.39) and Sortino (1.52) ratios of all hedge fund strategies. Key factors in the subsequent success of convertible arbitrage have been improving credit quality, increased dispersion, and increased volatility of volatility. Figure 7.3 illustrates the rising volatility from 2010 through 2020, and Figure 7.4 shows how the dispersion of the volatility of volatility across sectors jumped in the latter half of the 2010s.

As illustrated in Figure 7.5, relative to other hedge fund strategies since 1989, the convertible arbitrage Sharpe ratio (0.82) has been in the middle of the pack. The Sharpe ratios of other strategies such as macro, event driven, market neutral, equity hedged, distressed, relative value, and fund of funds range from 0.67 to 1.29. Yet, many hedge fund strategies

Figure 7.1   Cumulative return of convertible arbitrage, 1989–2020 (log scale, December 31, 1989 = 100)

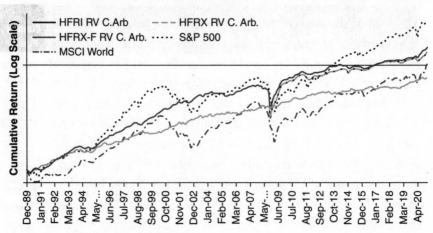

Sources: Bloomberg, Hedge Fund Research.

Figure 7.2   Return and volatility of convertible arbitrage relative to asset classes, 1989–2020

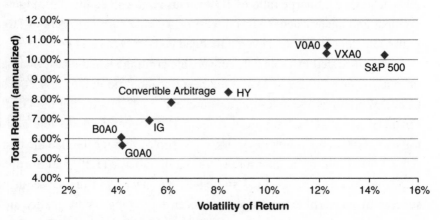

Sources: Bloomberg, Hedge Fund Research, ICE Data.

have suffered a decline in Sharpe ratios in recent years, whereas the Sharpe ratio of convertible arbitrage has increased significantly. With a Sharpe ratio of 1.39 since the end of 2008, other strategies such as macro (0.29), event driven (0.93), equity hedge (0.77), fund of funds (0.75), and even relative value (1.32) have paled in comparison. From 2014 to 2020, however, convertible arbitrage achieved better Sharpe and Sortino ratios than other hedge fund strategies as well as equities and both high-yield

Table 7.1   Convertible Arbitrage Has the Highest Sharpe and Sortino Ratios

	Relative Value: Convertible	HFRI Fund Weighted	Equity Hedge	Event-Driven	Macro	Relative Value	Fund of Funds
Total Return							
1989-1994	9.17%	18.24%	20.65%	15.61%	25.24%	15.89%	13.01%
1994-1999	13.80%	18.28%	26.92%	19.08%	15.97%	12.61%	12.13%
1999-2004	9.51%	7.13%	6.26%	10.56%	8.26%	8.57%	5.21%
2004-2009	4.24%	5.68%	4.52%	5.22%	7.02%	6.00%	2.78%
2009-2014	5.07%	4.54%	4.81%	6.02%	1.70%	6.57%	3.30%
2014-2019	4.54%	3.56%	4.55%	3.83%	0.82%	3.84%	2.36%
2020	12.05%	11.61%	17.49%	9.30%	5.22%	3.28%	10.27%
Full Period	7.80%	9.47%	11.14%	9.89%	9.38%	8.65%	6.50%
Since 2008	9.18%	5.91%	7.24%	6.83%	1.84%	6.61%	4.13%
Volatility							
1989-1994	3.72%	5.75%	7.73%	6.53%	10.15%	4.24%	4.72%
1994-1999	3.24%	8.01%	9.54%	6.91%	8.18%	3.99%	7.17%
1999-2004	3.11%	6.54%	8.75%	6.36%	6.08%	2.01%	4.45%
2004-2009	12.26%	7.33%	9.71%	7.62%	4.95%	6.36%	6.71%
2009-2014	4.63%	5.19%	7.56%	5.18%	4.43%	3.07%	4.02%
2014-2019	3.10%	4.43%	6.52%	4.50%	4.32%	2.86%	3.74%
2020	9.89%	13.82%	17.94%	16.89%	5.63%	11.68%	10.83%
Full Period	6.16%	6.82%	9.05%	6.94%	6.98%	4.53%	5.63%
Since 2008	6.21%	6.20%	8.64%	6.79%	4.51%	4.59%	4.81%
Sortino Ratio							
1989-1994	1.41	3.64	5.09	1.59	3.35	9.22	2.92
1994-1999	1.88	1.72	3.01	1.45	2.74	0.91	1.16
1999-2004	4.62	1.30	0.78	1.69	1.49	11.18	0.91
2004-2009	0.10	0.45	0.20	0.34	1.86	0.41	(0.01)
2009-2014	1.41	1.22	0.84	1.46	0.74	2.66	1.14
2014-2019	1.46	0.74	0.70	0.92	(0.08)	1.50	0.45
2020	inf	1.20	1.56	0.71	0.60	0.29	1.25
Full Period	0.62	1.14	1.18	0.97	1.39	0.90	0.68
Since 2008	1.52	0.87	0.87	0.80	0.25	0.90	0.64

(Continued)

Table 7.1   Convertible Arbitrage Has the Highest Sharpe and Sortino Ratios (*Cont.*)

	Relative Value: Convertible	HFRI Fund Weighted	Equity Hedge	Event-Driven	Macro	Relative Value	Fund of Funds
Sharpe Ratio							
1989-1994	1.13	2.31	2.03	1.63	2.00	2.58	1.70
1994-1999	2.63	1.63	2.27	2.00	1.31	1.84	0.96
1999-2004	2.17	0.67	0.40	1.23	0.91	2.89	0.55
2004-2009	0.11	0.39	0.17	0.31	0.84	0.50	(0.01)
2009-2014	1.08	0.86	0.63	1.15	0.37	2.11	0.80
2014-2019	1.12	0.57	0.54	0.62	(0.05)	0.98	0.35
2020	1.18	0.81	0.95	0.53	0.85	0.24	0.91
Full Period	0.82	0.99	0.93	1.03	0.95	1.31	0.67
Since 2008	1.39	0.86	0.77	0.93	0.29	1.32	0.75
Other Metrics (Full Period)							
Volatility	6.16%	6.82%	9.05%	6.94%	6.98%	4.53%	5.63%
Correlation to S&P 500	0.50	0.76	0.76	0.72	0.32	0.55	0.59
Beta to S&P 500	0.21	0.35	0.47	0.34	0.15	0.17	0.23
Downside Correlation	0.45	0.67	0.64	0.67	0.15	0.54	0.54
Downside Beta	0.34	0.42	0.51	0.47	0.09	0.30	0.31
Alpha vs. S&P 500	5.59%	5.61%	6.08%	6.21%	7.84%	6.80%	4.08%
Other Metrics Since 2008							
Volatility	6.21%	6.20%	8.64%	6.79%	4.51%	4.59%	4.81%
Correlation to S&P 500	0.58	0.86	0.89	0.78	0.39	0.67	0.78
Beta to S&P 500	0.24	0.36	0.52	0.36	0.12	0.21	0.25
Downside Correlation	0.25	0.68	0.73	0.61	0.09	0.47	0.58
Downside Beta	0.15	0.36	0.50	0.42	0.04	0.27	0.27
Alpha vs. S&P 500	5.43%	0.50%	−0.50%	1.44%	0.14%	3.46%	0.33%

Sources: Bloomberg, Refinitiv, Hedge Fund Research.

Figure 7.3   Volatility of volatility increased from 2010 through 2020

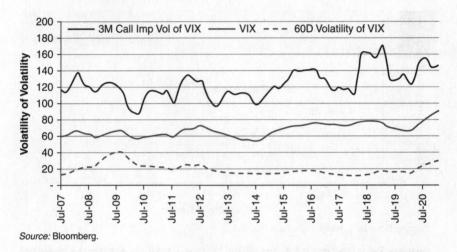

Source: Bloomberg.

Figure 7.4   Dispersion of implied volatility has increased since 2016

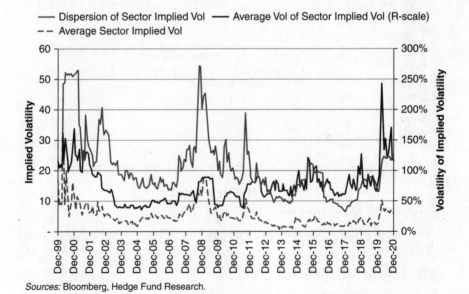

Sources: Bloomberg, Hedge Fund Research.

and investment-grade corporate debt. Figure 7.5 and 7.6 show the return relative to the volatility of various hedge fund strategies from 1989 to 2020 and from 2008 to 2020 respectively. While convertible arbitrage is in the middle of the pack over the longer time period, since 2008 the return relative to volatility stands out.

Figure 7.5 Return and volatility of convertible arbitrage relative to other hedge fund strategies, 1989–2020

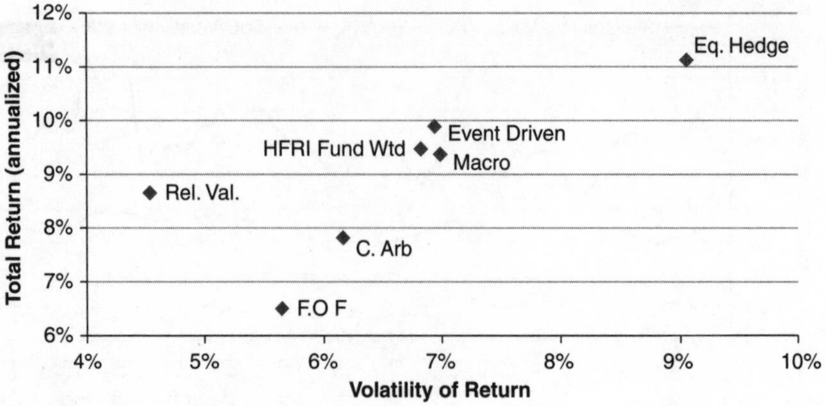

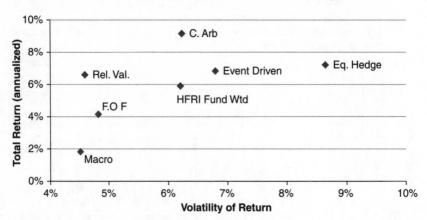

Sources: Bloomberg, Hedge Fund Research, Inc.

Figure 7.6 Return and volatility of convertible arbitrage relative to other hedge fund strategies, 2008–2020

Sources: Bloomberg, Hedge Fund Research.

Furthermore, convertible arbitrage has little correlation with equity markets, resulting in a beta of just 0.21 to the S&P 500 and 0.22 to the MSCI World. This gives it an alpha of 5.59% per year versus the S&P 500 and 6.13% versus the MSCI World 1989–2020.

7.3.3 Bear Markets: Peak-to-Trough Drawdowns

The strategy also has been a useful tool for limiting losses during market setbacks. Table 7.2 shows the peak-to-trough performance of the S&P 500 and the HFRI convertible arbitrage index over every 5% correction (from

Table 7.2 S&P 500 Peak-to-Trough Drawdowns Exceeding 5% (Monthly Data December 31, 1989–December 31, 2020)

Peak	Trough	S&P 500	HFRI RV-C.Arb
7/31/1997	8/31/1997	−5.6%	1.1%
1/31/2018	3/31/2018	−6.1%	−0.1%
6/30/1999	9/30/1999	−6.2%	2.1%
11/30/2015	2/29/2016	−6.6%	−3.0%
3/31/2012	5/31/2012	−6.6%	−2.9%
12/31/1989	1/31/1990	−6.7%	−1.5%
12/31/1999	2/29/2000	−6.8%	4.2%
1/31/1994	3/31/1994	−7.0%	−1.9%
7/31/2015	9/30/2015	−8.4%	−1.1%
11/30/2002	2/28/2003	−9.7%	5.3%
4/30/2010	6/30/2010	−12.8%	−2.5%
9/30/2018	12/31/2018	−13.5%	−4.7%
5/31/1990	10/31/1990	−14.7%	0.6%
6/30/1998	8/31/1998	−15.4%	−2.7%
4/30/2011	9/30/2011	−16.3%	−8.9%
12/31/2019	3/31/2020	−19.6%	−6.0%
3/31/2002	9/30/2002	−28.4%	2.3%
3/31/2000	9/30/2001	−29.3%	20.7%
10/31/2007	2/28/2009	−50.9%	−29.8%
Average		−14.2%	−1.5%

Sources: Bloomberg, Hedge Fund Research.

month end to month end) since 1989. On average, convertible arbitrage has participated in a tenth of the downside of the S&P 500. Excluding the singular GFC in 2008, convertible arbitrage average returns during S&P 500 drawdowns are *positive*.

Another way to evaluate the relative performance of convertible arbitrage versus equity markets is to consider average, minimum, maximum, and ±1 standard deviation convertible arbitrage returns by the S&P 500 return bucket. Figure 7.7 illustrates the consistent positive return of convertible arbitrage regardless of the equity markets. There were only three months in the 31 years through 2020 when convertible arbitrage suffered significant drawdowns.

Figure 7.7   Average convertible arbitrage return versus S&P 500 monthly return buckets

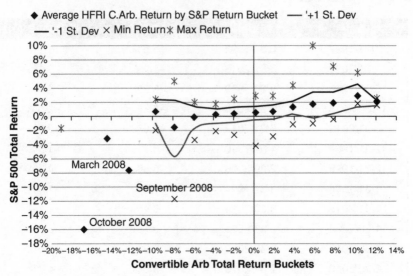

Sources: Bloomberg, Hedge Fund Research.

Because convertible arbitrage is exposed to credit risk, a widening of credit spreads—and the consequent reduction in market prices of convertible bonds—contributes to negative performance in extreme markets. Consider the peak-to-trough returns of the HFRI convertible arbitrage indices relative to the yield to maturity of high-yield bonds in Figure 7.8. The more spreads widen, the greater is the negative effect on convertible arbitrage.

The GFC saw a massive deleveraging of virtually all financial assets in 2008. Hedge Fund Research publishes several sets of indices with various inclusion criteria related to hedge fund size, liquidity, fund structure, and age—and these criteria have a significant effect on the track record of the convertible arbitrage indices. Some criteria make the index broader and some more narrow. For example, by 2007, there were literally hundreds of hedge funds involved in convertible arbitrage—some using very high leverage. Many of them collapsed during the GFC as the highly levered positions were unwound in fire sales called *bids wanted in competition* (BWICs) when hedge fund portfolios were being liquidated. These sales depressed the entire market—creating mark-to-market losses even for conservative managers and driving highly leveraged managers out of business as they were hit by huge losses, margin calls, and redemptions. The

Figure 7.8 Peak-to-trough performance HFRI Relative Value Convertible Arbitrage index versus change in high yield yield to maturity

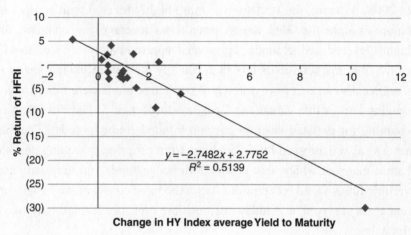

Sources: Bloomberg, Hedge Fund Research.

HFRI index posted a return of −34%, whereas the HFRX index—which included many more of the upstarts—was down −58%. Yet, the HFRX Global Hedge Fund index—which included only the 500 larger hedge fund managers—was down only −24%. For our purposes, we primarily use the HFRI because our goal is to explain the broad performance of hedged convertibles rather than attempt to analyze the reckless practice of overleverage. Two of the worst months for the HFRI convertible arbitrage indices were September and October 2008.

The Lehman Brothers bankruptcy on September 15, 2008, was a catalyst for a massive deleveraging of the entire financial system. Credit spreads widened dramatically. Lehman had been a top prime broker and provider of liquidity. Hedge funds in Lehman's large prime brokerage in London were frozen for an extended period because UK law had permitted Lehman to rehypothecate securities—that is, use *client* securities as collateral for loans to Lehman from banks—and the loans were *over*collateralized, so lenders were minimally price sensitive when dumping the collateral securities. Four days after Lehman went bankrupt, the Securities and Exchange Commission temporarily banned short selling of financial stocks,[5] which further depressed convertible prices by effectively outlawing hedging of convertibles in what was then the third largest economic sector of the US convertible market.

Because the convertible arbitrage strategy has a lower volatility than long-only portfolios, leverage is employed to increase targeted returns. In 2008, however, the strategy was more highly levered than at any time before or since the GFC. Six to seven times leverage was common, and highly levered hedge funds represented approximately 60% of the US convertible market versus less than roughly 40% in following years. As margin calls came in from prime brokers, hedge funds were forced to sell, sending convertible valuations far below theoretical valuations (even accounting for deflated stock prices and inflated credit spreads). The market was also depressed by liquidations from proprietary trading desks of banks, many of which shut down. Both hedge funds and long-only convertible funds faced redemptions. Only the most conservative hedge fund managers survived, and today positions are typically levered only two to three times.

In November 2008—two months after the Lehman bankruptcy—convertible arbitrage began to recover as credit spreads tightened while the equity market continued to drop. When the stock market finally turned up in March 2009, convertible arbitrage headed for its best year ever.

Eleven years later, another credit setback struck in March 2020 when the COVID-19 pandemic caused the global economy to suddenly tumble. What was common to both the GFC in late 2008 and the early months of the pandemic in 2021 was unprecedented widening of credit spreads *relative to the equity market declines*. If the ratio of credit spread widening to equity price decline had been more moderate, convertible arbitrage returns would have been more consistent with the historical relationship, that is, relatively uncorrelated with equities.

In both crises, credit spreads widened sharply and dramatically—increasing two- to threefold across the credit spectrum, as illustrated in Figure 7.9. In the 2008 crisis, the absolute level of high-yield credit spreads exceeded 2,000 basis points. Although the level in March 2020 was just over 1,000 basis points, the rate of change was twice as high as in October 2008. Relative to the historical relationship between stocks and bonds, these are the two most severe credit events since the Great Depression in the 1930s. Credit is a residual exposure in convertibles and therefore was a decisive impediment to convertible arbitrage under such extreme conditions.

Figure 7.9   High-yield credit spreads and 30-day change in spreads, 1996–2020

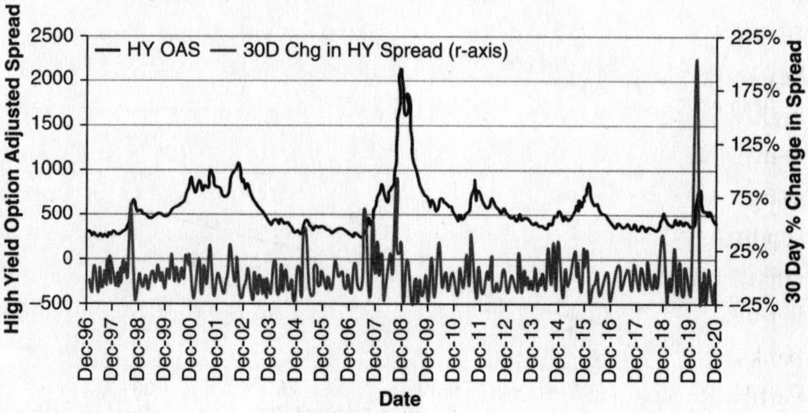

Source: Bloomberg.

7.3.4 Bull Markets: Trough-to-Peak Performance of Convertible Arbitrage

During bull markets, as markets recover from crisis and recession into a period of economic growth, convertible arbitrage returns are fueled by volatility and improving credit conditions. In the 19 periods after a 5% reversal in the S&P 500 (from month end to month end), the return of the convertible arbitrage strategy on an annualized basis has shown a 1.08 beta to the average level of the volatility index (VIX), which is based on the implied volatility of S&P 500 options. This sensitivity to the VIX explains a significant portion of the return resulting in an R^2 of 0.38, as shown in Figure 7.10, yet, a combination of volatility and change in credit spreads explains even more. A model based on the average VIX and the change in the yield to maturity of high yield results in an R^2 of 0.79 using a binomial curve, as illustrated in Figure 7.11.

7.3.5 Comparative Returns from Hedged Convertibles

In the 31 years that hedge fund return records have been kept, since the beginning of 1990, the economy has gone through several transformations. To analyze the performance, we have created six five-year comparisons, as well as a seventh focused on 2020, the year of COVID-19, to examine the

Figure 7.10   **Trough-to-peak Hedge Fund Research (HFR) relative value convertible arbitrage return (annualized) versus average VIX**

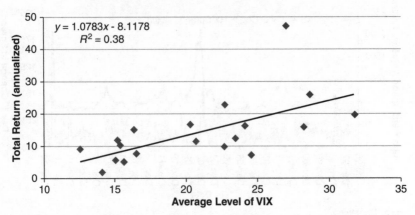

Sources: Bloomberg, Hedge Fund Research.

Figure 7.11   **Trough-to-peak Hedge Fund Research (HFR) relative value convertible arbitrage return (annualized) versus average VIX plus two times change in yield to maturity of high-yield bonds**

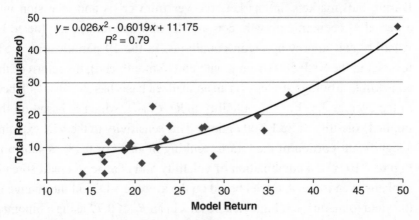

Sources: Bloomberg, Hedge Fund Research, ICE Data.

absolute and relative performance of convertible arbitrage under different conditions. We also analyzed the data in the five-year periods since inception as well as separately since 2008 in Section 7.3.6.

7.3.5.1 December 31, 1989–December 31, 1994

In spite of a brief recession (1990–1991) and rate-induced pullback in equity markets (1994), the convertible arbitrage strategy delivered 9.2%

annualized return, a 1.13 Sharpe ratio, and a 1.41 Sortino ratio. Interest rates were at the highest they have been since that time, which made interest income attractive but also made the cost of leverage expensive. Although total return performance lagged many of the main hedge fund strategies, convertible arbitrage outperformed equities, government and agency debt, and investment-grade corporate debt. In terms of Sharpe and Sortino ratios, it was superior to all the main asset classes by a wide margin—including high yield and unhedged convertibles.

7.3.5.2 December 31, 1994–December 31, 1999

Equity valuations rose sharply in this period, although there were periods of volatility related to the Asian currency crisis, Russian debt default, and failure of the biggest hedge fund in the world at that time, Long-Term Capital Management. The final quarter of the 1990s saw equity valuations—especially of technology stocks—skyrocket. Though Federal Reserve Chair Alan Greenspan had described the equity market as reflecting "irrational exuberance" in 1996, the bubble continued to inflate through the end of 1999. Equities provided a massive 29% per year return for the five years (1994–1999). Convertibles returned over 21%, and convertible arbitrage returned nearly 14%—well in excess of all other fixed-income categories. Other hedge fund strategies did well, too, with equity hedge returning almost 27% and event driven 19%. Despite having a lower total return, convertible arbitrage had an extraordinarily low volatility of just over 3%, giving the strategy the best Sharpe ratio (2.63) of any hedge fund strategy or asset class.

7.3.5.3 December 31, 1999–December 31, 2004

In early 2000, the technology bubble burst, deflating valuations and causing an army of day traders to seek new careers. The 9/11 attacks in 2001 caused the S&P 500 to plunge 11.6% when trading resumed on September 17.[6] The years through 2004 saw multiple high-profile corporate frauds, including convertible issuers Alltel, Enron, HealthSouth, Tyco, and WorldCom. Convertibles remained more than 2% cheap to theoretical valuation during this period, giving convertible arbitrage funds ample opportunity for profits. The HFRI Convertible Arbitrage Index was up 9.51% per year in 1999–2004, with a standard deviation of 3.11%, resulting in the highest Sortino ratios of all hedge fund strategies and asset classes and the second highest Sharpe ratio after relative value (of which convertible arbitrage is one component).

7.3.5.4 December 31, 2004–December 31, 2009

The first three years of this period saw a dramatic decline in risk premiums as investors took on more and more risk in the pursuit of vanishing yields. During this time, convertible valuations increased to within 25 basis points of fair value. Furthermore, volatility was low, and many new managers crowded into the strategy, which suppressed overall convertible arbitrage returns. Then, beginning in April 2007, credit spreads started to widen as credit markets began to price in a greater risk of recession, which finally arrived in the first quarter of 2008.

The S&P 500 peaked in October 2007 and then plunged −51% through February 2009 before beginning the longest and largest advance in history. Yet, by the end of 2009, the equity market had only recovered about half of its peak-to-trough losses. Many of the hedge funds that had recently crowded into convertible arbitrage had been overlevered, and as a result, the HFRX Convertible Arbitrage Index that included them declined −58% from peak to trough, although the HFRX index of the 500 largest hedge fund managers declined only 24%. Some convertible arbitrage funds that were lightly levered and that survived through 2009 generated positive returns during the GFC period of 2008–2009. The HFRI Convertible Arbitrage Index earned 4.24% per year during this five-year period through 2009 with 12% volatility.

7.3.5.5 December 31, 2009–December 31, 2014

While markets continued to recover in 2010 and the beginning of 2011, the summer of 2011 brought weaker economic metrics and lower market volatility. Yet, equity markets advanced 15.5% per year through 2014. The Federal Reserve Bank's suppression of interest rates was an apparent factor supporting equity markets but the reduction of interest rates was also an apparent factor in suppressed overall volatility, and a combination of lower new-issue coupons and reduced volatility weighed on the the returns from convertible arbitrage. The HFRI Convertible Arbitrage Index returned 5.07% per year with a Sharpe ratio of 1.08.

7.3.5.6 December 31, 2014–December 31, 2019

Equities continued to rally during this period, returning nearly 12% per year, apparently boosted by anticipation and passing of the Tax Reform Act of 2017. However, there were periods of retreat in late 2015 to early 2016 and in the fourth quarter of 2018 when interest rates temporarily rose.

7.3.5.7 December 31, 2019–December 31, 2020

The COVID-19 pandemic saw growth equities significantly outperform value equities in 2020, both on the downside in February and March and during the subsequent market recovery. Because the convertible asset class is significantly overweight growth, convertibles outperformed equities. Moreover, US issuance of convertibles soared partly because consumer discretionary companies such as airlines and cruise lines sought capital to tide them over until the economy recovered, and the new issues created ample opportunities for convertible arbitrage. The HFRI Convertible Arbitrage Index advanced by 12.05% in 2020 with volatility of 9.9%, giving it the highest Sharpe and Sortino ratios relative to other hedge fund strategies.

7.3.6 December 31, 2008 to December 31, 2020

Since 2008, convertible arbitrage has the highest Sharpe and Sortino ratios of all the primary hedge fund strategies at 1.39 and 1.52, respectively. At 0.58, its correlation to the S&P 500 is lower than all other strategies with the exception of macro. This correlation gives convertible arbitrage a low beta to the S&P 500 of 0.24. Downside correlation is even lower than overall correlation at 0.25, giving the strategy a downside beta of only

0.15. With the exception of macro, this is the lowest beta of all the main hedge fund strategies. Strong returns combined with a low beta gave the convertible arbitrage strategy a high positive alpha of 5.58% per year— much higher than macro, which generated alpha of only 0.14% per year; equity hedge, which generated a negative alpha −0.50% per year; event driven, which generated an alpha of 1.44%; or fund of funds, which generated an alpha of 0.33%.

7.3.7 Key Determinants of Return: Volatility, New Issuance

Two key determinants of return are market volatility and new issuance of convertibles. According to research by Michael Youngworth, equity-linked analyst at BofA Securities,[7] there is a strong correlation between return and the realized volatility of the S&P 500. Years when realized volatility was high, such as 2002 and 2020, saw strong returns for convertible arbitrage, whereas in years when realized volatility was low, such as 2004, 2005, 2014, and 2017, convertible arbitrage strategy performance was weaker.

The study also showed that years with significant convertible issuance coincided with higher returns, such as 2003, 2013, and 2020, whereas years with lower issuance coincided with weaker performance, such as in 2004, 2005, and 2011. This is not simply a result of hedge funds pocketing the new-issue discount but also because the conditions that lead to more issuance (higher volatility) also lead to higher returns.

7.3.8 More Drivers of Return: Crowding and Leverage

The convertible arbitrage strategy represents a small fraction of total hedge fund assets. According to Bank of America research, the strategy accounted for about 60% of the convertible market prior to the GFC but only approximately 36% in 2021. In 2004, hedge fund ownership was nearly equal to the size of the US convertible market, according to BarclayHedge. The overcrowding of the trade in the mid-2000s caused valuations to richen to fair value or above. Rich valuations of convertibles combined with diminished volatility probably explains the lackluster absolute performance in that period, although Bank of America research concludes that *risk-adjusted returns* in 1999–2007 were favorable.[8]

With hundreds of convertible arbitrage hedge funds using five to seven times leverage trying to squeeze out the last drops of volatility yield in the period of reduced volatility prior to the GFC, the strategy became overlevered, and the retrospective excessive leverage explains the horrendous performance of some managers in 2008—performance that drove most practitioners and investors out of the strategy.

7.4 BASICS OF CONVERTIBLE ARBITRAGE

In its most basic form, convertible arbitrage involves the purchase of a convertible bond and the sale of shares of the underlying stock short in order to neutralize the equity exposure or, as in the historical case of Jacob Little (in Section 7.3.1), short call options. The ratio of shares that need to be sold short is based on the theoretical delta of the convertible bond. Delta will be covered at length in Chapter 11, but as a preview, it is the equity price sensitivity of a convertible. Delta is calculated using convertible valuation models and differs depending on the model and assumptions. And there is a distinction in the way traditional long-only convertible managers and hedged convertible managers view delta. Long-only managers tend to think in terms of a *participation delta*, the percentage change in the value of the convertible relative to a change in the stock price. Hedged managers think in terms of *parity delta*, which is the percentage change in conversion parity (conversion ratio times the current stock price = conversion value) relative to a change in the stock price.

Mathematically, the relationship between the two deltas is as follows:

Participation delta = parity delta/(1 + conversion premium)

The lower the stock price, the larger is the conversion premium. The larger the conversion premium, the lower is the participation delta relative to parity delta. Once an arbitrageur determines an appropriate theoretical parity delta, the hedge ratio is simply the conversion ratio of the bond multiplied by the delta (see Chapter 11):

$$\text{Hedge ratio} = \text{conversion ratio} \times \text{parity delta}$$

When a convertible arbitrage position is first established, it is typically delta neutral, meaning that the dollar value of the parity delta is equal to the short market value of the stock. Being delta neutral means, hypothetically at least, that the value of the position will not change based on small movements in the price of the stock. In practice, the delta of a convertible bond is asymmetric; it changes when the price of the underlying shares change. When the stock price increases, the delta of the bond increases, and when the price decreases, the delta of the convertible decreases as well. The sensitivity of a convertible's delta to movements in the underlying stock price is called the *gamma* (see Chapter 11 for a refresher on gamma). As a result, the equity exposure of a convertible arbitrage position is constantly in flux.

As the delta of a convertible bond is a moving target, the number of shares sold short in a convertible arbitrage position needs to be regularly adjusted to keep the position equity neutral. When the delta of the long position exceeds the negative delta of the stock hedge, the position exhibits positive equity exposure. In order to regain delta neutrality, additional shares need to be sold short to keep the dollar delta of the short matched with the dollar delta of the convertible. Conversely, when the price of the stock decreases, the delta of the convertible also decreases, giving the arbitrage position as a whole negative exposure to the stock. To bring the hedge back into balance, shares in the underlying security need to be purchased, decreasing the size of the short position (i.e., *covering* a portion of the short position). Figure 7.12 shows the relationship between the price of a convertible and the underlying stock. The slope of the solid black line is the delta of the convertible bond at a given stock price.

The goal is for the dollar delta of the short position to match the dollar delta of the convertible bond. The consequent rebalancing has the benefit of creating a systemic process of buying low and selling high. The arbitrageur is reducing the short position (buying shares) when the stock price has gone down and is increasing the short position (selling shares) when the price has gone up.

Figure 7.12   Hedging activity results in buying low and selling high

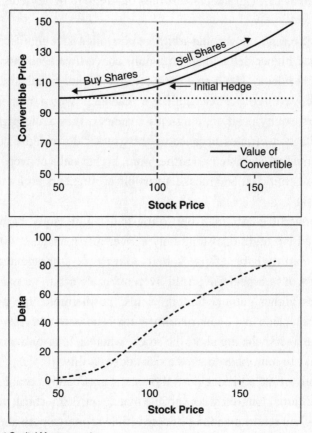

Source: Advent Capital Management.

7.5 CHARACTERISTICS OF TYPICAL CONVERTIBLE ARBITRAGE POSITIONS

BofA Global Research compared the characteristics of the holdings of the top 20 convertible arbitrage funds versus the holdings of traditional long-only convertible portfolios and reported the following differences in October 2020.[9] Convertible arbitrage managers tend to overweight higher-growth and higher-volatility sectors such as healthcare and technology and underweight sectors with low-growth and low-volatility stocks such as industrials, financials, and utilities. Convertible arbitrageurs also overweight sub-investment-grade and unrated convertibles that tend to trade cheaper to theoretical value and under-weight investment-grade convertibles that tend to trade richer, according to the BofA study.[10]

On average, convertible arbitrage portfolios have significantly higher prices and higher deltas than long-only convertible accounts: price, 166 versus 118; delta, 72% versus 56%. While higher prices and deltas can be attractive to convertible arbitrage managers whose risk is mitigated by a short equity position, long-only managers may avoid high-price and high-delta convertibles because of the greater downside risk, volatility, and diminished asymmetry. Furthermore, higher-delta convertibles tend to have less credit risk, and most convertible arbitrageurs prefer to minimize credit risk.

Convertible arbitrage portfolios had significantly higher realized volatility than traditional long-only convertible managers: 60 versus 47. While volatility is beneficial to both convertible arbitrage and long-only portfolios, it is especially prized by convertible arbitrage managers as it generates higher gamma trading yields. Furthermore, the potential for greater downside in a high-volatility stock is attractive to convertible arbitrage managers who are short the stock, whereas long-only manages usually prefer to minimize downside risk and volatility.

Convertible arbitrage portfolios had significantly cheaper valuations than traditional long-only convertible managers: 3.0% cheap versus 1.4%. The absolute return mandates of convertible arbitrage portfolios favor undervalued convertibles, whereas the relative return mandates of long-only portfolios favor issues that are similar to a benchmark.

Convertible arbitrage portfolios had slightly lower current yields than traditional long-only convertible managers: 1.4% versus 1.8%. Convertible arbitrage managers may be more tolerant of lower current yields because of the *volatility yield* generated through gamma trading. Furthermore, convertible arbitrage managers tend to underweight high-yielding mandatory and perpetual preferreds, which have higher yields but usually have less clearly defined downside protection and may be more difficult to hedge.

Convertible arbitrage portfolios had significantly lower stock dividend yields than traditional long-only convertible managers: 0.65% versus 1.44%. Convertible arbitrage portfolios are short common stock, and therefore, the dividend yield is a cost.

7.6 HEDGING FOREVER

Convertible arbitrage "has been around nearly as long as CBs have been issued,"[11] as confirmed by hedged convertible tactics in the nineteenth century (see Section 7.3.1). Yet, the strategy evolves as markets change, and a thorough knowledge of the many factors that influence the returns of hedged convertibles is essential. We go into more detail on hedged convertible strategies in Chapter 13.

ENDNOTES

1. Attributed to Winston S. Churchill, https://www.brainyquote
.com/quotes/winston_churchill_125996.
2. https://en.wikipedia.org/wiki/Jay_Gould.
3. $100,000 in 1855 would be worth more than $3 million in
2021.
4. Stewart H. Holbrook, *The Story of American Railroads*
(New York: Crown Publishers, 1947), p. 68.
5. https://www.sec.gov/news/press/2008/2008-211.htm.
6. https://www.investopedia.com/financial-edge/0911/how-
september-11-affected-the-u.s.-stock-market.aspx.
7. Michael Youngworth, *Convertible Arbitrage Primer* (New York:
BofA Global Research, October 19, 2020).
8. *Ibid.*, p. 13.
9. *Ibid.*, pp. 10–12.
10. *Ibid.*, p. 12.
11. *Ibid.*, p. 3.

CHAPTER 8

Convertible Valuation Basics

Options may seem like black magic, but understanding them could open the door to profits.

—Dan Colarusso[1]

8.1 INTRODUCTION

Valuing the conversion feature—essentially an embedded call option—is the most important task of evaluating a convertible bond. It is also a task that sometimes seems unintuitive and that almost always requires quantitative modeling. Yet, the concept of an option is ancient.

8.1.1 An Option 26 Centuries Ago

It was a bleak December in the Ionian city of Miletus in 575 BC. An especially cold spring had frostbitten the budding olive orchards and was followed by a sweltering summer and torrential autumn rains. The resulting poor olive harvest left many olive presses unused.

According to legend, an astronomer and mathematician named Thales had been studying weather and had concluded that the next olive crop would be especially bountiful. Because olives had been cultivated for more than 1,500 years prior to Thales's time, it's logical to imagine that he had information about prior harvests that enabled him to identify patterns in weather and production cycles.

Thales reasoned that he could profit from his prediction by contracting with the desperate olive growers to pay them a small up-front fee (effectively an option *premium*) in exchange for their guarantee that he would have the option to rent their presses the next year at a low fixed price. When the new crop arrived, it was bountiful, and demand for the presses skyrocketed. Thales exercised his right (*option*) to rent the presses at the low rate, and then he rented out the presses at a much higher rate.

From our quantitative perspective, the mystery of Thales's transaction is how he determined what to pay for the option to rent the olive presses at a fixed price. Because he was a great mathematician, he must have had a rational method, but the details are lost to history. Fortunately, we now have mathematical models that help us calculate the value of convertible securities and other investments with option features.

8.2 FINDING VALUE IN CONTEMPORARY CONVERTIBLE BONDS

A convertible bond is a hybrid security that includes the basic parts of a bond and an equity call option. Because the bond can be converted at any time, it is not a simple *European* option (which can be exercised only at maturity) but an *American* option (which can be exercised at any time); hence, the value of the option component of the convertible bond is *path dependent*. In other words, the value of the option depends not only on where the stock price is at expiration but also on how much it could fluctuate between issuance and expiration. Note that the hybrid nature of the convertible means that the bond is *usable* to exercise the option—no cash payment is required.

The simplest technique to value a convertible bond is to value the sum of its parts using a discounted-cash-flow approach to value the bond component and a form of the Black-Scholes-Merton model to value the option component. However, it is important to recognize that a model that works well for a majority of convertibles may not work for all convertibles. Some convertible bonds will appear significantly richer or significantly cheaper than fair value—not because these bonds really are over or undervalued, but *because the model is not properly capturing some condition or feature* of the bond. Caveat emptor! Yet, basic formulas are useful—we will use simple formulas as we progress to more complete and robust formulas.

8.3 OVERVIEW OF CONVERTIBLE MODELS

Certain primary variables are common to all convertible models: the underlying stock price, prevailing interest rates, the credit spread of the issuer, time to maturity, the call features, and the interest coupon. Most models also incorporate stock price volatility—which was introduced by Black-Scholes-Merton—and some incorporate interest-rate volatility or a parameter that models the credit spread or default probability as a function of the stock price. Some bonds have an embedded foreign exchange (FX) exposure (when the currency of the equity differs from the currency of the bond), and therefore, a complete model also would require both FX forward rates and FX volatility. In the rare instances where the underlying interest is a basket of two or more stocks, a complete model would require the covariance or correlation of the stocks in the basket. Many convertibles have dividend protection as well as a special *ratchet* feature (see Section 8.9) that provides compensation in the event of a takeover. A complete model would need to account for these features by calculating the possibility of special dividends as well as takeovers. Not every model takes all these factors into account, and therefore, the valuation results can differ significantly depending on the model used.

The most basic models ignore many features. Slightly better models assign some features a constant. Improved models assign additional components a variable, and even better models model variables stochastically—with second- or even third-order polynomials—and the most complete models capture interrelationships between multiple stochastically modeled variables. Black-Scholes-Merton, jump-diffusion, and constant elasticity of variance are in the middle of the spectrum of models because they use only one stochastically modeled variable (stock price).

8.4 BASICS OF CONVERTIBLE VALUATION

A good way to comprehend convertible valuation is to value the components of a convertible bond.

8.4.1 Bifurcating the Components: Bond plus Options

A convertible bond can be thought of as a straight bond plus an equity call option. If the option expires out of the money, the investor is effectively left with a straight bond. Alternatively, a convertible bond can be regarded as a stock plus a bond put option plus an adjustment for a difference in yield. If the convertible expires in the money, the put expires worthless, yet, the investor is left with the stock (and has received a higher yield during the life of the convertible). Each of these approaches involves bifurcating the components of the convertible: the former into bond plus call and the latter into stock plus put plus yield advantage.

8.4.1.1 Valuing the Bond Component

Straight (i.e., non-convertible) bonds are typically valued by discounting all cash flows at a yield to maturity that is appropriate for the term and creditworthiness of the instrument—in other words, the yield that fairly compensates investors for the risk of losses caused by default or by decline in market value in response to credit deterioration plus the risk of changes in prevailing interest rates prior to maturity. In liquid markets, the price of the bond may be directly observable, in which case the yield can be calculated from the expected cash flows and the prices.

The yield effectively reflects four distinct components:

1. The yield on a risk-free asset such as US Treasury securities.
2. The risk-free term premium, or the additional yield required for an investor to lend for a longer period of time; this compensates investors for the opportunity risk that short-term interest rates could increase faster than expected.
3. The systematic credit spread, or the additional yield required to compensate investors for the risk of not being repaid in full or on time.
4. The idiosyncratic spread, which is the difference between the bond-specific yield and the average yield for bonds with similar credit quality, maturity, interest coupon, and so on. Alternatively, the idiosyncratic spread is literally the difference between the bond-specific credit spread and the average credit spread of similar securities.

$$\begin{aligned} \text{Bond Yield} = {} & \text{Risk Free Rate} + \text{Term Premium} + \\ & \text{Systematic Credit Spread} + \text{Idiosyncratic Credit Spread} \end{aligned} \tag{8.1}$$

For a particular bond, the two components of spread are typically combined into a single credit spread, particularly for unrated bonds. When calculating the theoretical value of a bond, an appropriate discount rate is determined from these components, and the expected cash flows are present valued back to the present using this discount rate. More precise models will use a different discount rate for each individual cash flow corresponding with their distinct term and credit risk. All discounted cash flows are then summed to provide a theoretical fair value.

$$\text{Fair Value} = \text{Sum (All Discounted Future Cash Flows)} \qquad (8.2)$$

For a traditional bond, this is calculated by using a basic annuity formula for the coupon payments and adding the present value of the principal payment at maturity.

$$\text{Value of a Bond} = \text{Coupon} \times \frac{1 - \dfrac{1}{(1+r)^n}}{r} + \frac{\text{Principal}}{(1+r)^n} \qquad (8.3)$$

As a quick example, let's find the value of a five-year 4% traditional bond trading with a 5% yield to maturity. Thus:

$$40 \times \frac{1 - \dfrac{1}{(1+0.05)^5}}{0.05} + \frac{1,000}{(1+0.05)^5} = \$956.705$$

8.4.1.2 Valuing the Equity Option Component

There are two basic forms of an option, the right to buy, which is a *call*, and the right to sell, which is a *put*. Most of our explanations will focus on the call option.

The right to buy something at a fixed price can be quite valuable, even though it may require paying that agreed-on price at some point in the future. If the thing you are receiving is worth more than the price, then the right to buy it has a value roughly equal to the difference between the value of the thing and the fixed price you have the right to pay for it. At this point, we have to introduce some jargon. In a call option, that fixed price is called the *strike* (K). The difference between the strike and the current market price of the stock (S) expressed as a percent of (S) is called *moneyness*. The dollar difference between the stock and strike is called *intrinsic value* (for all values greater than zero). When the strike is less than the current stock price, it is said to be *in the money*, when it is greater than the stock price the call is said to be *out of the money*, and when the strike is equal to the current price, it is said to be *at-the-money*.

A call option is in the money when the call can be exercised on stock at a strike price that is *less than the market price* of the stock. A put is considered to be in the money when the stock price is *less than the strike price* and the stock can be purchased at a low market price and then the put can be exercised at the higher strike price.

A call is considered to be out of the money when the stock price is less than the strike price because there is likely to be no value at expiration, and hence, there would be no reason to exercise the option to buy the stock at the strike price. A put is considered to be out of the money when the stock price is above the strike price because at that price it would incur a loss to exercise the right to sell the stock at a price lower than what the market would pay.

Calls and puts are considered to be at the money when the stock price is equal to the strike price. An upward movement in the stock price will cause calls to move into the money and puts to move out of the money. Similarly, a downward move in the stock price will cause calls to move out of the money and puts to move into the money.

Option Valuation at Expiration.   For a more familiar example, let's say that you have a coupon for a pair of jeans that lets you buy the jeans for a certain price (rather than a percentage off the regular store price). If the coupon lets you buy the jeans for $60 instead of the regular store price of $90, then the coupon has a value of $30. If that coupon were a call option, we would say that it is $30 in the money and has moneyness of about 33%.

$90 Price without Coupon − $60 Price with Coupon = $30 Value of Coupon

When you are at the point of using the coupon (or *exercising* your call option), it is worth the following at expiration:

Call price = max(stock price − strike price, 0)   (8.4)

which gets abbreviated as:

$C = \max(S - K, 0)$

However, if the coupon didn't guarantee a price of $60 but just gave you the right to buy the jeans for $90 or more, it wouldn't really be worth much to you because you could buy the jeans without the coupon for the same or a better price. Again, if the coupon were a call option, we would say that it is at or out of the money and has no intrinsic value. But is that coupon really worthless?

Intrinsic Value Versus Time Value.   The jeans coupon would be worthless if it were expiring today, but if the coupon has a future expiration, say a month or a year from now, it might be worth something. Why? If the price of jeans goes up, and not just at one store, but everywhere—let's say to $120—then a $90 coupon would be worth $30. The real questions you have to ask are how much time do you have until the coupon expires, and what is the probability that the price of jeans will go up enough to make the coupon worth using before it expires?

A coupon that gives you the right to buy jeans for $90 when the current price is $90 has a value because the price may rise before the option expires five years from now. In five years, the price of the jeans might be $150, in which case the coupon would be worth $60. However, without knowing the future price of jeans, it is tricky to estimate the value of the five-year out-of-the-money coupon, yet, it is likely that it does have some *time value*. The total value of the coupon (or an option) is its intrinsic value plus its time value expressed as

Call option value = call intrinsic value + call time value   (8.5)

which is abbreviated as:

$C = C_i + C_t$

Figure 8.1 shows that the total value of the option is equal to the intrinsic value plus the time value at every point along the curve. Out of the money, the intrinsic value is zero, so the total value of the option is equal to its time value. In the money, the total value is the sum of time and intrinsic values. Note that time value is highest at and around the strike price. The reason for this is that the optionality becomes less meaningful for options extremely in or out of the money. Options that are far in the money will most likely expire in the money and provide intrinsic value. Options that are far out of the money most likely will expire out of the money and therefore expire worthless. The time value of a convertible *decays* or falls to zero by expiration, whereas the intrinsic value varies with the underlying stock price. Option *theta* is the measurement of time-value-premium decay, usually measured for a one-day period. Theta, as a percentage of time value, increases geometrically as the time to expiration decreases. In a convertible, option theta is combined with the accretion of premium or discount on the bond portion. Therefore, though option theta is always negative, convertible theta can be zero or even positive when option theta is low and the bond is trading at a *discount* to par.

Expected Future Value.   Moving beyond our jeans coupon example, let's consider a real call option with one year to maturity on a stock that could go either up or down. To make this example familiar, let's say that the stock price is $90 and that the strike of the option is $90. This means that it is an at-the-money option with $0 of intrinsic value. To use another simplifying assumption, let's assume that the stock could only go up or down $30 over the next year. If it goes up to $120, the option will be worth $30 at expiration, and if it goes down to $60, the option will be worth $0 at expiration because you wouldn't bother to exercise an option to buy for $90 when you can buy at $60 on the exchange.

The expected future value (EFV) of the call is the probability-weighted sum of potential intrinsic values. *This analysis occurs at expiration, when there is no further potential change in the stock price and hence, no time value.* If there is an equal chance of the stock going up or down,

Figure 8.1   Call and put values relative to stock price

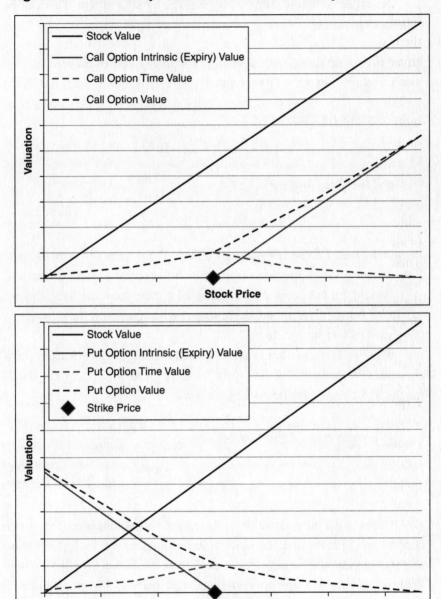

then the expected future value is the average of $0 and $30. This can be expressed as follows:

Probability of up move × up return + probability of down move
× down return = expected future value   (8.6)

We abbreviate this as:

$$P_U \times R_U + P_D \times R_D = \text{EFV}$$

and then we solve for it:

$$0.5 \times \$30 + 0.5 \times \$0 = \$15$$

Present Value of Expected Future Value.   What we really want to know is the value of the call option today. If the interest rate is zero, the present value would be the same as the expected future value of $15, and we would be finished with the calculation. For our purposes, let's assume a one-year US Treasury yield of 2.5%.

The $15 expected future value could be discounted back to its present value (PV) today using the 1-year Treasury yield. This is done by dividing the $15 by one plus the yield as follows:

$$\text{Present value of one-year option} = \frac{\text{EFV}}{(1 + \text{discount rate})}$$

$$= \frac{\$15}{1 + 0.025} = \$14.63 \qquad (8.7)$$

Because the intrinsic value of the option was $0, meaning that it was at or out of the money, all the value of the option was due to the likelihood of it moving into the money prior to expiration—this is also called the *time value of the option*. These are complementary parts of the option value.

Equation (8.7) is a simplified example because the term of the option (time to maturity) is one year and the rate we are using is also one year, and it is expressed as an annualized number. To generalize from Equation (8.7), we need to identify the term of the option and convert our yield into the same terms. Let's consider a call with the same expected future value but which expires in six months.

First, we would use the six-month Treasury yield rather than the one-year yield. Let's say that this is 2.01%. Next, we have to deannualize the 2.01%, which is not what would be earned in six months but is essentially what would be earned per year assuming that the money was reinvested in an identical bill when the first six-month bill expires. The deannualized rate would be 1% because compounding 1% for two periods results in total earnings of 2.01%.

$$\left[\left(\text{Period yield} + 1 \right)^{\# \, \text{periods per year}} \right] - 1 = \text{compounded yield} = 1.01^2 - 1$$
$$= 2.01\% \tag{8.8}$$

So our $15 EFV gets discounted to present value at 1% as follows:

$$\$15 \times \left(1 - 0.01 \right) = \$14.85$$

Again, this is still somewhat simplified because the term of the option coincides with a commonly quoted yield. The general formula for finding the correct discount rate over any period of time and assuming continuous compounding of interest is:

$$e^{-rT} = R \tag{8.9}$$

The constant e as it is commonly known or more precisely *Euler's number* 2.71828... is the limit of $\left(1 + 1/n \right)^n$ as n approaches infinity. It was described by Jacob Bernoulli but was named after Leonhard Euler who calculated its value in the early 1700s. It is useful in continuous compounding, but proving it is outside the scope of this text, and we show it here only so that it will be recognized in more advanced formulas later in this chapter. The main takeaway is that when you see this being multiplied by something, that thing is being discounted back to today at a risk-free rate. So adding that to Equation (8.5), we get the formula for the present value of a call option's expected value:

$$\text{EFV} \times e^{-rT} = \text{call present value, or just } C \tag{8.10}$$

Using a discount rate of 2.1% for half a year, we solve for the option value as follows:

$$\$15 \times 2.71828...^{-2.1\% \times 0.5} = \$14.84332$$

Another way to conceptualize the intrinsic value of the call is to consider that you are buying a stock in two steps. In step one, you pay an up-front premium today. In step two, you pay the strike price at expiration (assuming that the stock price still exceeds the strike price). Then you will receive one share of stock. Therefore, we can calculate the intrinsic value by subtracting the present value of the strike from the price of the stock:

Up-front payment (call premium) + present value of later payment (strike price) = stock price

$$Ci + K \times e^{-rT} = S$$

Then, rearranging this, we solve for the call value C:

$$Ci = S - K \times e^{-rT} \tag{8.11}$$

Put-Call Parity.   A useful maxim in considering option premiums says that the value of buying a European call option that confers the difference in value of a stock above a certain strike price at a future expiration date plus the value of selling a European put option that confers the difference in value of a stock below a certain strike price at a future expiration date is equivalent to buying a stock using money borrowed at the risk-free rate. It results in the following formula:

Call value − put value = stock value − present value of strike   (8.12)

If the present value of the strike price is above the stock price, the put will be worth more than the call because the put is in the money, whereas the call is out of the money. Conversely, if the present value of the strike is below the stock value, the call will be more valuable than the put because the call will be in the money, and the put will be out of the money.

Upside and Downside Returns of the Call Option.   Equation (8.4) shows us that above the strike price, the call expiration value moves one for one with the stock price. If the stock price moves up $30, the expiration value of the call moves up $30. However, if the stock price moves down $30, the expiration value of the call does not change. Because the initial stock price was at the strike price (at the money), the expiration value of the option is $0, and if the stock prices move down $30, the expiration value of the option is still $0. Equation (8.4) did not calculate the expiration value but the expected (probability-weighted) future value, which was $15. Therefore, if the stock price appreciates 30%, the expiration value ($30) is 100% higher than the expected future value ($15). And a stock price depreciation of 30% results in an expiration value ($0) that is 100% lower than the expected future value ($15). Setting interest and discount rates aside for the moment, the return of the call is +$15 when the stock appreciates ($30), and the return of the call is –$15 when the stock depreciates (–$30). Thus:

Upside return = upside expiration value – present value of the call   (8.13)

Downside return = downside expiration value
$$- \text{present value of the call} \qquad (8.14)$$

which we will abbreviate as

$$R_{CU} = C_{U \, \text{Exp}} - C = \$30 - \$15 = +\$15$$
$$R_{CD} = C_{D \, \text{Exp}} - C = \$0 - \$15 = -\$15$$

Replication Portfolio Valuation. The implicit agreement to pay for the stock at a later date in return for its performance in the interim is similar to taking out a loan for the expected future value of the call beyond the up-front premium. Therefore, we can approach call option valuation by treating it as a leveraged stock position. If we determine that a call option and a levered stock position have the same future value under all conditions, then both transactions will have the same present value. Hence, we can price the call option by calculating the value of the leveraged stock portfolio. This is the theory of arbitrage, which explains that the expected value of these two transactions should be equal; otherwise, it would be possible to buy one and sell the other making a risk-free profit. If the call were priced significantly lower than the leveraged stock position, this would present the market with such an attractive trade that the price of the call would get bid up and the price of the stock bid down until the opportunity for arbitrage disappeared. The first question, then, is how much stock?

How Much Stock: *Hedge Ratio/Delta.* To offset the gain or loss of the option is called *hedging*. We see from Equation (8.12) that the call option gain or loss on a ±$30 move in the stock is ±$15. From this we can calculate how much stock would be needed to offset the gain or loss on the option. The percentage of stock we would need to short to offset the call option return is called the *hedge ratio* or *delta*, and it can be expressed as:

$$\frac{\text{Change in value of call option}}{\text{Change in value of stock}} = \text{hedge ratio} = \text{call delta} \qquad (8.15)$$

which we will abbreviate as

$$\frac{R_C}{R_S} = \text{hedge ratio} = \frac{\$15}{\$30} = 50\%$$

One would need to be short exactly half a share of stock. In the downside scenario, the short half share of stock would gain $15 of value as the call fell $15, and in the upside scenario, the short half share of stock would lose $15 of value as the call gained $15.

How Much Loan? (Leverage).   The amount of leverage (or the loan one would need) is equal to the difference between the option payoff and the dollar value of the stock position. In our example, the option payoff is $15, and the dollar value of the stock is $45 (half of $90 share). Therefore, we would need a loan of $30. Technically, it should have a value of $30 at expiration, so if the term of the option is one year and the risk-free interest rate is 2.5%, we would need to borrow $29.27.

Valuation at Expiration.   If we have bought the right amounts of stock and loan, the values at expiration under all conditions should be exactly equal to that of the call option. The two outcomes we are considering are an up and down move of $30 from $90 to $120 or $60. As we have demonstrated, the value of the call option at expiration is $0 in a down move and $30 in an up move. The values of the stock position and loan are the same:

Call option value at expiration in up move =
stock − loan value in up move = (0.5 share × $120) − $30 = $30　　(8.16)

Call option value at expiration in down move =
stock + loan value in down move = (0.5 share × $60) − $30 = $0　　(8.17)

　　Valuation at present:

Present value of call option = present value of stock − present value of loan
= call delta × stock price − loan = 0.5 × $90 − $29.27 = $15.73

Probability of Up and Down Moves When Risk Premiums Are Zero.　Let's consider the same example in a non-zero interest-rate environment. We know from Equation (8.9) that the present value of the option when the interest rate is 2.1% per year is $14.83, which is the discounted expected future value. But let's make one more simplifying assumption: that we live in a world in which a stock's risk premium over Treasury securities is zero, a hypothetical situation in which equity investors do not charge a premium for the riskiness of the equity. The point is that the expected (probability-weighted) percent return on a stock would be equal to the risk-free rate. Thus:

Expected stock return = up return × probability of up + down return × probability of down　　　　　　　　　　　　　　　　　　(8.18)

which we can abbreviate and simplify as

$$R_U \times P_U + R_D \times P_D = R_U \times P_U + R_D \times (1 - P_U)$$

If we assume that the expected stock return is the risk-free rate, we can rewrite this as

$$R_f = R_U \times P_U + R_D \times (1 - P_U)$$　　　　　　　(8.19)

and then solve for the probability of an up move:

$$P_U = \frac{\left(\left[1+R_f\right]-\left[1+R_D\right]\right)}{\left(\left[1+R_U\right]-\left[1+R_D\right]\right)} = \frac{\left(\left[1.021\right]-\left[0.6667\right]\right)}{\left(\left[1.3333\right]-\left[0.6667\right]\right)} = 53.15\% \qquad (8.20)$$

Therefore, we can solve for the probability of a down move as

$$100\% - 53.15\% = 46.85\%$$

which means that the expected future value of the call option would be

$$\$30 \times 53.15\% \, \$0 \times 46.85\% = \$15.95$$

And the present value of the call option is

$$\frac{\$15.95}{1.025} = \$15.56$$

8.5 BRINGING TOGETHER THE BOND COMPONENT AND THE EMBEDDED CALL

As we noted in the beginning of this chapter, a convertible bond can be described as the combination of a traditional bond and a call option on the shares of the issuing company. The call option replicates the equity upside of a convertible bond that comes when the market price of the stock exceeds the conversion price of the convertible. Once the equity component of a convertible has been accounted for, what remains is simply a traditional bond.

By bifurcating a convertible bond into its two components, we can evaluate the equity component and the bond component as separate entities. Yet, in real-world trading, the values of the two components are usually correlated. Credit spreads and the underlying stock price are correlated with each other (unsurprisingly, given the fate of equity investors when a company goes bankrupt). This means that extreme movements in share prices—especially on the downside—usually are correlated with changes in the value of the bond component of a convertible.

Let's use a simple example to show exactly how a call option and a bond can replicate a convertible—ignoring correlation for the sake of simplicity. Say that an investor has a call option with a strike price of $90 and a bond with a par value of $1,000 that matures on the same day that the option expires. On the day of maturity, the investor will be left with the portfolio values in Figure 8.2, depending on where the stock price happens to be on that last day.

The combination of the bond and the call provides the bond floor of a convertible as well as the potential for equity upside that comes with the embedded call. When the share price moves above $90, the value of the option goes up one for one with any further increase in the stock price. On the downside, the value of the call option cannot fall below zero and the investor is left with the par value of the bond. The asymmetric return structure of the call option (you can never lose more than what you paid for the call, whereas the potential gains are unlimited) combined with the downside protection of the bond is what creates the positive asymmetry that convertible bonds enjoy. We will use the call option plus bond view of a convertible bond many times in further chapters because it allows for easy delineation of the equity and bond features of a convertible bond and how such bonds respond to changes in market conditions (i.e., changes in interest rates).

8.6 PONDERING THE PUT OPTION ON THE BOND COMPONENT OF A CONVERTIBLE

So far we have focused on the call plus bond model of a convertible bond. Another way to evaluate a convertible bond is to take the view that a convertible bond is a put option on the bond plus the underlying stock and an adjustment for the yield advantage of the convertible. The valuation of a put option works much the same way as the valuation of a call option but inverted. A put option gives the owner the right to sell a security at a predetermined price. Unlike a call option, a put only has value at expiration if the predetermined strike price is *higher* than the current price because otherwise you would be better off just ignoring the put option and selling the stock at the higher current price. Therefore, the intrinsic value of a put option at expiration is the difference between the strike price and

Figure 8.2   Call and bond components of convertible bond value

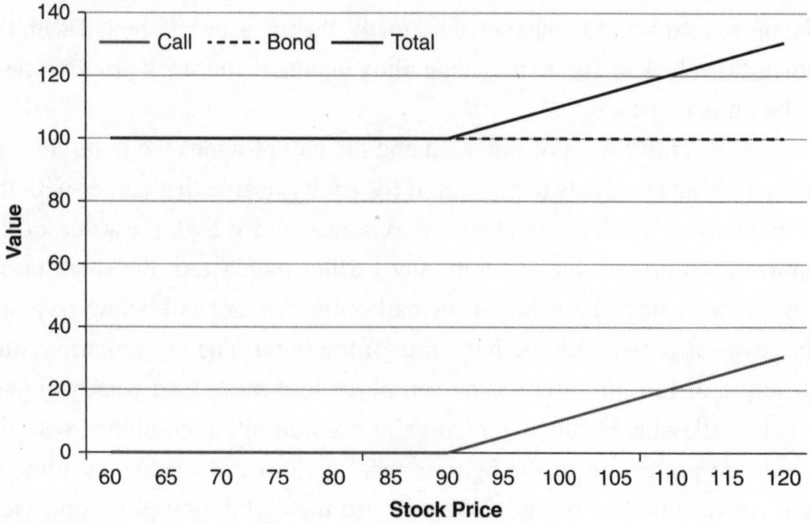

Data: Bloomberg.

the market price. With this in mind, we can adapt Equation (8.4) to fit the value of a put option at expiration. Thus:

$$\text{Put price} = \max(\text{strike price} - \text{stock price}, 0) \qquad (8.21)$$

which get abbreviated as

$$P = \max(K - S, 0)$$

In fact, all the equations we have covered for call options are applicable to put options. Just like a call option, the value of a put option prior to expiration is its intrinsic value plus its time value. Thus:

$$\text{Put option value} = \text{put intrinsic value} + \text{put time value} \qquad (8.22)$$

which can be abbreviated as

$$P = P_i + P_t$$

The value of an option at expiration can be simplified to just its intrinsic value. This is because the time value of an option shrinks toward zero as the time to maturity shrinks. Intuitively, this is logical because the time value of an option is ultimately the value of the potential for increases in the intrinsic value of the option. Once the option expires, it can no longer increase in intrinsic value; therefore, the time value is zero at expiration.

As we know, the intrinsic value of a put option at expiration is its strike price minus the current share price, but we can also calculate the intrinsic value of a put option prior to expiration. Prior to expiration, any sale of the underlying shares occurs in the future; therefore, we need to discount the strike price back to its present value in order to find the intrinsic value of the option. This can be expressed with the following formula:

$$K \times e^{-rT} - S = P_i \qquad (8.23)$$

It is notable that this shows that the intrinsic portion of a put option's value is worth less when the maturity is longer and when the risk-free rate is higher. This is distinct from the time value of an option, which, as we will see, increases when rates go higher and when the maturity of the option is longer.

A put option value also can be expressed as the present value of the probability-weighted average of expected future outcomes. Let's say that you buy a put option with a strike price of $30 on a stock that you know has a 50:50 chance of either going to $15 or $45 before the option expires (if only we could be so sure of what the stock market will do next). The expected future value of this option then can be solved as a probability-weighted average of the future outcomes:

$$P_U \times R_U + P_D \times R_D = \text{EFV} = 0.5 \times \$0 + 0.5 \times (\$45 - \$30) = \$7.5 \qquad (8.24)$$

We can then use the expected future value and the same periodic present value calculation from Equation (8.8) to find the present value of the put option. If we assume that our put option has a maturity of one year and that the risk-free rate is 2.5%, then the present value is solved as

$$\text{Present value} = \frac{\$7.5}{(1+0.025)} = \$7.317$$

Alternatively, you could discount the EFV back to the present using a continuously compounded rate instead. Thus:

$$7.5 \times e^{-0.025 \times 1} = \$7.315$$

Note that the present value found using a continuously compounded rate will be always be lower than the present value found using a periodic discount rate as long as we use the same value for the interest rate.

8.7 CONVERTIBLE VALUE = STRAIGHT BOND + CALL OPTION × NUMBER OF SHARES = (STOCK + PUT OPTION) × NUMBER OF SHARES + PRESENT VALUE OF YIELD ADVANTAGE

With a better understanding of basic put option valuation, we can return to the idea that a convertible bond can be modeled as a put option plus shares of the stock plus the value of any yield advantage in the convertible. When the share price goes above the strike price, the put option is worthless, but the investor keeps the gain on the shares. When the share price goes down, the gains made on the put option counteract the losses on the shares (recreating the effect of the bond floor in a convertible bond).

For example, let's say that an investor has a put option with a strike on a $30 stock as well as one share of the same stock. Depending on where the stock is trading once the option matures, the investor's portfolio would have the return dynamics in Figure 8.3.

As we can see, when the share price falls below the strike price of $30, the gains on the put option counteract any further losses on the stock, leaving the portfolio value unchanged. This is comparable to a convertible bond as there is upside participation if the underlying equity does well, but downside risk is limited to a set floor.

Of course, we are still ignoring the coupon payments of a convertible bond, which is why the put-stock portfolio needs to be adjusted for the yield advantage in order to accurately replicate the returns of a convertible bond. Most convertible bond issuers do not pay a dividend, and most of the issuers who do pay dividends have a dividend that is lower than the coupon payments on the convertible at issuance. In order for the put plus

Figure 8.3   Stock and put components of convertible bond value

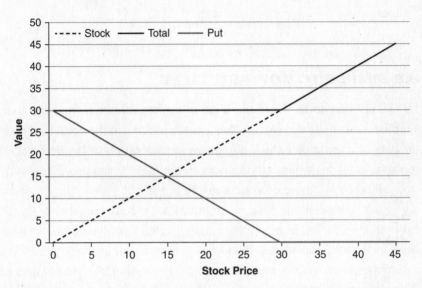

Data: Bloomberg.

stock model to work, there needs to be a third element to adjust for the difference in yield. Fortunately, this is a relatively simple adjustment because
the yield advantage is really just a finite series of cash payments over the
life of the convertible—in other words, an annuity with payments equal to
the difference between the bond coupon and the dividend flow (if any) of
the stock. Therefore, we can calculate the value of the yield advantage at
any point in the convertible's life simply by using the present value of an
annuity formula. (The following formula is for biannual payments using
an annualized nominal interest rate r.)

$$\text{Present value}_{\text{yield advantage}} = \text{yield difference} \frac{\left(1 - \left[1 + \dfrac{r}{2}\right]^{-2t}\right)}{\dfrac{r}{2}} \tag{8.25}$$

The preceding plugs into the stock plus put model to get the full
form:

$$\text{Convertible} = \text{put option} + \text{stock} + \text{present value}_{\text{yield advantage}}$$

This is functionally equivalent to our other model of a convertible bond:

$$\text{Convertible} = \text{call option} + \text{bond}$$

8.8 SIMPLE TO SOPHISTICATED

So far, in order to facilitate the logic of option valuation, we have used simplistic assumptions. We have been either looking at the option value on the date of expiration (which eliminates consideration of the time value) or we have made the simplifying assumption that we can predict not only what all potential future outcomes will be but also the probability of those outcomes. These simplifying assumptions are clearly unrealistic. Practical option valuation is much more complicated and dynamic than what we have thus far considered. In later chapters we will go far beyond these assumptions and analyze methods for option valuation that use a variety of different random distributions to model future potential outcomes and thus can be used to value convertible bonds.

The development of quantitative valuation models for various financial instruments, including convertibles, has been driven largely by the development of theories about the nature of the processes governing the movement of interest rates, stock prices, volatility, and credit spreads. Basic concepts such as the normal (or nonnormal) distributions of equity returns, the tendencies of interest rates to revert to a long-term mean, and the positive correlation between stock volatility and credit spreads have all been empirically tested, modeled, tweaked, and improved on over time. Some are based on assumptions once thought to be valid but now known to be false (the assumption that interest rates could never drop below zero is a key example of an assumption that has been disproven).

8.9 VALUING TAKEOUT TABLE/RATCHET FEATURES

Most convertible bonds come with some form of takeover protection. Without this protection, mergers and acquisitions have the potential to be a major risk to convertible investors because a takeover may prematurely place a ceiling on the value of the underlying shares. It's easy to see why an investor in a newly issued convertible with a conversion premium would not be thrilled if the company were bought the next day for *cash* because there's no option value, that is, *no conversion premium* on cash. Takeout protection prevents this by adjusting the conversion price in the event of a change of control. Depending on how the takeover protection is structured, the feature can be quite lucrative for convertible investors.

Takeout tables define the degree of protection for US convertibles. In a takeout table, the amount of benefit granted to the convertible holder in the event of an acquisition is based on the date and price of the acquisition and is found on a table of values that is created at issuance. For example, Table 8.1 is the takeout table from the Western Digital 1.5% 2024 convertible bond.

The values in the table represent the amount the conversion ratio of the bond will be increased if a cash acquisition occurs at that date and price. This convertible has a conversion price of $121.91 or a conversion ratio of 8.2026. If Western Digital were taken over at $105 cash on February 1, 2023, the conversion ratio would rise to 9.7826, reducing the conversion price of the bond to $102.22 and creating additional value for the convertible holder. Takeout protection adds value to a convertible bond, but it is difficult to calculate the additional value because an expected value calculation would require assigning a separate probability to every field in the takeout table. Realistically, few companies are likely to be taken over, so a takeover is not a meaningful risk for convertible investors. For companies that are likely takeover targets (e.g., small companies with valuable technology or market positioning), one can estimate an acquisition price based on the fundamentals of the company and comparable deals and assign a probability. From there, one can find the expected value of the adjustment on the takeout table and add it to the value of the convertible.

Other convertibles use a formula to calculate the increase in conversion ratio if the company is acquired for cash (rather than takeover protection predefined in a table). These formulas can be unique and can be based on time to maturity, trading price of the bond, and trading price of the stock or anything else. A good example of a convertible with this type of ratchet feature is the Inmarsat 3.875% 2023 convertible that was originally issued in 2016 (Inmarsat is a British satellite company that offers telecommunication services). The bond came with a conversion price of $13.409 for an

Table 8.1   Western Digital 1.5% 2024 Convertible Takeout Table

Share Price										
Date	87	95	105	122	140	159	180	200	225	250	275
2/13/2018	3.28	2.67	2.08	1.37	0.88	0.55	0.31	0.18	0.07	0.02	0
2/1/2019	3.28	2.63	2.02	1.29	0.80	0.48	0.25	0.13	0.05	0.01	0
2/1/2020	3.28	2.60	1.95	1.19	0.68	0.37	0.16	0.07	0.01	0	0
2/1/2021	3.28	2.56	1.89	1.09	0.54	0	0	0	0	0	0
2/1/2022	3.28	2.49	1.79	0.99	0.47	0	0	0	0	0	0
2/1/2023	3.28	2.34	1.58	0.77	0.31	0	0	0	0	0	0
2/1/2024	3.28	2.19	1.16	0	0	0	0	0	0	0	0

Data: Bloomberg.

initial premium of 32.5%. However, this conversion price was not set in stone because the bond came with an attractive ratchet feature that would activate if the company was ever acquired for cash: a new (lower) conversion price would be calculated by dividing the original conversion price by the result of the following formula:

$$A \times \frac{C}{B}$$

where A is average price of the convertible over the last 15 days (quoted as a percent of the premium), C is the conversion price, and B is the average trading price of the stock during the same 15-day period.

Not long after the convertible was issued, the shares in the underlying equity started to decline and never fully recovered. This made the takeover protection an interesting feature because at this point Inmarsat was a small, heavily leveraged company (the coupon on the convertible reflects the company's financial straits: nearly 4% for a European convertible is very high). But Inmarsat owned valuable assets—notably rights for spectrum usage in the United States that appreciated when telecommunications companies (and the US government) began planning to roll out fifth-generation (5G) coverage in the United States (see Figure 8.4).

While the stock performed badly, the convertible bond never fell below par value because it was supported by both the value of its bond component and the inherent value of the ratchet feature. Looking at

Figure 8.4 Price performance of Inmarsat convertible and common stock

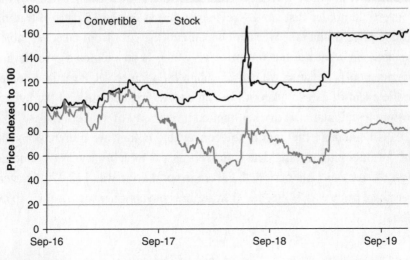

Data: Bloomberg.

Figure 8.4, the bond was trading at about 110 (ignoring the momentary spike in June 2018) for most of the second half of 2018—despite the stock languishing at a fraction of its price when the convertible was issued. The low share price meant that the bond had little option value remaining, yet, the convertible was still trading at a premium to par value.

We can isolate the value the market is placing on a ratchet option by valuing the convertible on its own and then comparing it with the market price of the convertible. To see this in action, let us use the Inmarsat bond as an example. In February 2019, the bond gained 10 points over the course of the month, suggesting that some market participants suspected that a takeover was coming. In order to value the bond, we used a credit spread of 237 basis points from a comparable Inmarsat straight bond and the historical 90-day stock volatility of 37.08 in a basic Black-Scholes-Merton convertible model. The results were that the convertible bond was worth 99.94, of which only 1.27 bond points came from the option portion, highlighting the lack of apparent value from the conversion feature. However, at the time, the market was trading the bond at 118.50, which was much higher than what the model would predict. Basic arithmetic gives the value of the ratchet option at a remarkable 18.56 bond points.

Because the Inmarsat convertible has a formula based on recent trading prices rather than a takeout table, there is an explicit gain to the convertible holder that can be calculated based on the 15 days of trading results prior to the takeover announcement (the gain from takeover tables depends on what the takeout price is, which is an unknown prior to announcement). Because we can calculate the gain to a convertible holder in the event of a cash takeout, we can use the market value of the ratchet feature to calculate the market implied probability of a takeover.

To calculate the gain to the convertible holder, we merely populate the formula with trading data from February 8 to February 28 (15 trading days). Over this time period, the average bond price was 112.37, the average share price was $4.98, and the original conversion price was $13.4093. Thus:

$$1.1237 \times \frac{13.4093}{4.98} = 3.0257$$

$$\frac{13.4093}{3.2057} = 4.4317$$

Hence, if Inmarsat had been taken over on exactly February 28, 2019, the new conversion price would have been $4.4317, a fraction of the original $13.4093 (and would give the bond a huge conversion ratio of 225.64). If we use the new conversion ratio, the option value of the bond would soar to 47.204 bond points (for a 45.934 point gain) using Black-Scholes-Merton. When added to the bond value of 98.67, the value of the convertible bond would surge to 145.871. Because the gain in the event of a takeover was 47.204 bond points and the market implied value of the ratchet feature on February 28 was 18.56 points, then the market implied takeover probability was 39.32%.

It is important to recognize that this process can be reversed. If a practitioner instead assumed a low takeover probability to calculate the value of the ratchet feature, it might turn out that the convertible was over-valued; the probability implied by the market could easily be too high compared with the probability assigned by a sophisticated investor. Hence, it is essential to evaluate takeover protection on a case-by-case basis, especially if one may have superior insight relative to the value implied by the market.

8.10 CONVERTIBLE VALUE IS THE SUM OF THE PARTS

As we explained previously, a convertible bond is functionally a straight bond combined with an embedded call option on the underlying stock (plus the value of any special bond features, e.g., call protection, puts, dividend and takeout protection, etc.). The value of the bond portion can be determined using a basic annuity formula that can be executed easily on any financial calculator. Any credit risk associated with the bond is incorporated as a higher credit spread by increasing the interest rate used in the formula. What credit spreads to use can be found by looking at the spreads of comparable bonds (ideally from the same company, if possible), looking at credit default swap (CDS) rates, if available (i.e., the cost to insure against default), or finding a way to classify the company and using the average spread of companies with that classification (e.g., BBB-rated consumer staples). Alternatively, you can sidestep credit spreads entirely if you decide to estimate the risk of default directly. If a bond worth 100 assuming no default has a 10% chance of default with an expected recovery of 50 percent of par, then the bond is worth 95.

Valuation of the equity option is more complex. The venerable Black-Scholes-Merton model is often used as a default option for equity option pricing because of its ease of use and broad applicability. There are many alternatives for pricing equity options that attempt to improve on the accuracy of the Black-Scholes-Merton model, as we will explore further in Chapter 9.

ENDNOTES

1. https://www.thestreet.com/investing/options/mirror-mirror-on-the-wall-explain-for-me-a-put-and-call-964257, p. 1.

CHAPTER 9

Advanced Convertible Valuation

An investment in knowledge pays the best interest.

—*Benjamin Franklin*[1]

9.1 VARIABLES AND STATISTICAL PROCESS

Valuation formulas all have *variables*, which are inputs into the original formula that vary based on the situation or data being modeled. A variable can be a simple data input (e.g., the volatility of a stock in an option model) or a random number, or it can even be represented by its own formula.

A simple bond calculation model assumes a discount rate that is comprised of a risk-free rate, a term premium, and a spread representing the credit and liquidity premium of the bond. The value is then calculated by discounting the future cash flows (the coupon payments and the principal repayments) at the discount rate and summing the results. A somewhat more advanced model incorporates the term structure by valuing each cash flow independently using a distinct discount-rate curve.

When a bond has optionality (i.e., callability or putability), it requires some assumptions about the possible range of changes in interest rates that follow various models of the rate movement process. In other words, what is the range of potential future interest rates, and what is the likelihood of each member of that range?

Similarly, the valuation of any financial instrument that has optionality on equity prices requires models that include some assumption about the range of changes in the equity price. The assumptions that are made follow models of the equity-price process. In other words, what is the range of potential future equity prices, and what is the likelihood of each price in that range?

A *process* is a mathematical formula that describes the movement of some element (e.g., a stock price) as a function of one or more variables. Investors have studied the rate and price movement processes for hundreds of years and have borrowed heavily from the discipline of mathematics that describes the movement of physical particles. Over time, models have been built and refined based on the application of higher mathematics, but occasionally events happen in the real world that alter our understanding and our models.

Historically, models have evolved based on research of empirical evidence, the intuition and experience of modelers, and advancements in mathematical theory and computational power. Some of the primary considerations of a model include the following: What is the subject being predicted or described (equity price, interest rate, movement of particles, etc.)? What factors influence the outcome of the subject? What is the relationship between the factors and the subject? How well does the model perform? While we will concern ourselves with process models pertaining to equity prices and price volatility, the aforementioned questions are relevant for any model.

9.1.1 Return Probability Distributions

Before we explain option models, we must explore the mathematics that describes the probability of achieving particular returns among a range of potential returns. The probability of certain returns occurring depends, in part, on what expectations we have about the distribution of returns. Are all outcomes equally likely, that is, a uniform distribution? Or are *average* returns more likely than extreme returns? This could be what is called a *normal* or *log-normal distribution*. Or is there an expectation of a very large (positive or negative) return that occurs suddenly and very infrequently. This would be called a *Poisson distribution*.

A single coin flip is an example of a *uniform distribution*. "Heads I win, tails you win" could be described as a 50% probability of a return of +100% and a 50% probability of a −100% return. Yet, when flipping that coin more than once, the return distribution is no longer uniform and begins to take on a normal-distribution profile. Let's examine the coin-flipping phenomenon up close.

Let's say that two people (your co-author and the reader) make a bet on the outcome of a coin flip. Heads the co-author wins $1, and tails you win $1. There are only two outcomes, and the chances are even. There is a 50% chance that you will win and a 50% chance that your co-author will win. In this case, the distribution of outcomes is said to be *uniform*, and the average expected value is zero (see Table 9.1):

$$50\% \times \$1 + 50\% \times -\$1 = 0$$

Now let's say that we decide to bet on the outcome of six coin flips. The co-author will pay you $1 for every tail, and you will pay the co-author $1 for every head. The chance that either bettor will win $6 from the other is fairly small. All six flips would have to be heads for your co-author to get your $6, and all six flips would have to be tails for you to win your co-author's $6. Table 9.1 shows that the probability of either bettor winning $6 is 1/64, or approximately 1.56%. We can also see the chance

Table 9.1   Coin-Flip Probabilities

	No. of Heads	No. of Trials	Probability		No. of Heads	No. of Trials	Probability
Flip 1	1	1/2	0.5	Flip 2	2	1/4	0.25
	0	1/2	0.5		1	2/4	0.50
					0	1/4	0.25
Flip 3	3	1/8	0.125	Flip 4	4	1/16	0.068
	2	3/8	0.375		3	4/16	0.250
	1	3/8	0.375		2	6/16	0.375
	0	1/8	0.125		1	4/16	0.250
					0	1/16	0.068
Flip 5	5	1/32	0.03125	Flip 6	6	1/64	0.01563
	4	5/32	0.15625		5	6/64	0.09375
	3	10/32	0.31250		4	13/64	0.20313
	2	10/32	0.31250		3	26/64	0.40625
	1	5/32	0.15625		2	13/64	0.20313
	0	1/32	0.03125		1	6/64	0.09375
					0	1/64	0.01563

Data: Bloomberg.

Figure 9.1   Distribution of coin flips

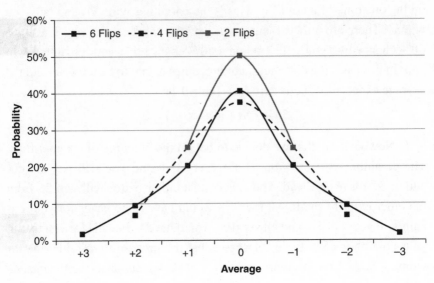

Data: Bloomberg.

of us breaking even because the odds that three of the flips are heads and three are tails is over 40%. And the chances of either bettor winning $2 or $4 are 20.3% and 9.4%, respectively.

Clearly, the probability of these outcomes is very different. Therefore, the probability distribution is no longer uniform. It has become what we call *normal* (see Figure 9.1). In fact, this happens any time a uniform distribution is repeated a number of times and the results are effectively added together. The distribution of the aggregated set is normally distributed; this is called the *central limit theorem*. The distribution of returns is also normally distributed.

Let's say that the next day your co-author offers you a similar bet (Table 9.2). We both start with $10 again, but this time your co-author offers to pay you 15% of your money every time the coin flip is heads, and you lose 15% every time it's tails. You can win more in this game because for every win, the amount of money you have (at risk) grows, making the next win that much bigger, and every time you lose, the amount of money you have (at risk) falls. Six straight wins would bring you a return of 131.3%, whereas six straight losses would lose you only 62.3%. Thus,

Table 9.2 Probabilities of Winning or Losing

	Betting $1 per flip	Return on $10 Capital	Probability	Expected (prob. Wtd.) Return
6	We win $6 from you	60%	0.01563	0.94%
5	We win $4 from you	40%	0.09375	3.75%
4	We win $2 from you	20%	0.20313	4.06%
3	We break even	0%	0.40625	0.00%
2	You win $2 from me	−20%	0.20313	−4.06%
1	You win $4 from me	−40%	0.09375	−3.75%
0	You win $6 from me	−60%	0.01563	−0.94%
				0.00%
	Betting 15% of Assets per flip	Return on $10 Capital	Probability	Expected (Prob. Wtd.) Return
6	1.15 ^ 6 − 1	131.31%	0.01563	2.05%
5	1.15 ^ 5 * .85 ^ 1 − 1	70.97%	0.09375	6.65%
4	1.15 ^ 4 * .85 ^ 2 − 1	26.37%	0.20313	5.36%
3	1.15 ^ 3 * .85 ^ 3 − 1	−6.60%	0.40625	−2.68%
2	1.15 ^ 2 * .85 ^ 4 − 1	−30.96%	0.20313	−6.29%
1	1.15 ^ 1 * .85 ^ 5 − 1	−48.97%	0.09375	−4.59%
0	.85 ^ 6 − 1	−62.29%	0.01563	−0.97%
				−0.47%

Source: Advent Capital Management.

$$1.15^6 - 1 = 131.31\%$$

$$0.85^6 - 1 = -62.29\%$$

Is this a good deal for you? Consider that winning three times and losing three times would cost you 6.6% of your money: $1.15^3 \times 0.85^3 - 1 = -6.60\%$. Indeed, the expected return (which is the sum of all the probability-weighted returns) is −.47%. If we assume $10 of initial capital, you could respond that you will only play this game if I give you 5 cents up front, which is fair because you expect to lose, on average, 4.7 cents each time you play ($10 \times -0.47\% = -0.047$ or -4.7 cents).

Figure 9.2 shows that the first bet is symmetrically distributed, and the second bet is asymmetrically distributed. This is because when

Figure 9.2   Normal versus log-normal distributions of returns

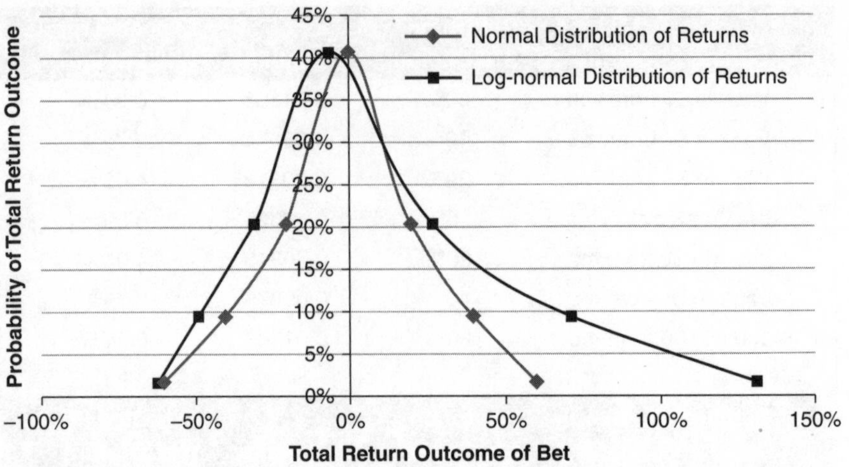

Data: Bloomberg.

normally distributed returns are added, the result is also normally distributed, and when normally distributed returns are multiplied, the result is log-normally distributed. Sequential returns of bets are similar to the period returns of financial assets. The returns get multiplied together as follows to determine the compounded return:

$$(1+r_1)\times(1+r_2)\times(1+r_3)-1 = \text{compounded}$$

Bringing this back to the realm of option valuation, let's consider the expected value of an option on our coin flips. If we were to offer you an option on the return of the six sequential coin flips, what would that be worth? Instead of having four negative outcomes and three positive ones, you need only consider the three positive outcomes. The expected (probability-weighted) value of those three outcomes is 14.06%, or $1.41, of your $10. If we offer you the option for $1.50 or more, you would decide that it is not worth it, but if we offer you the option for $1.30 or less, you might decide it is worth the risk. All the example models in this section were *discrete* in that there was always a set number of outcomes.

As we move into the realm of stochastic modeling, we will transition from discrete outcomes and probabilities to continuous ones. In other words, in stochastic modeling there are an infinite number of possible outcomes each with almost zero chance of occurring (technically most

Figure 9.3   Continuous normal distribution

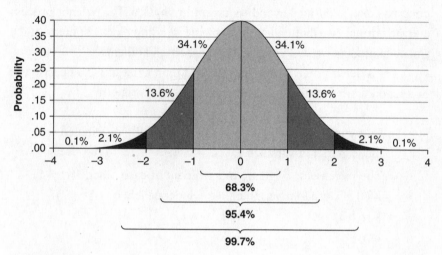

Data: Advent Capital Management.

financial data series violate this because prices and rates are rounded, limiting possible outcomes, but functionally the continuous assumption is effective). Figure 9.3 illustrates the continuous normal distribution—and the probability of outcomes at the mean and 1, 2, 3, and 4 standard deviations away from that mean. The figure shows that the probability of an observation being within 1 standard deviation of the mean is 68.3%; 2 standard deviations, 95.4%; and 3 standard deviation, 99.7%. The Black-Scholes-Merton formula uses this function to determine the probability of options expiring in or out of the money. The assumption is that stock returns are a random series of independent events, which means that the central limit theorem can be used to assume that the results are normally distributed.

However, the use of normal distributions to model a random series of events expands well beyond just equity returns. As we will see, normal distributions have been applied to interest rates, credit, and volatility, to name a few.

9.1.2 The Wiener Process

The Wiener process, defined by Norbert Wiener in the early 1900s, is closely related to Brownian motion. The Wiener process was originally designed to give a mathematical description to the random movements of a particle suspended in a liquid as it is buffeted by molecules in the fluid, the motion observed by Robert Brown. However, its use in statistical modeling has expanded far beyond its origin in physics. The Wiener process and the normal distribution are the two core building blocks of many of the financial models we will cover in this chapter and others.

The Wiener process [$dW(t)$ is the common notation] is a description of a random variable that follows a specific set of properties:

- Every increment $W(t + T) - W(t)$ is normally distributed with mean zero and variance T.
- The increments of W are independent of each other. $W(t + 1) - W(t)$ is a random variable that is independent of $W(t + 2) - W(t + 3)$.
- $W(0) = 0$.
- $W(t)$ is continuous.

The combination of these four criteria describes the movement of a random variable over time. Given the importance of Wiener processes, it is worth doing a simple example:

$$W(0) = 0$$

The movement from $W(0)$ to $W(1)$ is a randomly selected number from a normal distribution with mean 0 and variance 1 (see Figure 9.3 for an example of a normal distribution). Then

$$W(1) = 0 + 0.39 = 0.39$$

The movement from $W(1)$ to $W(2)$ is another randomly selected number from a normal distribution, independent of the prior movement, with mean 0 and variance 1 ($T = 1$ in these examples). Then

$$W(2) = 0.39 + -0.55 = -0.16$$

These movements can be scaled to the variance of that random variable, and drift elements can be added as well. Wiener processes will make an appearance in many of the models to come because modeling random uncorrelated movements of some element (e.g., stock returns, interest rates, etc.) is the goal of these models. With these concepts in place, we now have the tools we need to understand the variety of option models developed over time, beginning with the venerable Black-Scholes-Merton model.

9.2 BLACK-SCHOLES-MERTON

Myron Scholes and Robert Merton won a Nobel Prize in 1997 for the Black-Scholes-Merton option valuation formula that had revolutionized investment theory. Scholes and Merton had become principals and resident *quant* experts at a hedge fund called Long Term Capital Management (LTCM). In 1998, the fund had returned more than 100% cumulatively over the prior three years—*after performance fees of 27%*. Their models had been applied to the generation of profits by *arbitraging* the anticipated relationships between assets. Their success was unprecedented, and their assets under management had grown from $1 billion to more than $7.5 billion (which was levered to create more than $126 billion of market exposure).

By the end of the year, LTCM became the largest hedge fund failure in history—and the only hedge fund failure that ever threatened the financial system. LTCM received a $3.5 billion Federal Reserve bailout to avoid destabilizing the 14 global banks that were LTCM trading counterparties on more than $100 billion in derivative transactions.

Although the failure of a single hedge fund does not invalidate the models and formulas developed by these brilliant economists, it does serve as a powerful reminder that conclusions drawn from mathematical models are only as valid as the assumptions that the models are based on. All models make simplifying assumptions. As long as the assumptions hold, the models can be very useful and even profitable, but it is necessary to consider whether the assumptions are valid—and will *continue* to be valid.

We will first examine the model developed by Scholes, Merton, and their collaborator Fischer Black (who would have shared the Nobel Prize had he not passed away in 1995, prior to the award). Then we will analyze advanced methods for valuing equity options that challenged the assumptions made by Black, Scholes, and Merton.

The Black-Scholes-Merton model—commonly called *Black-Scholes* or *BSM*—is a differential equation for finding the value of an option. The BSM model was a breakthrough in financial theory at the time of its publication in 1973.

BSM requires five inputs: the current stock price, the term to expiration, the strike price of the option, the risk-free rate, and the volatility of the stock. The model assumes that stock prices are log-normally distributed and have a lower boundary of zero and that volatility and interest rates are constant. These assumptions are subject to challenge, but for the sake of understanding the model, let's assume that they are correct. BSM also assumes no dividend yield, but today there are simple extensions to the model that accommodate dividend yields. BSM evaluates European call options (which cannot be exercised prior to maturity) as well as American call options (which can be) and warrants (which are options that create new shares and therefore dilute the stock).

The main innovation of the BSM model was to apply the mathematics of normal distributions to assess the probability that a call option will expire in the money. The model applies the normal distribution by assuming that the asset prices follow a Brownian motion:

$$dS = \mu dt + \sigma dW \qquad (9.1)$$

where dW is a Wiener process that is normally distributed and follows continuous paths.

Although the BSM model looks complicated, the formula is simply an extension of the following equation:

$$\text{Call value} = \text{call delta} \times \text{stock price} - \text{loan} \qquad (9.2)$$

which adds expressions for the calculation of probabilities using normal distributions. In its full form, the BSM option formula is:

$$\text{Call value} = \left(N(d_1) \times S\right) - N(d_2) \times K \times e^{-rT} \qquad (9.3)$$

where $N(d_1)$ is a normal-distribution function representing the option delta, and

$N(d_2)$ is a normal-distribution function representing the likelihood of exercise. That is:

$$N(d_1) = \frac{\left[\ln\left(\dfrac{S}{K}\right) + \left(r + \dfrac{\sigma^2}{2}\right) \times T\right]}{\sigma\sqrt{T}} \qquad (9.4)$$

$$d_2 = d_1 - \sigma\sqrt{T} \qquad (9.5)$$

Again, this equation may seem intimidating, but at its core it is quite simple. The value of a call option is the value of the equity exposure from the option $\left[N(d_1) \times S \right]$ minus the present value of what the investor would have to pay to exercise the option $\left(K \times e^{-rT} \right)$ multiplied by the probability that the option will be exercised $\left[N(d_2) \right]$.

Using put-call parity, the call-option formula can be easily adjusted to provide a method to value a put option:

$$Put\ value = N(-d_2) \times K \times e^{-rT} - N(-d_2) \times S \qquad (9.6)$$

Let us consider two examples—an in-the-money and an out-of-the-money call option—and walk step by step through the BSM formula with these two numerical examples where the strike price is 100, volatility is 0.30, the risk-free rate is 3%, the term is 2 years, and:

1. Stock price = 120 (in the money)
2. Stock price = 80 (out of the money)

We have broken the valuation process into 12 small steps to make it easier to explain and comprehend:

1. (S/K) describes the current moneyness of the option. In the numerical example it would be:
   a. $120/100 = 1.2$
   b. $80/100 = 0.8$
2. The natural log of moneyness $\ln(S/K)$ is an expression of the logarithmic distance of the stock from the strike price. The logarithmic distance of plus or minus 20% would be expressed as:
   a. $\ln(1+0.2) = 0.182322$; *conversely* $e^{0.182322} = 2.71828^{0.182322} = 1.2$
   b. $\ln(1-0.2) = -0.223144$; *conversely* $e^{-0.223144} = 2.71828^{-0.223144} = 0.8$
3. Standard deviation (σ) scales with the square root of time $\sigma\sqrt{T}$ describes how much the stock can be expected to move because of its volatility and the term (but excluding the drift effect due to the risk-free rate).

$$\sigma\sqrt{T} = 0.30 \times \sqrt{2} = 0.4243$$

Given a volatility (annualized standard deviation) of 0.3, the stock can be expected to move 0.4243 over a two-year period.

4. Variance (σ^2) scales with time rather than the square root of time, as does the risk-free rate, which describes the expected drift of the equity price higher, which is why they can be combined as follows:

$$\left(r+\frac{\sigma^2}{2}\right)\times 2 = \left(0.03+\frac{0.3^2}{2}\right)\times 2 = (0.03+0.045)\times 2 = 0.15$$

5. The expected moneyness at expiration is therefore:

$$\ln\left(\frac{S}{K}\right)+\left(r+\frac{\sigma^2}{2}\right)\times T:$$

a. $0.182322 + 0.15 = 0.332322$

b. $-0.223144 + 0.15 = -0.073144$

6. The potential expiration moneyness expressed as a ratio of the volatility movement of the stock is then:

$$\frac{\ln\left(\frac{S}{K}\right)+\left(r+\frac{\sigma^2}{2}\right)\times T}{\sigma\sqrt{t}}$$

This is the number of standard deviations the upside expected value of the stock is from the strike price.

a. $0.332322/0.4243 = 0.7833$

b. $-0.073144/0.4243 = -0.1724$

In other words, the expiration moneyness could be 0.78 times the volatilty movement of the stock.

7. Delta uses the cumulative standard normal function N. Thus,

$$N(d_1) = N\left[\frac{\ln\left(\frac{S}{K}\right)+\left(r+\frac{\sigma^2}{2}\right)\times T}{\sigma\sqrt{t}}\right]$$

a. $N(0.7833) = 0.7833$, or a delta of 78

b. $N(-0.1724) = 0.4316$, or a delta of 43

8. Expected stock change in standard deviations: $d_2 = d_1 - \sigma\sqrt{T}$. This is the number of standard deviations the upside expected value of the stock is from the current price.

   a. $0.7833 - 0.4243 = 0.3590$

   b. $-0.1724 - 0.4243 = -0.5967$

9. The probability that the call will be exercised is the cumulative standard normal of the ratio.

   a. $N(0.3590) = 0.6402$

   b. $N(-0.5967) = 0.2754$

10. The present value of the strike price is $K \times e^{-rT}$:

$$100 \times 2.71828^{-.03 \times 2} = 94.1765$$

11. Loan value = Likelihood of exercise $\times$ present value of the strike price:

   a. $0.6402 \times 94.1765 = 60.29$

   b. $0.2754 \times 94.1765 = 25.93$

12. Call value = call delta $\times$ stock price − loan:

   a. $0.7833 \times 120 - 60.29 = 33.70$

   b. $0.4316 \times 80 - 25.93 = 8.59$

Comparing the two numeric examples, it makes sense that the in-the-money option would be worth significantly more than the out-of-the-money option. It is also interesting that they have a similar time value. While the in-the-money option has $20 of intrinsic value, it has $13.70 owing to the possibility of it moving further into the money and owing to the downside protection on a signficant pullback in the stock. The out-of-the-money option has no intrinsic value, yet, it does have time value of $8.59 based on the possibilty of the stock surpassing the strike price by expiration of the option.

9.2.1 Accounting for Dividend Yield and Warrant Dilution

The basic form of the BSM model does not account for dividends on common stock or the dilutive effects of warrants (which are options that, when exercised, require the issuer to fulfill by *issuing new stock*—akin to what happens when a convertible bond is converted). Two additions to the BSM model account for these situations. Let's assume an equity dividend yield of 2% and warrant dilution of 10% and continue with the numerical examples that we initiated in the preceding section.

The dividend yield reduces the expiration value of the stock because it represents value that is paid out prior to expiration. It is represented by the letter q, and it is simply subtracted from the risk-free rate as follows:

$$\left(r - q + \frac{\sigma^2}{2}\right) \times T = \left(0.03 - 0.02 + \frac{0.3^2}{2}\right) \times 2 = (0.01 + 0.045) \times 2 = 0.11$$

In our two numerical examples, this would reduce the deltas as follows:

1. $N(0.2923) = 0.7546$, or a delta of 75
2. $N(-0.1131) = 0.3949$, or a delta of 39

The reduced expiration value of the stock also affects the option delta; therefore, we make the follow adjustment:

$$\text{Call value} = \left(N(d_1) \times S \times e^{-qt}\right) - N(d_2) \times K \times e^{-rT} \tag{9.7}$$

1. $87.0 - 56.92 = 30.08$
2. $30.35 - 23.05 = 7.30$

A *warrant* is an option that, when exercised, adds to the total outstanding shares of the company. This dilutes the percentage ownership of all new and current shares, which decreases the intrinsic value per share. To account for the dilution, a ratio of $\frac{1}{1+\lambda}$ is multiplied by the option value to adjust for the dilution. *Lambda* is the ratio of warrants to outstanding shares (see Table 9.3).

Pondering how to use the model step by step highlights a key strength of BSM: the model is intuitive in its logic and is easy to implement (indeed, a quick search online reveals free BSM calculators). Volatility is the only input that is not directly observable. Unlike many alternative option models, no calibration process is necessary. This means that the BSM model can be applied to a broad array of securities without complex or time-consuming computations.

Table 9.3 Step-by-Step Numerical Examples of BSM Call/Warrant Valuation

Assumptions	Call (No Dividends)		Call w/Div & Warrants	
Risks free rate	3%	3%	3%	3%
Stock price	120	80	120	80
Volatility (σ^2)	0.3	0.3	0.3	0.3
Strike price	100	100	100	100
Term	2	2	2	2
Dividend yield (q)	0	0	2%	2%
Ratio of warrants to outstanding shares (λ)	0	0	15%	15%
Steps to Black-Scholes-Merton Value				
1. Moneyness (S/K)	1.2	0.8	1.2	0.8
2. Natural log of moneyness $\ln(S/K)$	0.1823	−0.2231	0.1823	−0.2231
3. Volatility/term movement $\sigma^2(T)$	0.4243	0.4243	0.4243	0.4243
4. Expected drift of equity price $(r - q + \sigma^2/2) \times T$	0.15	0.15	0.11	0.11
5. Expected moneyness at expiration $(\ln(S/K) + (r + \sigma^2/2) \times T)$	0.3323	(0.0731)	0.2923	(0.1131)
6. Ratio of expected moneyness to vol/term movement $(\ln(S/K) + (r + \sigma^2/2) \times T)/\sigma^2(T) = d_1$	0.7833	(0.1724)	0.6890	(0.2667)
7. Delta: change in call price to change in stock price $N(d_1)$	0.7833	0.4316	0.7546	0.3949
8. Expected stock change in standard deviations $d_1 - \sigma^2(T) = d_2$	0.3590	(0.5967)	0.2647	(0.6909)
9. Likelihood of exercise $N(d_2)$	0.6402	0.2754	0.6044	0.2448
10. Present value of the strike $K \times e^{-rT}$	94.1765	94.1765	94.1765	94.1765
11. Loan value $N(d_2) \times K \times e^{-rT}$	60.29	25.93	56.92	23.05
12. Call value (no dividends, dilution) $N(d_1) \times S - N(d_2) - K \times e^{-rT}$	**33.70**	**8.59**		
13. Expected value of stock adjusting for dividend yield $N(d_1) \times S \times e^{-rT}$			87.00	30.35
14. Call value adjusting for dividend yield $N(d_1) \times S \times e^{-rT} - N(d_2) \times K \times e^{-rT}$			**30.08**	**7.30**
15. Warrant value adjusting for stock dilution $C/(1+\lambda)$			**26.16**	**6.34**

Source: Advent Capital Management.

Beyond valuing options, the BSM model also can be used to find the implied volatility of an asset based on the current market price of its options. The *implied volatility* of an option is the level of volatility you need to assume in order for the BSM model to match the actual trading price of the option at that moment. The implied volatility of an *at-the-money* option (the distinction is important, as we will soon demonstrate) is a better estimator of the underlying security's future volatility than its historical volatility. Hence, implied volatility is often used as a proxy for volatility in other pricing models.

9.3 SHORTCOMINGS OF THE BSM MODEL

Although the venerable BSM option model is effective and popular, market participants have identified inconsistencies between the assumptions and results of the model when compared with real-world data. These inconsistencies cause the BSM model to potentially misprice deep out-of-the-money or in-the-money options.

9.3.1 Volatility Smile

The aforementioned problems have led to the formation of a *volatility smile* in the option implied volatility curve of most securities. Given the importance of volatility in financial markets and the widespread use of the BSM model, the volatility smile has been the subject of extensive academic research over the last several decades as researchers have attempted to explain and/or resolve the causes of the smile.

The graph in Figure 9.4 shows the implied volatility curve for JP Morgan Chase (JPM) shares in January 2020, which was generated from the market prices of a series of put options with a variety of strikes and a September 18, 2020, expiration date. We can clearly see the presence of a volatility smile with the implied volatility being higher at very high or very low strikes. The tilt to the smile shows that implied volatility is higher at very low strikes than at high strikes, which is a common phenomenon in options on equities; foreign exchange (FX) options are typically more symmetrical (some have referred to the tilted pattern as a *volatility smirk* to distinguish it from the volatility smile). In contrast, equity index options

Figure 9.4 Implied volatility of JPM 9/18/2020 puts as of 1/16/2020

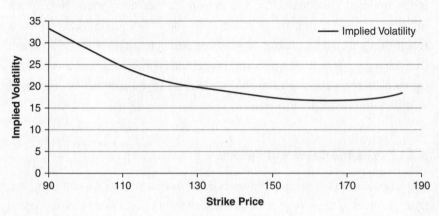

Data: Bloomberg.

series are typically asymmetrical with no uptick at all as option strikes become very high.

If the BSM model were an accurate predictor of the market price for options, we would expect the chart in Figure 9.4 to show a flat line because the true underlying volatility of JPM is the same regardless of what kind of option you buy. Realistically, therefore, the implied volatility should be the same for all JPM options at a given point in time. A small difference from one strike to the next could be explained as trading white noise, but with the $90 strike having *twice* the implied volatility of the $160 option, it is clear that this is a systemic issue.

Remember that the value of an option increases when volatility increases; in fact, volatility is often used as a proxy for the price of an option. With this in mind, the chart in Figure 9.4 shows that according to the BSM model, the low-strike options were more expensive than the options with strikes around $150. Essentially, there is a disagreement between the market and the BSM model on how to price the probability of extreme movements in the price of JPM shares. This disagreement is not unique to this particular series of JPM options; the volatility smile is seen in option series and securities of all types.

This disagreement is also not a constant fixture in the market. Prior to the 1987 market crash, the volatility smile of the S&P 500 Index was flat. In the aftermath of the crash, there was a dramatic and permanent change in the steepness of the left side of the implied volatility curve of index options; it appears that the option market now prices in a much higher chance of a significant move to the downside in the S&P 500 as a result of a permanent change in investor perceptions after the 1987 crash (this change affected international markets as well). Whether this is a rational change in expected return distributions or a symptom of increased risk aversion is difficult to tell.

9.3.1.1 Possible Causes of the Smile

One explanation for the gap between BSM option valuations and observed market prices is that *crash phobia* causes market participants to pay a premium for downside protection, which is why deep out-of-the-money puts in particular show high implied volatility. Alternatively, continuous supply and demand differences could be an explanation. People are more willing to buy out-of-the-money puts than they are to sell (write) out-of-the-money puts, which causes such puts to trade above theoretical fair value. The question then becomes, why is the volatility smile so persistent, and why does it prevail for nearly all securities? The smile is a global phenomenon. Structural mispricing on this scale would reflect a dramatic failure of the efficient-market hypothesis. Another explanation is that the smile is a reflection of inconsistencies in how the BSM models market returns and volatility versus real-world outcomes.

9.3.2 Non-normality of Stock Returns

The BSM model assumes that stock market returns follow a normal distribution. Assuming that results are normally distributed is common in statistical analysis, and it is mathematically convenient. But the prevalence and accessibility of historical financial data make it easy to confirm that the assumption of normal distributions is inconsistent with actual market returns.

A mountain of evidence demonstrates that stock market returns are not normally distributed and in fact are *leptokurtic*. Additionally, in the case of index returns, returns are negatively skewed. Put into plain language, *relative to what the BSM model assumes, broad market returns are*

Figure 9.5   Amazon (AMZN) 2009–2019 return distribution versus a normal curve

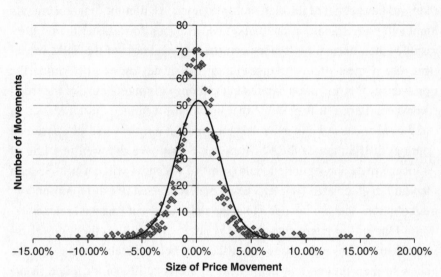

Data: Bloomberg.

much more prone to extreme movements and are more likely to be up than down, and extreme downward movements are more common than extreme upward movements.

Figure 9.5 shows the actual daily return distribution of Amazon (AMZN) shares from 2009 to 2019 compared with a normal distribution with the same mean and standard deviation. The plots show that Amazon's returns were what is commonly referred to as *fat tailed*. In essence, the gray dots are above the line, showing more events in the middle and the tails of the charts. To put some numbers to this observation, over this 10-year period, Amazon had an average daily return of 0.123% (this may not seem impressive at first glance, but for a daily equity return, 0.123% is remarkably high) and a daily standard deviation of 1.95%.

Based on the average volatility of Amazon's stock returns, a normal distribution would predict that there would be 26 days when Amazon shares moved more than ±5% in a 10-year period. In actuality, there were 64 days with movements of that magnitude. The difference between the normal distribution and what Amazon shares actually experienced is typical of most financial return series.

Experienced market participants know that stocks are prone to large price swings and that for broad market indices, extreme movements are skewed to the downside. Anyone who has spent decades in the stock market will have suffered through multiple "once in a lifetime" market crashes and will understand that the market usually goes down faster than it goes up. The non-normality of stock returns is a weakness of the BSM model because it means that the distribution the model uses to determine the probability that an option expires in the money is not reflective of true real-world conditions. It is possible that the volatility smile is just a reflection of the enhanced tail risk in actual stock market returns versus the assumed normal distribution of the BSM model. Some have followed this line of logic to create new option models (some of which we will cover in Section 9.4 and in associated supplementary materials) that use different random distributions that are intended to accurately represent financial returns.

One of the interesting things to note while still on the topic of return distributions is the question of skew. Indices typically have a negative skew to their returns that helps explain the volatility smirk found in the implied volatility curve. If large downward movements are more likely then large upward movements, then it's logical that deep out-of-the-money put options should have a higher price (and therefore show higher implied volatility) than deep out-of-the-money call options.

In contrast, individual security returns are often positively skewed, as is obviously characteristic of our example of Amazon. Despite this tendency of option series on individual securities to be positively skewed, we still see the same smirk on options on individual securities as on index option series; we cannot explain this smirk through return distributions. This leads us into the next possible cause of the smile that does offer a potential answer to the smirk question.

9.3.3 Relationship Between Volatility and Change in Equity Prices

The BSM model assumes that volatility is constant throughout the life of the option regardless of movements in the underlying stock. This ignores the effect of changes in equity prices on the leverage of a firm. Consider a company with a $10 billion equity market capitalization and $10 billion in outstanding debt. If this company suffers a 50% decrease in its share price, its debt-to-equity ratio will double to 2:1 (see Figure 9.6).

Figure 9.6 Debt-to-equity ratio after a change in stock price

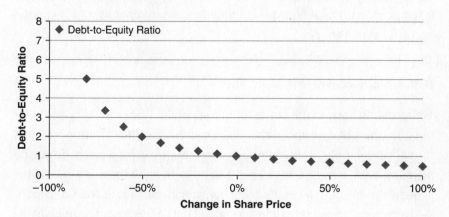

Data: Advent Capital Management.

In corporate finance, equity risk is seen as a function of operational leverage and financial leverage. Under this logic, the equity risk of this company has increased by virtue of its stock price having declined, thereby increasing its financial leverage. It follows that heightened equity risk will feed into higher stock price volatility, establishing a link between stock price movements and volatility. Regardless of how much weight one wants to place on the leverage argument, there is statistical evidence of a correlation between stock price declines and heightened volatility.

The leverage argument has the benefit of helping to explain the tilted nature of the volatility smirk in the implied volatility of individual securities. The BSM model does not allow for any kind of correlation between share level and volatility, implying that it underestimates the possibility of large downward movements. If the market recognizes the correlation and correctly prices options, we would expect to see higher implied volatilities for very low strikes, which we do. In Section 9.4.2 we will explain the constant elasticity of variance (CEV) model, which seeks to improve on the BSM model by including an elasticity parameter that ties together volatility and price level.

However, it's important to recognize that the leverage argument does not address the higher implied volatility we generally see at high strikes in individual securities. In fact, if we rely on leverage to explain the smile, we would expect implied volatility to be at its lowest at high strikes because volatility would go down relative to the BSM expectations as the company deleverages through stock price appreciation. The leverage idea also does not help us with FX options, which also have observable smiles. The leverage effect may help explain individual equity options, but it is not a universal explanation.

9.3.4 Non-constant Volatility

We repeat that one of the key assumptions of the BSM model is that volatility is constant and uncorrelated throughout the life of an option, yet, in reality, volatility is anything but constant. We have already discussed the correlation between price level and volatility, but there is also what is called *volatility clustering*. Philosopher/statistician/author Nassim Nicholas Taleb sums up volatility clustering and the deficiency of normal distributions in four words: "volatility comes in lumps."[2]

Figure 9.7 shows that the volatility of the S&P 500 not only changes but that it is also *sticky*. Once volatility spikes higher, which it can do quite sharply, it often remains high for an extended period. Once volatility exceeded 20% during the onset of the Great Financial Crisis in 2007, it stayed above that level until the fall of 2009, two years later. High volatility increases the probability that multiple extreme events may occur in a row.

The probability of extreme price movements in a row can be demonstrated in a quick example. Let's say that a stock has a 10% chance of

Figure 9.7   SPX Corporation rolling 90-day standard deviation

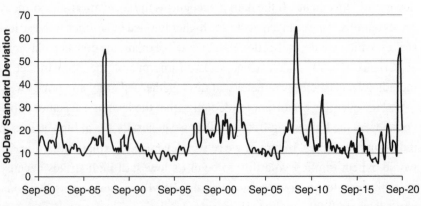

Data: Bloomberg.

moving down more than 5% in a day. The probability of this occurring three times in row would be:

$$10\% \times 10\% \times 10\% = 0.1\%$$

But historical volatility data show that stock volatility is correlated very strongly with past volatility. Once volatility goes up, it tends to stay up. Sticking with our example, let's say that after our first down day, volatility spikes higher, and the probability of the stock moving down more than 5% rises to 30%. Then:

$$10\% \times 30\% \times 30\% = 0.9\%$$

Obviously, our example is simplistic, yet, it clearly illustrates how assuming uncorrelated volatility leads to underestimating tail risk. An easy way to adjust for correlated volatility within the framework of the BSM model is to simply update the volatility assumptions being used in the model immediately after an extreme event has occurred. But this solution raises the question, how do you know what the volatility of a security is after that major event? Historical volatility typically has been an unreliable predictor, and without the use of option implied volatility, there is no way to directly observe volatility.

The generalized autoregressive conditional heteroskedasticity (GARCH) model (further explained in Section 9.4.3) accounts for the stickiness of volatility by forecasting volatility in a complicated process that is in part a function of the last period's volatility and the last period's forecast of volatility. The goal is to capture the volatility clustering that is observed in return distributions and use this tendency to forecast future volatility.

9.3.5 Time and Volatility

Another assumption of the BSM model (there certainly are quite a few assumptions) is that the distance that a price can move is a direct function of time and volatility. This is logical, an option with 30 days to expiration has twice as much time for the stock to move when compared with an option that has only 15 days to expiration. As the time to expiration of an out-of-money option decreases toward zero, the possibility that the option might end in the money also goes to zero. However, as is often the case, reality is a little more complicated.

Securities often experience very large changes in price in a very short period of time because of the release of new information. An option that is 10% out of the money with only two days to maturity still holds some value if the underlying stock is that of a pharmaceutical company that plans to announce the results of a major drug trial tomorrow. However, using the BSM model, this option likely will be mispriced because the model does not account for the possibility of a sudden instantaneous change in price. Following this logic, we would expect the BSM model to be more likely to misprice options with very short maturities. This theory is supported by data because the smile of an option series is generally more pronounced when the option maturity is shorter. We will begin Section 9.4 with an introduction to jump risk, which is the key feature of the jump diffusion model.

9.3.6 BSM in Context

Our discussions of the BSM model demonstrate that there are imperfections in the model. The question that follows is, what should we use instead? There is no easy answer. Option and volatility modeling that goes beyond BSM is an ongoing field of research. Many improvements to the BSM model have been proposed. A multitude of different option models and variations of those option models have been created since the BSM model was first popularized. Although we could easily fill chapter after chapter with detailed discussions of all the models, we will instead focus on the models that we regard as most useful and easy to apply, starting with the jump diffusion model.

But before setting aside the BSM model and moving on to the alternatives, it is important to recognize why BSM became so popular and why it remains in use despite the presence of many competitive models. (Original papers describing improved models appeared a couple of years after the 1973 publication of the BSM model.)

The BSM model is simple, easy to use, and useful. Meanwhile, most of the alternatives rely on complex mathematics and/or require a calibration process. BSM is effective at pricing at- or near-the-money options that have a reasonable amount of remaining time to expiration. The problems with BSM begin to arise as we move beyond these typical options. Other models do offer improvements over BSM on a theoretical level, yet, BSM does have meaningful utility as a general-use tool.

9.4 ADVANCED (AND IMPROVED) OPTION MODELS

All models are wrong, but some are useful.

—*George E. P. Box*[3]

This aphorism is popular among quantitative professionals and is credited to the famous statistician George E. P. Box. "'All models are wrong' is a reminder that models work by simplifying and idealizing real-world relationships in order to capture the most important features. In other words, any model is at best a useful fiction—there never will be an exact normal distribution or an exactly linear relationship. Nevertheless, enormous progress has been made by entertaining such fictions and using them as approximations."[4]

Box's message can be applied to the sophisticated and elaborate quantitative models that we have discussed so far as well as to others that we will consider shortly. We remind readers that quantitative models are essential for evaluating convertible securities. Unfortunately, space does not permit the full theoretical and step-by-step presentation of the more advanced valuation models such as jump diffusion, GARCH, CEV, Stable-Levy, or the Quartic-Damped-Sine models, but we will briefly describe them in this section. For a full review of each of these models including formulas and numerical examples, please visit www.AdventCap.com/SupplementaryMaterials.

9.4.1 Jump Diffusion

One of the underlying assumptions of the BSM model is that price movements are a continuous process. That is to say, if the price of a security is to rise from $5 to $10, that security needs to travel over every single penny between those two prices. This assumption makes the probability of a large price move in a short period of time very small (unless the volatility used is extremely high). In reality, the price progression of most securities is not purely continuous. Instantaneous changes in price—called *gaps*—occur often, typically in response to breaking news. The classic example of this would be a stock rising or falling sharply at the open following an earnings announcement after the market closed on the prior trading day. By not including these gapping price movements, the return distribution in the BSM model fails to accurately represent the way securities actually trade on the market. To correct this, the *Jump Diffusion model* includes a parameter that models the magnitude and frequency of a jump using what is called a *Poisson variable* to model tail risk. The Poisson is used to bring the normal distribution of the BSM model closer to the fat-tailed distributions observed in the actual trading history of financial securities.

9.4.2 Constant Elasticity of Variance (CEV)

The CEV model was introduced by John Cox in 1975[5] and can be regarded as a response to the BSM formula that was first published two years earlier. In a sense, the BSM formula is a special case of the CEV in which the elasticity between price level and volatility is *zero*. As the name would suggest, the CEV model is intended to redress the assumption that the volatility of the underlying stock is constant throughout the life of the option. (In economics and finance, elasticity often refers to the rate of change that occurs as a result of something else changing; for example, the elasticity of demand is the change in demand given a change in price.) The CEV model considers the connection between the price level of a stock and its volatility. This is why the CEV model can be said to be a level-dependent volatility model.

9.4.3 Generalized Autoregressive Conditional Heteroskedasticity (GARCH) Model

The GARCH, in contrast with the CEV model, ignores the price of the underlying asset and instead focuses entirely on the trading pattern prior to evaluating the option. GARCH is a volatility model first proposed in 1986 by Tim Bollerslev[6] as a generalization of the autoregressive conditional heteroskedasticity (ARCH) model. The idea behind both models is that volatility is not a constant, nor is it a random distribution. ARCH and GARCH are a response to the observation that many economic and financial time series have time-varying volatility and show strong signs of volatility clustering. Volatility clustering occurs when high volatility has a tendency to persist. For example, if you assume no volatility clustering if the market dropped 10% today, there would be no effect on your expectations of future volatility. With volatility clustering, your expectations for the next day's volatility would increase as a consequence of the extreme movement the day prior. There is a great deal of appeal to incorporating volatility clustering in economic and financial models because it is often observable in real-life data. If gross domestic product drops 8% because of a recession, you would generally expect growth during the rebound to be sharper than normal. Thus, *the central idea behind GARCH models is that volatility is not a constant (as it is in the BSM model), nor is it a random distribution (as the CEV model implies). Instead, past realized volatility provides information about future volatility* that can be used for forecasting.

9.4.4 Levy-Stable

Levy-Stable models are designed to address the inconsistency between a normal distribution and the trading patterns observed on the market, namely that market returns are typically fat tailed. Much of the interest in Levy-Stable models comes from the desire to develop an option model that offers an explanation for the volatility smile that is not time dependent, according to Carr and Wu.[7] To expand on this idea, let's reconsider the jump diffusion model. Jump diffusion expands on the BSM model by including the possibility of sudden instantaneous price movements (in other words, a *jump* in price). Inclusion of jumps clearly has a big effect on the evaluation of a short-term option. We used the example of an option with two days to expiration on a pharmaceutical company about to announce drug results. In the BSM model, the time value on this option is nearly worthless, but under jump diffusion, it still has value. However, what if that same option instead had five years left to expiration? With an expiration date that far in the future, the effect of jump risk is diluted away. This is a common theme in many option models, and it means that the implied volatility curves that those models create flatten out as maturity increases. The problem with this flattening effect is that the implied volatility curve observed in the market does not match this effect (according to Carr and Wu).[8] Thus, the goal of Levy-Stable models is to resolve the volatility curve in a process that does not depend on time.

9.4.5 Quartic and Damped Sine Adjustments (QDS Adjustments)

Regardless of the probability distribution process selected, the actual distribution realized over a period of time will have a distribution that differs to some extent from the model. We have observed that the difference between models is not entirely random and actually follows a predictable pattern. This means that process models fail to capture the true systematic distribution of stock prices. In other words, the difference between actual and predicted prices is not just noise. It is as if the model is near or farsighted. QDS Adjustment formulas model the predictable part of the discrepancy—essentially acting as a pair of corrective lenses for eyes that are near or farsighted. It is probably fair to call this the Partlow QDS Adjustment model as the co-author of this book developed the model based on the suggestions of two other Partlows. Please visit www.AdventCap.com/SupplementaryMaterials for a detailed paper on this and other methods.

9.5 CONCLUSION: THE CHOICE OF MODEL IS YOURS

The choice of which option model is most relevant to the needs of a convertible investor defies a simple answer. While natural processes can be described by mathematical models, there is usually some residual element that eludes explanation. The observation of G. K. Chesterton "the riddles of God are more satisfying than the solutions of man" seems particularly relevant to security prices. Nevertheless, CEV and jump diffusion models appear to be better than BSM for projecting stock price volatility, and in an ideal world, we would expect these two models to produce better results. Yet, CEV and jump diffusion require additional variables that need to be estimated. If these new variables are calibrated incorrectly, or if past data do not foretell the future, then the inaccuracy of the additional variable will undo any benefit that could have been realized from using a more sophisticated model.

The GARCH model offers great flexibility and a straightforward process for pricing an option but requires statistical software and the knowledge to use such software. Moreover, GARCH models have the same reliance as CEV and jump diffusion on past data being a viable predictor of future relationships. Levy-Stable models replace the normal distribution used by the BSM model with a Levy distribution that has tail risk that is more akin to what is observed in the market. Yet, the model entails infinite variance (creating options with infinite value) unless maximum asymmetry is assumed.

BSM is a functional default model that has performed well (as would be expected given decades of persistent use). With access to specialized software, GARCH is an attractive alternative, particularly in the case of asymmetric GARCH models such as the GJR-GARCH model.

CEV and jump diffusion are particularly good for pricing deep out-of-the-money options likely to be mispriced by the BSM model—assuming that their non-observable values can be estimated effectively, of course. For more information on selection of the right model, and for details on modeling special features of a convertible, visit www.AdventCap.com/SupplementaryMaterials.

ENDNOTES

1. https://www.brainyquote.com/quotes/benjamin_franklin_141119.

2. Nassim Nicholas Taleb, *Antifragile* (New York: Random House, 2012), p. 92.

3. https://en.wikipedia.org/wiki/All_models_are_wrong.

4. George E. P. Box and Alberto Luceño, *Statistical Control by Monitoring and Feedback Adjustment* (New York: Wiley, 1997).

5. J. Cox, "Notes on Option Pricing: I. Constant Elasticity of Diffusions," unpublished draft, Stanford University, Stanford, CA, 1975.

6. T. Bollerslev, "Generalized Autoregressive Conditional Heteroskedasticity," *Journal of Econometrics* 1986;31:307–327.

7. Peter Carr and Liuren Wu, "The Finite Moment Log Stable Process and Option Pricing," *Journal of Finance* 2003;58:753–777.

8. *Ibid.*

CHAPTER 10

Risk Management and Exposure Analysis

Damn the torpedoes, full speed ahead!

—*Attributed to Rear Admiral David*
Farragut of the Union Fleet during the
Battle of Mobile Bay

10.1 CONVERTIBLE RISKS, EXPOSURES, AND OPPORTUNITIES

What seems to be a rash statement on the part of a naval commander has become synonymous with ignoring risks in the pursuit of gains. Yet, this connotation is *not* true of Admiral Farragut—nor is it true of convertible investors who carefully examine their exposures and know which risks have been mitigated by the asymmetric properties of convertibles.

At the time of the Battle of Mobile Bay, a *torpedo* was a static mine. Farragut knew where the mines were laid, and he had ordered his ships to steer clear. Admiral Farragut also was aware of two greater risks to his fleet: a battery of land-based cannons, and a fleet of Confederate ships positioned just beyond the minefield. Farragut's fleet was more exposed to the cannons than to the mines. By commanding full speed, he was mitigating the two greater dangers by rapidly sailing out of range of the cannons on land while navigating around the torpedoes so that he could quickly engage the Confederate ships over which his fleet had numerical advantage. Admiral Farragut overcame his greatest risks and captured the Confederate fleet, which completed the strategic blockade of the South that was his ultimate mission.

Investors should understand how their investments are likely to perform under various circumstances. The biggest source of potential positive or negative returns from most convertibles is equity sensitivity. Analyzing the equity sensitivity of positions and portfolios, both on an absolute basis and relative to certain benchmarks or indices is the focus of Chapter 11.

A second significant source of expected returns and risk is the yield of convertibles. Chapter 12 analyzes the components of yield and considers the market price risk of convertibles in response to changes in interest rates, credit quality, and credit spreads.

A third significant source of returns and risk is the volatility of the underlying equity and, usually to a lesser extent, the volatilities of interest rates and credit spreads. This is also discussed in Chapter 12.

10.2 KEY QUESTIONS FOR INVESTORS AND PORTFOLIO MANAGERS

It is important to understand the risks in a portfolio and the potential performance relative to those risks. We should be able to answer the following key questions:

- Did the portfolio perform better or worse than an index on a risk-adjusted basis?
- Where did the relative performance come from—extra risk, sector allocation, or security selection?
- What is the expected future return of the portfolio on an absolute and relative basis?
- What are the best- and worst-case scenarios?
- What are the likely performance effects of various economic scenarios?
- How much asymmetry is there in upside versus downside scenarios?
- How quickly and at what cost can a position be exited under normal or stressed conditions?

10.3 RISK POLICY, STANDARDS, BENCHMARKS, GUIDELINES, AND LIMITS

Whether you are an individual investor, an institutional investor, a regulated asset manager, or a regulator, it is important to have a thorough and documented policy toward risk. Risk policy begins with having a clear rationale for investing in convertibles and an understanding of the specific convertible strategy being pursued. For example, some investors allocate to convertibles in place of equities in order to reduce overall portfolio downside and/or volatility. Others invest in convertibles in place of corporate or government bonds in pursuit of higher total returns from the appreciation potential of convertibles. Still others invest in hedged convertibles in pursuit of uncorrelated total returns. Some investors require daily liquidity, whereas others accept longer liquidation periods in anticipation of superior returns over time. Some investors want active asset managers to use their expertise to deliver positive alpha—and are willing to pay higher fees to achieve this goal—whereas other investors are content to earn index-like returns while minimizing fees. Some investors seek to incorporate externalities (indirect benefits) using environment, social, and governance (ESG) ratings and information in the investment process[1] (see Chapter 16). Such goals should be identified and prioritized.

Investors should be aware of their core competencies and use those to define strategic and non-strategic risks. An asset manager with an equity analyst mentality may choose to focus on balanced convertibles and avoid credit-sensitive convertibles. Similarly, a credit-focused convertible investor may prefer higher-yielding convertibles that trade at discounts. Some investors define currencies as a non-strategic risk to be fully hedged. Appropriate investment guidelines and risk parameters should be based on the convertible investment strategy and the definition of strategic and non-strategic risks. On a regular basis (pretrade if possible), the portfolio should be analyzed, and risks measured to ensure adherence to the parameters.

10.3.1 Regulatory Standards

Financial institutions such as regulated insurance companies and banks are required to measure risk in specified ways and to set aside capital to cover potential losses.

10.3.2 Benchmarks

It is instructive to compare the return and volatility of a strategy to an appropriate benchmark. This is often an index or a blend of multiple indices. The purpose of benchmarking is to evaluate the performance of the portfolio manager relative to the appropriate investible universe.

Broad convertible indices include the Intercontinental Exchange (ICE) Bank of America (BofA) All US Convertibles Index (VXA0), ICE BofA US Convertibles Index (V0A0), and the ICE BofA Global Convertible Index (CONV). These represent a market-capitalization-weighted return of all US convertibles (VXA0) or all US convertibles excluding mandatory preferreds (V0A0) or all convertibles issued globally (CONV) with the only constraints being size (a value of greater than $100 million at issuance). Alternatively, Refinitiv offers the Global Convertible and Global Focused Convertible Indices, which exclude many smaller, less liquid, and less balanced convertibles. Strategies focused on defensive or low-delta convertibles might choose the ICE BofA Yield Alternatives US Convertible Index (VYLD) of all US convertibles with a delta of less than 40% or the Refinitiv Global Defensive Index of all convertibles with a conversion premium that is larger than a minimum that is calculated as a function of the expected life. Hedged convertible strategies are frequently benchmarked against the HFRI Convertible Arbitrage Index that is published by HFR (Hedge Fund Research). Choosing a convertible benchmark can be challenging because individual convertibles run the gamut from bond-like to equity-like, and portfolio managers take extremely different approaches to using convertibles. It is best to select an index that approximates the strategy desired by investors.

While having a single or primary benchmark is the most common practice, many investors use a secondary benchmark, which can compare the performance of the strategy relative to broad equities, fixed income, or blended indices. Individual investors rarely have access to information about these indices and therefore may wish to consult Lipper or Morningstar mutual fund indices, or simply passive exchange-traded funds such as the SPDR Bloomberg Barclays Convertible Securities ETF (ticker CWB).

10.3.3 Guidelines

Guidelines can be specified either by the investor or by the asset manager and are then codified in an *investment management agreement* (IMA). Common guidelines for convertible portfolios include the prohibition of various security types such as mandatory or reverse convertibles that have unlimited downside risk. Credit ratings are also commonly used in guidelines to limit the amount of lower-quality convertibles. Other guidelines are often intended to ensure sufficient portfolio diversification, for example, maximum exposure to individual issuers and the maximum percentage of the portfolio that can be invested in any single economic sector or industry. Other guidelines may reflect various principles important to the investor, including environment, social, and governmental ratings and limits or prohibitions on certain industries such as firearms or tobacco.

Often guideline limits are established relative to the benchmark rather than absolute limits. For example, the limit on sector concentration might be no greater than twice the benchmark weight. The policy may be written to define tolerances of portfolio risk relative to the benchmark using Greek sensitivities, stress-test and scenario results, or various risk parameters such as value at risk, conditional value at risk,[2] or ex ante tracking error.

10.3.4 Measurement and Review

For an individual investor, measurement and review can be as simple as having accounts with decent analytical reporting and monitoring the reports. For an institution, a well-developed risk-management program will foster a culture of risk management by having clearly defined procedures involving reporting and review at regular frequencies. The rest of this chapter focuses on measuring investment risk, but operational risks such as trade or settlement errors and data or system errors can be just as costly and therefore are important to monitor.

10.3.5 Management and Mitigation

A sophisticated pretrade compliance process can prevent guideline breaches (either inadvertent or intentional). Yet, risks still arise either through routine trading or through passive breach. For example, a portfolio manager may choose to shift from a position in one currency into a position in another currency. If the guidelines are to avoid non-base-currency exposure risk, this requires simultaneously selling the first currency and buying the second to pay for the new position, it also requires adjustment of the forward contract hedges. Alternatively, some clients of global portfolios prefer to have *currency overlay specialists* manage currency risk. However, as a third party, the currency manager may not be immediately aware of changes in portfolio exposure, and therefore, the investor and manager may agree that the manager is responsible for maintaining the exact currency profile of the benchmark. When the benchmark profile changes, an exposure is created—this can result in a *passive* breach because no action of the portfolio manager created the exposure. Nonetheless, it is the portfolio manager's responsibility to adjust the hedge per the IMA. Some asset managers have a rigidly designed process that automatically adjusts currency hedges, and the process therefore becomes the responsibility of the operations department.

Other examples of passive breaches that can arise without portfolio manager actions are credit and liquidity risk limit breaches. If IMAs or the portfolio manager's internal risk policies limit the portfolio weight of low-liquidity positions or weak credits, passive breaches can occur as a result of falling market liquidity or credit deterioration. When this happens, it is the responsibility of the portfolio manager to reduce the offending positions to bring the portfolio back into compliance. Often a risk or compliance manager has the responsibility to make sure this takes place.

10.4 GREEKS AND EXPOSURE MEASUREMENT

As we saw in Chapters 8 and 9, the value of a convertible is a function of the equity price, credit spread, interest rate, and stock volatility. Changes in these metrics result in changes in the value of a convertible, but the relationships are not linear, and different models calculate different sensitivities to inputs.

The primary Greek sensitivities are as follows:

- *Delta:* The sensitivity of the value of the convertible to changes in the equity price.
- *Gamma:* The sensitivity of delta to changes in the equity price.
- *Vega:* The sensitivity of the value of the convertible to changes in stock volatility.
- *Rho:* The sensitivity of the value of the convertible to changes in risk-free interest rates.

- *Omicron:* The sensitivity of the value of the convertible to changes in credit spread.
- *Theta:* The sensitivity of the value of the convertible to changes in the time to maturity.

Calculation of these metrics is only part of the task of analyzing the risk. For example, the risk of delta is realized as a result of a decline in stock price. A way to measure the magnitude and likelihood of such a decline is to use the stock volatility. Therefore, the equity risk is the volatility times the delta. However, this is mitigated by the asymmetry of the convertible as measured by gamma.

Therefore, a more complete expression of equity risk would be as follows:

$$\text{Delta} \times \text{equity volatility} - \text{gamma} \times \text{equity volatility}^2/2$$

Similarly, credit, rate, and volatility risks can be measured as follows:

Credit risk:	Omicron × credit spread volatility
Interest-rate risk:	Rho × interest rate volatility
Volatility risk:	Vega × volatility of volatility

Chapters 11 and 12 describe the calculation and use of these metrics for individual convertibles and for the relative exposure of portfolios to benchmarks. The reason to calculate and to compare these values is to identify the greatest risks and avoid having more than the desired exposure either in aggregate or to individual companies. A common risk control is to limit individual position deltas and average portfolio deltas to ranges consistent with the overall strategy. The range can be defined on an absolute basis, but it is also helpful to define it relative to a benchmark because portfolio delta can swing significantly in bull or bear markets.

10.5 MACROECONOMIC AND SYSTEMATIC RISKS

Every few years there is a bear market when it seems as though the entire market is in freefall. Although some more financially stable companies may fall less than others, very few stocks avoid the throes of a general market rout. Such times expose the systematic risks: beta to the broad equity market and financial leverage.

In normal markets, some stocks are moderately correlated or even uncorrelated with the general ebb and flow of the broad market—responding primarily to the idiosyncratic drivers of return specific to the companies. Such drivers might be progress in the development of a new drug or the launching of some new technology. But when the entire market is retreating, such considerations take a back seat to the threats to the entire economy, and companies that normally have little correlation with the broad market suddenly show a high degree of correlation. This is an important consideration in managing risk because modern portfolio theory suggests that while idiosyncratic risks can be diversified away, systematic risk cannot. The mathematics of quantifying systematic and idiosyncratic risk are discussed in Section 11.11.4.

A silver lining of bear markets is that they provide information about the correlations of a particular industry or company with the broad market. Risk managers can study the anatomy of meltdowns and have a better understanding of the relative return of various asset classes—notably convertibles—over the course of a downturn. For more information on this topic, please visit www.AdventCap.com/Book/SupplementaryMaterial.

10.6 FUNDAMENTAL VALUATION

Equity fundamentals are valued and expressed primarily via price/earnings (P/E) ratio or price/earnings-to-growth (PEG) multiples while credit fundamentals are valued and expressed as interest rate spreads over a risk-free rate.

10.6.1 Equity Derating and Rerating

According to the P/E ratio, a stock is worth its earnings per share (EPS) times its P/E multiple. Companies with better growth prospects and less risk tend to be rewarded with higher P/E multiples. De- or rerating is simply the change in the P/E multiple, and this occurs when future earnings expectations or company leverage changes. Similarly, a PEG[3] model can be used that measures the P/E ratio per unit of expected EPS growth. As the perception of growth fluctuates, the de or rerating occurs via changes in the PEG ratio. In either the P/E or PEG model approach, risk management involves measuring two processes: an earnings process (either EPS or EPS growth) and a valuation process (either P/E ratio or PEG ratio). Both processes can be estimated using historical data—adjusted to reflect any structural changes such as acquisitions or legal disputes—to establish a mean and variance. The inherent risk in the stock then can be estimated by combining the earnings and valuation processes. Furthermore, as 2021 has clearly demonstrated to investors, higher levels of long-term earnings growth give stocks an effective "duration" to interest rates. Therefore, significant fluctuations in interest rates have caused stock prices, and therefore P/Es to fluctuate. Unprofitable firms with expected earnings in the distant future have been the most affected by rising interest rates.

10.6.2 Credit Spread Widening

Credit spreads can also rerate, either literally in terms of an agency upgrade or downgrade or in terms of a change in the credit spread derived from market prices. A credit transition matrix provides a macro approach to determine the probability of rerating, and a market credit surface can help determine how much a rerating would change credit spreads. In this case, the credit process is defined independently from the company's equity process. However, for a convertible, it is often necessary to link the two to understand how credit moves in relation to the equity. This can be done in two ways, either by using a leverage-based transition matrix (where changes in stock price affect credit spread through corporate leverage) or by modeling the credit as a function of the equity using a structural model (such as the Merton model).

10.7 EX POST RISK AND PERFORMANCE RATIOS

Risk and performance metrics can be categorized based on whether they describe past (ex post) performance or potential future (ex ante) performance. One way to think about risk is to consider historical performance. While this is a bit like driving by looking in a rearview mirror, it can be useful in describing historical relationships among portfolios, indices, and other determinants of return. It also tells an investor whether past risks turned out to be rewarding. If a portfolio is managed according to a consistent strategy, the strategy implies how a portfolio might perform under certain circumstances in the future. Examples of ex post values include maximum drawdown, volatility, beta, Jensen's alpha, Sharpe ratio, Sortino ratio, Treynor ratio, information ratio, tracking error, Modigliani[2] risk-adjusted return, and Brinson active return.

Market Drawdown Performance

The US stock market has had several routs since 2000: the dot-com bubble burst in the spring 2000, the 9/11 attacks of 2001, the correlation meltdown of 2005, the Great Financial Crisis of 2008–2009, the taper tantrum in the fall 2018, and the COVID-19 market collapse early in 2020. It is informative to weigh the total return of an investment during these specific events relative to key indices such as the S&P 500 Index. For fixed-income investments, it is also informative to look at periods of rising interest rates in order to determine downside risk during such trends. For example, from the February 2020 high on 2/19/20 to the trough of the COVID pullback on 3/23/20, the S&P 500 fell 33.9%, while the V0A0 convertible index fell 25.6%. In the GFC, from 8/28/08 to 3/09/09, the S&P 500 fell 47.1%, while the V0A0 fell 33.5%. Both of these examples show that convertibles draw down significantly less than equities, despite equity-like long-term performance.

Maximum Drawdown Performance

The maximum drawdown, or maximum negative cumulative return, usually occurs during a period of market decline. But not always: for example, long-volatility strategies suffered during 2017, whereas risk assets performed well, and short-volatility strategies suffered during the "volmaggedon" of early 2018, whereas other asset classes had relatively smooth sailing.

Volatility

Volatility measures price movement during a specific time frame. Whereas upside volatility is generally favorable, something that advances quickly (or instantaneously) can retrace its gains quickly. Volatility is calculated by taking the standard deviation of returns of daily, weekly, monthly, or intra-day data and then multiplying by the square root of the number of periods in a year. For monthly data, this is 12 periods, weekly is 52, daily 252 (the usual number of business days per year), and hourly 1,638 (252 × 6.5). (The New York Stock Exchange is open 6.5 hours from 9:30 a.m. to 4 p.m.) For example, as of 12/31/2020, twenty-year trailing annualized daily volatility of the V0A0 Convertible and the S&P 500 indices is 12.2% and 20.4% respectively. This comparison shows that convertibles are significantly less volatile than equities despite comparable to superior performance.

Beta

Beta describes how much an investment moves relative to an index—typically the local country large-cap index such as the S&P 500 or a global index such as the MSCI All Country World Index (ticker ACWI, sometimes referred to verbally as "Akwee"). It represents the *slope* if the return of the investment and return of the index were plotted on an XY scatter diagram and can be calculated by taking the covariance of the two-return series divided by the variance of the index return series. Some analysts use excess return series (backing out the risk-free rate), but this does not change the outcome (the two methods are mathematically equivalent). Beta is similar to correlation in that it describes correlated movement between the investment and the index, but it also explains the magnitude of the correlated movement of the investment relative to the index. For example, as of 12/31/2020, the twenty-year trailing beta of the V0A0 Convertible index to the S&P 500 is 0.5098. This tells us that, at the index level, convertibles have about half as much systematic risk as equities.

Correlation (R^2)

Correlation describes the degree to which an investment moves in the same direction as an index, but unlike beta, it does not necessarily describe the magnitude of the co-movement. An asset that moves 1% when an index moves 2% could be perfectly correlated (correlation = 1), but its beta would be 0.5 because it only moves half as much. As of 12/31/2020, the twenty-year trailing correlation of the V0A0 Convertible index to the

S&P 500 is 0.849. This tells us that convertibles directional movement is similar to equities, however this metric tells us less about the magnitude of movement relative to the index than beta.

Alpha

Alpha describes the excess return of an investment relative to an index. It backs out any correlated returns between the investment and the index using beta, and the residual is alpha, which can be either positive or negative. It can also be thought of as the annualized intercept in a linear regression model of asset to index returns. For example, as of 12/31/2020, the twenty-year trailing alpha of the V0A0 Convertible index to the S&P 500 is 4.69%. This tells us that convertibles have significantly higher return than equities relative to their systematic risk.

Fama-French Sensitivities

Like beta to a market index, Fama-French metrics determine the beta of a portfolio to valuation using the book-to-market ratio (high minus low [HML]) and market capitalization (small minus big [SMB]) based on a 1993 study published by Eugene Fama and Kenneth French.[4] More recent studies have extended the set to include profitability (robust minus weak [RMW]), research investment (conservative minus aggressive [CMA]), and momentum. To determine the historical betas, multiple regression analysis is performed using the time series of returns of the portfolio and indices representing the return of the broad market, the return of small-cap companies minus the return of large-cap companies, the return of growth companies minus the return of value companies, and so on. Excel provides a convenient tool for performing multiple regressions in the analytical tool pack. Using 20 years of daily data as of 12/31/2020, convertible (V0A0 index) multifactor market beta (to the Russell 3000 index) is 0.4664, SMB multifactor beta (to Russell 2000 minus Russell 1000 indices) is 0.1652, and the HML multifactor beta (to Russell 3000 Value minus Russell 3000 Growth indices) is –0.1991. Therefore, convertible portfolios are likely to outperform when growth is outperforming value or when small-cap stocks outperform large-cap stocks. In 2015, when

Fama and French extended their three-factor model to five factors, the model suggested that small, value, and profitable companies should deliver higher returns, but the succeeding five years saw large-cap growth deliver the best returns.

Sharpe Ratio

The Sharpe ratio, named after Nobel laureate William Sharpe, describes the excess return of an investment (over the risk-free rate) divided by the volatility of the investment. It describes how efficiently an investment earned its return relative to the actual risk (with risk defined as volatility). As of 12/31/2020, the twenty-year trailing Sharpe ratios of the V0A0 Convertible index and the S&P 500 are 0.71 and 0.34 respectively. This tells us that convertibles have about twice as much excess return per unit of volatility as equities.

Treynor Ratio

The Treynor ratio is similar to the Sharpe ratio except that instead of dividing excess return by volatility, it divides by just the systematic risk, beta. It describes how efficiently an investment earned its return relative to the systematic risk taken (ignoring idiosyncratic risk). For example, as of 12/31/2020, the twenty-year trailing Treynor ratios of the V0A0 Convertible index and the S&P 500 are 14.45% and 5.65% respectively. This tells us that convertibles have about 2.5 times as much excess return per unit of systematic risk as equities.

Sortino Ratio

The Sortino ratio is also similar to the Sharpe ratio except that instead of dividing excess return by volatility, it divides by only the downside volatility. The idea behind this is that volatility is only bad if it is to the downside. This metric highlights the downside protection of convertibles. As of 12/31/2020, the twenty-year trailing Sortino ratios of the V0A0 Convertible index and the S&P 500 are 0.919 and 0.435, respectively. This tells us that convertibles have had about 2.1 times as much excess return per unit of downside risk than equities.

Risk-Adjusted Return, M^2

This metric was proposed in a paper by Franco Modigliani and his grand-daughter Leah Modigliani,[5] which is why it is often referred to as the *Modigliani-Modigliani* or M^2 *metric*. It is used to compare the return of two investments of differing risks. It multiplies the return of the first investment by the ratio of the volatility of the second investment to the first. When the second investment has more volatility, it results in a risk-adjusted return that is higher than the actual return. For example, as of 12/31/2020, the 20-year trailing Risk Adjusted Returns (using S&P 500 volatility as the base volatility) of the V0A0 Convertible index and the S&P 500 are 14.5% and 7.0% respectively. This tells us that convertibles have had about 2.1 times as much risk adjusted return as equities. Alternatively, it can be calculated by taking the Sharpe ratio times index volatility and then adding back the risk-free rate. These two calculations are mathematically equivalent. One criticism of the model is that a risk-adjusted return is never actually earned, "You can't eat risk-adjusted return," but it is an approximation of the return if the size of the first investment had been adjusted using leverage to match the volatility of the second. Generally, convertibles have higher risk-adjusted returns than other asset classes. This metric also can be calculated using other divisors (beta ratio, downside volatility ratio, etc.).

Tracking Error

Tracking error measures the degree to which a portfolio return deviates from an index. It is the annualized standard deviation (or volatility) of the difference in return between the portfolio and index. Tracking error reveals how closely a portfolio manager hugs a benchmark.

Information Ratio

Information ratio is similar to the Sharpe ratio except that instead of dividing excess return by volatility, it divides by the tracking error. It helps answer the question, how efficient was the active share (differences in portfolio composition from the index) in generating excess return per unit of portfolio return deviation from the benchmark. A portfolio that outperforms the index with a high tracking error and a low information ratio may be taking excessive benchmark risk with insufficient outperformance to justify the deviation.

Brinson Active Return

Brinson active return measures how much of a portfolio's outperformance or underperformance is attributable to the individual positions selected or to allocations of capital to groups such as sector, industry, region, credit quality, and so forth. These metrics help explain relative performance over a particular period of time. The percentage returns, contribution to total return, and average weights are calculated for all positions in both a portfolio and an index for a period of time. This requires knowing the constituents of an index. Often it is possible to use subindex data instead. Start by calculating the return of each group (sector, region, etc.) relative to the overall index. The allocation alpha is calculated for each group by summing for all groups, the product of the portfolio excess weight (which may be positive or negative) and the relative return to the overall index. The selection alpha is calculated by summing for all groups, the product of the index weight and the difference in return between the portfolio and the index, group by group.

Unfortunately, these two values do not add up to the total difference in return. Therefore, a third value is calculated called *interaction* that is the difference in weight multiplied by the difference in return. The sum of all three values within a particular group is called the *total active return*. Whereas these values are quite helpful in understanding performance, weights based on total investment do not really reflect the way risk is allocated across the groups. For convertibles, it is helpful to recalculate average weights using one of three historical metrics—delta weights, beta-delta weights, credit-adjusted beta-delta weights—in order to calculate risk-adjusted Brinson metrics. For more information on this topic including numeric examples, please visit www.AdventCap.com/SupplementaryMaterial.

10.8. EX ANTE METRICS

Although it is useful to know the ex post risk and return metrics, it is still like looking in the rearview mirror. The risk that really matters is what could happen to the value of investments in the *future*. Ex ante metrics attempt to provide a reasonable and unbiased view of what could happen in the future based on what is known today. While there is an attempt to be forward looking, some ex ante models rely on past information such as correlations, volatility, and covariance. Some of the key ex ante metrics that do not use backward data are the Greek and cross-Greek sensitivities, active share, and diversification scores. Metrics that can incorporate some historical relationship parameters are stress tests, value-at-risk metrics, and ex ante tracking error.

Stress Testing/Scenario Analysis

A common risk-management tool is the stress test. It involves revaluing portfolios under different sets of assumptions and then assessing the potential outcome. Simple stress tests involve stressing a single factor *instantaneously*. For example, a stress might assume stock prices 20% below current levels and determine the change in the fair value of the positions. Generally, such stress tests are intentionally simplistic, ignoring the effect that an instantaneous 20% stock price plunge might have on the credit spread of the company or even the implied volatility of options on the stock. Yet, such a simple stress test may isolate equity sensitivity.

In contrast, some stress tests do incorporate multiple factors of return. Our firm uses a multifactor stress testing process that shocks equities in proportion to their volatility, then shocks the credit spread as a function of the equity stress, then changes the implied equity volatility as a function of the equity and credit-spread changes, then changes the risk-free interest-rate curve to reflect how it might respond to changes in all three other factors, and lastly cheapens or richens the convertible relative to the new theoretical fair value.

Value at Risk (VaR) and Conditional Value at Risk (CVaR)

VaR is intended to capture all portfolio risks, create a probability distribution of returns, and determine a near-worst-case estimate of loss given a fixed level of certainty and period of time. There are several related metrics that use a similar approach but provide different kinds of information, such as

CVaR, which provides an average expected loss beyond a given certainty threshold, as well as metrics allocating portfolio VaR to individual positions. VaR can be calculated on a single position, but the sum of position-level VaRs is greater than portfolio VaR assuming that the correlation between positions is less than 100%. Therefore, portfolio VaR is sometimes assigned on a pro-rata basis. Alternatively, marginal VaR is a value that explains how VaR changes with and without the position in the portfolio. The portfolio VaR is calculated both with the position and again substituting cash for the actual position and taking the difference between the two. Positions that have negative correlation to the rest of the portfolio—such as a hedge or countercyclical stock—can have negative marginal VaR because including such positions reduces portfolio risk. Typically, the lower the correlation with the rest of the portfolio, the less marginal VaR is from the position. Positions then can be evaluated on the basis of expected return versus marginal VaR. The higher this ratio, the greater is the potential positive effect on risk-adjusted returns.

Parametric VaR

The parametric approach to calculating VaR starts with a variance-covariance matrix to identify the relationship all positions in a portfolio have to each other. It is typically used only with stocks and straight bonds that tend to have a linear relationship with one another because it imperfectly evaluates the VaR of asymmetric instruments such as options and convertibles. There are, however, variations that accommodate the optionality of convertibles. One such is the *delta-gamma method*.

Historical VaR

Historical VaR involves using actual returns for each position or factor of return. It can be as simple as using the historical returns of positions in a portfolio. For example, a one-day 95% VaR can be calculated by multiplying the last 200 days' worth of daily returns for all positions in a portfolio by position weight and taking the tenth worst observation. This method has the same shortcoming as parametric VaR in that it ignores the dynamic nature of position asymmetry. A position that had little asymmetry on the tenth worst day in the historical observation period may have strong asymmetry at the time of VaR estimation. A more robust approach to a historical VaR process is to use historical factors of return (such as underlying stock price, interest rates, credit spreads, and volatilities) and then perform full theoretical revaluations using those historical factor returns. This will capture the potential future effect of historical factor movements in the context of the current properties of the convertible.

Monte Carlo VaR

Monte Carlo VaR is a third approach to calculating VaR. It is similar to historical revaluation VaR and also involves full revaluation based on factor movements. In this approach, instead of using n days of actual historical factor movements, each factor is modeled stochastically or parametrically—generating large sets of correlated random factor return sets (often the analysis requires more than 50,000 and as many as a million or more iterations)—and then revaluing each position (or the portfolio as a whole) using the factor return sets. Instead of looking at the tenth worst out of 200, 95th percentile VaR would be based on the fifth percentile worst return, that is, the 2,500th worst out of 50,000 or the 50,000th worst out of 1 million. Conditional VaR (CvaR) is a related metric that averages all the observations *beyond* a certain threshold. Both values are meaningful and complementary. VaR is meant to complete the statement, "We have 95% (or 99%) confidence that we will not lose more than x," whereas CVaR is meant to complete the statement, "If a left-tail event occurs (one with only a 5% or 1% likelihood), the expected loss is y." Elaborate and expensive systems are marketed to institutional investors to calculate these values, but these metrics also can be calculated in a spreadsheet. Go to www. AdventCap.com/Book/SupplementaryMaterial for some simple examples and instructions for building Monte Carlo processes in Excel.

Multifactor Horizon VaR

Multifactor horizon VaR is a third approach to VaR that is particularly useful for a convertible portfolio because it is a parametric-revaluation approach that uses a range of discrete equity index movements based on index volatility, the beta of each stock to the index, and credit spread, interest rate, and volatility values based on the observed relationships to equity prices. This allows a 95th or 99th percentile loss, as well as upside and downside comparisons, to be determined with relatively few calculations. It can even capture non-linear relationships between the factors, but it does not generally capture basis risk between factors without explicitly stressing those relationships. In other words, such an approach can specify that credit-spread change and volatility change increase geometrically with respect to equity price, but it does not allow for the possibility that relationships will be larger or smaller than the model predicts. For more information on this topic, please visit www.AdventCap.com/Book/SupplementaryMaterial.

Ex Ante Beta

Ex ante beta is a measurement of expected future systematic relative risk. A convertible is like a chameleon in that it can change its appearance based on its environment. In a bull market, it can look like a stock; in a bear market, it can look like a bond. When calculating the beta of the convertible to a stock index, if the delta has been high, the beta is likely to be high as well; if the delta has recently been low, the beta is likely to have recently been low as well. It is more useful to project what the beta will be in the future, and past correlation can be combined with current delta to obtain a more accurate ex ante beta.

Ex Ante Tracking Error

Ex ante tracking error measures expected future relative performance volatility. It is obtained through the use of a Monte Carlo process that models both the portfolio and the benchmark. Tracking error is calculated for every iteration in the Monte Carlo set, and the mean of all observations is the expected tracking error.

Active Share

Active share measures the deviation in portfolio holdings relative to an index. It is not a stochastic metric, subject to uncertain future return behavior, but rather a value that is known with certainty that suggests the opportunity for tracking error and positive or negative alpha. Active share is the sum of the difference in weight between the portfolio and the benchmark. In a convertible portfolio, it is useful to calculate active share using issuer weights because some issuers have multiple convertibles. It is also useful to substitute delta weights for capital weights because a manager may hold an overweight in a high-delta position and an underweight in a low-delta position rather than an equal weight in two convertibles from the same issuer.

Diversity Score

Diversity score[6] was developed by Moody's Investors Service as a way to analyze the level of diversification in a collateralized loan obligation, but it is a concept applicable to any portfolio. It is similar to active share in that it is a measurement based on the weights of current holdings rather than historical covariance of return. The metric is less useful when correlations rise—as they do in financial crises—and diversification temporarily is less effective in reducing risk. Use of the metric was criticized as encouraging risky behavior, yet, properly understood, it remains a useful data point. The metric is expressed on a scale of 1–100, with 100 meaning that the portfolio contains equal weights of 100 uncorrelated assets.

Liquidity Score

Liquidity score reflects the factors affecting the liquidity of a security. Advent Capital Management tracks eight values that combine to form a liquidity score, including lead dealer ranking (some dealers are better at providing liquidity than others), issue size, market capitalization of underlying, underlying equity volume, bond volume (tracked by the Trade Reporting and Compliance Engine [TRACE]), bid-ask spread, holders' data (a widely held bond tends to have greater liquidity, and being the biggest holder of an issue runs increased liquidity risk), and the stock borrow rate.

Creditworthiness

Approximately 75% of US convertibles are unrated.[7] Therefore, it is important for convertible managers to develop an internal credit-rating process.

Key ratios such as interest coverage and leverage are useful as well as market observations of the convertible's implied credit spread relative to the credit spreads of various credit indices. Beyond these basic metrics, it is often productive to focus on indicators *ignored* by most investors.

We recommend that investors focus on manipulation of reported earnings—which is a clue to deteriorating creditworthiness as well as to the prospects for the underlying common shares to underperform. "Think outside the box!" is a favorite admonition of co-author Tracy Maitland.

It's a red flag when company announcements emphasize *adjusted* earnings that are higher than generally accepted accounting principles (GAAP) earnings. Some cynics refer to such characterizations as "earnings before bad stuff." *The Economist* reported that "97% of firms in the S&P 500 in 2017 presented at least one metric of their performance in a way inconsistent with Generally Accepted Accounting Principles."[8] A large discrepancy between adjusted earnings and GAAP earnings is an especially strong warning—as is a pattern of chronic adjustments that raise earnings.

A quick indicator of earnings quality is the earnings footnotes in the 1,700 company reports in The Value Line Investment Survey. Companies with numerous footnotes that reflect exclusion of negative items from earnings per share are much more likely to be overstating earnings than companies with few or no earnings per share footnotes, based on our experience.

A useful clue to earnings quality in US disclosure is cash income taxes paid. Companies that report earnings while paying little or no cash income taxes may be pretending to be profitable in their reported accounts while telling the truth to the Internal Revenue Service. The *New York Times* reported that Enron had paid no cash income taxes in four of five consecutive years prior to its collapse.[9] Prior to Enron, perhaps the most famous bankruptcy in American history was the Penn Central railroad in 1970. The late Benjamin Graham noted in *The Intelligent Investor* that prior to its bankruptcy, Penn Central had been "paying no income taxes to speak of for the past 11 years!"[10]

Inconsistencies between cash flow and reported earnings are also warning signs. It is an especially powerful warning if these gaps are widening. An extremely useful aspect of disclosure in first-world countries is that audited accounts are nearly always *mathematically* accurate, no matter how creative (or even fraudulent) the accounting; deceit is enabled by *mislabeling* numbers. Diligent research can expose such trickery. A typical manipulation involves booking sales that have not taken place. This boosts reported revenues—but provides no cash flow. The collapses of Enron in 2001 and WorldCom in 2002 are extreme examples of misclassifying reported numbers.

We cannot overemphasize that accounting machinations do not affect cash flow; Enron and other fraudulent companies were hemorrhaging cash on their way to bankruptcy—while reporting "earnings." As co-author Tracy Maitland observes, "You cannot fake cash in the bank. We know of no US public companies faking cash in our decades of experience."

Red flags are easy to identify, but experience tells us that they are often ignored—which creates opportunities for sophisticated investors to avoid, hedge, or short the securities of companies with such warnings. On the positive side, cash flow often begins to recover *before* reported earnings—which may enable alert investors to anticipate securities price recoveries earlier than the market in general. Free cash flow relative to debt is a useful credit metric. Free cash flow relative to enterprise value is a useful valuation tool. Review Section 2.4 for further discussions of creditworthiness and the implications for convertibles.

10.9 RISK SYSTEMS AND SERVICES FOR CONVERTIBLE INVESTORS

While scores of fintech companies offer risk-analysis systems that are multi–asset class, relatively few provide useful tools for investors in convertibles—and even those rarely provide all the functionality a convertible risk manager would like to have. A few of the more popular are Black-Rock (Alladin), Bloomberg (OVCV and MARS), Imagine, KYNEX, and Monis. Each of these systems has valuation and risk tools, whereas some also provide performance attribution, trading, accounting, compliance, and back-office settlement and account-reconciliation tools. Other companies, such as MSCI RiskMetrics, offer turnkey risk-reporting services, yet, even some of the more well-known providers fail to capture the unique nature of certain convertible arbitrage positions that are delta neutral. Convertible risk managers should never be completely dependent on a single system and should be prepared to build internal models to validate, supplement, and in some cases replace third-party systems and services.

10.10 CONCLUSION

The financial risk management discipline has developed dozens of models for evaluating position and portfolio risk and return from various perspectives. They are all meaningful given their framework and assumptions, and can all provide useful insight and color to investors. Some take significant processing power to calculate, and person-hours to model properly, while others are easier to calculate. Many commonly used metrics show that convertibles compare favorably with other asset classes in terms of risk and risk-adjusted returns. For convertibles, the Greek exposure metrics discussed in Section 10.4 provide the most specific measurements relative to market factors. These are examined more fully in Chapters 11 and 12.

ENDNOTES

1. https://www.investopedia.com/terms/e/environmental-social-and-governance-esg-criteria.asp.

2. https://www.investopedia.com/terms/c/conditional_value_at_risk.asp.

3. https://www.investopedia.com/terms/p/pegratio.asp.

4. E. F. Fama, K. R. French, "Common Risk Factors in the Returns on Stocks and Bonds," *Journal of Financial Economics* (1993) 33: 3–56.

5. Franco Modigliani, "Risk-Adjusted Performance," *Journal of Portfolio Management* 1997 (Winter): 45–54.

6. https://www.investopedia.com/terms/d/diversityscore.asp.

7. Venu Krishna et al., *The Convert Renaissance*, Barclays Equity Research, New York, December 14, 2020, p. 61.

8. https://www.economist.com/business/2020/02/20/business-and-the-next-recession.

9. David Cay Johnston, "Enron Avoided Income Taxes in 4 of 5 Years," *New York Times*, October 6, 2020, https://www.nytimes.com/2002/01/17/business/enron-s-collapse-the-havens-enron-avoided-income-taxes-in-4-of-5-years.html.

10. Benjamin Graham, updated by Jason Zweig, *The Intelligent Investor* (New York: HarperCollins, 2006), p. 234.

CHAPTER 11

Understanding Sensitivity to Equity Prices: Delta, Gamma, and Vega

It's Greek to me.

—*Shakespeare*[1]

11.1 EQUITY-SENSITIVITY METRICS

Convertibles are usually more sensitive to the underlying stock price than to bond factors, and delta and gamma are the metrics, the so-called called "Greeks," that explain the sensitivity of the price of a convertible to changes in the price of the underlying stock. Understanding delta and gamma is essential to comprehending the asymmetry of convertibles. This chapter should convey more understanding of the meaning and usage of these metrics than poor Casca's understanding of the writing of Cicero in Shakespeare's *Julius Caesar* when Casca declared "It's Greek to me."

Delta represented rates of change in ancient Greek—precisely the meaning of delta in contemporary convertibles: the rate of change of the market price of a convertible relative to the rate of change of the market price of the underlying equity. The Talmud records that *gimel* ("gamma") is like a rich man giving his neighbors alms (*daleth*, "delta"). For convertible investors, gamma increases equity participation (*daleth*, "delta") as the stock goes up, thereby increasing gains while decreasing participation as the stock goes down, thereby mitigating losses.

Equity price movement (at least the portion of it that is not trending) is characterized as volatility, and the way that convertibles profit from volatility is known as *vega*. The word *volatility* derives from the Latin word *volare*, which means "to fly." While volatility can cause some

311

assets to "fly" higher, it also implies increased risk of loss. Vega is a Latin letter used in financial mathematics to describe the sensitivity of an asset value to the volatility of another asset. Vega is also the name of one of the brightest stars in the sky. Lucy Maude Montgomery, author of *Anne of Green Gables*, wrote of "Vega of the Lyre," "I've always loved it. It's my dearest among the stars" and described it as the symbol of faithfulness in the heavens,[2] which is an apt analogy for a property that faithfully produces positive returns in convertible securities when market volatility rises and other asset values decline. The positive return in such an instance reflects the fact that, *ceteris paribus*, increased volatility means that an out-of-the-money call option has a greater probability of exceeding the strike price prior to maturity. Vega exemplifies what author and investor Nassim Nicholas Taleb calls "Things That Gain from Disorder"[3] because it measures the relationship between value and uncertainty.

11.1.1 Basics of Delta and Gamma

Delta describes the sensitivity of a convertible to small changes in the price of the underlying stock. A convertible with a delta of 50% would be expected to increase in value by 1% on a 2% move in the underlying equity price. Delta becomes less accurate in response to bigger stock price changes because gamma causes delta to dynamically increase and decrease with upward and downward changes in the stock price. Delta also changes as equity prices approach or move away from the conversion price and as the convertible approaches a call or maturity.

When the underlying stock price is declining, the conversion premium rises because of the tendency of the convertible bond to stabilize near bond value rather than track the stock far below the conversion price. A high conversion premium suggests lower odds of the convertible expiring in the money. Delta decreases when the conversion premium rises. When the stock price rises, the conversion premium falls, the delta increases, and the odds increase that the convertible will expire in the money and ultimately will be converted (see Figure 11.1).

Gamma describes the change in delta as the equity price changes. It is useful to regard delta as a measurement of *speed* and gamma as a measurement of *acceleration*. A delta of 50% means that a convertible value

Figure 11.1 Evolution of delta and convertible value with respect to stock price

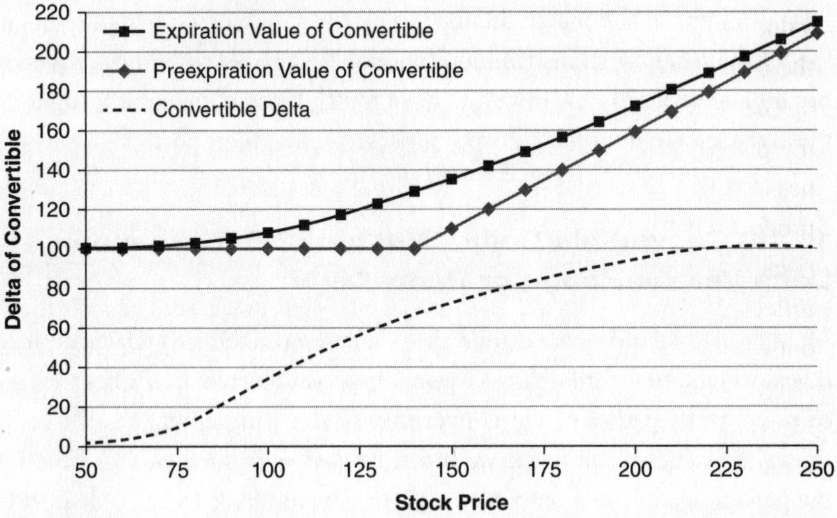

Source: Advent Capital Management.

increases 0.5% per 1% increase in the stock price. A gamma of 1.0 means that delta accelerates 1 delta point for every 1% increase in the stock price. Hence, a second 1% rise in the equity price would cause the convertible to rise 0.51% because the delta would have increased by 1 delta point to 51%, a third 1% movement would cause the convertible to appreciate 0.52%, and so on.

11.1.2 Volatility and Its Constant Companion, Time

Volatility creates the possibility of stock price movement in proportion to the square root of time to expiration of the option. Put another way, volatility (in unit terms) generally scales with the square root of time, not time. An implicit assumption of the Black-Scholes-Merton (BSM) option pricing model is that volatility is essentially constant over the life of an option. Since development of the BSM model, the constant-volatility assumption has been discredited, yet, the model is still in use, thanks to the development of volatility smile, skew, and surfaces. In other words, options are still priced using a constant-volatility assumption, but different volatilities are fed into the model for options of differing degrees of moneyness (described in Section 8.4.1.2) or different term because modeling dynamic volatility in a valuation model is challenging.

An important concept related to volatility is *tail risk*, which refers to the *left* tail in a normal distribution function associated with low-frequency but high-severity losses. Investors have multiple techniques for mitigating these risks, including the incorporation of vega in their portfolio analysis.

11.1.3 Convertible Delta: Outright or Participation Delta Versus Hedge or Parity Delta

Most investors hold a convertible as an *outright* (unhedged) position. Such investors tend to regard delta as a *participation* delta that describes the rate of price participation of the convertible in stock price changes. In order to define participation delta, we must use *hedge* or *parity delta*, which is the percentage of the *conversion ratio* that would have to be sold short to hedge the bond's equity sensitivity.

$$\text{Participation delta} = \frac{\text{hedge delta}}{(1 + \text{conversion premium})} \quad (11.1)$$

Convertible arbitrageurs who hedge the exposure to the equity by shorting the stock may like the structure of the convertible and/or may anticipate rising volatility of the underlying stock to increase the value of the convertible. Arbitrageurs may be positive, neutral, or negative on the prospects for the stock—but they are always hedged and almost always leveraged. Convertible hedging is explored in detail in Chapter 13.

Figures 11.2 and 11.3 show the evolutions of participation delta, hedge delta, and gamma of a two- and a five-year convertible, each with a conversion premium of 40%, coupon of 2%, and implied volatility of 30. The chart in Figure 11.2 shows that the participation delta is lower than the hedge delta and that the delta of the two-year convertible is lower than the delta of the five-year convertible. Delta represents both a rate of price change relative to the stock and also a probability of the convertible expiring in the money. If the stock price is considerably lower than the conversion price and the conversion premium is high, then having less time to maturity means that there is a lower probability of the stock appreciating enough for the convertible to be in the money by expiration—hence the convertible has a lower delta.

Figure 11.2   Evolution of participation delta and hedge delta with respect to stock price change and term to maturity

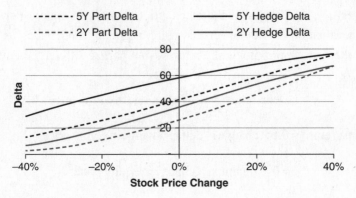

Source: Advent Capital Management.

The hedge delta is higher than the participation delta because it pertains only to the conversion value of the bond, whereas the participation delta pertains to the value of the convertible bond as a whole. Figure 11.3 shows that the gamma of a shorter-term convertible is generally higher than the gamma of a longer-term convertible except when the conversion premium is very high and the likelihood of reaching the conversion price is *de minimis*. Unless otherwise specified, we will use the term *delta* to refer to the outright or participation delta of the convertible.

Figure 11.3   Evolution of gamma with respect to stock price change and term to maturity

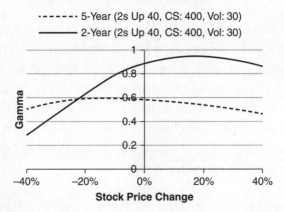

Source: Advent Capital Management.

11.1.4 Deciphering Delta and Gamma Returns

There are two primary ways to estimate future price returns of a convertible relative to changes in the stock price. One is to simply perform a full reevaluation of the convertible using a pricing model such as BSM. The other is to approximate the return using partial differential equations (PDEs):

$$\text{Delta return} = \text{delta} \times \text{change in equity price} \qquad (11.2)$$

$$\text{Gamma return} = 0.5 \times \text{change in delta} \times \text{change in equity price} \qquad (11.3)$$

$$= 0.5 \times \text{gamma} \times \text{change in equity price}^2 \qquad (11.4)$$

So, for convertible with a 50% (0.5) delta and 0.5 gamma, a 20% increase in equity price return would lead to a total return of:

$$\text{Delta return}: 20\% \times 0.5 = 10\%$$

$$\text{Gamma return}: (20\%)^2 \times 0.5 = 2\%$$

$$\text{Total return}: 10\% + 2\% = 12\%$$

Similarly, on a 20% decline in stock price return would be:

$$\text{Delta return}: -20\% \times 0.5 = -10\%$$

$$\text{Gamma return}: (-20\%)^2 \times 0.5 = 2\%$$

$$\text{Total return}: -10\% + 2\% = -8\%$$

While delta and gamma give us excellent ex ante (forward-looking) measurements for projecting the price movements of convertibles relative to their underlying equities, there is also an ex post technique to evaluate the actual effective delta, which helps validate the ex ante models by calculating a beta of the convertible relative to its underlying stock. The beta is the slope of the regression of convertible returns and equity returns, which is calculated by dividing the covariance of convertible and equity returns by the variance of the equity returns.

$$\text{Ex post delta} = \frac{\text{covariance}(\text{convertible returns, equity returns})}{\text{variance}(\text{equity returns})} \qquad (11.5)$$

Since delta changes as the equity price fluctuates, it is best to calculate ex post delta using only short periods of time when changes in the equity price are small.

11.2 AN EXAMPLE OF CONVERTIBLE EQUITY SENSITIVITY: THE FIVE-YEAR LIFE OF THE RESTORATION HARDWARE 0% OF 2020

Figure 11.4 shows the returns of the stock and the Restoration Hardware convertible from the issuance of the convertible (both rebased to an initial value of 100) in the chart on the left. The chart on the right plots the bond's cumulative total return since inception on the y-axis versus the total return of the stock since inception on the x-axis.

11.2.1 Year 1: Falling Stock Price and Delta

The Restoration Hardware convertible was issued with a conversion premium of 23%. This gave the convertible a delta of 54% and a gamma of 0.54. Within one year, the stock fell −73% and the price of the convertible declined −28%. The initial delta times the stock price change would have resulted in a decline of −39.4% in the price of the convertible:

$$\text{Delta return} = \text{stock price change} \times \text{delta} - 73\% \times 0.54 = -39.4\%$$

Figure 11.4   Timeline of total return of Restoration Hardware 0% 2020 convertible and common stock

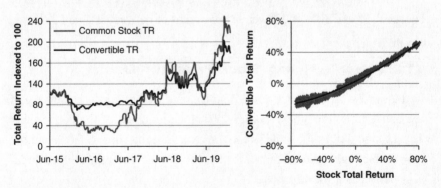

Data: Bloomberg.

The convertible held up better than suggested by the initial delta because gamma reduced the delta on the downside:

$$\text{Delta and gamma return} = \text{stock price change} \times \text{delta}$$

$$+ \text{stock price change}^2 \times \frac{\text{gamma}}{2}$$

$$= -73\% \times 0.54 + -73\%^2 \times \frac{0.54}{2}$$

$$= -25.0\%$$

The market value of the convertible declined 3 percentage points more than the –25% calculated by the delta and gamma return model presumably because deterioration in the company's creditworthiness reduced the investment value of the convertible bond independent of its conversion premium. Yet, the market loss for the convertible was only 38% of the decline in market value of the stock. Gamma had reduced the delta from 54% to 13%, so the participation of the price of the bond relative to the equity price at its nadir was only 13%.

11.2.2 Year 2: Low Delta

During the second year, the stock remained depressed, and therefore, the delta remained low. In the first seven months of the second year, the convertible appreciated 2.7% while the stock fell another –12.6%, but in the last five months of the year, the stock rebounded 157%, though it was still well below its price at the time the convertible was issued, and therefore, the convertible recovered only 11% in the year as a whole because it had ex ante deltas of between 5% and 30% and lower ex post deltas of between 0% and 23%.

11.2.3 Year 3: Rising Stock Price and Delta

In the third year, the stock price doubled, and by the third anniversary of the convertible, the stock was up 45% since issuance of the convertible. The ex ante delta rose to 84% and the ex post delta rose to 64%, and the convertible had captured 60% of the stock appreciation during the three-year period as a whole.

11.2.4 Year 4: Balanced Convertible

The fourth year saw the stock decline a further −17.0%. The convertible had a higher delta at this point and participated in 60% of the decline (−10.4%). From issuance to the peak, the convertible had captured 66% of the upside while participating in only 30% of the downside of the stock: 2.2 times ex post upside/downside ratio.

11.2.5 Year 5: Low Premium, High Delta

During the fifth year, the stock rose from $116 to more than $190 in late October, before settling in the $170s in November. The conversion premium shrank from 18.5% to 1.3% at the peak, and the outright delta rose from 54% to 94%. See Figure 11.4 for the fluctuations in the total return from the convertible during this turbulent period when the convertible briefly traded with a single-digit conversion premium (as an equity surrogate).

11.3 UNDERSTANDING ASYMMETRY OF RETURNS

Asymmetric performance relative to the return of the underlying common stock is a key rationale for investing in convertibles. A convertible with a higher upside/downside ratio exhibits more positive asymmetry.

11.3.1 Ex Ante Asymmetry

Delta and gamma can be used to project the expected upside/downside ratio of the prospective returns of a convertible relative to changes in the price of the underlying stock. If a stock has a delta of 50% and a gamma of 0.5, the upside/downside ratio (on a ±20% move in the stock price) would be:

$$\text{Ex ante upside / downside ratio} = \frac{\text{upside return}}{\text{absolute value of downside}}$$
$$= \frac{12\%}{8\%} = 1.5 \qquad (11.6)$$

11.3.2 Ex Post Asymmetry

On an ex post basis, actual returns may be biased toward the upside or downside. In such a case, we use upside and downside participation rates:

$$\text{Ex post upside / downside ratio} = \frac{\text{upside participation rate}}{\text{downside participation rate}} \quad (11.7)$$

While gamma is a useful metric for projecting forward, historical upside and downside returns are used to illustrate ex post asymmetry. Table 11.1 analyzes the returns of the Restoration Hardware convertible bond over the first four years of its existence.

Table 11.1 shows that as Restoration Hardware stock declined, the delta declined considerably from issuance to the end of the first year. While gamma fell, it remained significant at 0.32. Despite a lackluster second year, gamma increased to 0.53. Then, as the stock price recovered in year three and eventually rose significantly above the conversion price, delta surged. In year four, both delta and gamma fluctuated because of the considerable volatility in the stock price. Although delta ended lower in the fourth year, gamma remained resilient, as occurs in the final year of a convertible that is trading close to parity. The ex post upside/downside

Table 11.1   Delta and Gamma of Restoration Hardware 0% 2020

	Chg. Stock Price	Delta	Gamma	Ex Post Delta Range	Participation
Issuance	N/A	54	0.54	N/A	N/A
Year 1	−73%	13	0.32	9–58	35%
Year 2	125%	30	0.53	0–23	11%
Year 3	166%	80	0.32	8–65	46%
Year 4	−17%	55	0.66	27–79	61%
Issuance to low	−74%				30%
Issuance to peak	68%				66%

Data: Bloomberg.

ratio then would be the participation rate on the upside divided by the participation on the downside:

$$\text{Ex post upside/downside ratio} = \frac{66\%}{30\%} = 2.2$$

11.4 HOW ACCURATELY DO DELTA AND GAMMA PROJECT POTENTIAL RETURNS?

Table 11.2 compares the upside and downside return estimates using partial differential equations (PDEs), delta, and gamma versus a full revaluation BSM model and the constant elasticity of variance model (CEV). The PDEs do a reasonable job of estimating returns and asymmetry but are necessarily imprecise. For example, at issuance, the downside return estimate on a −25% move in the underlying stock is −12.06% using PDEs, which is very close to the −12.13% estimate using BSM full revaluation. Yet, the PDE estimate is 148 basis points (bp) less than the −13.54% reduction in value predicted by the CEV model. The upside PDE estimate of 15.44% is 52 bp higher than the BSM full revaluation result of 14.92% but is 298 bp less than the CEV full revaluation calculation of 17.42%.

11.4.1 Speed: Gamma Varies

One reason for the disparity between the PDE estimate of return and the full reevaluation estimate is because gamma varies as the stock price increases and decreases. Typically, gamma is at a maximum if the expected expiration value of the stock price (based on the upward time-dependent drift) is equal to the expected conversion price. If the stock price is below the conversion price, gamma typically increases with an increase in the stock price. If the stock price is above, gamma typically decreases with an increase in the stock price.

The instantaneous change in gamma is called *speed*, meaning that it is the first derivative of gamma with respect to a change in the stock price. While it is useful to know whether rising stock prices will increase or decrease the amount of gamma, investors should remember that this metric is itself dynamic and can swing from positive to negative as the stock price

Table 11.2 Return Estimates of Restoration Hardware 0% 2020 Convertible Using Historical Delta and Gamma and Upside/Downside Ratios on ±25% Stock Returns

	Delta and Gamma (PDEs)			Full Revaluation (BSM)			Full Revaluation (CEV Using Elasticity of 0.65)		
	Upside	Downside	UD Ratio	Upside	Downside	UD Ratio	Upside	Downside	UD Ratio
Issuance	15.44%	−12.06%	1.28	14.92%	−12.13%	1.23	17.42%	−13.54%	1.29
Year 1	4.25%	−2.25%	1.89	3.50%	−2.98%	1.17	2.86%	−1.76%	1.63
Year 2	9.16%	−5.84%	1.57	8.60%	−6.47%	1.33	8.80%	−5.64%	1.56
Year 3	21.00%	−19.00%	1.11	20.66%	−18.74%	1.1	23.44%	−20.92%	1.12
Year 4	15 19%	−11.81%	1.29	15.28%	−11.78%	1.3	17.77%	−13.52%	1.31

Source: Advent Capital Management.

Figure 11.5   Booking Holdings 0.9% of 2021 speed: the change in gamma versus a change in price as of October 9, 2019

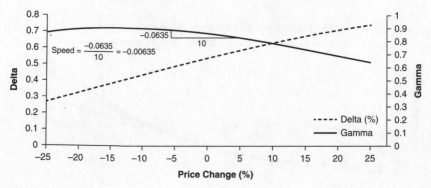

Data: Bloomberg.

crosses above or below the present value of the expected conversion price. Figure 11.5 depicts the speed of a Booking Holdings convertible.

Speed can be used to fine-tune expected returns, but it is so dynamic that the outcome is not always better. We can see in Figure 11.6 for the Fortive (FTV) 0.875% convertible of 2022 that the delta-gamma estimate of downside price is significantly greater than the full reevaluation approach on a –30%, –40%, or –50% decline in the stock price. In fact, the downside participation is nearly 2.25 percentage points too deep on a –50% move. Incorporating speed of 0.32 in the estimate greatly improves the accuracy of the downside. However, incorporating speed on the upside makes the price estimate *less* accurate. The delta-gamma model price of 111.9 is about 1% higher than the full revaluation price of 110.9, but the incorporation of 0.32 speed pushes the estimate in the wrong direction—raising the upside price to 114.1. Figure 11.6 demonstrates that the bifurcation of speed into upside and downside improves the accuracy only on the upside—and only slightly—while *impairing* the accuracy on the downside.

Full reevaluation is certainly best practice when it comes to calculating stress-test results, yet, PDEs still provide meaningful information—especially when summing them across an entire portfolio or a subset of positions. For example, a portfolio manager armed with a portfolio weighted-average delta of 50%, weighted-average gamma of 0.60, and

Figure 11.6   Fortive 0⅞ of 2/15/22 participation delta of 14, gamma 0.41, speed 0.32 (upside speed 0.01 and downside speed 0.62) as of October 10, 2019

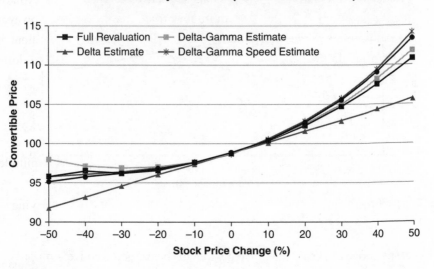

Absolute Devision of Delta from Full Revaluation	−50	−40	−30	−20	−10	0	10	20	30	40	50	Mean
Delta Estimate	4.00	2.73	1.62	0.75	0.18	-	0.21	0.85	1.80	3.36	5.20	1.89
Delta-Gamma Estimate	1.02	0.48	0.18	0.05	0.01	-	0.01	0.05	0.09	0.15	0.18	0.20
Delta-Gamma Speed Estimate	0.04	0.02	0.03	0.01	0.00	-	0.01	0.02	0.12	0.35	0.80	0.13
Delta-Gamma Up/Dn Speed Estimate	1.09	0.50	0.23	0.07	0.01	-	0.01	0.04	0.09	0.12	0.13	0.21

Data: Bloomberg.

speed of 0.01 could perform a quick back-of-the-envelope calculation: on a 20% rise in stock prices, the portfolio would rise 10% on delta, 2.4% in gamma, and 0.4% in speed (increase in gamma), for a total appreciation of 12.8%. Although a full reevaluation stress test would reveal similar (perhaps slightly more accurate) information, it would not tell the portfolio manager that after that 20% rise, the portfolio delta would be 64% and the gamma would be 0.8.

11.5 THREE APPROACHES TO SETTING THE MAGNITUDE OF UPSIDE/DOWNSIDE ANALYSIS

While gamma measures instantaneous convertible asymmetry, we have also described asymmetry in the preceding examples in terms of ex post upside and downside participation rates. These ex post calculations were based on total returns over a period of time and incorporated the effects of yield and other factors. These metrics are useful for explaining the past but inherently inaccurate for projecting the future. However, it is possible to calculate the effect of an instantaneous movement in share price on the price of a convertible. The three approaches to doing this are:

1. A fixed-magnitude movement in underlying equities, that is, ±20%

2. A beta-adjusted change in equity prices given a fixed-magnitude movement in an equity index

3. A change in equity prices based on the volatility of underlying equities

Furthermore, the upside and downside values can be estimated using PDEs, or they can be calculated using a full-revaluation methodology. For a thorough review of these three methods, visit www.AdventCap.com/ SupplementaryMaterial.

11.5.1 Which Beta and Volatility?

Both beta and volatility can be calculated over different time periods on an ex post basis and can also be estimated on an ex ante basis. For a complete review of the topic, visit www.AdventCap.com/Book/Supplementary Material.

11.5.2 Cross Greeks: Measuring the Exposure to Factors That Change Delta and Gamma

Stock option mathematicians have considered cross Greeks for many years. For a full review of delta and gamma cross Greeks and how they apply to convertibles, please visit www.AdventCap.com/Supplementary-Material.

11.6 PORTFOLIO DELTA WEIGHTS

It is useful to know weights of convertibles on a delta-adjusted basis. A delta weight of a position is the weight of the position in the portfolio times the delta of the convertible:

$$\text{Position delta weight} = \text{weight}\% \times \text{delta of position} \qquad (11.8)$$

The delta weight of an economic sector in the portfolio would be the sum of all the delta weights for the positions:

$$\text{Issuer A delta weight} = \text{sum}_{\text{all issuer A cvts}}(\text{position delta weight})$$

$$\text{Sector B delta weight} = \text{sum}_{\text{sector B cvts}}(\text{position delta weight})$$

Assuming the same weights as the equity portfolio and index and an average portfolio delta of 20% and an average index delta of 30%, we can estimate portfolio effect of delta of −1%, an index effect of −1.125%, and a relative return of +0.125%:

$$\text{Delta adjusted return} = \text{sum of delta weight} \times \text{sector equity return} \qquad (11.9)$$

$$\text{Portfolio delta-adjusted return} = 20\% \times -20 \times 25\% = -1\%$$

$$\text{Index delta-adjusted return} = 15\% \times 30 \times -25\% = -1.125\%$$

$$\text{Relative return} = -1\% - (-1.125\%) = 0.125\%$$

The comparison of delta weights allows us to examine how a convertible portfolio differs from an index with greater clarity than if we simply considered weights because delta weight incorporates the sensitivity of the convertibles to equity returns. Delta weights therefore can be summed, or *bucketed*, in different dimensions. It is useful to know sector delta weights and also useful to bucket delta weight by industry, credit quality, region, and even issuer.

Some issuers have multiple convertible bonds outstanding, which usually have been issued at different times and with different terms and therefore have significantly different deltas. Booking Holdings (formerly Priceline.com) issued three different convertible bonds between 2012 and 2014, and as of June 30, 2017, their deltas ranged from 50.66% to 99.57%, as illustrated in Table 11.3.

Table 11.3 Sample Portfolio and Index Weights

Bond	Delta	Index Weight	Portfolio Weight	Index Delta Weight	Portfolio Delta Weight
Booking 1% 2018	99.57	0.79	0	0.79	—
Booking 0.9% 2021	50.66	0.96	0	0.49	—
Booking 0.35% 2020	86.31	0.61	2.21	0.53	1.91
Total		2.36	2.21	1.81	1.91

Data: Bloomberg.

If we assume that a convertible index contains all three Booking Holdings issues and a portfolio contains only the 2020 maturity, we can compare the relative portfolio weight of Booking Holdings, as well as the relative portfolio delta weight. While in the example, the portfolio is underweight the index by $0.15\%(2.36\%-2.21\%)$, it is actually delta *overweight* versus the index by 10 delta points $(1.81\%-1.91\%)$. Therefore, on a 25% advance in the stock price of Booking Holdings, one would have expected $25\%\times0.10=0.025\%$, or 2.5 bp of outperformance of the portfolio versus the index due to delta.

The average delta of the multiple convertibles of a single issuer can be determined by dividing the sum of delta weights by the sum of the weights:

$$\text{Average delta} = \frac{\text{sum of delta weights}}{\text{sum of weights}} \qquad (11.10)$$

The average delta weights for the portfolio and index are as follows:

Average delta of Booking Holdings in portfolio = 76.69

Average delta of Booking Holdings in index = 86.31

11.6.1 Comparing Overweight and Underweight Positions by Issuer

It is important to monitor the weights of individual portfolio positions. Table 11.4 provides an example of a comparison of the weight, delta weight, and beta-delta weight of three issuers with a total of seven out-

Table 11.4 Relative Issuer Weight, Delta Weight, and Beta-Delta Weight

	Portfolio			Benchmark			Difference		
	Sum of Weight	Sum of DWt	Sum of BDWt	Sum of Weight	Sum of DWt	Sum of BDWt	Sum of Weight	Sum of DWt	Sum of BDWt
Tesla	1.21	0.34	0.27	2.92	1.27	1.02	(1.70)	(0.93)	(0.74)
TSLA 1 1/4 03/01/21	1.21	0.34	0.27	0.92	0.26	0.21	0.30	0.08	0.07
TSLA 2 05/15 /24				1.32	0.72	0.57	(1.32)	(0.72)	(0.57)
TSLA 2 3/8 03/15/22				0.68	0.30	0.24	(0.68)	(0.30)	(0.24)
Deutsche Wohnen	2.01	0.36	0.14	1.26	0.25	0.09	0.75	0.12	0.04
DWNIGY 0.325 07/26/24				0.63	0.12	0.05	(0.63)	(0.12)	(0.05)
DWNIGY 0.6 01/05/26	2.01	0.36	0.14	0.63	0.12	0.05	1.38	0.24	0.09
Twitter	1.73	0.65	0.55	1.42	0.35	0.30	0.31	0.29	0.25
TWTR 0 1/4 06/15/24	1.73	0.65	0.55	0.80	0.30	0.25	0.94	0.35	0.30
TWTR 1 09/15/21				0.62	0.05	0.05	(0.62)	(0.05)	(0.05)

Source: Advent Capital Management.

standing convertibles. With three bonds in the index, Tesla had a combined weight of 2.92% of the benchmark but only 1.27 delta points on a delta-weighted basis. The portfolio is significantly underweight on both a notional and delta-weighted basis, resulting in a notional difference of 1.70% of the portfolio and 0.93 delta points. This means that we would expect that a 20% increase in the market price of Tesla stock would generate 18.6 bp more for the benchmark than for the portfolio $(20\% \times 0.93)$. This could be a significant source of positive or negative alpha for the portfolio relative to the benchmark depending on the performance of Tesla stock relative to other underlying stocks in the portfolio or benchmark.

Although the portfolio is underweight Tesla, it appears to be overweight Deutsche Wohnen and Twitter, which presumably represents the fundamental views of the investor; however, the investor should be aware that if Deutsche Wohnen and Twitter stocks underperform by 20%, it could cost 2.4 and 5.8 bp, respectively, of relative performance $(0.12 \times -20\%, 0.29 \times -20\%)$ *just considering weight and delta in isolation and ignoring gamma or other factors.*

11.6.2 Portfolio Exposure by Weight, Delta Weight, and Beta-Delta Weight

Investors often deliberately overweight sectors. Other investors are *bottoms up* and do not pick sectors per se, yet, the consequences of bottoms-up analysis usually favor one sector or another. In Table 11.5 we can see that technology is the largest sector by weight in the portfolio but is only the second largest weight in the benchmark, behind financials. However, on a delta-weight basis, the technology sector stands out as the highest delta weight for both the portfolio and the benchmark (8.27 versus 6.01). Media is underweight for the portfolio versus the benchmark (6.00 versus 7.19), and industrials are overweight on a notional basis (7.22 versus 5.76), but industrials are actually slightly underweight on a delta-weight basis (1.04 versus 1.11). In aggregate, the portfolio has somewhat more delta than the benchmark (21.96 versus 17.27) and beta delta (22.37 versus 18.50). This tells us that on a 10% increase in the S&P 500, we would

Table 11.5 Sector Weight, Delta Weight, and Beta-Delta Weight

	Portfolio			Benchmark			Difference		
	Sum of Weight	Sum of DWt	Sum of BDWt	Sum of Weight	Sum of DWt	Sum of BDWt	Sum of Weight	Sum of DWt	Sum of BDWt
Cash	3.65						3.65		
Consumer Discretionary	6.96	1.68	1.74	3.91	0.88	0.77	3.05	0.80	0.97
Consumer Staples	2.43	0.74	0.49	2.00	0.59	0.39	0.43	0.15	0.10
Energy	2.06	0.07	0.08	5.92	0.55	0.73	(3.86)	(0.48)	(0.65)
Financials	17.48	2.26	2.21	30.10	2.81	2.63	(12.62)	(0.54)	(0.42)
Healthcare	15.45	3.56	3.63	15.20	2.71	3.10	0.25	0.84	0.52
Industrials	7.22	1.04	1.23	5.76	1.11	1.32	1.46	(0.07)	(0.09)
Materials				0.34	0.00	0.01	(0.34)	(0.00)	(0.01)
Media	6.00	1.78	1.92	7.19	2.07	2.43	(1.19)	(0.29)	(0.51)
Technology	33.00	8.27	8.89	26.72	6.01	6.60	6.28	2.26	2.29
Telecommunications	2.62	1.45	1.30	2.00	0.48	0.42	0.62	0.97	0.88
Transportation	1.32	0.29	0.25	0.86	0.06	0.09	0.46	0.23	0.16
Utilities	1.81	0.82	0.62				1.81	0.82	0.62
Grand Total	100.00	21.96	22.37	100.00	17.27	18.50	0.00	4.68	3.87

Source: Advent Capital Management.

expect the portfolio to outperform the benchmark by approximately 39 bp. Thus:

$$\frac{(22.37-18.50)}{100}\times 10\% = 39\,\text{bp}$$

The "Difference, Sum of Delta Weights" column in Table 11.5 makes it easy to estimate the effect on relative return of a 10% increase in the market prices of the stocks of any sector. For example, a 10% sector equity return would lead to outperformance of 23 bp in technology, 10 bp in telecommunications, and 8 bp in each of the healthcare and consumer discretionary sectors but underperformance of 3 to 5 bp in media, energy, and financials—each of which was calculated as the difference in delta weight times 10%.

The purpose of the weight, delta weight, and beta-delta weight comparisons is to compare exposure by portfolio bucket (sectors, regions, etc.) These metrics can be further adjusted to incorporate the downside protection and additional upside participation owing to gamma. Also, rather than using beta, which is a measure of systematic risk, a measure of total risk such as relative volatility can be used. For a thorough discussion of weight adjustments, please visit www.AdventCap.com/SupplementaryMaterials.

11.6.3 Gamma Returns in a Portfolio Context

When estimating the return of a portfolio, it is tempting to multiply the average stock return squared by average gamma times one-half, but this misses a significant part of the portfolio gamma return. Imagine a portfolio of stocks that has a weighted-average return of 0%. Some stocks are up, some are down, but, on average, the returns are flat. The portfolio return, of course, would be 0%, *ceteris paribus*. However, a portfolio of convertibles on those underlying stocks would have a positive return (even if none of the convertibles paid interest) because gamma will increase the positive returns of convertibles with rising stocks and decrease the negative return of convertibles with falling stocks. The effect of positive gamma on returns is always positive whether stocks are rising or falling. Therefore, even if the average underlying stock return is zero, one would expect a positive convertible portfolio return due to gamma. This effect is not captured in the average gamma minus average stock return calculation. It is a function of gamma *and the dispersion* of underlying stock prices.

11.7 EFFECT OF DISPERSION ON CONVERTIBLE PORTFOLIO ANALYSIS

Dispersion is a lack of uniformity in a result set. *Dispersion of return* is a measurement of the degree to which stock prices deviate from the mean. For example, in an equal-weighted portfolio of two stocks that return 5% and 15%, the average return is 10%, and therefore, the mean absolute deviation is 5%. This value can be measured for broad indices and indicates whether stocks are moving together with a high degree of correlation or idiosyncratically with a low degree of correlation.

Dispersion was highest in the three years with the highest equity market returns in Figure 11.7: 1999, 2009, and 2020. In such strong markets, the more highly levered and more cyclical stocks tend to outperform defensive or stable stocks—and because price movements are so sharp, dispersion is at a maximum. In the 2020 market advance, however, more highly levered value stocks initially underperformed the stocks of growth companies (some of which benefited from economic conditions during the COVID-19 pandemic).

Sharp *declines* in the stock market often cause lower levels of dispersion, as described in the old maxim, "In a crisis, all correla-

Figure 11.7   Dispersion of the S&P 500 and VXAO underlying equities, 1995–2020

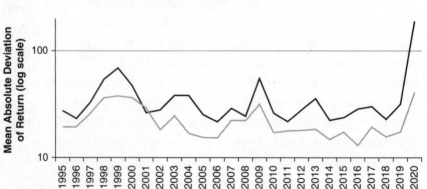

Data: Bloomberg.

Figure 11.8   VXAO and S&P 500 dispersion relative to the average daily VIX, 1995–2020

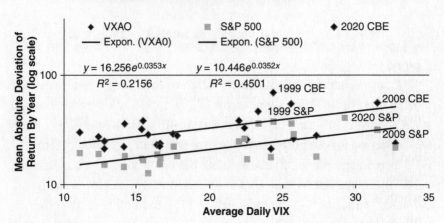

Data: Bloomberg.
CBE, Convertible Bond Underlying Equity

tions go to one." Figure 11.8 shows dispersion year by year relative to the average daily S&P 500 Volatility Index (VIX). Although the trend lines for both convertible dispersion and S&P 500 dispersion are upward sloping, there are some years when high levels of the VIX are accompanied by lower levels of dispersion (e.g., 2008). The stocks underlying convertibles have high dispersion, possibly due to the idiosyncratic uncorrelated growth rates of companies that issue convertibles.

11.7.1 Estimating Total Gamma Return Using Dispersion

The dispersion of returns has an important implication for convertibles that is absent in all other asset classes. Because gamma returns are dependent on the magnitude of movement of each stock, and because gamma returns increase exponentially with magnitude, any amount of dispersion of stock price returns *increases* total expected gamma returns.

There are two ways to arrive at total gamma returns: (1) either take the sum of all gamma returns of each position independently, or (2) add together the gamma returns on an average price movement plus the gamma returns due to dispersion as follows:

Method A: Sum of all positions $\left(\text{stock price return}^2 \times \dfrac{\text{average gamma}}{2} \right)$

$$\text{Method B: } \left(\text{Average stock price return}^2 \times \frac{\text{average gamma}}{2} \right) +$$
$$\left(\text{dispersion}^2 \times \frac{\text{average gamma}}{2} \right)$$

Consider an example in which there are two energy-sector convertibles in a portfolio. The energy sector is down −25% on average, but one stock is down −10% and the other is down −40%. The *dispersion*—which we can define for our purposes as the mean absolute deviation of return— is 15 percentage points. Mean absolute deviation measures the absolute value of the amount by which each observation deviates from the mean. Because the mean of −10% and −40% is 25%, each of these two observations deviates 15 percentage points from the mean. Let's assume that both positions are equal weight and that each has a gamma of 0.5.

Dispersion = mean absolute deviation

$$= \text{average} \left[\text{absolute} \left(\text{return}_i - \text{return}_{\text{index}} \right) \right] \qquad (11.11)$$

$$= \text{average} \left\{ \text{absolute} [-10\% - (-25\%)], \text{absolute} [-40\% - (-25\%)] \right\}$$
$$= 15\%$$

Method A would be to calculate the exact gamma return for each position, which would be $(10\%)^2 \times 0.5 / 2 = 25$ bp for one position and $(-40\%)^2 \times 0.5 / 2 = 400$ bp for the second position. Multiplying these returns by the position weights results in a total gamma return of $2.125\% = 25\% \times 50\% + 4\% \times 50\%$.

Method B would be to calculate the portfolio gamma return on the average stock price movement and add to it the return from dispersion. In the example in which the two energy stocks moved exactly −25% (and dispersion therefore was zero), the expected gamma return was zero. Yet, in the second example, where the average stock is down 25%—but one stock is down −10% and the other is down −40%—dispersion would be 15 percentage points, and gamma return would be 2.125%. The return due to the average stock price return of −25% and the average gamma is 1.5625%. The incremental gamma return due to dispersion of underlying stock price returns is 0.5625%. The two added together result in 2.125%, which is the same result as obtained in method A. Granted, if the amount

Figure 11.9   Convertible return generated by gamma and change in underlying equity price

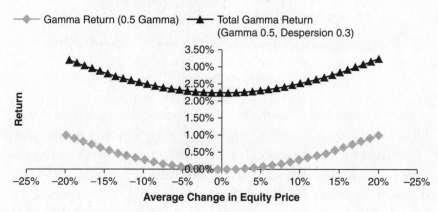

Source: Advent Capital Management.

of gamma differs between positions, the results of these two methods will diverge.

When the annual return of stocks is either highly positive or highly negative, the effect of dispersion gamma return tends to be small relative to that of the average-price-change gamma returns. Yet, in years when the average price change of stocks is near zero but dispersion is high, dispersion gamma returns can be substantially higher than the average-price-change gamma return. Figure 11.9 shows both average-price-change gamma returns and total gamma returns (including the effects of dispersion). The example is a typical balanced portfolio that starts with a delta of 55% and a gamma of 0.5. This means that for a 20% increase (or decrease) in equity prices, one would expect convertibles to appreciate (or depreciate) about 11% because of delta (20% change in equity prices × 0.55) and delta to increase (or decrease) by 0.10 because of gamma (which is a 20% change in equity prices × 0.5).

The reduction in delta on the downside cushions convertible returns by 1% and adds 1% to the upside, so the upside and downside returns become +12% and −10%. Furthermore, the dispersion of underlying stocks adds to both the upside and downside. If dispersion is 0.3, it adds ±2.25 percentage points to return, extending the projected upside to +14.25% and truncating the projected downside at −7.75%. Therefore, on a ±20% move, the total upside would be +14.25%, and the downside would be −7.75%.

$$\text{Dispersion return} = (\text{dispersion})^2 \times \text{gamma} \times 0.5 = 2.25\%$$

$$\text{Upside: } 11.0\% + 1.0\% + 2.25\% = 14.25\%$$

$$\text{Downside: } -11.0\% + 1\% + 2.25\% = -7.75\%$$

$$\text{Upside/downside ratio}: \frac{14.25\%}{-7.75\%} = 1.84$$

A skeptic might argue that the effects of dispersion are temporary. Take, for instance, the situation in which we have a portfolio with a target delta of 50% and a target gamma of 0.5. The fund manager owns two convertibles on two different stocks, each having a delta of 50% and a gamma of 0.5 and each having 50% weight in the portfolio. In the first period, one is up 25% and the other is down –25%, and in the next period, the stock returns revert back to their initial levels such that they both end the second month unchanged over a two-month period. Dispersion return would be positive in both months, but both the stock and the convertible would essentially be back to zero.

11.7.2 How Could Dispersion Return Only Be Positive?

There are three key parts to the answer. First, the weight of the positions at the end of the first period would be different. The weight of the advancing position would be significantly higher than the weight of the declining position, and as a result, portfolio delta would be higher. If no rebalancing were done, then the reversal in the second period would result in significant negative delta returns. If, for the two periods delta return is negative and total return is zero, then gamma returns must be positive. But, in reality, to maintain the target delta of 50%, active managers sticking to their discipline likely would rebalance positions at the end of the first month.

Second, if the stock prices reverted to their prior levels, the returns in the second month would not be ±25% for the two stocks. They would be +33.3% for the stock that declined and −20% for the stock that advanced. As a result of the rebalance, the position that declined in the first period might be larger, and the position that advanced in the first period might be smaller.

Third, gamma would have changed for both positions. Indeed, gamma might be lower on both the advancing and declining convertibles, necessitating the inclusion of a third convertible in the portfolio to restore the portfolio gamma to the 0.5 target level. An active manager maintaining gamma discipline would have factored this into the rebalancing in order to maintain target levels of both delta and gamma. The reward for consistent levels of gamma through rebalancing is that even if stocks oscillate back and forth, *if gamma levels are maintained, the net effect of dispersion will be positive, even if there is frequent reversion to the mean of stock prices.*

Therefore, calculation of sector or industry upside and downside adjusted deltas should include the effects of dispersion:

$$\text{Adjusted delta}_{up} = \frac{\left(\text{delta return}_{up} + \text{gamma return}\right)}{\text{average stock price change}} \qquad (11.12)$$

$$\text{Adjuster delta}_{down} = \frac{\left(\text{delta return}_{down} + \text{gamma return}\right)}{\text{average stock price change}} \qquad (11.13)$$

This is illustrated in Table 11.6 assuming a starting delta of 50%, gamma of 0.5, and dispersion of 25%.

Because dispersion is an annualized number, the inclusion of dispersion gives the analysis an implicit horizon of one year. Adjusting the horizon can be accomplished by multiplying the annualized dispersion by the square root of the relative period. In other words, if the desired horizon is just one quarter, one would multiply dispersion by the square root of one quarter (which is 0.5). So an annualized dispersion of 0.3 would be transformed into a quarterly dispersion of 0.15.

$$\text{Dispersion}_{horizon} = \text{Annualized dispersion} \times \text{horizon}^{0.5} \qquad (11.14)$$

Table 11.6   Adjusted Delta

Avg. Stock Price Change	Delta Ret	Gamma Ret (Avg. Chg.)	Gamma Ret (Disp)	Adj. Delta
20%	10.00%	1.00%	1.56%	62.8
−20%	10.00%	1.00%	1.56%	47.2

Source: Advent Capital Management.

11.8 INCORPORATING GAMMA RETURNS IN PORTFOLIO UPSIDE/DOWNSIDE METRICS

The principles of analyzing the delta and gamma of a single convertible are generally applicable when analyzing a portfolio or index of convertibles, with the exception of dispersion, as described in Section 11.7. The weighted-average delta of a portfolio gives a reasonable approximation of the degree of equity sensitivity. Delta weights and beta-adjusted delta weights measure portfolio equity sensitivity across sectors, regions, credit qualities, issuers, and other subsets:

$$\text{Portfolio delta weight}_{\text{sector1}} = \text{sum}_{\text{sector1}}\left(\text{position weight} \times \text{position delta}\right)$$

$$(11.15)$$

$$\text{Portfolio beta} - \text{delta weight}_{\text{sector1}}$$

$$= \text{sum}_{\text{sector1}}\left(\text{position weight} \times \text{position delta} \times \text{position beta}\right)$$

$$(11.16)$$

Comparing the portfolio beta-delta weight of a given sector versus the index beta-delta weight shows us whether the portfolio is relatively overweight or underweight a particular sector.

It is possible to be relatively underweight a particular sector on a capital-weight basis while being relatively overweight that same sector on a delta-weight basis if the deltas of the positions in the portfolio are significantly higher than the deltas of the positions in the index. Hence, the investor can create comparable or greater exposure to a sector while devoting less of the capital weight of the portfolio to that sector.

$$\text{Upside delta weight}_{\text{sector1}}$$

$$= \text{weighted average delta}_{\text{sector1}} + 0.5 \times \text{average gamma}$$

$$\times \left(\text{upside return} + \text{dispersion} \times \text{horizon}^{0.5}\right)$$

$$(11.17)$$

$$\text{Downside delta weight}_{\text{sector1}}$$

$$= \text{weighted average delta}_{\text{sector1}} - 0.5 \times \text{average gamma}$$

$$\times \left(-\text{downside return} + \text{dispersion} \times \text{horizon}^{.5}\right)$$

$$(11.18)$$

Effective delta can be estimated based on the change in delta due to gamma over the course of an upside or downside movement by using the assumed average stock price change and an assumed dispersion. Table 11.7 is based

Table 11.7 Upside and Downside Sector Delta Weights of Hypothetical Portfolio Versus a Benchmark

	Portfolio Sum of Weight	Sum of DWt	Sum of UpDWt	Sum of DnDWt	Benchmark Sum of Weight	Sum of DWt	Sum of UpDWt	Sum of DnDWt	Difference Sum of Weight	Sum of DWt	Sum of UpDWt	Sum of DnDWt
Cash	3.65								3.65			
Consumer Discretionary	6.96	1.68	2.37	0.98	3.91	0.88	1.24	0.53	3.05	0.80	1.14	0.45
Consumer Staples	2.43	0.74	0.98	0.50	2.00	0.59	0.77	0.41	0.43	0.15	0.21	0.09
Energy	2.06	0.07	0.27	-	5.92	0.55	1.08	0.01	(3.86)	(0.48)	(0.80)	(0.01)
Financials	17.48	2.26	4.01	0.52	30.10	2.81	5.52	0.10	(12.62)	(0.54)	(1.50)	0.42
Healthcare	15.45	3.56	5.10	2.01	15.20	2.71	4.08	1.34	0.25	0.84	1.02	0.67
Industrials	7.22	1.04	1.76	0.32	5.76	1.11	1.62	0.59	1.46	(0.07)	0.14	(0.27)
Materials					0.34	0.00	0.03	-	(0.34)	(0.00)	(0.03)	-
Media	6.00	1.78	2.38	1.18	7.19	2.07	2.72	1.43	(1.19)	(0.29)	(0.34)	(0.24)
Technology	33.00	8.27	11.57	4.97	26.72	6.01	8.42	3.61	6.28	2.26	3.16	1.36
Telecommunications	2.62	1.45	1.71	1.19	2.00	0.48	0.66	0.30	0.62	0.97	1.05	0.89
Transportation	1.32	0.29	0.42	0.16	0.86	0.06	0.13	-	0.46	0.23	0.29	0.16
Utilities	1.81	0.82	1.00	0.64				-	1.81	0.82	1.00	0.64
Grand Total	100.00	21.96	31.59	12.46	100.00	17.27	26.27	8.32	0.00	4.68	5.32	4.14

Sources: ICE BofA, Advent Capital Management.

on the initial weights and deltas in Table 11.5, adjusting for a gamma of 0.5 for the portfolio and 0.45 for the benchmark, annual dispersion of 0.3 for both the portfolio and the benchmark, and a horizon of one quarter.

In Table 11.7, the sum of the relative upside delta weights of 5.32 is 0.64 delta points higher than the sum of the relative delta weights of 4.68. Downside relative delta weight is 0.54 delta points lower than the relative delta weight of 4.68. These differences in upside and downside delta weights relative to the delta weight of the index reflect the higher gamma in the portfolio than in the benchmark (0.5 versus 0.45).

11.9 WHAT CAUSES EQUITY VOLATILITY?

Volatility describes the change or instability in the price of an asset; hence, volatility is influenced by anything that could affect the value of that asset. Following are brief descriptions of 10 popular models of stock valuation. The stochastic or probabilistic nature of every variable in each of the models means that valuation is subject to change as the inputs of each model fluctuate. Uncertainty, or instability in model inputs, creates valuation volatility. For the formulas associated with each model and descriptions of the volatility and stochastic nature of each input variable, visit www.AdventCap.com/Book/SupplementaryMaterial.

11.9.1 Price/Earnings Ratio

The *price/earnings (P/E) ratio* models a stock price as a function of price divided by earnings per share. The P/E ratio is also called the *earnings multiple* and is sometimes expressed as the more intuitive *earnings yield*, which expresses earnings per share as a percentage of share price. Equity analysts model future earnings and potential changes to the multiple (also called *rerating*) to project a target price for the stock. In an arithmetic sense, stock price volatility is a function of earnings per share volatility and P/E ratio volatility.

11.9.2 P/E-to-Growth (PEG) Ratio

The *P/E-to-growth (PEG) ratio* models a stock price as a function of its earnings growth and what the market is willing to pay for growth. Because a slight change in the earnings growth can have a large effect in the long run, changes in earnings growth or in the PEG ratio (which is based on the market's perception of future growth) have a large effect on price volatility.

11.9.3 Capital Assets Pricing Model

The capital assets pricing model (CAPM) was developed to explain the performance of individual stocks relative to the overall market or an index. Beta is a key component of the model. The beta of a stock relative to the index, which is the covariance of a stock to the index divided by the variance of the index, determines how much a stock price is expected to change given a change in the index. Beta is a measurement of both directional correlation (do the two things move consistently?) and magnitude (does the stock move more or less than the index?). But beta is not static; it can be high during market dislocations (as everything falls in tandem), and it can fall in more normal markets, especially if the stock is prone to reacting to idiosyncratic factors. When beta is low, alpha (the idiosyncratic return—either positive or negative) tends to dominate. Therefore, price volatility is a function of market or index returns, the volatility of beta, and the volatility of alpha.

11.9.4 Price/Book Ratio and an Old Saying in Banking: "The Balance Sheet Is the Income Statement"

The properties of the assets (loans) and liabilities (deposits) on a bank's balance sheet determine the bank's income. In the most basic case of a bank, the loans provide interest income (ultimately net of losses from defaults), and the deposits provide the funding for the loans. The primary source of profits is the resultant net interest income (minus loan losses). *Book value* is the value of assets minus liabilities, and some financial stocks can be valued as a function of the *price/book ratio*; hence, changes in book value may induce volatility. As recently as the 1950s, US banks reported balance sheets only, and it was necessary to subtract the prior year balance sheet figures (adjusted for dividends paid) in order to calculate income.

11.9.5 Earnings Leverage Model

The *earnings leverage model* says that the *enterprise value* (EV) of a company, including both stock market capitalization and the value of all the company's net debt, is equal to a multiple of the earnings before interest, taxes, depreciation, and amortization (EBITDA). If the stock price, and hence, the EV, declines, then leverage increases. If EBITDA falls, leverage also increases. Increased financial leverage increases stock price volatility. Ultimately, of course, EBITDA ignores the need for capital investing to replace physical assets that depreciate; for example, evaluating a capital-intensive business such as a railroad on EV/EBITDA might make the EV appear undervalued even if the company was cash-flow negative after replacing worn-out track and equipment. Hence, EV relative to free cash flow is a more realistic (if less popular) measure of financial leverage.

11.9.6 Discounted Dividend Model

The *discounted dividend model* says that a stock price is worth the net present value of all future dividend payments or, alternatively, the present value of a fixed number of future dividends plus the present value of a terminal stock price. Therefore, stock price volatility is a function of dividend volatility, as well as volatility in the discount rate and the volatility of earnings growth.

11.9.7 Equity Risk Premium Model

The *equity risk premium model* says that the market expects a return on a stock commensurate with its riskiness (volatility or market beta) over and above the risk-free rate. Therefore, stock price volatility is a function of the volatility of the risk-free rate and the risk premium.

11.9.8 Merton Model

The *Merton model* regards the stock as an option on the future earnings of the company over and above the level of debt. This framework uses the same stochastic process as is used in option valuation in the BSM model (presented in Section 9.2), except that expected future earnings is substituted for the stock price and the level of net debt is substituted for the strike price. In this framework, stock price volatility is a function of the cumulative standard normal distribution of future earnings. The model assumes fixed interest rates and fixed volatility as simplifying assumptions. Therefore, the Merton model implies that risk-free-rate volatility and earnings volatility are sources of price volatility.

11.9.9 Free-Cash-Flow Valuation Model or Operating Free-Cash-Flow (OFCF) Model

The *free-cash-flow model* regards the stock price as a function of earnings before interest less cash required for operations such as capital expenditures and working capital divided by the discount rate adjusted for the expected growth rate in OFCF. Therefore, price volatility is a function of any changes in cash flow, cash-flow growth, or the discount rate.

11.9.10 Cyclically Adjusted P/E (CAPE) Model

The *cyclically adjusted P/E model* suggests that the stock price is a function of long-term real earnings (trailing 10-year earnings adjusted for inflation) and the cyclically adjusted P/E. In other words, a stock price will gravitate toward its current earnings and its CAPE ratio. Therefore, price volatility is a function of changes in earnings and the relative valuation of the stock versus its CAPE.

11.10 VALUATION AND VOLATILITY DUE TO MARKET CONDITIONS

Value is not only a function of the 10 fundamental models we have described; it is also a function of market dynamics. There is an old saying that something is only worth what someone else is willing to pay for it—and this truism introduces the behavior of market participants into the equation. The following is a list of ways in which behavior affects volatility.

11.10.1 Active Versus Passive Participants

Whereas active investors pay close attention to at least some of the models listed earlier, passive broad market or index exchange-traded funds (ETFs) exist simply to buy or sell all securities in their mandate as money flows in or out. Passive investing may reduce volatility, but when a stock qualifies (or gets disqualified) from inclusion in an index, passive funds are forced to transact regardless of price—which *increases* volatility.

11.10.2 High-Frequency Traders (or Algos, Because They Use Algorithms)

The Dow Jones Industrial Average crashed 600 points in five minutes on May 6, 2010, and then recovered most of the 600-point loss in the next 20 minutes—an event that came to be called a *flash crash*.[4] Within two years, the US Justice Department had brought a 22-count indictment against a trader for *spoofing*—a practice of entering and then canceling fake orders in an effort to move markets. In two minutes on October 6, 2016, the British pound lost 6% versus the US dollar and then immediately recovered—possibly the result of a *fat-fingered trade* or an errant algorithmic trade. These and several other examples demonstrate the brief but shocking consequences of automated trading. In general, the increased trading volume created by algorithmic trading is thought to enhance liquidity and therefore reduce volatility. Yet, occasionally the algos create *more* rather than less volatility.

Because convertible bonds are almost exclusively traded by humans rather than computers, a flash crash in the convertible market seems inconceivable. Given that convertible trading often involves hedging, the convertible market benefits from increased liquidity of common stocks, yet, at the same time the convertible market is obviously susceptible to stock price dislocations—which may be a consequence of algorithms that enable buying in milliseconds when a large buy order is detected and equally quick selling in front of a significant sell order—as described in *Flash Boys*.[5]

Figure 11.10   Average and maximum VIX versus the volatility of the VIX by quarter (Q1 1990–Q1 2021)

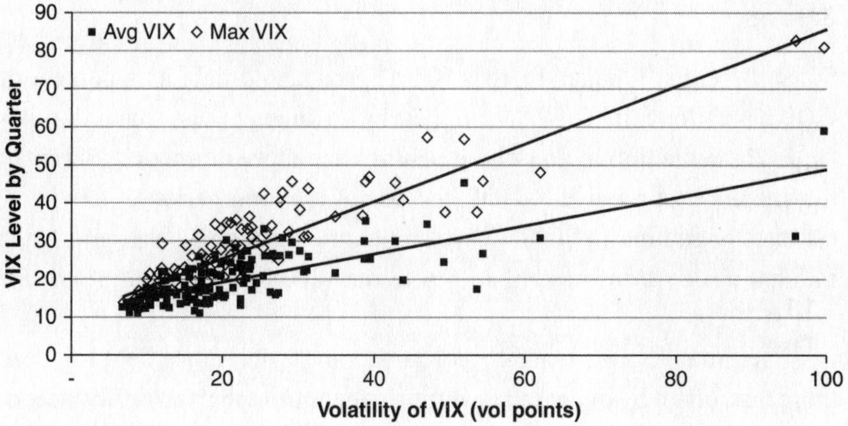

Data: Bloomberg.

11.10.3 Volatility Trading

The Volatility Index (VIX) quadrupled from its open at 12.5 on February 1, 2018, to more than 50 on February 6, 2018. Prior to the 2018 *volatility spike*, the index had had an unprecedented run of low volatility. The VIX had been less than 11 on 70% of the trading days over the prior nine months—despite the fact that the long-run average volatility of the VIX was 15. Furthermore, the volatility of volatility had fallen to very low levels, as depicted in Figure 11.10. It is likely that widespread shorting of volatility by selling options led to the extraordinary low levels of the VIX in the second half of 2017. Such a strategy can be very profitable—until it isn't. In February 2018, a sharp spike in volatility led to a collapse in the short volatility trade. The ProShares short VIX ETF (SVXY) fell more than 80% on February 6, 2018.

The unwinding of the short volatility trade in February 2018 was doubtless very expensive for the short-volatility speculators, but within about a week, the VIX had returned to a level below 20. The shorting of volatility by selling options reduces the cost of hedging either long or short positions in the underlying stock or index. If the cost of the hedge increases, it can lead to unwinding of the original hedged position, thereby increasing volatility in the underlying.

11.10.4 Systemic Leverage: Total Debt to Gross Domestic Product (GDP) and the Economic Balance Sheet

Since the Great Financial Crisis (GFC), household debt as a percent of GDP has fallen almost 40% from nearly 1.3 times to less than 0.8 times GDP. The reduction in household debt is even more dramatic in terms of the interest cost relative to GDP because of the long period of low interest rates beginning in 2008. For example, the average 30-year mortgage rate had fallen from more than 6% in mid-2008 to less than 3% at the end of 2020.

Yet, the progress made by consumers in paying down debt has been more than offset by increased government debt in support of deficit spending and increased corporate leverage. Total debt, including household, corporate, and government debt, has increased from 2009 through the COVID-19 pandemic. Hence, the economy as a whole is even more levered in 2021 than it was at the time of the GFC.

11.10.5 Systemic Liquidity and Central Bank Response

Central banks control the supply of money, adding and removing liquidity according to their mandate. In September 2019, liquidity evaporated in the repurchase agreement (repo) markets and momentarily pushed money-market rates above the Federal Reserve's target. The Fed responded by injecting $128 billion of liquidity. Six months later, when COVID-19 had afflicted the markets, the Federal Reserve provided $2 trillion of support to keep markets functioning. Without such drastic measures, liquidity-induced volatility could have spiked.

11.10.6 Hidden Volatility: Not All Markets Are Liquid

Private equity and credit positions can be traded in normal markets. There is no expectation that positions can be traded at any time. And there is no marking to market of positions. While this can create an appearance of stability, when positions must be traded in stressed markets, significant losses may occur.

11.10.7 Best House on a Bad Street

Even when everything fundamental and technical seems more volatile, sometimes volatility abates as money pours out of the riskiest markets and into those that are regarded as relatively safe havens, for example, currencies such as the US dollar and Japanese yen, defensive/non-cyclic sectors, lower-leverage companies, and higher-growth companies.

11.10.8 Market Friction: Taxes, Trading Costs, and Volatility

Occasionally, politicians float the idea of transaction taxes with the hope that this might reduce volatility by discouraging speculation. However, an important cause of volatility is low trading volumes, and if transaction taxes impeded trading—which seems inevitable—reduced trading volume would *increase* market volatility.

11.11 TYPES OF VOLATILITY

Volatility is often used as a euphemism for market setbacks. (No one complains about volatility when markets soar.) Severe downside volatility is frightening.

11.11.1 Actual Stock Volatility (Movement Versus Uncertainty)

There is a minor debate as to whether volatility is a result of uncertainty. To an extent, it is. Consider a high-quality bond with a maturity in one year versus the stock of a small-cap growth company. The value of the bond is going to be more stable (have less volatility) because the principal that will be paid at maturity is known with relative certainty. That future value can be discounted to today, and unless the discount rates change, the value will not vary much from day to day. Institutional investors have access to the relevant information, so there is little deviation based on perception of the facts. The stock, however, has greater volatility because its value in one year is far from certain. Multiple factors pertaining to the health of the company's industry or competitiveness of its products and so on determine the longer-term value of its stock. The flow of economic news, or idiosyn-

Figure 11.11   Implied versus historical volatility

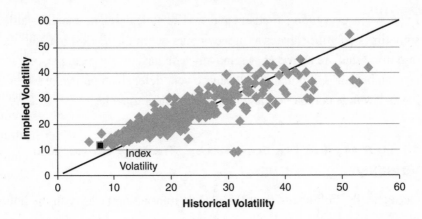

Data: Bloomberg.

cratic company news, and the way investors *perceive* the news can cause significant volatility (see Figure 11.11).

11.11.2 Correlated Volatility Versus Uncorrelated and Negatively Correlated Volatility

The price movement of an asset can be either correlated or uncorrelated with equity market indices. Whereas volatility measures the movement of the price of an asset on an absolute basis, beta measures the movement *relative to* an index. If the asset is more volatile and highly correlated with an index, its beta is usually greater than 1.0. In other words, when the index is down, the asset is likely to be down *more*, and when the index is up, the asset is likely to be up *more*.

If all members of an index are perfectly correlated, then the index volatility would be the same as the index average member volatility, but because correlations are usually less than 1, the diversification effect makes the volatility of the index (or portfolio) significantly less than the average volatility of the individual members. Generally, the lower the correlation of a security with the index (or portfolio), the greater the diversification benefit the security brings to the whole—especially if the low correlation is accompanied by high volatility. Companies that issue convertible bonds are prone to low correlation and high volatility.

If the drivers of the return are *uncorrelated* and based on the idiosyncratic growth of the company (which comes from rapid or unpredictable innovation), then returns can be significantly positive—even when the economy is weak. Hence, convertible bonds may reduce the volatility of the index (or portfolio) without sacrificing expected long-run returns.

Furthermore, if a driver of return is *negatively correlated*, this means that the driver boosts performance at exactly the time when the overall index (or portfolio) is falling. Convertibles have two properties that are *negatively correlated* with equity indices. *Both the low/non-correlated nature of convertible issuer fundamentals and the negatively correlated nature of convertible bond properties harness volatility to create positive returns in a vega strategy.*

11.11.3 Single-Issue Versus Portfolio or Index Volatility

As noted in Section 11.11.2, the diversification effect in portfolios and indices means that group-level volatility is always less than the average volatility of the individual members (so long as average correlation is less than 1). In other words, while an index such as the S&P 500 typically has volatility in the midteens, the average volatility of all its members is typically in the twenties to thirties (roughly double that of the index). This is generally true of both observed price movements of the individual equities and the index, as well as the volatilities implied by option prices.

Both index and individual-equity volatility can vary significantly over time. For example, Cardtronic's stock actual 30-day volatility varied between 23 and 71, whereas option implied volatility varied between 21 and 42, the S&P 500 actual 30-day volatility varied between 5.5 and 19, and implied volatility varied between 6 and 24. *For a complete discussion of the periodicity of volatility, please visit* www.AdventCap.com/Book/ SupplementaryMaterial.

11.11.4 Calculating Systematic and Idiosyncratic Volatility

Idiosyncratic risk can be determined by "backing out" systematic risk from total risk according to the following formula: $\sigma_{\text{IdiosyncraticA}} = (\sigma_{\text{AssetA}}{}^{2}$

$- (\sigma_{\text{Index}} \times \beta_A)^2)^{0.5}$. For example, if an index has volatility of 0.2, a stock has volatility of 0.4, and a beta of 1.5 to the index, it will have systematic volatility of 0.3 which is index volatility times the beta of the stock. It will also have idiosyncratic volatility of 0.2646 which is the square root of the square of 0.4 minus the square of 0.3. Since idiosyncratic volatility is by definition uncorrelated to systematic volatility, the stock volatility can be modeled as the sum of a process with a volatility of 0.3 and a process with a volatility of 0.2646. The combination of the two will result in a process with the desired volatility of 0.4.

11.11.5 Option Implied Volatility

A convertible bond is essentially a straight bond with an attached equity option (or warrant). Equity options have what is called an *implied* volatility. Because the volatility of the equity changes over time, historical measurements of volatility are not necessarily the same as market expectations of future volatility. While the market expectation is not directly observable, it can be deduced (implied) from option prices.

$$\text{Price of option} = f \left(\text{strike, stock price, volatility, risk-free rate} \right)$$

Therefore,

$$\text{Implied volatility} = f \left(\text{strike, stock price, risk-free rate, price of option} \right)$$

11.11.6 Convertible Implied Volatility

A convertible bond, like an equity option, has an implied volatility. This is the volatility at which the theoretical price of the convertible is equal to the actual market price. However, unlike an equity option, there is a second variable necessary to determine theoretical price, which is not necessarily directly observable in the market—credit spread. If a *pari passu* straight bond or liquid collateralized debt security exists, the credit spread of such a security can be used to infer an appropriate spread for the convertible. If not, a spread can be assumed from the credit rating or from credit fundamentals. Because a very significant percentage of convertible bonds are not rated, different market participants will use different spread assumptions depending on the conclusions (or absence) of their credit research.

$$\text{Price of bond} = f\left(\text{cash flows, risk-free rate, credit spread}\right)$$

and

$$\text{Implied spread} = f\left(\text{cash flows, risk-free rate, price of bond}\right)$$

Therefore,

$$\text{Convertible implied volatility}$$
$$= f\left(\begin{array}{l}\text{price of convertible, strike, stock price,}\\ \text{cash flows, risk-free rate, assumed spread}\end{array}\right)$$

When convertible bond implied volatility has fallen relative to historical averages, and convertible volatility remains well below the three-year moving average, the probability of a reversion to the mean is significant if volatility is more than 5 volatility points below the three-year moving average. In such an instance, history suggests a 3 volatility point reversion over the course of one year. Similarly, when implied volatility spikes higher, as it does in a crisis such as the GFC or the onset of COVID-19, or even in a more moderate market correction, history suggests a significant, if not complete reversion to the mean over the course of one year. (See Section 5.1.)

11.11.7 Convertible Assumed Volatility and Richness/ Cheapness

Once an implied volatility is determined, a volatility trader will compare that to the historical or expected volatility to determine if the volatility is rich or cheap. In other words, if the implied volatility is 25 and the actual or expected volatility is 30, a bond can be regarded as *5 volatility points cheap*. This cheapness also can be expressed in terms of the price of the convertible relative to theoretical value (i.e., a bond with a theoretical value of 115 and an actual market value of 110 can be said to be *5 bond points cheap*). Alternatively, those 500 bp of cheapness can be expressed in terms of spread (i.e., a bond with an assumed spread of 300 bp and an effective duration of 3, with a cheapness of 500 bp, can be said to have an implied spread of 500).

Convertible implied spread

$$= f \left(\begin{array}{l} \text{price of convertible, strike, stock price,} \\ \text{cash flows, risk-free rate, assumed volatility} \end{array} \right)$$

Therefore,

Cheapness

$$= f \left(\begin{array}{l} \text{price of convertible, strike, stock price, cash flows,} \\ \text{risk-free rate, assumed spread, assumed volatility} \end{array} \right)$$

11.11.8 Shape of Volatility: Term Structure, Skew, Smile, and Surface

Generally speaking, equity price movements increase with respect to time or, to be more precise, the square root of time. For example, a stock with an annualized standard deviation of 30 might be expected to move 30% over the course of a year, or 60% over the course of four years, or 15% over the course of 3 months.

$$30 \times \sqrt{1\,\text{year}} = 30$$
$$30 \times \sqrt{0.25\,\text{year}} = 15$$
$$30 \times \sqrt{4\,\text{years}} = 60$$

However, the implied volatilities of various maturities on the same underlying equity rarely reflect a constant/flat term structure. There can be a variety of reasons for these irregularities, ranging from supply/demand for shorter-term instruments to idiosyncratic reasons pertaining to corporate debt maturities, licenses, or production schedules. S&P 500 call option volatility is upward sloping, likely due to a supply/demand relationship (see Figure 11.12).

In contrast, convertible implied volatility is downward sloping (see Figure 11.13), which is consistent with the higher short-term actual and realized volatility relative to longer-term convertible implied volatility.

Figure 11.12   S&P 500 call option implied volatility

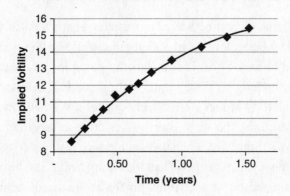

Source: Bloomberg.

Figure 11.13   Average convertible implied volatility

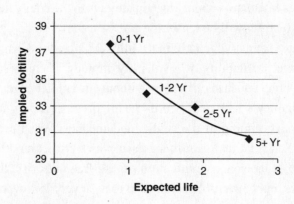

Sources: KYNEX, Advent Capital Management.

Volatility varies not only with respect to term but also with respect to moneyness (i.e., magnitude of in- or out-of-the-money). The shape of a chart of implied volatility is generally referred to as *skew* or a *smile*.

When volatility tends to increase as an option moves away from the strike price in either direction, the chart is called a *volatility smile*. Listed call options tend to have more "expensive" volatility for significantly out-of-the-money options, whereas convertibles (which are always issued out of the money) tend to offer relatively cheap volatility. A *volatility surface* is simply a three-dimensional graphic of volatility with respect to term and moneyness.

11.11.9 Actual Versus Realized Volatility

A *volatility strategy* is a method of monetizing equity volatility. This is accomplished by being long vega and gamma while hedging out delta (and potentially rho) exposures. This is done by going long a convertible bond and short the underlying shares equal to the amount of delta in the convertible. This volatility strategy effectively creates a *synthetic put*. When the stock price declines, the stock short makes more money than the convertible bond loses. Similarly, when the stock price rises, the convertible bond gains more money than the loss from the equity hedge. As the equity hedge is adjusted up and down over time, profits are realized. Actual volatility is the volatility of the equity over the holding period of the strategy. If the hedges are adjusted continuously or at least at local peaks and troughs, all this actual volatility can be converted into realized volatility. However, if equity prices fluctuate without any adjustments to the equity hedge, not all the actual volatility will be realized.

Rho exposures (which are more fully explained in Chapter 12) also can affect the profitability of a volatility strategy. If credit spreads on a convertible bond widen significantly without any credit hedge, the strategy could lose money, which underscores the importance (and value) of having a proper understanding of the credit fundamentals. When credit spreads widen, implied volatility tends to increase, which creates an offsetting gain in the value of the conversion feature. If risk-free rates rise, that can also create losses, but convertible bonds tend to have very low overall effective durations (due to the fact that the optionality has negative duration), and convertible hedge fund managers tend to hedge rate exposure.

11.12 VEGA IS THE SENSITIVITY OF AN OPTION OR A CONVERTIBLE TO CHANGES IN VOLATILITY

In option valuation mathematics, an increase in volatility is very similar to an increase in the term of an option. This is because both term and volatility pertain to the likelihood of an option expiring in the money. A more volatile stock is more likely to have gone up significantly. Vega describes the extent to which an increase in volatility increases the value of the convertible bond. As volatility is a measurement of magnitude, not

Figure 11.14   Vega: change in value due to volatility

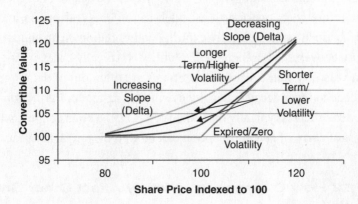

Source: Advent Capital Management.

directionality, volatility can increase (or decrease) as markets advance or decline. Vega is independent of market direction—which makes it effectively uncorrelated with the direction of equity prices. The profitability of realizing an increase in volatility depends on the magnitude of the vega of a position (see Figure 11.14).

11.12.1 Similarity to Theta: Cost of Optionality

The attractive ratchet properties of convertibles (see Section 8.9) are not entirely "free." The costs associated with vega and gamma come in the form of theta. Theta is the change in value of the optionality given the passage of time, and it can be thought of as a reduction of the effective yield of the convertible bond, but it should be noted that theta is much lower on longer-term options, such as those embedded in convertible bonds, than it is in short-term listed equity options. The magnitude of theta reflects the fact that the passage of one day has more of an effect on the probability that an option will surpass the strike price when an option is near maturity than when an option has years to go.

Theta scales with the square root of term to maturity; therefore, a quarterly expiring equity option (rolled four times a year) typically will cost twice as much as a one-year option $(0.25^{0.5 \times 4}/1^{0.5})$. In contrast, an at-the-money convertible bond with a maturity of four years "uses up" only

13% of its premium value $\left(4^{0.5} - 3^{0.5} / 4^{0.5}\right)$ over the course of the next year and therefore costs one-fourth as much as the one-year option and one-eighth as much as the quarterly expiring equity option on an annual basis. Because convertible bond implied volatility is typically cheaper than listed option volatility, and because convertibles are often out of the money, the difference in theta decay is usually even more dramatic. Furthermore, the convertible theta is typically more than offset by the bond coupon, whereas the cost of carry of an equity option can be well over 10% per year.

11.12.2 How Changes in Volatility Affect Other Greek Sensitivities

The measurement of how much Greek sensitivities change relative to other factors is called a *cross Greek*. It is useful to know how these properties evolve over time and with respect to various factors. For a complete discussion of the relationship between volatility and other Greek sensitivities, please visit www.AdventCap.com/SupplementaryMaterial.

11.13 CONCLUSION

The interactions of delta, gamma, and vega explain why convertible securities demonstrate positive asymmetry; that is, convertibles tend to capture more of the upside when the underlying stocks rise, and suffer less of the downside when the unerlying stocks decline. Positive asymmetry is the key attraction of convertible securities, and positive asymmetry is the reason why convertible indices have demonstrated equity-like returns over time with lower volatility and less downside than equity indices. It is essential to comprehend the relationships of the various Greek measures in individual positions as well as in portfolios as a whole.

ENDNOTES

1. From "Graecum est; non legitur" (translated literally as "This is Greek; it cannot be read), which was a common annotation used by medieval scribes who were unable to translate Greek quotations that appeared in texts that were predominantly written in Latin. This quotation is the source of Shakespeare's phrase, "It's Greek to me."
2. Lucy Maud Montgomery, *Emily's Quest* (1927), p. 13, https://www.fadedpage.com/showbook.php?pid=20170224.
3. Subtitle of *Antifragile: Things That Gain from Disorder* by Nassim Nicholas Taleb (New York: Random House, 2012).
4. https://en.wikipedia.org/wiki/2010_flash_crash.
5. The perception of trading disadvantages inspired Brad Katsuyama to found the IEX stock exchange, as explained in *Flash Boys* by Michael Lewis (New York: W.W. Norton, 2014).

CHAPTER 12

All-in Yield and Sensitivity to Credit and Rate Markets

Then the land will yield its fruit, and you will eat your fill and live there in safety.

—*Leviticus 25:19*

12.1 INTRODUCTION

Yield may seem like a simple concept. Yet, yield has confusingly numerous definitions: it can mean to produce, pay for, reward, return, render, rent, respect, submit, surrender, worship, serve, or sacrifice. A common thread to all these definitions is that, in some way, yield is earned, and in the realm of finance, it implies period earnings for the use of an asset. In a sense, it is the period price the owner of an asset requires to lend the asset. When that asset is money, yield is in essence the price of money, and it reflects supply and demand as well as the risk of default. Low default rates of convertibles are a secondary reason (after the conversion right) why convertibles yield less than other fixed-income securities (see Figure 12.1).

The form in which the yield is received varies by asset class. Bonds provide cash interest and/or an accretion to par from a discount or an amortization to par from a bond that is acquired at a premium. *Equity yield* almost always refers to the cash dividend yield paid by the company, but the amount of earnings per year per share of stock is sometimes described as *earnings yield*.

Because convertibles are hybrid securities, an investor in convertibles must consider the preceding concepts plus the additional considerations of the costs or returns due to hedging and the borrowing or lending of positions, as well as the tax implications, all of which affect the yield

Figure 12.1   Annual default rates by fixed-income asset class

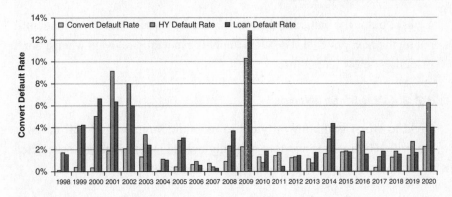

Sources: Credit Suisse, JP Morgan, BofA Securities.

provided by a convertible bond. This chapter describes the components of yield in typical long-only convertibles portfolios and how this increases the asymmetry profile over time. Chapter 13 describes the additional considerations for convertible arbitrage in a hedge fund.

12.2 YIELD TO WHAT?

The yield calculation requires a holding-period assumption. This can be either the maturity date or any earlier call or put date according to the call and put schedules. Calculations of yield to maturity and other yields to specific redemption dates assume that interest coupons can be reinvested at the same compounded rate over the remaining life of the bond. This is an essential rule of thumb for evaluating individual bonds and especially for comparing different bonds.

12.2.1 Yield to Maturity

Yield to maturity is the projected annualized compounded return of a security if held to maturity (see Section 12.3.4 for details).

12.2.2 Yield to Call

Yield to call is the annualized compounded return of a security if held until called on the next call date. It incorporates any premium (called a *call* or *redemption premium*) that would be paid over par as a result of the call.

12.2.3 Yield to Put

Yield to put is the annualized compounded return of a security if held until put on the next put date. The yield to put is especially relevant when a bond is trading below its put price.

12.2.4 Yield to Worst

Yield to worst is the lowest yield to redemption among all call dates or maturity. High-yield investors typically use this yield (and the associated credit spread to worst) as a base-case assumption.

12.2.5 Yield to Put/Maturity

Yield to put/maturity is used by convertible investors to understand their downside (assuming that the bond does not default). It represents the minimum return that can be expected if the stock is below the conversion price.

12.2.6 Current Yield

Current yield is simply the annualized interest coupon rate as a percentage of the market price of a bond. Convertible bond investors typically use current yield as a base-case yield of the income portion of the bond—independent of the value of the conversion right. Current yield ignores compounding and reflects the actual cash flows from the convertible—which are often an important investment consideration (see Section 12.3.3 for further details).

12.3 COMPONENTS OF BOND YIELD: YIELD PLUS ACCRETION OR MINUS AMORTIZATION TO PAR

Although it all boils down to the single appellation *yield*, the components can be complicated.

12.3.1 Coupon Rate

The most fundamental concept of borrowing and lending is that the borrower pays the lender interest—usually at a predetermined fixed rate. Historically, these interest payments were receivable on presentation of semiannual clipped coupons that had been physically attached to the paper bond certificates of yore. Hence, the appellation *coupon*.

12.3.2 Premium or Discount to Par

Bonds are most frequently issued with a *par* or *face value* of 100, which technically refers to 100% of par. Typically, bond principal is $1,000, so a change in par value of 1 bond point changes the dollar value of the bond by $10. If the bonds mature at par, this means that bondholders will receive the initial face value or principal. When bonds trade above par, they are said to trade at a *premium*, and when they trade below par, they are said to trade at a *discount*. Under normal circumstances, the discount or premium will fall to zero as the market value of the bond converges on par at the maturity date. The expected or actual change in the premium or discount over a period of time is called *amortization* or *accretion*, respectively. Amortization of premium or accretion of discount is part of the total return.

The accretion of a discount specifically relates to the principal cash flow at maturity, and it is calculated as par minus the price (as a percent of par) divided by the length of the period as a percent of the term to maturity. For a bond with two years to maturity bought at 90, the annual accretion is 5.41%. Thus

$$\text{Yearly accretion of discount on principal} = \left(\frac{\text{par}}{\text{price}}\right)^{1/\text{term}} - 1 \qquad (12.1)$$

$$\text{Yearly accretion of discount on principal} = \left(\frac{100}{90}\right)^{1/2} - 1 = 0.0541$$

The annual amortization of premium can be calculated with the same formula by substituting *amortization* for *accretion* and *premium* for *discount*.

12.3.3 Current Yield

Buying a bond at a discount does not just entitle the investor to a discounted principal payment; the investor is also receiving the coupons at a discount as well. For example, if a bond pays a 5% coupon and an investor is able to buy the bond for 90, the investor is effectively earning a 5.56% current yield:

$$\text{Current yield} = \frac{\text{coupon}}{\text{price as a percent of par}} \qquad (12.2)$$

$$\text{Current yield} = \frac{5\%}{90/100} = 5.56\%$$

12.3.4 Yield to Maturity

Yield to maturity is the rate that discounts all future cash flows to the present such that the sum of the present values is equal to the price. The two values explained earlier, annual amortization/accretion of premium/ discount and current yield, are complementary values in that they can be added together. However, this will *not* equal the yield to maturity of the bond. This is because yield to maturity assumes that cash interest payments are *reinvested*—that is, *compounded*—at the calculated yield-to-maturity rate. Yield to maturity is calculated by combining an annuity formula for the coupon payments and a present-value calculation for the return of principal at maturity (or other redemption).

Take, for example, the same 5% annual coupon bond and assume a five-year maturity. If investors were able to purchase the bond at 90, they would receive a yield to maturity of 7.47% for those five years.

$$90 = \left\{ 5 \times \left(\frac{1 - \dfrac{1}{1 + \text{yield to maturity}}}{\text{yield to maturity}} \right) + \left[100 \times \frac{1}{(1 + \text{yield to maturity})^5} \right] \right\} \qquad (12.3)$$

Solving for yield to maturity gives 0.0747. Note that the assumption that interest is reinvested at the same yield to maturity is inherently unrealistic because interest rates fluctuate and opportunities to reinvest cash interest will vary.

12.4 YIELD IS COMPOSED OF A RISK-FREE RATE PLUS SPREADS

In section 12.3, we explained that bond yield reflects the interest coupon rate and the price paid. The second approach is to think of the yield in terms of a riskless rate plus a yield spread over the risk-free rate that reflects the market's view of compensation for the various risks taken. Once we know the yield to maturity, we can dissect the yield into components reflecting the risks of holding the bond to determine whether the yield and the price associated with that yield are reasonable. The basic components of the yield are the risk-free rate for the currency of the bond, the term premium, the credit spread, and the liquidity spread. It is worth defining each before getting into precise calculations.

12.4.1 Risk-Free Rate

The *risk-free rate* is the rate at which an entity that is free of credit or liquidity risk can borrow for one day. Only entities that have the ability to print money are considered to be completely risk free because under any circumstance they can repay their debt with currency that they alone can create. For example, the US Federal Reserve controls the money supply, and hence, the Federal Funds Rate is the primary risk-free rate. However, US Treasury notes and bonds are also considered to be credit risk free because of the taxing authority of the US government. Yet, when Treasury securities have a maturity of greater than one day, there is interest-rate risk, and therefore, such issues are not entirely risk free. For example, a 10-year Treasury bond might fall in value significantly if interest rates were to rise (in order to boost the yield to maturity to the new—higher—prevailing market rate of interest). This forces the prices of older bonds downward until an equilibrium price is reached. This risk is minimal for bonds nearing maturity, therefore, one-month Treasury bond yields are also used as a proxy for the US dollar risk-free rate.

Low-risk short-term US Treasury bonds have one risk, and that is the value of the US dollar relative to other currencies. Foreign investors selling their home currency in order to buy dollars for purchasing US Treasury securities would lose some of their investment if the dollar were to fall. However, currency risk is generally considered an exogenous risk because the risk-free rate is specific to each currency.

In Japan, it is the Bank of Japan that sets the rate for the Japanese yen; in China, the Peoples Bank of China sets the rate for the yuan and renminbi (China has two currencies, one for internal trade and one for external trade); in the United Kingdom, the Bank of England sets the rate for the pound sterling; but in the Euro zone of the European Union, it is the European Central Bank. Because each country in the Euro zone has its own government debt-issuing authority but not money-printing authority, the debt of certain countries has sometimes been considered to be *not* credit risk free.

12.4.2 Term Premium

Term premium is the additional yield required by investors to hold bonds to maturity. Generally, nearer maturities have low term premiums and longer maturities have higher term premiums because of the risk that rising interest rates could impair the market value of longer-duration bonds. For example, a Treasury bond maturing in five years paying 3% interest will be worth less if newer issues, also maturing in five years, are paying 3.5% interest. The price of the older bond will fall to the point where its yield is equal to the yield of the newer bond. Although there are some minor deviations from this in practice (*off-the-run* versus *on-the-run* issues), such inconsistencies reflect liquidity rather than term premium.

Yield curves reflect the yields of different bonds from the same issuer (e.g., the US Treasury), and the different bonds usually have different yields for different terms to maturity. When the yields are plotted (on the *y*-axis) relative to the terms (on the *x*-axis) and the points are connected by a line, that line is called a *yield curve*. Usually this is an upward-sloping curve, and the size of the term premium determines the *steepness* of the yield curve. If all term premiums are zero, the curve would be said to be *flat*. Rarely, but as happened in the second half of 2019, the term premium is negative, and the yield curve is *inverted*.

12.4.3 Credit Spreads

Different issuers can issue identical bonds on the same date, but there will almost certainly be a significant difference in the yield investors demand to buy their bonds. This is a reflection of the difference in the respective credit qualities of the two issuers. The essence of a *credit spread* is that it reflects the additional yield required for an investor to purchase a nongovernment bond of the same term to maturity as a risk-free bond.

A number of factors go into market perceptions of credit quality, including the existing debt levels or leverage of the issuer, the amount of cash or liquid assets, the capital structure and the seniority of the debt issue, the current and near-term earnings and cash-flow potential and risks of the issuer, the likelihood of default, and expectations of recoverable value in the event of default. Issuers frequently pay for ratings agencies, known as *nationally recognized statistical ratings organizations*,[i] to rate their credit quality or that of a specific issue. Many institutional investors are prohibited from investing in securities that are not rated or are rated below a certain quality. Equivalently rated securities tend to have similar credit spreads in the market, but credit quality is subjective and subject to change, so there is significant dispersion of spreads among bonds with identical credit ratings. Furthermore, because risk increases with respect to time, longer-term securities tend to have wider credit spreads than shorter-term securities.

12.5 APPROACHES TO CALCULATING CREDIT SPREAD

The concept is consistent, but the techniques are various.

12.5.1 Synthetic-Market Approach

Many liquid bonds can be insured with what are called *credit default swaps* (CDS).[ii] The buyer of this insurance-like protection pays a percentage of the notional value of the bond in return for a payment of interest plus that principal (less the recoverable value the bond receives during bankruptcy) by the seller of protection in the event of default. The rate paid to insure the bond is essentially the credit spread, but the CDS market is not as extensive as it was before the GFC, and no CDS market exists for the vast majority of bond issuers. The way the market operates for issuers with a high probability of default is somewhat different, but when it exists, a usable CDS spread can be determined regardless of different settlement methods for CDS on stressed bonds.

12.5.2 Cash-Market Approach

One could also measure the yield of a bond and back out the risk-free rate, the term premium, and an estimate of the liquidity premium. Or one could simply ignore liquidity rather than attempt to bifurcate the credit spread and the liquidity spread of the bond.

12.5.3 Adjusted-Credit-Quality Average Spread

One could also determine the market average credit spread for a bond with the same credit rating, industry, and term to maturity. The difference between the average spread and the spread determined by the cash-market approach could be thought of as the *idiosyncratic spread* of the bond, which would include any differences between the risk suggested by the rating and market-perceived risks. This would include changes in credit condition after the rating was assigned as well as adjustments for the liquidity of the issue.

12.5.4 Liquidity Spread

The liquidity of a bond can affect the yield, and the degree to which it does is called the *liquidity premium* or *liquidity spread*. Typically, the smaller the bond, the higher is the liquidity premium, but even large issues can incur a liquidity premium depending on market conditions. As mentioned earlier, it can be difficult to distinguish between liquidity and credit spreads in a particular bond, and it is often unnecessary. However, when a credit spread can be firmly established (because of the existence of either an active CDS or a highly liquid *pari passu* bond), the liquidity spread can be distinguished from the credit spread.

During the GFC, it was striking to observe tremendous differences between synthetic- and cash-market spreads. Bond spreads were widening much more quickly and severely than the spreads on the CDS on the same bond. This reflected a crisis in liquidity. Credits were certainly being priced lower (hence, the widening CDS levels), but in general, bonds were declining in price more severely than was suggested by the CDS. Various accounts were being forced to liquidate positions, even entire portfolios, and there were very few buyers. In effect, much of the credit market was hit with a margin call as well as redemptions.

Bond investors who had counted on CDS to offset any mark-to-market losses on their bond portfolios were disappointed because *CDS were designed to compensate for credit-spread widening—not for liquidity-spread widening.*

12.5.5 CDS Spread

The *CDS spread* is a useful benchmark because it represents what the CDS issuers charge to insure a bond against default. It is the purest credit-spread indication in that it isolates an issuer's credit from other risks such as duration, liquidity, or any embedded options. Unfortunately, the CDS market is not always liquid, and active CDS spread levels are unavailable for many bonds. Furthermore, the quoting convention differs for bond issuers that have greater credit risk. The CDS market is also subject to occasional regulatory constraints because some countries prohibited CDS activity in some issuers during the GFC. There have been lawsuits over the procedures involved in triggering a CDS claim in the event of default that may adversely affect the usefulness of CDS in the future.

12.5.6 G-Spread

G-spread is the bond yield minus the interpolated yield to the same maturity on the government (Treasury) rate curve. This is meant to back out the risk-free rate and the term premium of a longer-term risk-free bond adjusted for any differences in the term to maturity.

12.5.7 I-Spread

I-spread is the bond yield minus the interpolated yield derived from a swap-rate curve. The swap market is made up of participants with high credit quality that are nonetheless not entirely credit risk free.

12.5.8 Z-Spread

Both the G-spread and I-spread are based on curves built with bonds or instruments that have coupons. Such securities have variable durations that may not align perfectly with the duration of the bond being analyzed. It is a better practice to create curves of yields that are effectively stripped of any coupons and represent a true fixed duration. This is done in a process called *bootstrapping*, which is beyond the scope of this book. Zero-coupon bonds do not have duration-altering coupons and therefore are a useful point of comparison; the duration of a zero-coupon bonds is equal to its years to maturity. The *Z-spread* is the bond yield less the interpolated point on the zero-coupon curve.

12.5.9 Asset-Swap Spread

The *asset-swap spread* (ASW) is the difference between the bond coupon and offsetting swaps fixed coupon.[iii] Typically, the structure involves the transfer of cash bonds rather than just a synthetic rate. This means that the swap captures not only the credit spread but also the liquidity spread *and, in the case of convertible bonds, any changes in value due to the appreciation of the underlying equity*. This spread therefore differs from CDS spreads, which do not involve any exchange of physical bonds.

12.5.10 Option-Adjusted Spread

The *option-adjusted spread* (OAS) is the spread over the benchmark adjusted for put or call options. Note that standard OAS models typically calculate only changes in yield and generally ignore the equity optionality embedded in convertible bonds.

12.5.11 Discount Margin to Maturity

The leveraged loan market reserves the term *spread* to refer to the spread over the London Interbank Offered Rate (LIBOR) that determines the interest rates on the loans. Using classic banking terminology, the market credit spread is called a *discount margin*. Historically, this discount margin was calculated to an assumed refinancing term such as three or four years. With LIBOR rates at extremely low levels, and with the existence of LIBOR floors that effectively suspend interest-rate resets when rates are low, the 2020s began with the discount margin more commonly evaluated relative to the maturity date. Note that most use of LIBOR for the US dollar is scheduled to be replaced by the Secured Overnight Financing Rate (SOFR) in June 2023.[4]

12.5.13 Implied Credit Spread (Convertible Bond Model)

The *implied spread* of a convertible bond is derived from the market value of the convertible after the value of the option has been subtracted from the price. Because option valuation requires assuming a specific volatility, implied spreads are therefore subject to changes in assumed volatility. Conversely, it is possible to determine the option implied volatility by subtracting a bond value based on an assumed spread from the market price of the option. Because convertible evaluations require both credit spread and volatility to be priced, it is impossible to imply both simultaneously. If both spread and volatility are assumed, a *theoretical value* of the convertible can be calculated and compared with the market price to determine *richness* or *cheapness* relative to theoretical/fair value.

12.6 UNDERSTANDING CONVERTIBLE YIELDS

A key component of yield calculations is the price of the bond. The price of the convertible bond, however, reflects the value of both a bond component and an equity call option, and the embedded call option can make the price of the convertible bond substantially higher than par. Straight bonds also can have prices in excess of par, which reduces the yield to a level below the coupon and in some cases below zero. This typically happens under the following three circumstances:

1. If prevailing interest rates drop below their level at the time of issuance
2. If the credit quality of the issuer improves
3. If the bond is issued at a premium to par and the premium amortizes downward (negative interest rate)

With a straight (non-convertible) bond, there is a limit to the premium over par and therefore the reduction in yield. The yield to maturity tells investors what they will earn *ceteris paribus* (and the bond is not called) if they hold the bond to maturity.

With convertible bonds, however, the value of the option can in-crease the value of the convertible many hundreds of percent if the eq-uity soars—as demonstrated in 2020–2021 when Tesla convertible bonds soared to over 1,000. Without making any adjustment for the option value, this results in an apparent negative yield to maturity. Artificially lower or negative yields on convertibles are not very informative because these simple calculations ignore the reality that at expiration the holders of such issues will convert into underlying shares worth an amount substantially greater than par. The only thing a negative yield tells the convertible holder is what the maximum loss would be if the underlying stock collapsed and the convertible matured out of the money; therefore, a negative yield on a convertible bond is not a reflection of what the investor will earn *ceteris paribus*.

In the convertible market, it is more common to consider the current yield, which isolates the coupon portion of the yield from the premium or discount. What is also more useful than simply yield to maturity is to consider what yield to maturity would be on the bond portion of the con-vertible independent of the embedded equity option. This can be done by using the investment value of the bond to calculate the yield rather than the price. Investment values reflect the credit spread, term premium, and risk-free rate and are often well below par, even when the market prices of the convertible bonds are well above par.

12.6.1 Theta

Another important piece of information in calculating the all-in yield of a convertible is how much the option premium would change because of the passage of time. This is called *theta decay*. Theta decay of a convertible bond differs from theta decay in an equity call option in four important ways:

1. Convertible bonds usually have much longer-terms than listed call options. Because theta decay increases as expiration approaches, the longer-term of convertible embedded calls means that they lose less value in the same period of time than short-term equity options.

2. Implied volatility is typically lower in a convertible bond than in a listed equity option. This reduces the option premium attributable to time value but not intrinsic value. But intrinsic value does not decay, only the time value does, so convertibles with lower implied volatilities experience less theta decay.

3. Convertible embedded call option premiums are already *paid for* because a convertible bond inherently has a lower coupon than an equivalent non-convertible bond. The flip side of this diminished yield is that the convertible is less exposed to theta decay.

4. Credit-spread widening results in reductions to the intrinsic value of the bond, creating a discount of the bond portion relative to par. Over time, this discount accretes back to par, just as a discount straight bond accretes to par. Most convertible evaluation models work in such a way that the accretion of discount reduces convertible theta—so much so that theta can even flip from a negative to a positive.

Therefore, the all-in yield of a convertible must incorporate theta. But it is essential not to double count discount accretion. Because convertible theta *includes* discount accretion, we do not add theta to yield to maturity; rather, we add theta to current yield, which excludes discount accretion.

12.6.2 Effects of Foreign Exchange Hedging on Yield

Convertibles are a global asset class. Yet, every portfolio has a base currency—the currency of the investor. Investing in non-base-currency convertibles involves exchanging base currency for foreign currency in order to purchase the bond. When the bond is sold or reaches maturity, the foreign currency is exchanged back into base currency. This creates an exposure to exchange rates for the investor. If the foreign currency weakens relative to the base currency, the investor will suffer foreign exchange (FX) rate losses. Frequently, but not always, investors seek to minimize the perceived currency exposure using FX forward contracts. This gives the investor the right to sell the foreign currency at a future date at a fixed price, thereby eliminating much of the risk. There is, however, either a cost or a positive gain that gets locked in when buying an FX forward contract.

The reason for a cost or a gain is because the FX forward rate is rarely the same as the FX spot rate, meaning that the rate you pay to exchange the foreign currency back to your base currency in the future is different from the rate you pay for the currency in the present. The difference reflects the difference in risk-free rates between the two currencies, which is called *interest-rate parity*. Investors whose base currency has a higher risk-free rate than the foreign currency receive a gain when entering an FX forward contract, and investors whose base currency has a lower risk-free rate receive a loss, or a cost. The gain or cost is called *FX forward points*. The effects of the gain or loss should be included in calculating the all-in yield for portfolios that have non-base-currency exposures and hedges.

FX has become a substantial component of yield in global portfolios over recent years through 2020 because of the disparity in interest rates between currencies. US dollar investors have earned as much as 4% per annum by hedging bond investments in euros and Swiss francs back into US dollars. On the flip side, euro and Swiss franc investors have had to pay that amount in order to hedge their investments in US dollars. This has made buying low-yielding European bonds relatively more attractive for US dollar investors, but it has made investing in higher-yielding US dollar bonds more costly for Europeans. The result has been that many European investors have chosen to leave all or part of the exposure to US dollar investments unhedged, choosing to accept the exchange-rate risk rather than pay the cost of hedging. In some cases, European investors outsource the task of hedging to currency overlay specialists who are given some discretion to increase and reduce hedges opportunistically.

12.6.3 Interest-Rate Parity

Interest-rate parity assumes that each currency is exchangeable and that investors can finance and invest at the risk-free rates in either currency. When currencies have different risk-free rates, investors can borrow in the lower-rate currency and invest in the higher-rate currency, but they take on the risk that the higher-rate currency will depreciate. If the FX forward hedge contract were free or negligibly low, it would be possible to make risk-free arbitrage profits by borrowing in the lower-rate currency and investing in the higher-rate currency. Because no risk-free arbitrage can last for very long, a widely used principle in finance and economics is that prices and rates will adjust until the opportunity for risk-free arbitrage is gone. Hence, the cost of the FX forward increases until it is equal to the difference in the risk-free rates.

12.6.4 Dual-Currency Convertibles

An oddity of the global convertible market is that convertibles sometimes are issued in two currencies. This typically occurs when a foreign company seeks to tap the large convertible markets in the United States or the Euro zone. Such a bond will be denominated in US dollars or in euros, whereas the underlying stock will primarily trade in its home currency. Such convertible bonds provide a built-in hedge on the downside because the interest and principal of the bond will be paid in US dollars or euros. The investor is, of course, exposed to fluctuations between the currency in which the underlying shares trade and the US dollar or euro denomination of the bond. Of course, dual-currency convertibles are almost always issued by large multinational companies that generate revenues in multiple currencies that may mitigate FX risk. Institutional investors typically establish FX hedges immediately after purchasing such bonds; such hedges are particularly important for hedged convertible strategies that attempt to isolate the volatility of the stock.

12.6.5 Equity Yield

Because convertibles can be converted into common shares, appreciation of the underlying stock price results in capital appreciation. For straight bonds trading at a discount to par (or put), the expected capital appreciation is the accretion of the bond price upward—the so-called pull to par. This is used in calculating the yield of the bond. If a bond trades at a discount to par of 3%, and there are three years to maturity, then the additional yield of price accretion is approximately 1% per year. For convertibles, however, the value at redemption is higher than par if parity—that is, the stock price times the conversion ratio—exceeds par at maturity. The appreciation potential of a convertible is uncertain— but is potentially unlimited—because investors in the convertible will convert rather than accept par redemption in cash if the conversion value exceeds par.

12.6.6 Asymmetry Yield (Volatility-Gamma Yield)

As described in Chapter 11, equity participation of convertibles is asymmetric; it is higher on the upside and lower on the downside because of gamma. *Such asymmetry is a key reason that convertibles have provided equity-like returns over time.*

There are four points about gamma that makes it relevant to the discussion of yield:

1. There is a yield-like return that is generated by the interaction of volatility and gamma at the security level.
2. There is a yield-like return that is generated by the interaction of dispersion and gamma at the portfolio level.
3. While the theoretical value of this yield can be predetermined (or estimated) based on expected volatility and dispersion, it also requires a simple prescribed trading behavior.
4. This trading behavior can take two forms, the long-delta and the delta-neutral forms.

Points 1 and 2 were described in detail in Chapter 11. The assumed trading behavior referred to in point 3 is that the portfolio manager trades the portfolio to maintain an assumed level of gamma.

The long-delta approach is applicable to portfolios where investors seek some positive exposure to the underlying equities. Typically, positions will be held while the convertibles possess a desired amount of delta and gamma. For a balanced convertible portfolio, this might imply a range of deltas from 40% to 80%; for a defensive convertible portfolio, this might imply a range of deltas from 15% to 55%. As convertible deltas move beyond the upper or lower boundary of the ranges, the positions are reduced or eliminated. As they move back into the balanced discipline, they are bought back. Because delta is lower when the stock and convertible prices have declined and higher when the stock and convertible prices have appreciated, delta can be used to create an organic buy-low, sell-high discipline. Not only is the average delta maintained at a fairly stable level, but average gamma is as well. Because convertibles become too bond-like when sinking to discounts or too equity-like when soaring far above par, the level of gamma is reduced. Therefore, the automatic trimming of convertibles moving out of the delta discipline helps to maintain the level of gamma. As described previously, stock-price volatility and dispersion are catalysts that create trading opportunities. The more volatility and dispersion, the more trades will occur as convertibles move in and out of the balanced discipline. Because this trading discipline leads to a stable level of gamma, it is possible to draw conclusions about the natural yield given the expected levels of volatility and dispersion as follows:

$$\text{Long-delta volatility gamma yield} = 0.5 \times \text{gamma} \times$$
$$\frac{\text{dispersion}^2 + (\text{equity index volatility} \times \text{average beta})^2}{\text{portfolio value}} \qquad (12.4)$$

The delta-neutral approach achieves a similar gamma yield, but it is employed in a very different way:

$$\text{Delta-neutral volatility gamma yield} = \frac{\sum\left(0.5 \times \text{gamma}_i \times \sigma_i^2\right)}{\text{portfolio value}} \qquad (12.5)$$

12.6.7 Accretion of Convertible Theoretical Cheapness

Convertibles typically come to market cheap relative to theoretical value. In other words, the embedded equity option is sold using an implied volatility that is cheap relative to the actual expected volatility or the listed equity option volatility. This cheapness accretes to zero by the expiration of the convertible, adding to the overall yield. If a convertible is issued 2.5% cheap with a five-year expected life, the accretion of cheapness is approximately 0.5% per year:

$$\text{Cheapness accretion yield} = \frac{\text{theoretical cheapness}}{\text{expected life}} \qquad (12.6)$$

12.7 METHODS OF CALCULATING EQUITY YIELD

Various models have been advanced to estimate the value and expected return of a stock. A portion of the return of the underlying equity passes through to the convertible, and therefore we can consider these models while making the appropriate adjustment for the convertible structure. These models include discounted dividend yield, earnings yield, equity risk premium, and adjusted equity index forecast. While space does not permit a thorough examination of each of these models here, please visit www.AdventCap.com/SupplementaryMaterials for a detailed review of each of these models.

12.8 ALL-IN CONVERTIBLE YIELD

Multiple yields can be calculated for convertibles. The *all-in yield* represents the expected return from all the various parts of a convertible.

12.8.1 Standstill Yield

Standstill yield is the expected portfolio yield if average equity prices remain unchanged. This is a useful value to consider for the purposes of adjusting upside-downside ratios to incorporate yield because the upside-downside ratios already have an explicit expectation of underlying equity return. The standstill yield incorporates the convertible current yield, theta decay, asymmetry yield, convertible cheapness, and FX currency hedging cost, as described in Equation (12.7).

Standstill yield =

current yield + theta + asymmetry yield + FX cost + cheapness accretion yield

$$(12.7)$$

12.8.2 All-in Expected Yield (Gross)

The all-in expected yield incorporates the four elements of the standstill yield plus the delta-adjusted earnings yield and is useful in describing the expected return on an unlevered long-only convertible portfolio:

All-in expected yield (gross) = standstill yield + delta-adjusted equity yield

$$(12.8)$$

12.8.3 Leverage, Cost of Funding, and Rebate

Hedged convertible strategies employ *leverage*, borrowing to finance long convertible positions in excess of the portfolio net assets under management (AUM). Such a strategy also borrows and sells short shares of stock to hedge some or all of the equity exposure. Furthermore, the long positions in the convertibles can in turn be lent out. The interest cost of borrowing the incremental long positions and the short stock minus the income earned from lending long positions is the *cost of funding*. These costs taken as a percentage of AUM represent a reduction of total yield (see Section 13.10 for more detail).

Cost of funding =

$$\frac{\left(\text{cost of borrowing} \times \text{amount borrowed} - \text{stock rebate rate} \times \text{short stock}\right)}{\left(\text{assets under management}\right)}$$

$$(12.9)$$

12.8.4 Fees and Expenses

Management fees (assessed on AUM), performance fees (assessed on fund performance), and expenses are added together and taken as a percent of AUM.

$$\text{Fees \%} = \frac{\left(\text{management fee} + \text{performance fee} + \text{fund expense}\right)}{\left(\text{assets under management}\right)} \quad (12.10)$$

12.8.5 All-in Expected Yield (Net)

The all-in expected yield on a net basis starts with the gross yield and subtracts the funding costs as well as any fund fees and expenses. For hedged convertible funds that are essentially delta neutral, the standstill yield might be used in place of the all-in gross yield. Furthermore, because such a strategy typically finances non-base-currency positions by borrowing, there is less FX currency hedging involved. Nonetheless, non-base-currency unrealized gains and losses can be hedged, and any associated forward point cost would be included in the standstill yield.

$$\text{All-in yield (net)} = \text{all-in yield (gross)} - \text{cost of funding (\%)}$$
$$- \text{fees and expense (\%)}$$
(12.11)

12.9 COMPARISON OF YIELDS AND SPREADS

Yield is always an important component of convertible returns, and a useful way of comparing different securities.

12.9.1 Types of Convertibles

The charts in Figure 12.2 describe the differences in current yield between (starting in the upper left-hand corner and progressing clockwise) different types of convertibles, types of global bonds, types of investment-grade bonds, and types of speculative-grade bonds. Note that because mandatory preferreds tend to have more downside risk than other types of convert-

Figure 12.2   Convertible current yield

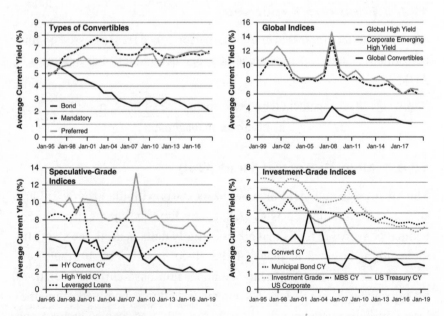

Sources: ICE Data, Bloomberg.

Figure 12.3　Equity yield and delta-adjusted equity yield

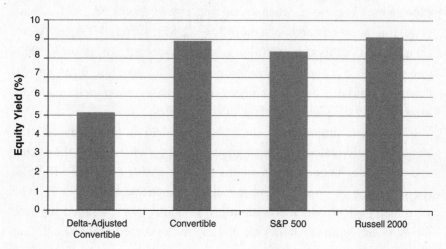

Source: Bloomberg.

ibles, they typically offer a higher yield. Furthermore, the change in yields in convertibles has been less pronounced than the change in straight bond yields.

The chart in Figure 12.3 shows the equity yield and delta-adjusted equity yield of US convertibles versus the S&P 500 and Russell 2000. While the equity yield of convertible equities surpasses that of both the S&P 500 and the Russell 2000, it is less on a delta-adjusted basis, which represents the equity yield adjusted for the equity sensitivity of the convertible. Furthermore, this adjusted equity yield is only one of several components of convertible all-in yield (see calculations in Section 12.8).

12.10 HOW YIELD ENHANCES CONVERTIBLE ASYMMETRY

We discussed the instantaneous upside and downside of convertibles that depend on gamma for their positive asymmetry in Chapter 11. However, when considering the upside and downside of a convertible over time, it is important to include the yield that is earned whether the underlying stock goes up or down.

Although the all-in convertible yield incorporates a market expectation of equity appreciation, an upside/downside analysis makes explicit assumptions about the price change of the equity that may vary from the expectation. Therefore, when enhancing upside/downside analysis with yield, it is necessary to use standstill yield, which excludes equity yield. Chapter 11 described a portfolio in which expected upside on a ±20% move is +14.25%, and the downside is −7.75%, resulting in an upside/downside ratio of 1.84. This analysis is essentially *instantaneous*, without incorporating the yield advantage of convertibles.

A simple approach to incorporating yield is to simply add the standstill yield (calculated without asymmetry yield) to both the upside and downside. Assuming a yield of 1.5%, the upside becomes +15.75%, the downside is −6.25%, and the upside/downside ratio is 2.52. The asymmetry yield and the delta-adjusted equity are excluded because the delta and gamma returns are already incorporated in the upside and downside.

An alternative approach is to perform a full revaluation upside and downside using a future valuation date (setting the calendar forward one year) and then adding the current yield, cheapness accrual, and foreign-currency hedging cost. In this case, theta can be ignored because the valuation one year in the future will result in lower option valuations—essentially duplicating the effects of theta decay.

12.11 YIELD SENSITIVITY: DURATION, CONVEXITY, RHO, AND OMICRON

> Learning is rooted in repetition and convexity, meaning that
> the reading of a single text twice is more profitable than reading
> two different things once.
>
> *–Nassim Nicholas Taleb*[5]

A water droplet is a natural *convex* lens that splits white sunlight into its component colors, creating a rainbow on the horizon opposite the sun—a phenomenon that is fittingly fleeting in *duration* (*durus*, Latin for "hard" or "to harden"; *endure*, "to be steadfast, unmovable for an extended period, longsuffering through something negative, or loyal in both good and bad times"). In plain English, duration is a quantity of time. Duration also carries with it the connotation of what can be experienced during that period of time. In this sense, duration can either be good or bad given the context. If it is a measurement of the time of something pleasurable, such as time spent with a friend, we generally consider the more duration the better. Yet, if it is the measurement of time of something excruciating, then duration implies a negative connotation or bad times.

For bonds that have a fixed rate of interest until maturity, the context can either be positive or negative depending on the movement of interest rates. For example, if you own a bond that pays 3% interest for three years and rates of other newly issued three-year bonds suddenly jump to 5%, the context is negative because you have to suffer through the next three years earning only 3%, while those who bought just after you are earning 5%. In other words, you would end up with about 6 percentage points less interest, and if you had to sell your bond, you would find that the market price of your bonds would have fallen about 6%.

However, if the interest rate of newly issued three-year bonds fell to 1%, then you would have the joy of receiving 3% while all those who bought the newly issued bonds received only 1%. During the three years until maturity, you would receive about 6 percentage points more than the buyers of the 1% bonds. This means that if you decide to sell your bond, you will likely find that the market price of your bond relative to others would have increased about 6%.

Thus far we have examined the components of the yield of a convertible. Yield, however, is not static. As market yields change, the new yields affect the market prices of convertibles, just as changes in the underlying equity prices change the market value, as discussed in Chapter 11. For the purposes of this chapter, we will specifically focus on changes in value due to changes in the risk-free rate, term premium, credit spreads, and assumed recovery rates.

12.11.1 Greek Symbols for Interest-Rate Sensitivity

Just as mathematicians and quants use delta and gamma to describe the change in value of a derivative (or convertible) relative to an underlying interest (equity price in the case of a convertible), quants commonly use the terms *duration* and *convexity* to describe the change in value relative to interest rates. However, duration is always represented as a positive number because it is similar in concept to the average amount of time (in years) until cash flows are received—and time is always a positive number. Duration, however, causes the value of bonds to decline as rates rise.

Words are less convenient than letters for the purpose of writing mathematical formulas. A letter or symbol used for rate sensitivity is the Greek letter rho, which—like delta—represents the first derivative, albeit with respect to change in interest rates rather than change in equity price. Rho—unlike duration—can be either a negative number (as it is for all straight bonds that decline when rates rise), or it can be a positive number (as it is when rising rates cause an increase in value, as in the case of options). Because convertibles have both bond and option properties, the rho of a convertible bond can be positive or negative and generally is much lower than the rho of a straight bond with a similar duration.

Rho, just like delta, is a dynamic value, and the measurement of its change is described by a second derivative. For changes in delta, the second derivative is called *gamma*; for changes in duration, or rho, the second derivative is called *convexity*. While there is not a common Greek letter assigned to convexity, we will use the letter q because it is a "neighbor" of r in English, just as delta is a neighbor of gamma in Greek. Unfortunately, we cannot use the Greek neighbors of rho because it is preceded by pi and followed by sigma, both of which are already doing double duty in quantitative analysis. Pi is used as an operator symbolizing the product of a series. Pi has been especially widely used since 1706, when a Scottish school teacher named William Jones decided to use it as a symbol for the Archimedes constant that describes the ratio of the circumference (or perimeter) of a circle relative to its diameter. Jones did posterity a favor because the only alternatives were to use the clumsy Latin expression *quantitas in quam cum multiflicetur diameter, proveniet circumferencia* ("the quantity which, when the diameter is multiplied by it, yields the circumference") or to write out the entire number, which actually goes on forever: 3.1415926535897…. Likewise, sigma is used both as the symbol of volatility and as an operator symbolizing the summation of a series.

There is precedent for using q in that it precedes r in ancient Phoenician, Egyptian, and Hebrew as well as in Germanic languages such as English. In fact, the Egyptian hieroglyph gives us the perfect justification for its use in that it resembles a hillside that is positively convex at the base and negatively convex (or concave) at the top. It also means "food," which is the perfect antecedent to the letter rho, which is represented by the glyph of a mouth.

Other first-derivative Greek sensitivities related to yield are omicron (O), phi (Φ), and upsilon (Y). Omicron is the sensitivity of convertible price relative to a change in credit spread rcs, and it is a fitting letter because it represents an eye or watchfulness in ancient languages. Investors should certainly keep an eye on quality credit, especially of lower-delta convertibles. Phi is the sensitivity of convertible price relative to the underlying stock dividend yield rd. Phi makes the "ef" sound and is used as a symbol for the golden ratio—a constant that is frequently seen in exponential expansions in nature such as the growth of a nautilus shell. Upsilon is the sensitivity of convertible price relative to a change in the recovery rate of a convertible in the event of default. Upsilon looks like the modern letter Y, which resembles a path that diverges. Ancient writers, including Pythagoras, saw this as symbolic of the divergent roads of vice and virtue, life or death. Certainly upsilon is used in convertibles to describe performance under a "death" or worst-case scenario to the credit (default).

12.11.2 Convertible and Straight Bond Example During the Taper Tantrum

Following the Great Financial Crisis, the US budget deficit swelled, and as a result, the US Treasury issued several trillion dollars of new Treasury bonds and notes. To accommodate the issuance, the Federal Reserve (and other central banks) bought a substantial portion of the new Treasury debt along with mortgage-backed securities; these purchases had the effect of increasing the money supply. While households and businesses initially reduced debt levels and delevered their balance sheets, the Federal Reserve helped maintain the total amount of debt outstanding, which kept interest rates lower than they would have been otherwise, stimulating the economy in the process. The central bank bond purchases constituted an ever-increasing bond purchase program that continued to swell the Federal Reserve Bank balance sheet by $70 billion per month. The market understood that this would be a temporary situation, but it was not clear how or when the Federal Reserve would begin to unwind or reduce its purchases of debt, which would effectively shrink the money supply and be antisimulative to the economy.

The chart in Figure 12.4 plots the growth of the balance sheets of key central banks, that is, the European Central Bank (ECB), the US Federal Reserve Bank, and the Bank of Japan (BOJ). On May 22, 2013, Federal Reserve Board Chair Ben Bernanke announced that the Federal Reserve would begin to taper bond purchases over subsequent months. While this would not reduce the money supply immediately, it signaled that the stimulative effect of bond purchases was coming to an end *because economic prospects had improved*. Because the federal government still had substantial deficits, the market feared that reduced central bank purchases would result in higher interest rates, and this fear apparently led to the *taper tantrum*: from May 22 to May 28, 2013, the 10-year Treasury yield surged 54 basis points, which was a 33% increase.

In response, investment-grade corporate debt fell −2.14% because significant increases in interest rates on Treasury bonds cause most high-quality bonds to lose value. However, investment-grade convertible bonds

Figure 12.4   Central bank balance sheet growth

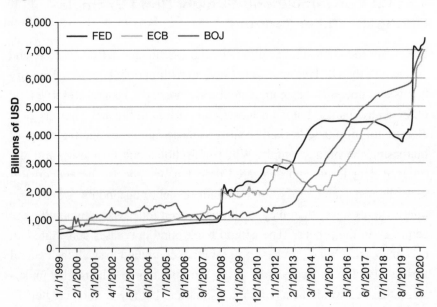

Data: Bloomberg.

Figure 12.5   Anthem stock, convertible, and bond (2042 maturity) total return from May 1, 2013 to October 1, 2013

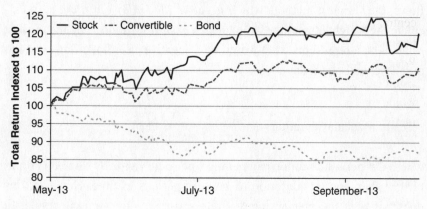

Data: Bloomberg.

returned +2.88%. The favorable return from investment-grade convertibles happened in part because of the good performance of the underlying equities—which naturally strengthened in anticipation of a stronger economy—but also because convertibles have less interest-rate sensitivity than straight bonds.

A case in point was Anthem, a health insurer (Figure 12.5). In the prior year, Anthem had issued both a convertible bond and a straight bond, each with a 30-year maturity (unusually long for a convertible bond). The convertible had a coupon that was 188 basis points less than the straight bond. Normally, a lower coupon would mean greater exposure to interest rates, but this convertible had an effective duration of only 5.51 years versus the straight bond modified duration of 16.01 years, almost two-thirds less rate exposure for the convertible. The straight bond was down 6.8% by May 28, whereas the convertible was up 6.2%. The 10-year Treasury yield continued to rise to almost 3% in September. While the Anthem straight bond was down as much as 14% in late August, the convertible was up more than 9%, thanks to strong equity performance and the significantly lower interest-rate sensitivity of the convertible.

12.12 CALCULATING THE YIELD GREEKS

There are multiple ways to estimate the interest-rate sensitivity of bonds.

12.12.1 Interest-Rate Sensitivity: Duration and Rho

Because straight bonds are essentially a collection of fixed future cash flows, the simplest method, which is called *Macaulay duration*, is to calculate the weighted-average time to each cash flow divided by the current price (which represents what would be a negative cash flow if one were to purchase the bond today).

$$\text{Macaulay duration} = \frac{\int_{t=1}^{n} \frac{t \times C}{(1+y)^t} + \frac{n \times M}{(1+y)^n}}{\text{current bond price}} \qquad (12.12)$$

where C = periodic coupon payment, y = periodic yield, M = the bond's maturity value, and n = duration of bond in periods of time. However, this does not give the precise interest-rate sensitivity for straight bonds. In order to obtain rate sensitivity, one must modify the formula to account for the yield to maturity; hence, the second method is called *modified duration* and is calculated as follows:

$$\text{Modified duration} = \frac{\text{Macauley duration}}{\left(1+\text{yield to maturity} / k\right)} \qquad (12.13)$$

where k = number of coupon periods per year. The key observation for our purposes is that higher rates lead to losses on a straight bond.

Although modified duration works well for calculating the interest-rate sensitivity of straight bonds, modified duration ignores the interest-rate sensitivity that convertibles derive from the embedded option to convert into common shares. To calculate convertible duration, or rho, one must incorporate the rate sensitivity of the embedded call option. Recall from Chapter 8 that an option's value has two basic parts—the expected intrinsic value at maturity (which is essentially the delta) and the present value of the loan needed to obtain the delta. Rho is focused on the latter and is calculated as follows:

$$\rho = Kte^{-n}N(d_2) \qquad (12.14)$$

where

$$d_1 = \frac{\ln(S/K) + t \times \left(r - q + \frac{\sigma^2}{2}\right)}{\sigma \times \sqrt{t}}$$

$$d_2 = d_1 - \sigma \times \sqrt{t}$$

$$N(x) = \frac{1}{\sqrt{2\pi}} \int_{-\infty}^{x} e^{-d_1^2/2}$$

The key observation is that higher rates *increase* the value of rho for an option, which is the opposite effect of higher rates on a straight bond. This is because the preceding formula assumes that the underlying stock price drifts higher at the risk-free rate minus the dividend yield plus one-half the variance $[r - q + (\sigma^2/2)]$. A higher figure for the risk-free rate increases the likelihood of conversion. Note that this is distinct from an increase in credit spreads, which does not affect option value.

So let's consider the effect of convertibility on the interest-rate sensitivity of a bond by comparing a straight (non-convertible) bond with a convertible bond that has the exact same maturity and coupon payment dates. Say that we have a straight bond that matures in 10 years and pays 5% coupons annually. We also have a convertible bond that matures in 10 years and pays 3% coupons annually but is also convertible and has a 40% conversion premium at issuance. Let's assume that the stock has a volatility of 35%, the risk-free rate is 2%, and both bonds are priced at par.

Using the formula for modified duration, the interest-rate sensitivity of both the straight bond and the bond portion of the convertible would be

$$\frac{\int_{t=1}^{10} \frac{t \times 50}{(1+0.05)^t} + \frac{10 \times 1,000}{(1+0.05)^{10}}}{1,000} = 8.108$$

$$\text{Modified duration} = \frac{8.108}{(1+0.05)} = 7.722$$

Using the formula for rho, the interest-rate sensitivity of the call option would be

$$\rho_{\text{call}} = K \times t \times e^{-rt} \times N(d_2)$$

$$d_2 = \frac{\ln\left(\frac{S}{K}\right) + t \times \left(r - q + \frac{\sigma^2}{2}\right)}{\sigma\sqrt{t}} - \sigma\sqrt{t}$$

$$d_2 = \frac{\ln\left(\dfrac{100}{140}\right) + 10 \times \left(0.02 - 0 + \dfrac{0.35^2}{2}\right)}{0.35 \times \sqrt{10}} - 0.35 + \sqrt{10} = -0.6767$$

$$N(d_2) = N(-0.6767) = 0.2493$$

$$\rho_{\text{call}} = \frac{1}{100} \times 140 \times 10 \times e^{-0.02 \times 10} \times 0.2493$$

$$\rho_{\text{call}} = 2.858$$

This means the value of the underlying option increases by $2.858 per 1 percentage point increase in rates. This is different from duration, which enables calculation of the percent increase/decrease in bond value given a percent change in rates. In order to determine convertible interest-rate sensitivity, we need to make sure that our units of measure are identical before calculating a weighted average.

Using the BSM formula, the *per contract* (i.e., an option for 100 shares) of the call option is $38.07, so the percent increase in the call option is $2.858/$38.07 = 0.07513, or 7.513%. Therefore, the interest-rate sensitivity of the convertible would be

$$\rho_{\text{convertible}} = \left(\frac{845.57}{1,000} \times 8.245\right) + \left(\frac{154.43}{1,000} \times -7.513\right) = 5.811, \text{ or } 5.811\%$$

We can then see that despite the similarity of term and coupon, the rate sensitivity of the straight bond is 32.89% higher than that of the convertible.

$$\rho_{\text{bond}} / \rho_{\text{convertible}} = \frac{7.722}{5.811} = 1.329$$

If the stock price were to advance by 40% in the first two years, the conversion premium would be reduced to zero, and the convertible rho would drop significantly.

Rate sensitivity in the straight bond would be reduced because of the passage of two years to maturity to 6.46. Rate sensitivity in the convertible would be reduced because of both the passage of time and a significant increase in the value of the option to 4.31. Therefore, the relative rate sensitivity would increase from 1.329 to 1.499.

12.12.2 Interest-Rate Convexity

The rate sensitivity of bonds changes as rates fluctuate. To illustrate this rate sensitivity, let's consider the straight 10-year bond with a 5% coupon as well as a bond with a 4% coupon and one with a 6% coupon. We can immediately see that Macaulay duration will be higher for the bond with a 4% coupon because less of the total cash flow of the bond occurs prior to maturity (26% instead of 30%), resulting in a Macaulay duration of 8.628 instead of 8.416. We can also see that the duration should be smaller for the bond with the 6% coupon because a greater portion of the total cash flow of the bond occurs prior to maturity (34% instead of 30%), resulting in a Macaulay duration of 8.230 instead of 8.416 (see Table 12.1). Similarly, modified duration is higher in the 4% bond (8.306 instead of 8.025) and lower in the 6% bond (7.774 instead of 8.025).

When yields move about 1 percentage point higher or 1 percentage point lower, the change in modified duration enables us to estimate the convexity of the bond. When rates increase 1 percentage point, modified duration falls by 0.251, and when rates decrease by the same amount, modified duration increases by 0.281. The average of these two values is our finite-difference estimate of convexity 0.266. The convexity of a normal bond also can be calculated via the following formula:

$$\text{Convexity} = \frac{1}{P \times (1+y)^2} \times \sum_{t=1}^{T} \left(\frac{CF_t}{(1+y)^2} \times (t^2 + 1) \right) \qquad (12.15)$$

where
P = bond price
y = yield to maturity
T = maturity in t years
CF_t = cash flow at time t

There are bond features that might interfere with the preceding duration and convexity calculations (Figure 12.6). If a bond is callable, there is a chance that the issuer will pay off the bond prior to maturity if interest rates fall and enable refinancing at lower rates. This can cause convexity to be reduced or even go negative. A call prior to maturity is much more common among high-yield straight bonds than it is among investment-grade straight bonds, and as a result, for the last few years through

Table 12.1   Duration and Convexity

	Cash Flows			Relative wt. of Cash Flows			Wt. years		
	Bond A	Bond B	Bond C	Bond A	Bond B	Bond C	Bond A	Bond B	Bond C
Year price	5% coupon 101	4% coupon 101	6% coupon 101	5% coupon	4% coupon	6% coupon	5% coupon	4% coupon	6% coupon
1	5	4	6	3.33%	2.86%	3.75%	0.033	0.029	0.038
2	5	4	6	3.33%	2.86%	3.75%	0.067	0.057	0.075
3	5	4	6	3.33%	2.86%	3.75%	0.100	0.086	0.113
4	5	4	6	3.33%	2.86%	3.75%	0.133	0.114	0.150
5	5	4	6	3.33%	2.86%	3.75%	0.167	0.143	0.188
6	5	4	6	3.33%	2.86%	3.75%	0.200	0.171	0.225
7	5	4	6	3.33%	2.86%	3.75%	0.233	0.200	0.263
8	5	4	6	3.33%	2.86%	3.75%	0.267	0.229	0.300
9	5	4	6	3.33%	2.86%	3.75%	0.300	0.257	0.338
10	105	104	106	70.00%	74.29%	66.25%	7.000	7.429	6.625
Total cash flow	150	140	160	Macaulay duration			8.416	8.628	8.230
Prior to maturity	45	36	54	Yield to maturity			4.876	3.881	5.871
% of total prior	30%	26%	34%	Modified duration			8.025	8.306	7.774
				Difference from A			0.266	0.281	(0.251)
				Convexity approximation					

Source: Advent Capital Management.

Figure 12.6   High-yield and investment-grade convexity

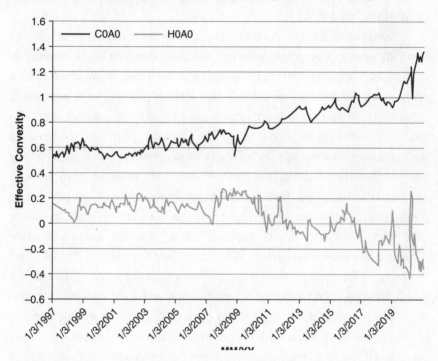

Data: Bloomberg.

2020, high-yield corporate bonds have, on average, had negative convexity, whereas investment-grade corporate bonds have enjoyed positive convexity.

Convertibles typically have lower coupons than straight bonds, which is the trade-off for having the embedded optionality. The lower coupon increases the rate sensitivity of the bond portion of a convertible. If the coupon in our example were 2% rather than 3%, such a convertible would have a rho of 6.02—which would be higher than the rho with a 3% coupon but would still be only 78% of the rho of the straight bond.

12.12.3 Spread Duration and Spread Convexity

For straight bonds, a change in yield—whether due to a change in rates or a change in credit spreads—has the same effect if the change in yield is measured in basis points (bp). In other words, if yield increases 10 bp because of an upward shift in the risk-free curve of 10 bp, or if yield increases

10 bp because of a 10 bp widening of the credit spread, the change in the value of the bond is the same.

However, duration can be expressed in terms of a basis point change in yields or as a percentage point change. Let's consider a 1% increase in rates and a 1% increase in credit spread for a bond that yields 5% and has a credit spread of 300 bp over the risk-free yield of 200 bp. A 1% increase in spreads means that spreads are increasing 3 bp, but a 1% increase in rates means that rates are increasing 2 bp. The 1% increase in spreads therefore has a greater effect on the yield of the bond than the 1% increase in interest rates. Hence, one would expect spread duration (as measured on a percentage basis) to be higher than rate duration (as measured on a percentage basis). This effect is carried through to spread convexity and rate convexity.

With convertible bonds, however, spread duration and rate duration differ for one additional reason. While both credit spreads and rates affect the value of the bond portion, only rates influence the value of the call option (unless the credit-risk rate is being used to value the option). Remember that our option rho formula used the risk-free rate in its calculations, not the actual market rate of the bond. This means that an increase in credit spreads will cause a larger decrease in price than an equivalent increase in rates. To return to our example, the rho of the convertible under a change in credit spread is

$$\rho_{\text{convertible}} = \left(\frac{845.57}{1,000} \times 8.245 \right) + \left(\frac{154.43}{1000} \times -0 \right) = 6.972$$

Another important consideration is what portion of the convertible value is attributable to the option and what portion is attributable to the bond. Our readers may have noticed that the final step in calculating the rho of a convertible comes in the form of a weighted average of the two pieces. For convertibles that are more in the money, the option represents a greater percentage of the value of the convertible as the negative rate duration and zero spread duration of the option become a bigger percentage of the convertible, which pushes overall duration down. For more out-of-the-money convertibles, the option becomes worth relatively little, the convertible becomes more bond-like, and the positive durations of the bond dominate. (If a convertible bond becomes distressed, however, the influence of duration will fade, the influence of credit spread will increase, and ultimately the bond will become more equity-like if the market anticipates a cents-on-the-dollar recovery of the face value of the bond in a bankruptcy or other financial restructuring. It is extremely difficult to model such situations quantitatively.)

12.13 HISTORICAL EXAMPLE: TEVA PHARMACEUTICAL

In 2006, generic drug producer Teva issued a $575 million 0.25% 2026 (puttable on February 1, 2021) convertible bond and a $750 million 1.75% convertible bond, also with a 2026 maturity. The two bonds were issued in order to refinance short-term debt associated with Teva's acquisition of IVAX Corporation. The 1.75% convertible bond was called for redemption in 2011, but the 0.25% convertible remained outstanding until it was put back to the company on February 1, 2021. (With a coupon payment as low as 0.25%, it's easy to see why Teva did not call the bond.)

Figure 12.7 focuses on the period from the start of 2013 to 2019, which tracks the rise and then collapse of Teva's stock price. Teva initially benefited, as did the generic drug industry as a whole, from the increased demand for generic drugs as a method of controlling rising healthcare spending. Then Teva acquired Allergan for a hefty $40.5 billion (nearly $34 billion of which was cash) in 2015. This left Teva with a leveraged

Figure 12.7 Timeline of performance (total return) of Teva .25% convertible 2026 in 2013–2019

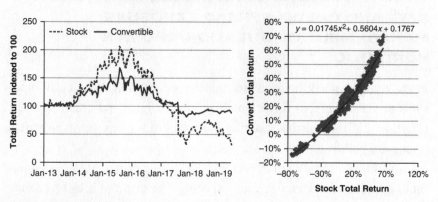

Data: Bloomberg.

balance sheet and ill equipped to face accelerating generic drug price deflation that began shortly thereafter.

For our purposes, it is interesting to consider what happened to the rho of the convertible over this time period using what we have learned about how convertible interest-rate exposure works. In 2015, after Teva's share price had doubled since the start of 2013, much of the convertible's value was coming from the option value associated with the conversion feature. As we have seen, the lower rho of convertible bonds comes from the counteracting force of the option value and from the fact that the bond value is only a portion of the total value of the convertible.

So, in 2015, when Teva's stock price (and therefore the conversion value as well) was at its peak, the rho of Teva's convertible bond was very low, potentially even zero. Later on, when it became clear that Teva had overpaid for Allergan, Teva shares collapsed 80%, wiping out the option value of the bond in the process (though it appears that Teva was not considered a major credit risk despite the business problems because the bond floor held). By 2017, the chances of Teva recovering to the conversion price had become remote, and most of the convertible's value came from the bond component, so the convertible's rho was nearly the same as the rho of a straight bond. The overarching point of this example is that interest-rate sensitivity is not a set and forget characteristic. The rho of a convertible security (or a portfolio of convertible securities) can change dramatically based on the performance of the underlying equity.

12.14 CALCULATING AND MANAGING INTEREST-RATE AND CREDIT-SPREAD EXPOSURE: MANAGEMENT OF DURATION/RHO IN A PORTFOLIO

In managing a portfolio, it is desirable to understand the overall exposures to various macro factors such as interest rates and credit spreads. Duration and rho metrics describe the relationship between convertible prices and yields.

Yields can change either because of a change in market rates of interest or because of a change in credit spreads. The effect of a 10 bp change in yields is nearly identical whether the change is due to an increase in spreads or an increase in rates (for an unhedged convertible portfolio). It is convenient to calculate rho in terms of basis points, but it is also common to calculate rho relative to a 1 percentage point change in rates or a 1 percentage point change in spreads. Because the relevant rate and spread are rarely the same, the rho effect of a 1 percentage point change differs, whereas the rho effect of a 10 bp change is identical. For example, consider a convertible with a spread of 300 bp, duration of two years, and rho 10 bp of −0.2%, and the prevailing two-year Treasury is 1%. A 10 bp increase in either the rate or the spread will reduce the value of the convertible by 0.2%, *ceteris paribus*. A 1 percent increase in rates increases the yield by 1 bp, whereas a 1 percentage point increase in spreads increases the yield by 3 bp. Therefore, rate rho of 1% is −2 bp, and spread rho 1% is −6 bp.

12.14.1 Negative Correlation Between Rates and Spreads

Because corporate bond yields are a function of both rates and spreads, understanding rate and spread exposure requires an understanding of the relationship between rates and spreads. The ICE high-yield and investment-grade corporate bond indices have spread data since December 31, 1996. Both have demonstrated negative correlation with Treasury yields. Linear regression of quarterly data suggests that a 100 bp increase in the 10-year Treasury yield is consistent with a 57 bp decrease in investment-grade spreads and a 213 bp decrease in high-yield spreads. Convertibles are more sensitive to the two-year Treasury because the duration of a convertible is significantly less than that of straight bonds. A regression versus the two-year Treasury yield suggests that a 100 bp increase in rates is consistent with a 47 bp decrease in investment-grade spreads and a 178 bp decrease in high-yield spreads.

Therefore, any increases in interest rates have been partly offset by a spread decrease for investment-grade convertibles and more than offset for high-yield convertibles. Thus, while periods of rising rates generally result in capital losses for Treasury bonds, the negative effect on investment-grade bonds is muted, and the effect is *positive* for high-yield bonds. In 20 quarters with the biggest increases in two-year Treasury yields, the rate

**Figure 12.8   Quarterly high-yield and investment-grade spread
change versus 10-year Treasury yield change,
1996–2020**

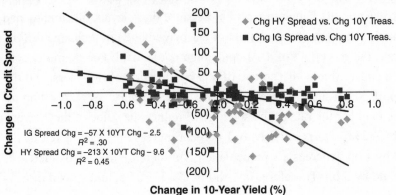

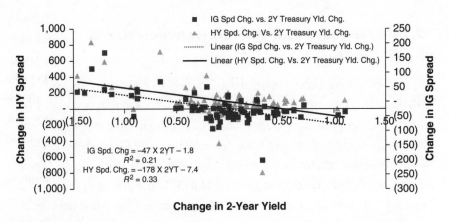

Data: Bloomberg.

increase was more than offset by high-yield spreads tightening, and about two-thirds of the increase was offset by investment-grade spreads.

Similarly, during periods of market volatility, increases in investment-grade and high-yield spreads have been at least partially offset by decreases in rates—mitigating corporate bond portfolio losses. Considering the 20 quarters with the highest spread widening, over 30% of high-yield spread widening has been offset by two-year Treasury yield declines, whereas all the investment grade spread widening was offset. Yet, in an era of very low Treasury rates, this relationship may not continue indefinitely (see Figure 12.8).

Therefore, when considering rho risk, it is important to consider the negative correlation between rates and spreads (historically) but also whether the negative correlation can persist in the future. If the concern is rising interest rates, then falling spreads are certainly likely, but if the concern is widening spreads and interest rates are near all-time lows, it is unlikely that the negative correlation will recur.

12.14.2 Spread Volatility and Beta

Although the spread is the market metric that measures credit risk, it is the change in this spread, rather than the actual level, that causes gains and losses in the market prices of bonds. Understanding spread rho risk requires understanding the propensity for individual spreads to widen (spread volatility) as well as the propensity for an index to do so (spread beta).

Just as equity portfolios have both systematic risk, represented by the overall portfolio beta (or beta-adjusted delta) to the market, and idiosyncratic risk, related to each individual security in the portfolio, fixed-income portfolios also have both systematic and idiosyncratic risks. The theory of diversification is that systematic risks are additive across all positions, but idiosyncratic risks are reduced, if not eliminated entirely, by diversification because the idiosyncratic risk is by definition uncorrelated with systematic risks.

Systematic risks include risk-free rate and term-premium duration as well as duration to the systematic portion of credit spreads. The idiosyncratic risk is represented by exposure to the idiosyncratic portion of the credit spreads. While it is informative to know the weighted-average portfolio spread relative to the index, it is perhaps more informative to know the weighted-average beta of portfolio spreads relative to the index because beta incorporates the covariance of individual spreads to index-spread variance.

In the example in Table 12.2, the spread, spread beta, spread volatility, and idiosyncratic portion of the spread are provided for 10 large high-yield bonds. If a portfolio held these bonds in equal weight, it would have a spread about 29% less than the high-yield index, but the average beta is only 11% less than the index.

While an investor is earning 29% less spread than the index, he or she has only 11% less systematic spread risk than the index. A more efficient portfolio might earn more spread than the index with less spread beta.

Table 12.2   Spread Beta of 10 High-Yield Bonds

	Spread	Spread Beta	Index Beta (Spread BP)	Idiosyncratic (Spread BP)	Spread Volatility
HY Index	555	1	555	–	
S 7 7/8	314	0.32	179	135	159%
TDG 6 1/4	536	1.02	568	–32	141%
SFRFP 7 3/8	448	0.93	518	–70	174%
CHTR 5 1/8	370	0.6	334	35	102%
KHC 4 3/8	345	0.35	194	152	50%
HCA 5 3/8	307	0.67	374	–68	169%
WDC 4 3/4	294	0.52	289	5	134%
NFLX 5 7/8	341	0.33	184	157	100%
THC 8 1/8	462	1.65	913	–451	166%
OXY 2.9	506	2.35	1,306	–800	248%
Average	392	0.88	486	–94	144%
% of Tot. Spd	71%		89%	11%	

Data: Bloomberg.

12.15 RATE AND CREDIT CROSS GREEKS

As in the Teva example, interest-rate sensitivity (and therefore spread sensitivity as well) is not constant. Changes in equity prices, equity volatility, and term to maturity all influence yield sensitivity. The measurement of the effect of these other factors on rho (rates) and omicron (credit spreads) are called *cross Greeks*. These can give investors a sense of how rate exposure and spread exposure change over time and with inflections in equities.

The most obvious example of the effects of cross Greeks would be a new-issue convertible in which the equity either increases or falls significantly. If the stock price doubles, the convertible becomes an equity surrogate and loses almost all yield sensitivity. In contrast, if the stock falls by 80%, the option becomes worth much less, and the investor is left with what is essentially a straight bond that is much more credit and rate sensitive. Space does not permit describing cross Greeks here, but for a thorough review of the subject, please visit www.AdventCap.com/SupplementaryMaterials.

12.16 RATE AND CREDIT PARAMETRIC FACTOR MODELING

So far we have been assuming that our different variables are uncorrelated with each other (e.g., that an increase in volatility is not associated with a change in rates). However, this assumption is faulty, particularly when it comes to equity price changes and their correlation with changes in spread. Intuitively, it's easy to see why the two might be correlated; something that drives the shares down 30% likely will carry credit implications—and the same is true for a large increase in stock prices.

We have also covered the idea that the leverage of a company increases as its share price decreases because the equity of the firm is now smaller relative to its outstanding debt, which effectively means higher financial leverage in the sense of market price. Moreover, a company's ability to borrow becomes impaired as the market value of its equity declines. Hence, a company becomes a weaker credit as its share price decreases, which leads to wider credit spreads in order to compensate debt holders for the risk. There is empirical evidence that an inverse correlation between equity price movements and credit spreads does exist. The enterprise value of a company that has debt is akin to the relationship of the market price of a house to its mortgage, as we explained in more detail in Chapter 2. It's obvious that a house with a large mortgage is a riskier investment than a house with a small mortgage; both the downside and the upside potentials of the equity in the house are higher with a large mortgage. Space does not permit a more complete review of rate and credit-factor parameters here, but for a thorough review of the subject, please visit www.AdventCap.com/SupplementaryMaterials.

12.17 SUMMARY AND CONCLUSION

- While the yield of straight debt is often calculated as yield to maturity, yield to call, or yield to worst, convertible investors usually prefer to use current yield, yield to put/maturity, or all-in yield.
- The yield can be thought of as the risk-free rate plus a number of risk-based spreads or premiums, including the term premium, credit spread, and liquidity spread.

- A number of specialty spread calculations exist that express the credit spread relative to various base rates. For convertibles, the implied spread incorporates both the credit risk of the bond and the cheapness of the equity option embedded in the convertible.
- While convertibles are typically thought of as a way to reduce the interest expense of the issuer, the all-in yield of convertibles can be as high as or higher than the yield on comparable straight debt.
- Straight debt can only have total returns greater than the coupon—because of capital gains—when interest rates fall or credit spreads narrow. Convertibles typically provide capital gains because of the rising prices of the underlying equity.

The length of time until the maturity of the bonds in this example is essentially the duration. In one scenario, when interest rates fell, duration was pleasurable; in the other scenario, when interest rates rose, duration was painful.

There are things in life that make bad duration more tolerable like reading a good book *about convertibles* or playing a game on your smartphone during a long flight—effectively they make the duration shorter, or at least they make the passing of time seem quicker. There are also things that make happy moments last longer—effectively increasing good duration—such as a photograph.

For bonds, this property, which diminishes bad duration and makes good duration even better, is called *convexity*. Convexity, like its antonym concavity, is a property of a curve relative to the starting point or location of the observer. When the curve appears to be inward sinking, it is called *concave*, like a cave that sinks into the Earth. When the curve appears to be outward bending, as a rainbow in the heavens, it is called *convex*—like the diluvian covenant. Cave and covenant are useful mnemonic devices to remember which is inward sloping and which is outward sloping.

In the physical world, convexity is a property that brings distant objects nearer—like the convex lens of a telescope, which brings the tiny speck of a merchant ship on the horizon into full view of a buccaneer captain. Or like the rainbow, convexity also brings color to an otherwise gloomy overcast sky. When you gaze at the sun through a thick cloud, as sunlight passes through a cloud, its rays become diffused—or partially blocked—but the light that passes through remains white light, without being refracted into its component colors. However, when the sun is at your back, such as when you are looking westward in the morning or eastward in the afternoon, and it encounters water vapor in front of you, it does refract backward. In other words, you will see a rainbow in the opposite direction of the sun. Irish lore suggests that a pot of gold can be found at the end of a rainbow. Financial acumen suggests that it is actually convexity (like the refracting property of water) that builds and preserves wealth.

ENDNOTES

1. https://www.investopedia.com/terms/n/nationally-recognized-statistical-ratings-organization.asp.
2. https://www.investopedia.com/terms/c/creditdefaultswap.asp.
3. https://www.investopedia.com/terms/a/assetswap.asp.
4. https://www.economist.com/finance-and-economics/2021/05/22/learning-to-live-without-libor.
5. Philosopher, statistician, and author of popular books, including *New York Times* best-sellers *Antifragile* (2012) and *The Black Swan* (2007).

CHAPTER 13

Convertible Hedging Techniques and Analysis

Nature has provided us a spectacular toolbox... and we now have the ability to use it.

— *Barry Schuler*[1]

13.1 TRADITIONAL CONVERTIBLE ARBITRAGE

The overall structure of a hedged convertible position and the long-term strategy performance were presented in Chapter 7. This chapter focuses on the components of return and hedging alternatives. Convertible arbitrage is possible because of the asymmetric return of convertibles relative to the price movement of the underlying stock, that is, the appreciation potential from the conversion feature, the downside support from the bond floor, and the ability to isolate these properties by hedging out unwanted risks. Financial markets provide a "spectacular toolbox," and this chapter provides the instructions for using these tools.

There are four key sources of returns from a convertible arbitrage position: (1) the current yield of the convertible, (2) the rebate on the stock short position, (3) the *volatility yield* as the hedge is adjusted (see further details in Section 13.9), and (4) the richening of the value of the convertible as its market price reflects increased volatility and/or improved credit quality. The characteristics of the convertible and the thesis for setting up the hedge determine how a hedged position is structured. Delta measures equity sensitivity and is determined using theoretical models (described in Chapters 7 and in this chapter). High, medium, and low-delta convertible positions have vastly different properties in terms of the magnitude of hedge required, and they also have different sensitivities to interest rates, credit spreads, volatility, and the capacity to generate gamma trading gains from asymmetry.

13.2 CLASSIC CONVERTIBLE ARBITRAGE USING BALANCED CONVERTIBLES

The most common delta-neutral convertible arbitrage position is long a highly asymmetric convertible with gamma of 0.4 or higher and a delta in the 40%–80% range on a stock with medium to high volatility and an issuer with a stable credit profile. This is the "sweet spot" for a convertible arbitrage position because gamma and volatility combine to generate the volatility yield. The higher the delta, the more short shares are required by a delta-neutral position.

After the hedge is set up, most arbitrageurs regularly adjust the positions by buying back (covering) some of the short stock when the shares decline and by selling (shorting) more stock when the shares rise. These adjustments help to maintain a delta-neutral hedge and help to realize small trading profits. Some sophisticated arbitrageurs have developed algorithms to automate the rehedging activity. Such adjustments are intended to provide a relatively consistent stream of realized gains.

New convertible issues usually provide the ideal hedging profile of balanced delta and relatively high gamma and are typically issued below theoretical value. Yet, to implement the strategy, an arbitrageur must be able to short the underlying stock. Sometimes smaller-cap issuers and companies that already have a significant percentage of their stock shorted have shares that are expensive to borrow. Convertible arbitrageurs can be accommodated if the issuing company plans to use a portion of the proceeds of the new convertible to buy back stock. The company might satisfy the demand of arbitrageurs without incurring downside pressure on the stock by issuing a package of long convertibles while concurrently arranging for the arbitrageurs to establish stock hedges. Such a combination is nicknamed a *happy meal* after the McDonald's product that includes a toy. See Section 1.6.9 for further details on happy meals.

The issuing company usually uses a portion of the proceeds from the new convertible to purchase a call spread from the underwriter, which minimizes the potential dilution from the convertible by synthetically raising the conversion premium. The investment bank therefore becomes the natural buyer of the stock to hedge the call option it is writing and then lends the shares to convertible arbitrageurs participating in the convertible issuance. Call spreads are favorably regarded by both issuers and investors (see further discussion in Chapter 16).

13.2.1 Trade Example: Twitter 0.25% of 2024

To demonstrate the workings of a high-gamma, delta-neutral position, we have created a hypothetical arbitrage of the Twitter 0.25% convertible of 2024 from late June 2020 through January 2021.

The Twitter position represented a classic long convertible bond and short stock hedge. The thesis was that the embedded option was trading at a discount to both realized volatility and to the implied volatility of long-dated long-term equity anticipation securities ("LEAPS."[2]) There was also the potential for spikes in volatility because of social media regulation or merger and acquisition activity. In mid-June 2020, the bond had a parity delta of 52.9%, a conversion premium of 68.6%, and a gamma of 0.434.

The 100-day realized volatility rose to 66.8, and the listed equity option implied volatility reached 52.8 versus an implied volatility of only 42.2 on the convertible bond. Hence, the convertible was *theoretically cheap* because it was trading at a discount to the theoretical value of the combined components of the bond and the embedded equity option.

An alternative way to evaluate the arbitrage position is to estimate the relative cheapness of the implied credit spread over Treasury bonds, which represents the default risk. The basic delta-neutral position hedge is affected by the credit risk of the issuer, so credit research is important. Twitter had a strong credit profile with a free cash flow of more than $1 billion. The Twitter straight-bond credit spreads had recovered after the COVID-19 trough, and in mid-June 2020, the 3% straight bond of 2027 traded at a spread of only 304 basis points (bp) over Treasury bonds, whereas the 0.25% convertible bond of 2024 implied a much wider credit spread of 465 bp. Discounted implied spread is an alternative way of determining whether the convertible is trading at a discount from theoretical value (see Figure 13.1).

Assume that on June 23, 2020, the arbitrage position was established with a neutral delta. By June 26, Twitter's stock price had fallen to $29.05 from $32.91 in just three days, and the convertible bond had declined 2.8 bond points. As a result of these price movements, the arbitrage position

Figure 13.1   Realized and listed call implied volatility of Twitter through June 23, 2020

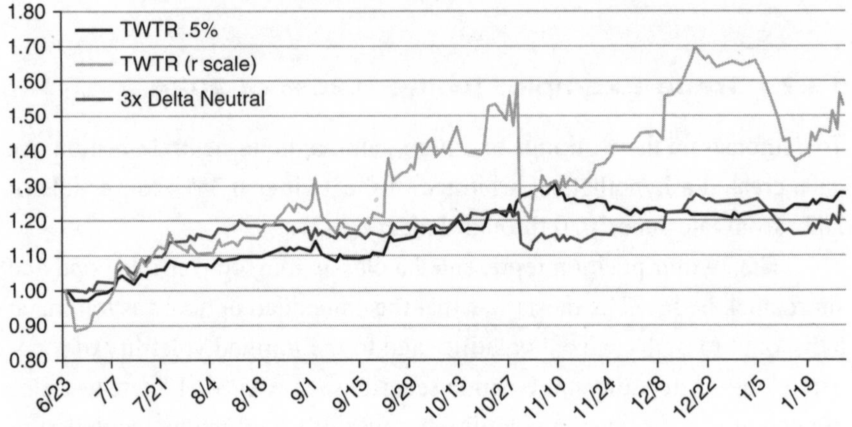

Data: Bloomberg.

was now net short Twitter because of the lower delta (as a result of the stock declining), hence, requiring an adjustment of the hedge position. Accordingly, shares of Twitter would have been purchased to reduce the size of the short position to compensate. By July 8, the price of Twitter had risen to $35.41, which meant that the hedge needed to be adjusted again in order to be kept equity neutral. This would have been accomplished by selling shares of Twitter to increase the short position. Over this two-week period, an arbitrageur could have benefited from the volatility in Twitter's equity price through the hedging process of the convertible arbitrage position. The arbitrageur would have systematically bought at the lows and sold after a recovery, thereby generating gamma trading profits.

The stock weakened amid high volatility after third-quarter earnings were disappointing, followed by a recovery on anecdotal evidence of improving usage. High stock volatility continued through January 2021 and propelled our hypothetical delta-neutral convertible arbitrage position to a total return of 28% compared with 23% on the convertible and 54% on the stock. As illustrated in Table 13.1, the convertible arbitrage position had a fraction of the volatility of the stock, and as a result, the Sharpe ratio was nearly double that of both a long stock and long convertible position, and the Sortino ratio was nearly three times as high as that of the stock and the convertible.

Table 13.1   Delta-Neutral Arbitrage Position Has Much Higher Sharpe and Sortino Ratios

	Stock	Cvt	3x Delta-Neutral
Return	53.5%	22.7%	27.8%
St. Dev.	51.6%	21.7%	13.9%
Sharpe	1.04	1.05	2.00
Sortino	1.16	1.10	2.98

Source: Advent Capital Management estimates.

13.3 HIGH-DELTA HEDGED CONVERTIBLES AND SYNTHETIC PUTS

In-the-money convertibles (where the stock price is well above the conversion price) typically have deltas greater than 80. This means that creating a delta-neutral position involves shorting an equal amount of stock as the long position represented in the convertible. The position therefore has a lower net market value than the balanced delta-neutral position in the preceding example, which was short considerably less stock than the value of the convertible. Consequently, small movements in the stock price do not change the delta significantly, and therefore, the position will generate a lower volatility yield.

Yet, some high-delta convertibles will generate gamma trading profits on moderate and high levels of volatility because maintaining a delta-neutral position generates profits as a result of slight modifications of the hedge, although such adjustments are significantly less than for lower-delta (hence, higher-gamma) convertibles. Even when gamma is low, if the *cross-Greeks speed* (the change in gamma with respect to stock price) or *zomma* (the change in gamma in response to a change in volatility) is high, then gamma will increase rapidly in a downward movement in the stock. This is generally the case when a stock price is near the conversion price and the bond is within a year or two of maturity. If there is increased volatility or a sharp correction in the stock price, this sort of trade can be highly profitable.

Tesla convertible bonds became high-priced and high-delta equity surrogates just prior to the COVID-19 shock in early 2020. A *synthetic put* hedge comprised of the 2% 2024 convertible bond, bought at 305, and 16.14 shares of Tesla stock shorted per bond, with the position levered four times, would have yielded a positive return of about 24% as Tesla stock plunged −60.6% from February 19 to March 18 while the convertible fell 6 percentage points less than the stock at −54.6%.

A portfolio of positions with high deltas can be used as a *tail-risk* hedge. Consider what would happen to a hypothetical synthetic put in the event of default. The position has equal parts long convertible (trading at 160) and short stock. In bankruptcy, the stock will decline 100% and the convertible will decline to some recovery rate—say 40% of par. In this example, the convertible will fall 75% (from 160 to 40). The position therefore will net a 25% return on the original bond value on an unlevered basis or 100% on a four times levered basis. If the stock falls 90% and the bond is repaid at par, the position will net 51.5% on the original bond value on an unlevered basis $[0.9 - (1 - 100/160) = 0.515]$ or 206% on a four times levered basis.

In-the-money high-credit-quality convertibles with near maturities and significant equity volatility work well as synthetic puts. As of November 15, 2020, the Illumina (ILMN) 0.5% 2021 had a price of 131.23, with parity delta of 82.3, participation delta of 79.4, and gamma of .85. The stock, at 322, was 20% higher than its trough 10 weeks earlier and 54% higher than the COVID-19 trough in March 2020. The convertible implied a credit spread of zero because high-credit-quality, high-delta convertibles have minimal bond-like properties, and the price behavior is influenced more by the equity option properties. The implied volatility was 42.5. For every dollar of convertible owned, the synthetic put would be short about 80 cents of stock.

The Bloomberg OVCV convertible valuation model indicated that if ILMN stock fell to the September low, it would cost the bond 11.9%, even assuming a 50 bp widening of the credit spread. A fall to the March low would cost the bond 20.6%, even with a 100 bp widening in the credit. However, starting from delta neutral and using four times leverage, a drop to the September low would earn a synthetic put 12%, and a drop of $113 to the March low of $209 would earn 67.8% because the short stock position would earn significantly more than the loss on the convertible because the convertible declined—as expected—far less than the stock. In contrast, an equivalent increase in the stock to $435 would increase the value of the convertible 31% while costing the stock short 27.85%; at four times leverage, this is a positive return of 12.72%, which demonstrates that price swings *in either direction* are positive for synthetic puts.

The worst-case scenario is a decline in implied volatility. If volatility were to fall from 42.5 to 20, the bond would cheapen 4 points, or about 3%, costing a four times levered position 12%. Even a deterioration in the credit would not have as significant an effect given the short maturity and high delta; an increase in the spread of 1,000 bp would cost the bond less than 1% and a four times levered synthetic put position about 3.85%. Even the simultaneous 1,000 bp widening of the credit spread with the drop of the stock price to $209 would still return nearly 60% because of the near maturity and the relative solidity of the bond floor. It should be noted that this analysis is instantaneous. Over time, a convertible experiences theta decay as the time value of the option decreases. With synthetic puts, almost all the option value is intrinsic value, which does not decay. Very little of the option value is time value, and therefore, theta decay is negligible.

13.4 CONVERTIBLES APPROACHING MATURITY: AVERAGING PERIODS

Some convertibles do not exercise into shares at expiration, but rather the issuer has the option of paying the par value in cash and the residual value in cash or shares. Calculation of the cash value is not based solely on the price of the stock at expiration but on its *average* price during an *averaging period*. This period may range from 20 to 40 trading days or longer. The properties of the convertible change significantly as the convertible enters the averaging period. For a convertible with a 20-day period, properties such as delta are reduced by 1/20th on the first day, 1/19th on the second day, 1/18th on the third day, and so on until the final day. This change in properties should be reflected in the size of the hedge. This feature is not always properly evaluated in online convertible models, but models that do evaluate averaging periods essentially divide the convertible into N slices, where N is the number of days in the averaging period, and one slice *matures* each day in the averaging period.

13.5 DEFENSIVE CONVERTIBLES

Even moderately low-delta convertibles (delta 20–40) can have high gamma. Moderate deltas combined with high stock volatility, theoretical cheapness, and coupon income can create attractive opportunities if the credits hold. Although most *defensive convertibles* are the consequence of a decline in the price of the underlying stock since issuance, defensive convertibles are occasionally provided by the new-issue market.

An example of an attractive low-delta convertible for a convertible arbitrage strategy is Fortive, an investment-grade manufacturer. At the end of April 2020, the interest spread over the yield on equivalent Treasury bonds on the Fortive 3.15% straight bond 2026 had widened to 269 bp from 231 bp on March 23 at the bottom of the market and only 119 bp a year earlier despite the fact that the market capitalization of the company had rebounded from a low of $14 billion to nearly $22 billion. At the same time, the Fortive 0.875% convertible 2022 had an implied volatility of 20.18, parity delta of 14.7%, conversion premium of 92%, participation delta of 7.3%, and gamma of 0.47. The convertible was trading at 96.4, which was just above the estimated bond floor of 96.1. The implied volatility at 20 was well below the one-year equity option implied volatility of 37 and the six-month realized stock volatility of 49.

By January 31, 2021, the spread on the straight bond had compressed to 53 bp, and the convertible price had increased 5.35 bond points to 101.75. About 1.75 bond points of this was due to delta—which is hedged away in a delta-neutral position—but about 360 basis points was attributable to the tightening of the credit spread and the richening of volatility, with the bond implying a volatility of 29, gamma expanding to 0.89, and the premium falling to 40.5%. A three times levered position would have returned 10.8% on the richening of the bond $(3 \times 3.6\%)$ while also earning 2.00% $[(3 \times 0.875 + 1)^{0.75} - 1]$ on the coupon and 7.4% (the result of simulating the daily rehedging of the bond), less the cost of leverage for nine months of approximately 1.00%—altogether a return of about 18.2% with an annualized standard deviation of less than 2.

13.6 DISCOUNT CONVERTIBLES

Discount convertible bonds, with stocks far out of the money, are used with less frequency in convertible arbitrage because the delta-neutral position calculated in evaluation models almost always will calculate a low delta and a light hedge. Yet, credit risk in such situations is usually high and is sometimes paramount; this residual credit risk is exceptionally difficult to model. Lower-delta bonds generally have more *rho* (rate risk) and even more *omicron* (credit risk).

In the case of discount convertibles, if the convertible bond becomes stressed and then distressed, the bond and the stock usually begin to decline *in tandem*—as though the delta were *rising*—which makes traditional hedging with the stock exceptionally difficult. If a heavy hedge is used—short a lot of stock—such a position may be profitable as the stock tumbles. But if the stock rebounds, such a development can be positive from a credit perspective, and sometimes the convertible rebounds with the stock. So a heavy hedge (i.e., a hedge that will be especially profitable if the stock delinces) on a deeply discounted convertible can result in losses. Typically, companies with discount convertibles have suffered a significant decline in market capitalization, and credit spreads have widened since issuance.

13.7 HEDGING CONVERTIBLE PREFERREDS AND MANDATORY CONVERTIBLE PREFERREDS

Convertible arbitrage classically involves convertible bonds. It is possible to hedge convertible preferreds, of course; such hedges seek primarily to capture the yield advantage of the preferreds. The superior yield makes it possible to hold large short positions in the underlying stock while still earning a positive carry after the cost of borrowing the stock (and paying any dividends on the borrowed stock). However, convertible preferreds are rare in the contemporary convertible market. The challenges of hedging convertible preferreds are twofold: (1) the typically long duration of the preferreds and (2) the weak credit protections that are inherent in the preferred structure. When credit markets require wider credit spreads, the downside protection of convertible preferreds is exceptionally weak. And from a hedged convertible perspective, short-term performance is vital—and will be undermined by the plunging prices of convertible preferreds. The $1,000-par Bank of America 7.25% convertible preferred plunged from over par before the Great Financial Crisis (GFC) to a low of around $250 in the aftermath—and an advance to well over par in ensuing years.

Preferreds with such market risk are inappropriate for hedged convertible strategies. No quantitative model could have accurately calculated an appropriate number of Bank of America common shares to hedge against such a collapse in the price of the preferred, nor could a model have anticipated the need to almost eliminate a short stock position once the preferred began to recover.

Mandatory convertible preferreds are commonplace. Options can be easily used to hedge mandatory preferreds because most of the issuers of mandatory securities are larger companies that have liquid listed options on their common stock. Moreover, mandatory preferreds sometimes deviate from theoretical value partly because of the yield illusion that is created by their quarterly distributions (i.e., at issuance, there are merely 12 quarterly distributions until mandatory conversion after three years, and as the remaining time until mandatory conversion declines, the remaining distributions become fewer and fewer, and the concept of yield becomes a misnomer). The *yield illusion* may cause the mandatory preferreds to trade *rich*—overvalued—which creates opportunities for profitable hedging. Yield per se is attractive to certain institutional accounts. And mandatory preferreds are widely held by individual investors who are attracted by the apparent yields—and who lack access to sophisticated quantitative models that properly value mandatory securities. Some financial advisors misunderstand mandatory characteristics and may make inappropriate recommendations of mandatory preferreds to their retail clients. Hence, retail trading may cause mandatory preferreds to become overvalued, which creates opportunities for arbitrageurs.

Mandatory preferreds are avoided by many convertible arbitrage managers because of their propensity to exhibit negative gamma, or *gamma-neg* in the lingo of convertible traders, meaning that the delta of the mandatory may increase as the underlying stock goes down and decrease as the underlying stock rises. This relationship between the mandatory and its underlying stock exists because a mandatory has a *range* of *strike prices* in what is called the *dead zone*. At issuance, the conversion ratio is at its maximum; that is, the strike price is at the low end of the dead zone. If the underlying stock begins to rise, the conversion ratio declines to a minimum; that is, the strike price rises toward the high end of the range. The dead zone effectively provides a conversion premium at issuance.

If the mandatory matures while the stock is in the dead zone, there is no participation in either stock upside or downside. Therefore, between the strikes, delta is low—especially as the mandatory approaches maturity. However, delta *increases* as the stock approaches either strike price. This creates positive gamma closer to the upper strike and negative gamma closer to the lower strike. In fact, gamma flips from positive to negative approximately midway between the two strikes. Because positive asymmetry (i.e., positive gamma) is the source of most convertible arbitrage profit, negative gamma is a source of loss—or at least increased risk of loss—for convertible arbitrageurs, which is why mandatory preferreds are less frequently used by arbitrageurs. See Section 1.4 for further details on mandatory preferreds.

13.8 USE OF TOTAL RETURN SWAPS, ASCOTS, AND SYNTHETICS

While convertible arbitrage positions are usually held as cash long and short positions with the prime broker of a hedge fund, occasionally the position is structured as a *total return swap* (TRS). The economics of the trade are exactly the same as holding the cash bond and stock short. Yet, for regulatory reasons, it is sometimes impossible to short; for example, European undertakings for the collective investment in transferable securities (UCITS) funds must structure delta-neutral positions as TRS because of regulations against shorting. India, Taiwan, and some other countries prohibit short sales, so TRSs are used to create delta-neutral positions for convertibles in those countries.

Asset swapped convertibles option transactions (ASCOTs) are swaps issued primarily on Asian convertibles where the credit of the issuer is replaced by that of a high-credit-quality financial institution. When an issuer's bank is more familiar with the credit quality of the issuer—and is therefore relatively more comfortable with its credit than overseas investors—the ASCOTs enable global convertible arbitrage funds to go long the issuer's stock volatility without exposure to the issuer's credit. The ASCOT market developed in the 1990s and was a major catalyst for growth in Asian convertible markets in the early 2000s because arbitrageurs had previously avoided these markets. ASCOTs were also widely used in Europe prior to the Great Financial Crisis (GFC) of 2008. ASCOTs are occasionally used by US hedge funds. In general, asset swap bids are available for investment grade (or implied investment grade) issuers.

An ASCOT bifurcates a convertible bond into two components. The credit component is the convertible asset swap and the option/equity component is the convertible call option. The bond component (credit exposure) is sold to a fixed income investor at an agreed upon spread and the call option on the convertible is retained. The convertible is sold at "bond value" (i.e. the present value of the bonds future cash flows). The value of the "equity option" is the difference of the discoverable price (i.e., the market price of the convertible) and bond value. The difference is what is retained by the convertible investor. The buyer of the ASCOT (a credit investor) assumes both the credit and the interest rate risk. That investor earns a higher yield from the stripped asset than is available in the market, while the convertible investor sources cheap volatility and employs leverage to achieve the targeted returns.

Exchangeable convertibles are issued by entities other than the issuer, sometimes convertible into an entity that has been spun off by the issuer. The credit is that of the bond issuer rather than the issuer of the stock—which mitigates the correlation between the credit and the stock price that is observed in traditional convertible bonds. Exchangeables can trade cheap relative to theoretical value; hence, they can be especially attractive to convertible arbitrageurs.

Synthetic convertibles are issued by entities—usually banks—that do not own the underlying stock. Synthetics are typically structured in Europe. Synthetics increase the pool of potential investments for convertible investors—especially for accounts that have investment grade mandates, since the credit quality of the convertible carries the rating of the issuer. Synthetics are rarely attractive for convertible arbitrage funds because the issuer of the synthetic needs to earn a spread, therefore synthetics are issued "rich" to theoretical value. The issuer must mark up the volatility of the underlying stock in order to earn a profit from structuring the synthetic—whereas an operating company that issues a convertible is a natural seller of its own volatility and will attract buyers for the new convertible by issuing it at a price that is cheap to theoretical value.

13.9 GAMMA TRADING

Gamma trading is the process of adjusting the hedge on a delta-neutral convertible arbitrage position. When the stock price goes up, delta on the bond increases, which means that to return the position to delta neutral, one must sell more stock. When the stock price declines, delta on the bond declines, which means that to return the position to delta neutral, one must buy back or cover a portion of the short stock position. As stock prices fluctuate over time, there is a continuous process of buying stock at lower prices, and selling it at higher prices. This natural buy low, sell high activity generates a profit. The amount of this profit depends on the volatility of the stock price and the magnitude of the asymmetry (gamma) in the convertible, which is why this aspect of return can also be called a "volatility yield." The relationship between expected profit, volatility, and gamma is as follows:

$$\text{Expected return (annualized)} = \text{volatility}^2 \times \text{gamma}/2$$

13.9.1 Gamma Trading Frequency: A Machine to Generate Profits

Consider two convertibles of the same underlying company, delta hedged with stock, one with a gamma of 0.4 the other with a gamma of 0.8, as depicted in Table 13.2. Assume that the stock price begins at 1 and swings between 1.05 and 0.95 before ending the day unchanged. A rehedge threshold of 5% would perfectly match the daily high (up 5%) and low (down 5%). The 0.4 gamma position would sell 2% of the stock at 1.05 and buy it back at 1.00, after which it would buy 2% stock at .95 before selling it at 1.00, netting 20 bp on the day. The 0.8 gamma position trades would be double the size of the 0.4 gamma trades because the delta change would have been twice as much as the lower-gamma bond. Therefore, the 0.8 gamma position would have made 40 bp.

However, top ticking sales and bottom ticking purchases are rare, and it was coincidence that the daily range perfectly matched the rehedging thresholds. Consider the same two bonds and the same intraday stock swings but with a rehedging threshold of 2%. Rather than making 20 and 40 bp, the return would be only 6.2 and 12.7 bp. The return is less for two reasons. First, rather than making 5% on each of the trades, only 2% is made, and second, the total quantity of stock traded is 20% less. And if the rehedging threshold is 1%, the returns are 4 and 8 bp, respectively.

This does not mean that wider thresholds are always better. If the daily price movement had been from 1.0 to 1.04 to 1.0 to 0.96 and back to 1.0, a threshold of 5% would have missed out on all gamma trading profits because the threshold would have never been reached on either the high or low side.

13.9.2 Trending Versus Non-trending

When there is an expectation of a directional trend, less frequent and wider rehedging thresholds are more profitable. In uptrending markets, as the stock hits increasing rehedge thresholds, the wider the threshold, the higher is the price that will be obtained for each sale of stock (increasing the hedge to match a higher convertible delta). In downtrending markets, the wider the threshold, the lower is the price that will be obtained for each repurchase of stock (reducing the hedge to match a falling convertible delta). When a stock is trading in a tight range, wide thresholds could lead to the loss of profitable gamma trading because up and down movements are quickly reversed. In this case, narrower thresholds are the better option because they capture more of the volatility (see Table 13.2).

Short-term volatility can far exceed daily volatility. Therefore, a volatility trader monitoring and continuously trading can "realize" volatility beyond the annualized daily volatility over a given period, particularly in *sideways* markets when stock prices close well inside the daily high-low range.

Historical volatility is the annualized standard deviation of return over a specified period of time. *Implied volatility* is the volatility number

Table 13.2 Gamma Trading Returns by Threshold Level and Position Gamma (Unlevered)

Threshold	Stock Price	Quant Traded .4 Gamma .8 Gamma		Realized PnL .4 Gamma	.8 Gamma
5%	1.00				
	1.05	−2.00%	−4.00%		
	1.00	2.00%	4.00%	0.095%	0.190%
	0.95	2.00%	4.00%		
	1.00	−2.00%	−4.00%	0.105%	0.211%
	1			0.201%	0.401%
2%	1.00				
	1.02	−0.80%	−1.60%		
	1.04	−0.80%	−1.60%		
	1.05				
	1.02	0.80%	1.60%	0.015%	0.031%
	1.00	0.80%	1.60%	0.015%	0.031%
	0.98	0.80%	1.60%		
	0.96	0.80%	1.60%		
	0.95				
	0.98	−0.80%	−1.60%	0.015%	0.032%
	1.00	−0.80%	−1.60%	0.015%	0.033%
				0.062%	0.127%
1%	1.00	0.00%	0.00%		
	1.01	0.40%	0.80%		
	1.02	0.40%	0.80%		
	1.03	0.40%	0.80%		
	1.04	0.40%	0.80%		
	1.05	0.40%	0.80%		
	1.04	−0.40%	−0.80%	0.004%	0.008%
	1.03	−0.40%	−0.80%	0.004%	0.008%
	1.02	−0.40%	−0.80%	0.004%	0.008%
	1.01	−0.40%	−0.80%	0.004%	0.008%
	1.00	−0.40%	−0.80%	0.004%	0.008%
	0.99	−0.40%	−0.80%		
	0.98	−0.40%	−0.80%		

(Continued)

Table 13.2 Gamma Trading Returns by Threshold Level and Position Gamma (Unlevered) (Cont.)

Threshold Stock	Price	Quant Traded .4 Gamma .8 Gamma		Realized PnL .4 Gamma	.8 Gamma
	0.97	−0.40%	−0.80%		
	0.96	−0.40%	−0.80%		
	0.95	−0.40%	−0.80%		
	0.96	0.40%	0.80%	0.004%	0.008%
	0.97	0.40%	0.80%	0.004%	0.008%
	0.98	0.40%	0.80%	0.004%	0.008%
	0.99	0.40%	0.80%	0.004%	0.008%
	1.00	0.40%	0.80%	0.004%	0.008%
				0.040%	0.080%

Source: Advent Capital Management estimates.

that reconciles the theoretical (model-based) value of an option or convertible with the actual market price. If the model represents reality, then it provides an unbiased market representation of expected future standard deviation of return from the present to the expiration of the option.

One can calculate the historical volatility using data on various periodicities (i.e., daily, weekly, monthly, or one of several intraday increments). Theoretically, volatility scales proportionally with the square root of time (or periodicity), and therefore, any periodicity with a sufficient number of observations can be used to provide a valid expression of volatility. Yet, it is certainly possible to see intraday volatility much higher or lower than daily, weekly, or monthly volatility.

Table 13.3 illustrates the volatility of Restoration Hardware (RH) stock from August 7, 2020 to September 25, 2020, using weekly, daily, and hourly data. A volatility trader who adjusted delta hedges weekly would have realized volatility of 58. Adjusting the hedge daily, the trader would have realized volatility of 61, and adjusting the hedge every two hours, the trader would have realized a volatility of 76. Hourly returns produce even higher volatility of 80. This shows that a continual monitoring of equity markets can allow volatility traders to capture higher volatility profits than daily end-of-day returns would suggest.

Table 13.3   Volatility of Restoration Hardware Stock Calculated Using Weekly, Daily, and 2-Hourly Periodicity

	Week 1	Week 2	Week 3	Week 4	Week 5	Week 6	Week 7
Weekly Returns							
	0.85%	2.27%	3.25%	–4.47%	20.43%	–0.79%	–6.30%
Standard Dev.	**8.12%**	**Annualized Vol.**		**58.52%**			
Daily Returns							
Monday	0.10%	0.19%	0.69%	–0.30%		–0.24%	–1.70%
Tuesday	–2.29%	2.19%	–1.32%	3.11%	–1.51%	–1.65%	0.00%
Wednesday	1.88%	0.44%	1.74%	–1.46%	2.93%	1.95%	–5.19%
Thursday	1.54%	0.35%	0.52%	–4.71%	20.05%	–0.52%	–0.41%
Friday	–0.33%	–0.90%	1.60%	–1.03%	–1.04%	–0.30%	0.97%
Standard Dev.	**3.86%**	**Annualized Vol.**		**61.21%**			
2-Hour Returns							
Mon – A	–0.31%	1.54%	0.35%	–1.25%		–2.60%	–3.30%
Mon – B	0.91%	0.22%	0.22%	0.67%		–0.24%	0.10%
Mon – C	–0.58%	–1.13%	–0.46%	0.60%		1.72%	0.94%
Mon – D	0.08%	–0.41%	0.58%	–0.31%		0.93%	0.61%
Tue – A	–0.41%	3.72%	–2.08%	3.74%	1.22%	–0.66%	0.40%
Tue – B	0.56%	0.26%	0.21%	0.18%	–1.03%	–0.54%	–0.50%
Tue – C	–1.51%	–1.59%	0.76%	–0.62%	–0.96%	–0.22%	–0.39%
Tue – D	–0.94%	–0.14%	–0.19%	–0.17%	–0.74%	–0.25%	0.49%
Wed – A	1.31%	–0.06%	0.21%	–3.46%	2.63%	3.92%	–1.75%
Wed – B	–0.33%	0.26%	0.21%	–0.02%	–0.30%	–0.01%	–0.63%
Wed – C	0.56%	–0.14%	1.15%	1.47%	0.79%	–1.38%	–1.36%
Wed – D	0.33%	0.38%	0.16%	0.61%	–0.19%	–0.51%	–1.55%
Thu – A	2.91%	0.50%	–0.19%	–6.51%	22.79%	–0.69%	0.27%
Thu – B	–0.62%	–0.20%	0.03%	1.70%	0.45%	0.08%	0.93%
Thu – C	–0.37%	0.11%	0.90%	–0.47%	–2.86%	–1.08%	–2.02%
Thu – D	–0.34%	–0.06%	–0.22%	0.69%	0.20%	1.18%	0.42%
Fri – A	0.50%	–0.80%	2.13%	–4.79%	–2.97%	0.24%	0.56%
Fri – B	–0.56%	–0.30%	–1.06%	1.70%	–0.80%	–2.13%	0.25%
Fri – C	–0.42%	–0.02%	0.32%	2.29%	3.28%	0.41%	0.07%
Fri – D	0.16%	0.22%	0.23%	–0.09%	–0.45%	1.21%	0.08%
Standard Dev.	**2.40%**	**Annualized Vol.**		**76.20%**			

Source: Advent Capital Management.

13.10 COST OF LEVERAGE AND STOCK REBATE

Hedged convertible funds typically use leverage to concentrate and increase returns. While leverage is a cost, the cost is somewhat offset by the rebate earned from shorting stock. That is, stock is shorted and the proceeds are invested at a short-term interest rate of return. The amount paid on the leverage is typically a risk-free rate plus a spread, whereas the amount earned on the stock rebate is typically a risk-free rate minus a spread. When risk-free rates (i.e., Federal Funds) are near zero, the rebate on the stock short is minimal, but when rates increase, it can be significant. Consider Table 13.4, where we assume that the Fed Funds rate starts at 1% and increases to 1.5%, the spread paid on leverage is Fed Funds plus 25 bp, and the rebate earned is Fed Funds minus 25 bp. The example shows that for the six-month period, the cost of leverage is 101 bp, whereas the stock rebate offsets 92 bp, leaving a net cost of only 9 bp.

While most stocks provide a rebate rate equal to the Fed Funds rate minus 25 bp, some stock is harder to borrow, and therefore, the borrow rate may be 250–500 bp or more over Fed Funds.

13.11 STRUCTURED WITH A LONG STOCK BIAS

When a portfolio manager perceives positive asymmetry in the fundamental or technical character of a stock, there are multiple ways to express the view while minimizing the risk of loss.

13.11.1 Widening Rehedging Bands

A rehedging threshold of 10% on a 0.5 gamma bond would allow the net delta to rise as high as 5 delta points on a position, giving it some participation in the upside movement of the stock.

13.11.2 Using Puts and Put Spreads

Alternatively, the position could be fully or partly hedged by buying puts or put spreads. This could make sense on a tactical basis if the investor perceives a short-term upward movement in the price of the stock or if the implied volatility on the put option is below the implied volatility of the convertible. A put spread would hedge delta losses on the convertible for small to mod-

Table 13.4 Cost of Leverage Versus Stock Rebate

	Cost of Leverage: Fed Funds + 25							Stock Rebate: Fed Funds - 25	
Month	Avg. Delta	Long MV CB	Avg. Short MV Stock	Portfolio Leverage	Position Capital	Fed Funds	Long Leverage Cost	Stock Rebate	Carry
1	0.800	1,000,000	800,000	2.10	476,190	1.00%	(546)	500	(46)
2	0.700	1,000,000	700,000	2.20	454,545	1.10%	(614)	496	(118)
3	0.750	1,000,000	750,000	2.30	434,783	1.20%	(683)	594	(89)
4	0.800	1,000,000	800,000	2.40	416,667	1.30%	(753)	700	(53)
5	0.850	1,000,000	850,000	2.50	400,000	1.40%	(825)	815	(10)
6	0.800	1,000,000	800,000	2.60	384,615	1.50%	(897)	833	(64)
Total $					427,800		(4,318.15)	3,937.50	(380.65)
Total % Avg. Capital							−1.01%	0.92%	−0.09%
Annualized					427,800		−2.01%	1.85%	−0.18%

Source: Advent Capital Management.

erate downside moves, which might be sufficient if the investor regards the upside as a more likely outcome. Or if the investor is willing to incur small delta losses on a small downside move but wants to be hedged against more significant declines, out-of-the-money puts might be sufficient. With either the put spread or the out-of-the-money put, if the investor is correct and the stock moves higher, the position will have captured all the upside less the small premium paid for the options. If the investor is wrong and the stock moves lower, the options offer some downside protection while the asymmetric properties of the convertible also reduce delta-related losses.

13.11.3 Proxy Hedging

Occasionally, it is impossible to sell the stock short either because of liquidity or local regulations. It is possible to use an alternative stock or even an index product in the same industry and region to create a hedged convertible position. The correlation between the two should be high, and the beta of the proxy hedge to the convertible underlying should be taken into account. Such a position must be carefully monitored because of the *basis risk*, which is the potential for deviation between the return of the convertible issuer and the proxy hedge. Furthermore, the position should be sized to reflect the additional risk in the position.

13.11.4 Hedging Beta

Alternatively, an investor could choose to hedge the exposure to systematic equity risk (beta) while keeping the idiosyncratic (alpha) risk. In this case, the investor would use a short position on a market index such as the S&P 500 using futures, or by shorting the SPY exchange-traded fund (ETF), or by buying puts on the S&P 500. Because index volatility is typically much less than individual stock volatility, the cost of these options will be much less, but they will only protect against downside beta movements and not negative alpha in the stock. One way to reduce the idiosyncratic risk in this sort of a position is to use a sector hedge rather than a broad market hedge. In this case, the basis risk in the trade is only the idiosyncratic risk between a stock and its sector, which is typically less than the idiosyncratic risk between a stock and the broad market.

13.11.5 Partial Stock Short, Half a Hedge

One of the simplest ways to express a bullish stock view in the context of a hedged convertible portfolio is to reduce the hedge ratio by some percentage. For a convertible with a 60% delta and 0.5 gamma, putting on half a hedge would mean retaining net 30 delta points long. The return of such a position on a ±30% stock price move would be +11.25% on the upside and −6.75% on the downside not including coupon or gamma trading returns (which are positive on both the upside and downside). If the portfolio is intended to be uncorrelated with the equity market, this particular approach might be more appropriate for stocks that have a relatively low correlation or beta to the equity index or lower volatility and should be avoided or limited for higher-beta stocks.

13.12 HEDGING WITH A SHORT-STOCK BIAS

When a portfolio manager perceives negative asymmetry in the character of a stock, there are multiple ways to express the view while minimizing the risk of loss.

13.12.1 Widening Rehedging Bands

Widening the rehedging threshold allows delta to build in an upside move, but it also allows net delta to become negative in downside moves. This negative delta generates delta gains in continued downside stock movement. Rather than waiting for negative delta to accumulate, an investor could simply start by overhedging the position such that net delta is negative from the start.

13.12.2 Using Puts and Put Spreads

The position could be overhedged by buying puts or put spreads in addition to the delta-neutral stock hedge. This could make sense on a tactical basis if the investor perceives a short-term downward movement in the price of the stock or if the implied volatility on the put option is below the implied volatility of the convertible.

13.12.3 Using Calls and Call Spreads

If option implied volatility is higher than convertible implied volatility it also could be profitable to sell calls or call spreads in the context of a negative stock outlook. If the investor is correct, the premiums will be pocketed, and if the stock price jumps unexpectedly, the gamma in the convertible will increase the delta—creating the long exposure against which the calls have been sold—similar to a covered-call strategy. If the notional value of the calls remains below the incremental dollar delta of the convertibles plus the received premium, then the position should not lose money on an unexpected jump in the stock price.

13.13 CASE STUDY: SQUARE

Consider a delta-neutral position on the Square .5% May 2023 convertible bond. The bond was issued in May 2018 with an initial conversion premium of 42.5%. When the bond was priced, shares of Square were trading at $54.63, meaning that the conversion price for the bond was $77.8477. This gives the bond a conversion ratio of 12.8456 . On May 23, 2018, the bond had a delta of 64.44%, which means that the hedge ratio that would fully neutralize the equity risk exposure on that day was 8.28.

$$8.28 = 12.845 \times 0.6444$$

Assume that the arbitrageur purchases a single convertible bond and initially shorts 8.28 shares to neutralize any equity risk of the position. Arbitrageurs typically trade throughout the day, but for the sake of simplicity, our example assumes that at the end of the trading day the arbitrageur readjusts the short position based on how the delta has moved during that day. Even with this simplified assumption, the arbitrageur generates a profit of $179 over the life of the position (from May 2018 until September 9, 2020).

Two things to note from the chart in Figure 13.2—besides Square's impressive performance—is the low correlation between the position's return and the underlying stock performance and the sudden fall in the total profits that occurred during the market swoon as the COVID-19 pandemic struck. The goal of convertible arbitrage is to earn a good return without taking an equity market risk. With the exception of early 2020, this position accomplishes the goal. The convertible arbitrage generated relatively consistent returns largely irrespective of the performance of the underlying shares.

Figure 13.2   Square stock and convertible bond performance, June 23, 2020–January 31, 2021

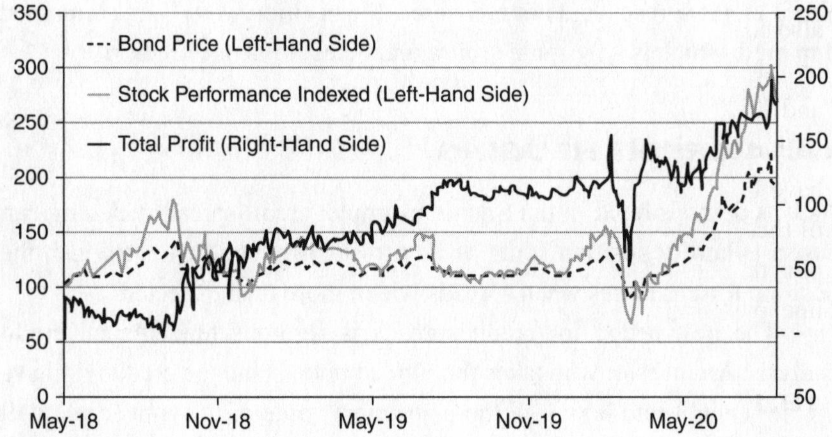

Data: Bloomberg.

From September 28, 2018, until December 21, 2018, shares of Square fell from $99.01 to $52.51, a 47% decline. Because of its inherent asymmetry, the convertible bond fared better with only a 28.4% drop in price. In contrast, the convertible arbitrage position benefited from the volatility, and profits increased from $7.45 to $49.62 during the same time period. This is how convertible arbitrage is supposed to function. However, Figure 13.2 shows that in early 2020 something happened that caused the convertible arbitrage position to lose money as Square's stock and convertible bond fell.

The contraction in the arbitrage profits during the early months of the COVID-19 pandemic were caused by a sharp increase in the implied credit spread of the convertible bond. Either because of broad market concerns or specific considerations related to how COVID-19 would affect Square's business, bond investors began to demand higher returns from Square's debt in order to be compensated for increased credit risk. On March 2, 2020, the Square convertible had an implied credit spread of 238 bp. By March 19, the implied spread had surged to 665.5 bp, which drove the bond below par. After this trough, credit spreads recovered over the course of several months; moreover, convertible arbitrage positions tend to benefit from high volatility, so the position recovered faster than credit spreads. As the position is long the bond and short the stock, anything that reduces the value of the bond but not the value of the stock (such as rising credit spreads or higher rates) hurts the convertible arbitrage position. In the case of Square, the expansion in credit spreads proved transitory, and the convertible arbitrage position regained all its profits (and then some). Yet, if credit spreads had not recovered, the position would have remained impaired, which is why some arbitrageurs elect to hedge credit risk.

13.14 CREDIT HEDGING

As was demonstrated in the Square example, credit-spread widening can cost a volatility position some of its profitability and can even push the position toward losses when spreads widen more than expected.

The best hedge for credit spreads is rigorous fundamental credit analysis. An investor who takes the time to understand the credit will have greater insight into how well the investment value of the convertible will hold up when the stock declines. An investor who understands credit dynamics is also more likely to avoid convertibles that have excessive credit risk, which is the biggest source of loss in a credit crisis.

Every bond has some credit risk, and credit hedges come at a cost that reduces the portfolio carry. Yet, there are times when it is worth the cost of credit hedging. By hedging credit risk, one can isolate the volatility and simplify the exposures of the position.

The ultimate credit loss is the default of the bond. If you assume that a bond is worth some recovery value in the event of default and the loss is equal to the current value less the recovery value, then the hedge should be constructed to earn a profit equal to the loss given default. Consider just the bond floor or investment value of the bond—which is unhedged by a delta-neutral stock short. For a bond with a bond floor of 90, or $900, and an expected recovery of 30, or $300, the hedge should earn at least $600 in the event of default to compensate for the loss on the bond. Mark-to-market losses due to credit deterioration have greater frequency than default, and therefore, the credit hedge should offset all or part of the mark-to-market losses even when the bond does not default.

13.14.1 Single-Name Credit Default Swaps

The first method to hedge credit risk is to use *credit default swaps* (CDSs) to eliminate the credit risk of a specific issuer. CDSs effectively provide insurance against the risk of the issuer defaulting. Active CDS markets vary over time, and CDSs may not exist for every convertible issuer.

If the issuer has an actively traded *single-name* CDS, it can be used to hedge the credit exposure. The cost of the hedge will be similar to the current credit spread on the bond, assuming that the reference bond is *pari passu* and of a similar maturity to the convertible. If the convertible and the reference bond default, then the convertible investor will be compensated by the swap counterpart.

Market losses can be incurred even if the bond merely suffers credit deterioration and spread widening. Therefore, one must hedge in a way that fully compensates for spread widening. A CDS is a very convenient tool for doing so because the swap increases in value as the spread widens, just as the bond decreases in value. There is basis risk, however, in that a bond is a cash instrument, and a CDS is a synthetic instrument. In a crisis, cash instruments can be significantly discounted because of a lack of liquidity. When this occurs, the CDS does not fully compensate the investor for the loss on the bond.

13.14.2 Index CDSs

Alternatively, an arbitrageur could use index swaps to hedge credit risk at a portfolio level. Index swaps are effective for hedging out broad market credit risk but do not protect the investor from idiosyncratic credit deterioration of an individual position. Essentially, index swaps reduce the credit beta (systemic credit risk) of the portfolio but leave the idiosyncratic credit risk untouched. The theory behind this method is that a well-diversified portfolio will protect the investor from exposure to idiosyncratic credit risk; therefore, idiosyncratic credit risk is mitigated through diversification rather than hedging. However, it is important not to conflate spread equivalence with a unit beta. In other words, a bond that has an implied spread equal to the spread of an index should not be presumed to have a beta of 1 to that index. This can be seen in the behavior of the Square implied credit spread in the months leading up to the COVID-19 crisis. Although the Square spread remained well below that of the High-Yield (HY) CDS Index (CDX), Square spread change tracked the Hight-Yield CDX closely (see Figures 13.3 through 13.5).

Over the course of the COVID-19 pandemic, the Square implied credit spread behavior was very similar to that of the HY CDX, with a correlation

Figure 13.3   Delta-neutral position on Square

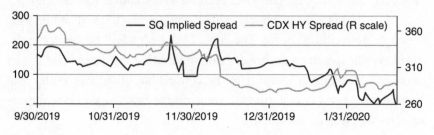

Data: Bloomberg.

Figure 13.4   Square and CDX high-yield spreads

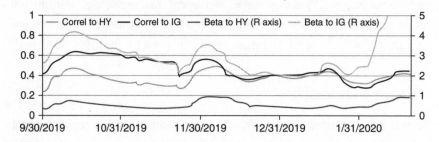

Sources: Bloomberg, Advent Capital Management.

Figure 13.5   Beta and correlation of Square credit spread to investment-grade (IG) and HY CDX

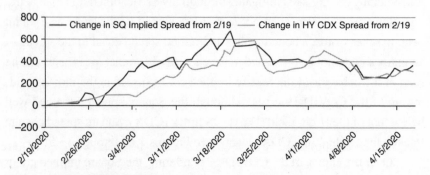

Sources: Bloomberg, Advent Capital Management.

of 0.85 and a beta of 0.91; hence, the index would have been an effective hedge. Using the equation rho($) × beta to CDX gives us the unit size of the appropriate hedge. Furthermore, this dollar amount is additive across positions because beta represents the portion of the credit spread that is perfectly correlated with the index and excludes the idiosyncratic portion that cannot be reduced through diversification. An appropriately sized CDX HY hedge would be equal to the sum of all rho($) × beta to the CDX HY index—assuming that this is the only form of credit hedging in the portfolio.

13.14.3 Short Stock

Arbitrageurs can create a synthetic credit hedge by overhedging the convertible arbitrage position. This is plausible because credit spreads and equity prices are correlated, meaning that expanding credit spreads typically coincide with a decrease in equity prices. If credit spreads widen, then the gain from the excess equity hedge counteracts the credit losses, leaving the arbitrageur unimpaired. The benefit of this method is that it is easy to implement (the arbitrageur is already shorting shares, so this is just more of the same activity) and cost efficient. However, this method is not without flaws. The relationship between credit spread and equity price is not linear. If the stock moves higher while the credit quality of the issuer does not improve, then an overhedged arbitrage position could perform poorly because the bond will not richen enough to offset the loss on the incremental stock short.

13.14.4 Put Options

Assuming that a stock price falls to zero in the event of default, one can purchase options that would have a value of $800 at a stock price of zero. If the stock price is $100, then being short eight shares would fully hedge the bond against its loss given default. Alternatively, a put struck at 50 would be worth $50 in the event of default, and a put struck at 80 would be worth $80 in the event of default. Therefore, 16 puts struck at 50 or 10 puts struck at 80 also would compensate for the loss given default on the bond.

Hedging idiosyncratic credit exposure therefore often involves the use of stock or put options and an estimate of how credit spread is likely to respond to changes in stock price. As discussed in Chapter 12, there are several models for estimating this relationship, all of which predict a nonlinear ratio between stock price change and credit spread. In other words, a model might suggest that a 5% drop in the stock price would coincide with a 1% increase in credit spreads (a 5:1 ratio), but a 25% drop in the stock price would coincide with a 50% increase in credit spreads (a 1:2 ratio), or a 75% drop in the stock price would coincide with a 450% increase in credit spreads (a 1:6 ratio). Hence, the size of the stock short that is necessary to hedge the credit exposure depends on the expected movement in the stock price, and the size of the stock position increases as the stock price falls.

As a company loses the stock market value cushion in its capital structure, the outstanding debt causes the firm to become more highly leveraged, which will further increase its stock volatility. The higher the volatility, the more likely default becomes because higher volatility makes extreme changes more likely. Options increase in value as volatility increases, and put options increase in equity sensitivity as the stock price falls—these two relationships cause a put to behave more like a bond than a pure stock short. The more out of the money a put option, the less it will cost—but more options will be needed to protect against default. Furthermore, a significantly out-of-the-money option will offer little hedging value until the stock price approaches the level of the strike. If a put option is struck at 50% out of the money and the stock price declines only 40%, it will offer no protective value as the bond tumbles in value due to spread widening. The challenge for hedging credit risk with puts is to identify a put option strategy with a value profile that approximates the cost of credit spread widening as the stock price declines. Put spreads can be significantly less expensive than being long a single put, but put spreads provide only limited protection, increasing in value until the lower strike is reached, but no further (see Table 13.5).

Table 13.5   Square Put Prices During COVID-19 Crisis

	Stock	Mar-80 Put Price	Mar-80 Put Delta	Apr-80 Put Price	Apr-80 Put Delta
3-Feb	79.8	5.01	−47	6.29	−46
19-Feb	85.24	2.48	−30	4.13	−33
20-Mar	38.09	41.91	na	40	−100
17-Apr	61.09	na	na	61.09	na

Data: Bloomberg.

13.14.5 Applying Excess Short Stock from Delta Hedge

So far we have ignored the delta-neutral stock short held to hedge the convertible delta because we are discussing the credit hedge. Yet, as the stock falls, delta will decline. If the credit spread were expected to be stable, the stock short would be reduced to remain delta neutral. This would normally generate a profit because the stock was shorted at a higher price and the short was covered at a lower price. However, another possibility is to maintain the excess stock short as a hedge against credit-spread widening. The further the stock drops, the more of the short stock position becomes "available" to hedge the credit risk. The amount of short stock available as a credit hedge may not match the target size based on the expected path of the credit spread, but it can be incorporated. The chart in Figure 13.6 shows that as the stock price declines and the excess short delta accumulates, further price declines generate positive returns that can offset credit-spread widening losses on the bond.

Figure 13.6 shows the cumulative return from the excess short delta hedge held against credit losses. To measure the credit loss, we compare actual bond price change with that stemming from bond delta and stock price declines. Note that if interest rates are falling or implied volatilities are widening, these trends will affect the residual non-delta bond price change as well as the credit. Therefore, this residual loss may be less than a pure credit spread analysis would imply; in other words, volatility vega and rate rho also constitute partial credit hedges.

From late February until March 10, 2020, the excess short added just 73 bp of return to the position, which failed to fully offset the 149 bp

Figure 13.6   Change in Square and HY CDX spreads

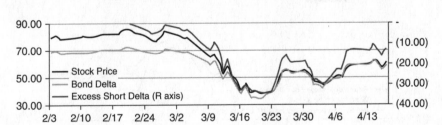

Sources: Bloomberg, Advent Capital Management.

non–delta bond loss. This is because the excess short delta was still relatively light for most of that period. However, from March 10 to March 16, the excess short delta increased to 35%, delivering nearly 600 bp of incremental return—far surpassing the non–delta bond loss of 145 bp. From March 16 to March 20, the excess short delta increased further to 37%, delivering another 204 bp of return relative to the non–delta bond loss of an additional 38 bp. At this point, it was clear that the credit was overhedged, and a recovery of the credit could result in position losses. If the hedge remained unadjusted, the excess delta would lead to a 1,575 bp loss as the credit rebounded from the trough of the COVID-19 crisis—far in excess of the 779 bp non-delta gain on the bond from its low on March 23 through April 17. However, if the excess short delta hedge had been cut by 50%, the hedge would have lost only 705 bp—effectively neutralizing the cumulative credit performance (see Table 13.6 and Figure 13.7).

Table 13.6   Excess Stock Short Return Versus Bond Return (Ex Delta)

	Excess Stock Short Return	Bond Return x-Delta
10-Mar	0.73	−1.49
16-Mar	6.68	−2.94
20-Mar	8.72	−3.32

Source: Advent Capital Management estimates

Figure 13.7   Excess short delta available for use as credit hedge

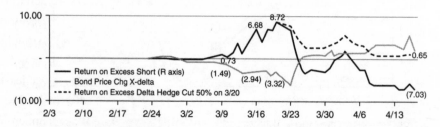

Sources: Bloomberg, Advent Capital Management.

13.14.6 Credit Hedging with Equity Index Options

Credit spreads are negatively correlated with equity prices. Credit risk has an idiosyncratic component as well as a systematic component, just as stocks do. And, like equity portfolios, credit portfolios can reduce idiosyncratic risk through diversification. Therefore, a convertible arbitrage manager can calculate the credit-spread beta to equity indices and hedge it using equity index options. Equity indices are generally less volatile than individual equities; therefore, equity index options are usually much cheaper than single-name options. Granted, this is only a partial hedge because it only covers the systematic component of the risk, but it is nonetheless a convenient and cost-effective way of adding protection quickly.

13.15 INTEREST-RATE AND FOREIGN CURRENCY HEDGING

Convertible hedging often goes beyond hedging equity risk. Interest-rate fluctuations have significant effects on the market prices of many convertible, and some convertibles are issued in a different currency from that of the underlying stock.

13.15.1 Interest-Rate Rho Hedging

Rho exposures can affect the profitability of a volatility strategy. If risk-free rates rise, this can create losses, although convertible bonds tend to have very low overall effective duration. Although the bond component of the convertible has duration similar to that of a straight bond, the equity option portion of the convertible has *negative* duration because the option is worth more when interest rates are higher. The economics of a convertible are similar to borrowing an amount of stock equal to the delta, as described in Chapter 11. The duration of borrowing is negative because the option owner is doing the borrowing, whereas the owner of a straight bond is doing the lending.

Furthermore, convertible hedge fund managers tend to hedge at least a portion of interest-rate exposure. The portion of the rho risk hedged reflects a manager's approach to credit omicron risk because rho and omicron

Table 13.7 Correlation with and Beta (Slope) of Credit Yield to Maturity Versus Treasury Yield to Maturity (2008–2020)

Credit Quality	AAA	AA	A	BBB	BB	B	CCC
Avg. Dur	8.8	6.7	7.0	7.1	4.7	3.9	3.4
vs. Treasury	10Y T	7Y T	7Y T	7Y T	5Y T	5Y/3Y T	3Y T
Correlation	0.82	0.61	0.51	0.26	(0.10)	(0.22)	(0.28)
Slope	0.64	0.49	0.44	0.31	(0.19)	(0.63)	(1.62)
Upside Slope	0.78	0.64	0.70	0.74	0.26	0.93	0.69
Upside (>10bp) Slope	0.74	0.68	0.76	0.78	0.15	0.37	(3.87)

Sources: Bloomberg data, Advent Capital Management estimates.

have a relatively predictable correlation. When rates rise, spreads tend to fall, and vice versa. Because there is some counterbalancing between rho and omicron, most managers hedge only a portion of the interest-rate risk, especially managers with unhedged credit exposure.

Credit spreads are negatively correlated with risk-free interest rates. Hence, when Treasury rates rise, credit spreads typically fall, so the overall effect on credit-risky yields is either mitigated or in some cases positive, meaning that some credit yields *fall* even as risk-free rates *rise*. It is instructive to consider the correlation of the change in credit yields to the change in similar-duration Treasury yields. As illustrated in Table 13.7, from December 31, 2008, to December 31, 2020, the correlation was high for high-credit-quality yields (AAA and AA), moderate for lower-quality investment-grade (IG) yields (A and BBB), and negative for speculative-grade yields (BB, B, and CCC). The same is true of the beta of credit yields to Treasury yields. These correlations suggest that the rho of speculative-grade convertibles should remain unhedged or that it could even be deducted from IG convertible rho.

The primary motivation for holding a rho hedge is to prevent losses due to rising interest rates. Yet, the correlations during periods of rising rates are significantly different across the credit spectrum—especially for speculative-grade credits. The beta of BBB convertibles during rising rates is more than twice what it is for all periods, whereas the beta of speculative-grade convertibles reverses from negative to positive. These correlations suggest that all credit-quality rho risk should be hedged, at least in some proportion to the upside beta. Yet, minor increases in risk-free rates have little effect on returns. It is only when Treasury rates jump 10 bp or higher that the correlations of BB and B convertibles weaken and the correlation of CCC convertibles turns negative. The weakest credits benefit because bigger increases in Treasury rates typically occur in periods of robust economic growth. Rho hedging policy ultimately depends on the judgment of fund managers. A general rule is that rho risk should be adjusted according to coefficients such as AAA to A: 1.0; BBB: 0.75; BB: 0.5; B: 0.25; and CCC: 0. If a manager has significant credit hedges in place, the amount of credit offset to rho risk is reduced. In this case, a manager should estimate the percentage of credit risk hedged and compensate for reduced credit risk with the rho hedge. Numerous instruments hedge risk-free rate exposure, including interest-rate swaps, interest-rate futures or options on futures, and short Treasury bond ETFs.

13.15.2 Currency/Foreign Exchange Hedging

An unlevered long-only investment portfolio typically pays cash for its investments. An investor who buys a non-base-currency security must first buy the foreign currency to pay for the security. Then holding the foreign-denominated security creates a risk of foreign currency losses. But hedge funds that pay for foreign currency investments with foreign currency borrowed from their prime brokers create a natural foreign exchange (FX) hedge.

Currency risk is mitigated in cross-currency exchangeables, where the bond is typically denominated in US dollars while the underlying stock trades primarily in foreign currency; for example, Siemens issued a US dollar convertible that converted into its euro-denominated stock. A US investor was exposed to the effect of euro fluctuations on the price of the stock when translated into US dollars, but the downside protection of the bond was defined in US dollars. Hence, the exchangeable essentially provided a free FX option that would be profitable if the stock price was driven up by the euro advancing relative to the dollar.

Currency risk is typically hedged with FX forward contracts with maturities of up to 12 months. For a US dollar portfolio with $5 million of euro exposure, a forward contract locks in a rate at which the euro can be converted into US dollars at some point in the future. The forward contract rate will either cost something or pay something to the investor depending on the levels of risk-free interest rates in the two currencies. In recent years, the level of US dollar interest rates has been higher than that of euro interest rates. This means that a US dollar investor earns a premium by entering into a forward contract to sell euros, whereas an euro investor would pay a premium for entering into a forward contract to sell US dollars. The cost or earnings of the forward contract should be considered when calculating the yield of a position.

13.16 RISK MANAGEMENT, LEVERAGE, POSITION SIZING

Convertible arbitrage typically uses leverage to optimize the return per dollar of capital invested. Being long equity-sensitive convertibles and short an equivalent amount of stock minimizes equity risk by neutralizing the exposure to the stock. Furthermore, being long both credit and volatility—two factors that tend to offset each other—means that the value of unlevered convertible arbitrage is relatively stable. When seeking to exploit small relative value opportunities, it is often necessary to use leverage to realize meaningful gains.

A basic principle is that higher-risk positions should remain unlevered, whereas the lower the risk of a position, the more leverage can be safely used to amplify the potential return. Because both correlated and uncorrelated risks are present in a position (credit risk and convertible valuation have both a positively correlated component and an idiosyncratic component, whereas volatility is generally negatively correlated), the lower the correlated risks are relative to total risk, the more leverage can be applied. In other words, a company whose credit risk is completely idiosyncratic can be more highly levered than one whose credit spread has a high beta to the index. However, because correlation itself is volatile, risks should be measured using maximum historical correlations rather than current or stable market correlation.

The quantity of leverage employed should be in proportion to the current opportunity set. In other words, if volatility, credit spreads, and convertible valuations are at historically rich levels, leverage levels should be reduced. And if volatility, credit spreads, and convertible valuation are at historically cheap levels, leverage can be increased commensurate with the opportunity. It is wise to change leverage gradually because cheapness can always get cheaper and richness can always get richer.

Stress testing the portfolio and individual positions and the calculation of both portfolio value at risk (VaR) and position marginal VaR are useful ways to assess portfolio leverage and individual position sizes. See Chapter 10 for details of these risk-control methods. For the purposes of leverage and position sizing, what is important is that the negative portfolio contribution of individual positions should be limited to a fixed amount (e.g., 50 bp). Therefore, a position that represents 5% of capital should lose no more than 10% of its value under a worst-case scenario. If the position is three times levered, this means that the position cannot lose more than 3.33% on an unlevered basis. If a stress test reveals that a 5% position could lose more than this on an unlevered basis, say, for example, 4%, then three times leverage would mean that the position could lose 60 bp of capital. To comply with the maximum-loss principle, the position size should be reduced by 20% (from 5% to 4% of capital), which, in turn, would reduce leverage.

13.16.1 Stock Borrow and Liquidity Monitoring

A key aspect of risk management is monitoring the liquidity of a position. In stressed markets, illiquidity can cause credit spreads to widen more than on more liquid bonds of the same credit quality. Furthermore, illiquidity can reduce the ability to short stock and raise the cost of borrow significantly. Consider a hypothetical example using the Wayfair convertible bond, which had a low stock borrow rate of 0.5% in February 2021.

Modeling indicates that if the stock borrow rate were to increase to 2.5%, the fair value of the bond would fall from 102.2 to 99.7, and if the borrow were to increase to 5%, fair value would fall to 97.05. In a three times levered position, this could create a loss of more than 15%, *ceteris paribus*.

A useful way to monitor the liquidity of a convertible is to score it on the basis of observable values such as the amount outstanding, the market capitalization of the company, the trading volume of the bond, the trading volume of the underlying stock, the bid-ask spread, and the stock borrow rate. For larger convertible investors, it is also helpful to score the various dealers on their ability to provide liquidity—especially in stressed markets—and then to adjust the liquidity score of their bonds accordingly. Lastly, it is helpful to know how large a position you own relative to other holders of the bonds. Being the largest investor in a bond can make it more difficult to reduce the position without moving the market.

13.16.2 Leverage Function of Credit Quality and Moneyness

The risk of a delta-neutral position is a function of its credit quality and the *moneyness* (i.e., the percent difference between the conversion price and the current market price of the stock). The higher the moneyness, the more stock that is shorted, and consequently, the lower is the net position size. Higher-risk positions, such as those on low-credit-quality or low-delta (high-net-market-value) positions may be dangerous to leverage, whereas higher-credit-quality and high-delta (low-net-market-value) positions are more worthy of leverage. Managers should establish guidelines for leveraging that consider these two factors.

13.16.3 Historical Leverage Levels

In a study published by Bank of America in October 2020,[3] the historical leverage of convertible arbitrage funds was estimated; from the fourth quarter of 2003 to the beginning of the GFC in 2008, convertible arbitrage represented most of the ownership of US convertible bonds, whereas since then convertible arbitrage has represented a much smaller part of the US convertible market. Many hedge funds failed to survive the GFC, and the convertible arbitrage funds in the post-GFC years have reduced the use of leverage. Prior to the GFC, hedged convertible leverage of six to seven times was common, whereas two to three times was more typical by 2021.

13.16.4 Portfolio Diversification and Concentration Limits

An important function of risk management is ensuring sufficient diversification to minimize the potential effects of negative alpha in individual positions. It is therefore desirable to establish guidelines limiting position size as a percent of total long-market value, or net market value. It is also beneficial to have diversification of economic sectors, regions, and investment themes. Although technology and consumer sectors are the largest issuers of convertibles, it is possible to obtain diversification between subsectors. For example, semiconductor and software companies are both *technology* companies, but they do not move in lockstep. Dispersion across several subsectors increases portfolio diversification.

13.16.5 Shorting Convertibles

Some convertibles are more suited to a long volatility strategy than others because of the cheapness of their volatility or the stability of their credit. But convertibles that lack these properties could be candidates for shorting. A bond that is especially rich relative to its theoretical value can be shorted in a delta-neutral position to extract the richness, which will diminish to zero by expiration.

There are two key advantages to having what can be categorized as *alpha shorts* in a hedged convertible portfolio.

First, alpha shorts provide some protection against portfolio credit deterioration if the credit of the alpha shorts deteriorates faster than the overall portfolio in a period of spread widening. Such convertibles falls by more than the deltas suggest.

Second, if the implied volatility declines or the bond cheapens, an alpha-short delta-neutral position gains. Having such an offset in a portfolio can insulate against volatility collapse.

There are, however, inherent risks in alpha shorts.

First, such a position tends to be gamma negative, meaning that the position has negative asymmetry with respect to stock price movements—and gamma-negative price behavior may result in losses in the context of normal buy high, sell low delta hedging. Hence, it is preferable to short convertibles with low gamma. Deeply discounted bonds with high premiums have little gamma and therefore are candidates for short credit positions. In-the-money bonds with low premiums also have less gamma but almost no credit exposure and therefore better serve as implied volatility shorts. If volatility falls, gamma in the convertible will fall further, thereby reducing negative gamma in the short position.

Second, shorting rich convertibles as a credit hedge may be ineffective in a downturn because the richest convertibles tend to have the highest credit quality, and such high-quality bonds tend to suffer less credit-spread widening and valuation cheapening in a downturn; therefore, the hedge against credit deterioration may be inconsequential.

Another source of short candidates is reverse or contingent convertibles (CoCos; see Section 1.7.4). CoCos are rarely used as a long position in a convertible arbitrage portfolio because they are inherently gamma negative; they mandatorily convert into equity if the stock price falls. Therefore, shorting CoCos creates a *positive*-gamma position. CoCos offer higher coupons as compensation for negative gamma, which makes them more expensive to short. Furthermore, to be delta neutral, one must be long the stock—which entitles the investor to dividends. However, in the event of a plunge in market capitalization, a cut in the dividend becomes more likely.

Mandatory convertibles are gamma negative when the stock price is near or below where it was at issuance, whereas gamma can turn positive as the stock price rises toward the upper end of the dead zone. Such positive gamma can quickly turn negative, however, if the stock declines. By shorting the mandatory and delta hedging with a long stock position, a positive-gamma strategy can be created. However, like CoCos, mandatory convertibles generally have high yields and are therefore more expensive to short.

13.17 CONCLUSION

Convertible arbitrage seeks to generate relatively stable returns regardless of market fluctuations—and usually has achieved this goal over the longer term. The primary tool for achieving this goal is to determine the relative value of individual convertibles and hedge accordingly. This strategy is potentially rewarding because market setbacks are frequent—and are beyond the control of investors. Losses are disconcerting to most investors. But convertible arbitrage is not for beginners; it requires active trading and dynamic rebalancing of hedges—and a panoply of research and insights into credits, equities, and capital markets.

ENDNOTES

1. https://amara.org/zh-cn/videos/xj382Ap64VRc/info/ genomics-101/ 11:41.
2. https://www.investopedia.com/terms/l/leaps.asp.
3. Michael Youngworth, *Convertible Arbitrage Primer*, BofA Securities, New York, October 19, 2020, p. 8.

CHAPTER 14

Convertibles and Convertible-like Structures in Private Capital Markets

. . . private credit markets are due a growth spurt.

— The Economist[1]

14.1 INTRODUCTION

Globally, private capital markets exploded in size in 2020 and 2021. In the United States, total annual capital raised in private markets grew from $44 billion in 2016 to almost $283 billion in just the first three quarters of 2021.[2] The Europe, Middle-East, and Africa (EMEA) market grew from issuance of just $30 billion of privately placed equity in 2018 to $99 billion in just the first three quarters of 2021.[3] Similarly, Asian private capital markets grew to over $110 billion in just the first three quarters of 2021, up from only $60 billion in 2019.[4] Note: figures for the size of the private capital markets *exclude* bonds issued under Securities and Exchange Commission (SEC) Rule 144A, which technically are private placements, but typically are actively traded obligations of major public corporations. Today, most US convertible bonds are issued under Rule 144A, which exempts the issues from registration and prevents purchase by individual investors for six months. These 144A issues effectively constitute an institutional convertible bond market that is both liquid and transparent.

Private convertibles represent a subset of the private capital markets. The appellation *private* describes the nontradable security itself— not necessarily the issuer. There are essentially three types of private investments: Private Investments in Public Entities (PIPES), Pre-IPO Investments, and Private Investments in Private Companies. The US PIPE market saw issuance of over $80 billion in the first three quarters of 2021. Convertibles are found in each of these categories of the private markets.

While the public convertible market is highly liquid and transparent, private convertibles are less-so. Since transactions are private, or involve companies that have no public reporting requirements, data collection is sparse, and there are no listed prices or indices. It is therefore more challenging to compare the performance to public asset class returns. Be that as it may, the explosive growth in private capital is unquestionably due to advantages perceived by both investors and issuers.

Few individual investors are familiar with *private* convertibles—unregistered securities that are issued in private placements—because such issues are rarely publicized. Private convertibles are not tradable in public markets, except for unregistered securities issued under the aforementioned SEC Rule 144A, which are actively traded by institutional investors.

While the market for public convertibles and for 144A issues is highly liquid and transparent, private convertibles often involve companies that have no public reporting requirements, and there are no public price quotations or indices. An exception is PIPESs, which have gotten a huge boost from the surge in issuance of private securities by Special Purpose Acquisition Companies (SPACs). The typical SPAC IPO is a unit that includes a common share plus a warrant—and this combination constitutes a convertible-like structure. SPACs are further discussed in Section 14.2

Private convertibles provide an important source of capital for a wide range of companies from tiny startups to large public corporations. Issue sizes range from trivial to more than a billion dollars. Public companies issue private convertibles in order to speed the process of issuance and/or to satisfy demand from specific investors. Some private convertibles are sold to a single entity, as in the case of several large public companies that created multibillion-dollar private convertibles for Berkshire Hathaway (see Section 14.2.2); these bespoke convertibles were examples of PIPEs.

Greater flexibility in structuring private convertibles may serve the interests of both issuers and investors. The basic advantages for both issuers and investors parallel those of publicly traded convertibles, with investors gaining additional favorable terms that compensate for the illiquidity and limited disclosures that typify private issues. Issuers benefit from fewer regulatory restrictions.

Private convertibles often include potentially rewarding features for both investors and the issuing companies, for example, coupon rates that escalate if a future IPO or other valuation event is delayed, conversion prices that represent discounts from the prices of future IPOs, caps on conversion prices that ensure significant participation if the future valuation is much higher than at issuance of the convertible, and non-debt Simple Agreement for Future Equity (SAFE) and Keep It Simple Securities (KISS) convertibles (see Section 14.4).

In the United States, only *accredited investors*[5] may purchase private securities (excluding Rule 144A issues, which may be purchased only by *qualified institutional buyers*[6] [QIBs]). We estimate that about half the value of the private convertible market is PIPEs. Estimates of the size of the private debt market refer *exclusively* to non-tradable private securities—and *exclude* the huge market for actively traded debt issued under SEC Rule 144A.

The tradable convertible market in the United States is dominated by convertible bonds issued under Rule 144A that are actively traded by institutional investors. These bonds are *not* regarded as private convertibles by market participants. Yet, convertibles issued under Rule 144A are exempt from registration at issuance and are technically private convertibles.

It is easier to introduce new features in private convertibles than in public issues.[7] Like conventional non-convertible debt, private convertible bonds are financial obligations that require a borrower to pay periodic interest payments and repay principal at maturity. In cases of startups and early-stage private companies, of course, the creditworthiness is inherently subject to doubt—which justifies favorable terms for the early investors.

In the case of issuance by a private company that has not yet gone public, the conversion price is usually defined as a preset discount from the price of the stock once the stock valuation is established by an injection of additional private-equity funding or an IPO; when such discounts include capped conversion prices, the upside participation in the valuation of the company above the cap becomes essentially 100%.[8] Some private convertibles are simply convertible into a percentage of the issuing company.

14.2 PIPES (SPAC AND NON-SPAC)

PIPES can be structured in a number of ways. Because of the surge in IPOs of Special Purpose Acquisition Company (SPACs) in 2020 and 2021, PIPEs are currently categorized into SPAC and non-SPAC forms, but the non-SPAC forms come in numerous forms including private convertibles into public equities.

The US PIPE market has grown rapidly. There have been $240 billion of PIPEs created in the last five years, one third of which were issued in just the first three quarters of 2021. SPACs have become the dominant form of PIPEs at 70% of all PIPE issuances while convertible preferreds and convertible debt constitute about 12% of the total. Furthermore, 64% of all PIPEs have been in the technology sector, and another 16% in healthcare.

14.2.1 SPAC PIPES

SPACs are shell companies created to acquire or merge with private companies, which effectively takes the acquired companies public in the process. Despite their grouping with otherwise private investments, SPAC managers raise money through a public equity IPO. This takes place before any acquisition target has been identified, which is why SPACs are also called blank-check companies. Investors receive units of both common shares and warrants, typically one share of stock and one quarter to one half a warrant per unit. The SPAC manager holds the cash generated from the IPO in short-term Treasury notes until the cash is deployed in an acquisition or merger. Investors have the right to either participate in the acquisition or redeem and get their initial investment back with interest. The right to redeem and the inclusion of the warrant makes the structure economically similar to a low-yield convertible trust preferred with a two-year put, in our opinion. In addition to the SPAC, a side PIPE structure may exist which also participates in the acquisition. The side SPAC provides capital to complete the acquisition if a significant percentage of SPAC investors choose to redeem. If a large enough percentage of SPAC investors choose to redeem, however, the acquisition could fall through, in which case the SPAC warrants would become worthless.

SPACs have become a popular alternative to a public IPO. Once an acquisition target has been identified, due diligence has been completed, terms have been agreed, and the deal has been publicly announced, the vehicle is referred to as a de-SPAC, since the entity transitions from an acquisition shell vehicle to a publicly traded company with operations.

For example, on January 2, 2021, a SPAC entity called Gig Capital 4 was listed on NASDAQ at an initial price of $10.00 per unit, trading under the symbol GIGGU. A unit comprises one share of equity plus one third of a warrant. Each warrant has a strike of $11.50, which is equivalent to a 15% conversion premium at the IPO price, and is callable at $18. The SPAC raised $359 million. Subsequently, a $200 million PIPE was created in the form of a five-year 6% convertible bond. After a brief period, the equity and warrant shares traded separately under the symbols GIG and GIGGW. On June 4, 2021, the SPAC announced it would merge with a defense sector data analytics firm, BigBear.ai. The transaction valued the firm at $1.57 billion, and had a minimum cash provision of $300 million. Given that the SPAC investors have the option of participating (keeping their shares) or redeeming at $10 plus whatever returns have been made on the investment in Treasury bills, the SPAC had ample capital from the $200 million PIPE convertible bond; only $100 million of the $359 million from the SPAC IPO investors needed to participate to meet the $300 million minimum cash provision for the deal to proceed. Note that the redemption feature provides strong downside protection— akin to a put.

14.2.2 Non-SPAC PIPES

A more traditional approach to a PIPE is a privately negotiated deal offering financing to a public company. These are similar to liquid convertibles in form, but simply have a single investor and do not trade except in privately arranged transactions. Classic examples of this come from a series of private investments made by Berkshire Hathaway following the great financial crisis (GFC).

Berkshire Hathaway Investments in Private Convertibles

Long-term investors with limited liquidity needs are amenable to buying and holding attractive but illiquid investments in private convertibles. An extreme example is Berkshire Hathaway CEO Warren Buffett, who has said, "Our favorite holding period is forever."[9]

During the early post-GFC years, major companies that needed capital had suffered from depressed stock prices. Berkshire Hathaway took advantage of this market opportunity by negotiating six multibillion-dollar PIPEs with different issuers. The returns from these investments were excellent as a whole (see Table 14.1). Berkshire had previously negotiated a private convertible in Salomon Brothers in 1987 and another in USAir in 1989.

The companies that sold the bespoke convertibles to Berkshire Hathaway presumably benefited from the prestige of having Berkshire as a major investor, which must have been especially valuable to the financial issuers—Bank of America, Goldman Sachs, Salomon Brothers, and Swiss Re. Confidence is essential to the success of financial companies in attracting and retaining clients. The fact that the private convertibles in Table 14.1 were structured as preferreds rather than bonds was also important to financial issuers because preferreds are equity rather than debt. The terms of the new convertibles, of course, were favorable to Berkshire, with the preferred dividends presumably qualifying for the corporate dividends received deduction (DRD).

The Berkshire investment in Bank of America (BAC) was structured as a $5 billion private 6% cumulative perpetual preferred that was usable to exercise 10-year warrants to buy 700 million BAC common shares at $7.14; the deal closed on August 25, 2011. The high dividend and low conversion price reflected continued market concerns following the GFC of 2008–2009 as well as worries in 2011 that Europe's economic travails

Table 14.1 Berkshire Hathaway Negotiated Large Private Convertibles in 2008–2013

	Year	Size	Convertible Preferred Share Structure	Outcome
Goldman Sachs	2008	$5 bn	Perpetual preferred shares with a 10% annual dividend and warrants at $115/share.	In 2015, Berkshire reduced its stake. After Goldman redeemed the preferred shares, Berkshire renegotiated the warrants.
General Electric	2008	$3 bn	Preferred shares with a 10% annual dividend, callable in 3 years with warrants to acquire shares at $22.25/share that can be exercised through 2013.	In 2017, Berkshire Hathaway sold its shares.
Dow Chemical	2009	$3 bn	Convertible preferred shares with an 8.5% annual dividend and a conversion price of $58.35/share.	In 2016, Berkshire announced its intention to convert into common stock at the end of the year and sell the stock.
Swiss Re	2009	CHF 3 bn	Convertible preferred shares with a 12% annual dividend and conversion price of CHF 25 after 3 years.	In 2015, Berkshire announced its intention to sell its investment in Swiss Re.
Bank of America	2011	$5 bn	Preferred shares with a 6% annual dividend usable to exercise warrants to buy common stock at $7.14/share for 10 years.	In 2017, CEO Buffett announced that Berkshire would use the preferred shares to exercise the warrants with the stock about $24/share.
Kraft Heinz	2013	$8 bn	Convertible preferred shares with a 9% annual dividend and warrants that were callable in 3 years.	In 2016, Berkshire announced it would redeem the preferred at the earliest date allowed later in the year.

Source: Advent Capital Management.

might spread globally.[10] Unusually, however, Bank of America had the right to redeem the preferred at a 5% premium at any time.[11]

Prior to the deal with Berkshire, Bank of America had reported losses in 2009 and 2010 and was heading for earnings per share in 2011 of only 1 cent. BAC shares had plunged from more than $15 early in 2011 to less than $7 at the time the PIPEs were issued. The dividends paid on the common stock had been cut from more than $2.40 in 2007 to only 4 cents in 2009, 2010, and 2011. Bank of America CEO Brian Moynihan denied that the company *needed* the Berkshire investment: "We have the capital and liquidity we need. . . . At the same time, I also recognize that a large investment by Warren Buffett is a strong endorsement."[12] The $5 billion proceeds of the Berkshire investment was a minor capital boost in the context of Bank of America's $230 billion of shareholders' equity.[13]

We infer that the Bank of America preferred shares were usable to exercise the warrants; Buffett explained in a letter to shareholders that the transaction would be "a cashless exchange of our preferred into common." Berkshire executed the warrants after just under six years because Bank of America had raised the quarterly dividend from 1 cent a share to 12 cents; hence, the new dividends were $336 million a year on the 700 million BAC shares into which the preferred could be effectively converted—which was $36 million more than the $300 million in dividends on the preferred shares that were used to execute the warrants.

The combination of the usable preferred and the warrants had effectively created a 6% convertible preferred with a conversion premium of only 6.9%, albeit with a 10-year expiration—which resembled the time limits on convertibility of some nineteenth-century convertibles (discussed in Section 3.1).

The Bank of America warrants provided the classic upside participation of convertibles. With BAC shares around $24 when the warrants were exercised on August 24, 2017, Berkshire's $5 billion investment had returned $1.8 billion in preferred dividends that presumably qualified for the DRD plus an $11.5 billion unrealized capital gain on the exercise of the warrants that presumably was tax deferred (see explanation of warrant taxation on the Startup Log Blog[14])—a tax-favored gain of $13.3 billion on a $5 billion investment in less than six years.

Berkshire Hathaway announced a $10 billion PIPE in Occidental Petroleum in April 2019, which followed the Berkshire pattern of negotiating a preferred plus warrants from a company that needed capital. Occidental was pursuing Anadarko Petroleum and ultimately paid $57 billion in August 2019. We assume that the $10 billion face value of the preferreds is usable to exercise the warrants, and therefore, the two securities effectively constitute a private convertible. The exercise price is $62.50. The preferred dividend is a lofty 8%, but the dividend has a pay-in-kind feature that enabled Occidental to initially pay in common shares, although Occidental subsequently paid a cash dividend.[15]

14.3 PRE-IPO CONVERTIBLES

Startup companies often issue private convertibles structured as relatively short-term notes that are especially useful for private companies that have become successful enough to place pre–initial public offering (pre-IPO) convertibles in anticipation of an IPO. These issues are structured to provide a potential payoff for investors in the event of an IPO, while enabling the issuing companies to raise capital at minimal interest expense without meaningfully diluting existing equity investors. Pre-IPO convertible bonds typically have a coupon rate (or dividend in the case of convertible preferreds) that increases over time, which gives management an incentive to IPO before the rate increases to punitive levels. These issues also typically reward investors by allowing them to convert into common shares at a discount to the IPO price. This discount is what gives the convertible its delta, for example, a 20% discount increases in dollar value as the value of the company rises. If the company were to triple in value prior to going public, the 20% discount would also increase threefold.

Uber

In January 2015, Uber issued a $1.6 billion six-year pay-in-kind (PIK) private convertible note with a 20% to 30% discount on stock issued in the future IPO in addition to a coupon that would escalate if Uber did not go public in four years.[16] The notes were sold to clients of Goldman Sachs[17] at a valuation of $40 billion. The provisions of the payment of interest in either cash or PIK were complicated and are disclosed in detail in an SEC exhibit[18] that describes interest of 2.5% for the first four years, followed by an increase to 12.5%. Uber went public at a valuation of $77.5 billion in May 2019, which was 89% greater than the valuation at issuance of the private convertible, so the IPO provided a worthwhile IRR for the convertible. See Section 14.6.1 for an approach to estimating IRRs of Pre-IPO convertibles.

14.4 PRIVATE CONVERTIBLES (ON PRIVATE COMPANIES)

The final category of Private Convertibles are truly private in that they represent an investment into the equity of private companies. Since the companies do not have listed shares, the deals are structured to provide a percentage of ownership to investors at a fixed price.

Startup companies often obtain seed capital by issuing private convertible notes to high-net-worth *angels* and to venture capitalists[19] who qualify as *accredited investors*[20] under SEC Regulation D. These notes are designed to convert into common or preferred shares upon a subsequent *qualified financing* that establishes a valuation of the company. The notes typically convert at a discount to the established valuation.

Such notes often include a valuation *cap* that ensures that the early investors will participate if there is a dramatic increase in the valuation of the company between the time of issuance of the private convertible and the next financing. Above a predetermined threshold valuation, the conversion price is capped.

The rationale for caps is that early investors deserve to participate in subsequent appreciation given the risks of investing in a startup that may have a binary outcome, that is, success or failure. A cap effectively limits the potential increase in the conversion price that would otherwise occur if the conversion price were based solely on a discount from a subsequent valuation. Once the valuation rises above the cap, the conversion price is fixed, so the convertible investor participates 100% in the valuation increase. Caps are less common among private companies that have obtained multiple funding rounds that establish clear valuations. Further details of valuation caps are explained by the law firm of David Wright Tremaine in a paper entitled, "What Is a Valuation Cap?," in July 2020.[21]

Private convertibles to fund startups and early-stage companies include SAFE and KISS products, which were introduced in 2013 and 2014, respectively. These instruments are contractual agreements that promise future conversion into equity but are not debt instruments (and pay no interest and have no maturity). Such agreements are similar in risk profile to convertibles that are issued by companies that have not yet established creditworthiness. The paperwork for arranging such securities is relatively basic. According to Carta, the first half of 2020 saw such non-debt convertible securities reach dollar parity with debt convertible securities among prefunding companies.[22] A glossary of terms for private convertibles and SAFE securities was published by Carta on January 13, 2021.[23]

Initial private fundings of startups and early-stage companies tend to be tiny. "The typical range for a healthy initial convertible debt round is $500,000 to $1,250,000," according to a post by Peter Werner,[24] a partner of the Cooley law firm, which specializes in venture capital.[25] The rest of our discussion will focus on later-stage companies that have issued private convertibles as large as several billion dollars.

Private convertibles structured as preferred shares lack the protection of debt instruments; hence, the yields on preferreds tend to be higher to compensate for the reduced safety. Regulators and rating agencies usually favor preferred equity over debt liabilities. Taxable individual investors may benefit from reduced taxation of dividends as qualified dividend income, and corporations may be able to claim the DRD on preferred dividends—advantageous tax provisions relative to the full tax rates on interest income, assuming that these provisions continue in an era of rising tax rates.

The Economist described a hypothetical example of a venture-capital firm buying a 20% stake in an early-stage company for $20 million in the form of preferred shares with a liquidation value of $20 million, convertible into 20% of the equity if the company goes public or is acquired.[26] The venture-capital investor earns a minimum of the preferred dividends and has some downside protection from the $20 million liquidation value. If the company commands a value exceeding $100 million, the convertible preferred can be converted into 20% of the equity of the company, which provides the upside participation.

14.5 PRIVATE ATTRACTIONS AND GROWTH

The overall private credit market—including private convertible preferreds as *debt*—has grown rapidly in part because banks have deemphasized corporate lending and loan syndication since the 2008–2009 Great Financial Crisis (GFC). By 2018, non-bank lending—including issuance of private convertibles—accounted for 42% of commercial lending,[27] which was up from less than 5% in 2009. The lending shift toward private markets has included growth in private convertibles, and banks have underwritten a growing amount of public and Rule 144A convertible securities, including record convertible issuance in the United States in the 12 months through March 2021.

We estimate that global private convertible ex-144A issues constituted approximately $100 billion of new issuance value at year-end 2020—more than 10% of the entire private credit market, which was $880 billion per the 2021 Preqin Global Private Debt Report.[28] (The global tradable convertible market including Rule 144A issues in the United States was $659 billion at year-end 2021 per Refinitiv.)

We estimate that roughly half the value of the private convertible market comes in the form of PIPEs. The remaining private convertibles are obligations of private companies, and around half of these are pre-IPO convertibles. Investors in a pre-IPO private convertible should confirm provisions for the future conversion value to reflect the possibility that the private company is acquired by a public entity (possibly a special-purpose acquisition company [SPAC][29]) or arranges a direct listing of its common shares (rather than additional private-equity funding or an IPO).

The basic structures of private convertibles mirror those of public convertible securities, with the exception that preferred shares represent a significant part of the private convertible market—in contrast with the tiny percentage of traditional convertible preferreds (as opposed to mandatory preferreds) in public markets. Individual issues of private convertibles tend to be customized, unlike the relatively standardized structures in public markets.

We theorize that one attraction of private securities (excluding Rule 144A issues that are actively traded) is the emotional advantage of being valued by sophisticated investors—not by momentary emotions that roil public markets. When the stock market drops, we may feel demoralized and want to sell. When the market surges, we may feel euphoric and want to buy regardless of rich valuations because of fear of missing out (FOMO; see Chapter 5).

As in the public market for US convertibles, the private convertible market tends to attract growth companies in general and technology companies in particular. Private securities are especially important for early-stage companies that need capital.

Private convertibles are issued by every sort of private company from tiny startups to household names such as Airbnb, Spotify, and Uber, which issued private pre-IPO convertibles before going public. Private convertibles are also issued by public companies, including multibillion-dollar PIPEs negotiated by Berkshire Hathaway as vehicles for investing in such household names as Bank of America and Goldman Sachs (see Table 14.1). Microsoft purchased a $150 million private convertible preferred in Apple in 1997 (see Section 4.2.2)

14.5.1 Graduating to Rule 144A

Private convertibles issued under Rule 144A—and hence, available for re-sale to QIBs—are typically issued by publicly traded companies. Although the SEC characterizes Rule 144A securities as *private placements*, such issuers usually are large and well known to investors, and their securities are liquid. The issuers of Rule 144A convertible bonds take advantage of minimal regulatory requirements compared with issuing registered bonds. Many Rule 144A bonds are issued overnight, announced after the close of the New York Stock Exchange, and allocated to institutional buyers prior to the open the next morning.

Rule 144A bond trading is confined to QIBs for six months for Rule 144A obligations of public companies. Afterwards, the Rule 144A issues are free to trade. Yet, brokerages often are reluctant to allow individual investors and other non-QIB accounts to trade bonds that were issued under Rule 144A even after six months. In practice, only high-net-worth individuals who transact through sophisticated advisors are able to trade Rule 144A securities. Prior to 2008, Rule 144A issues were not free to trade for the first two years, and many of the issues came with registration rights. Bonds issued under Rule 144A that are subsequently registered are clearly eligible for trading by non-QIBs.

We found an excellent report on the characteristics of Rule 144A issues by DDJ Capital Management that focused on high-yield bonds,[30] but the implications for Rule 144A convertible bonds are essentially identical.

Uber Technologies and Spotify each graduated to issuance of large convertible bonds under Rule 144A after they became public: a $1 billion Uber convertible in December 2014 and a $1.3 billion Spotify convertible in February 2021.

14.6 PRIVATE CONVERTIBLE RETURN PROFILE

Following the GFC, the average life of a late-stage startup technology company was more than 10 years because the market for IPOs had been weak. As a result, private issues often provided needed capital. The recovery of IPOs in recent years has shortened the length of the pre-IPO period of private ownership, which also shortened the wait for private convertibles to be in the money following an IPO or acquisition by a SPAC.

Private *mezzanine* investments—a type of subordinated debt that ranks just above preferreds in the corporate capital structure—sometimes provide equity upside through an equity coinvestment or warrants that mimic the equity upside of convertibles. Mezzanine investors generate most of their return from current interest.[31]

Private convertibles are global, notably with issues from technology companies in China and other areas of Asia, including Alibaba in 2012 and a company backed by Tencent Holdings in 2016.[32] Spotify is a Swedish company.

14.6.1 Calculating Expected Pre-IPO Convertible Internal Rate of Return (IRR): Uber Example

In January 2015, Uber issued a $1.6 billion six-year pay-in-kind (PIK) private convertible note with a 20% to 30% discount on stock issued in the future IPO in addition to a coupon that would escalate if Uber did not go public in four years.[33] The notes were sold to clients of Goldman Sachs at a valuation of $40 billion.[34] The provisions of the payment of interest in either cash or PIK were complicated and are disclosed in detail in an SEC exhibit that describes interest of 2.5%[35] for the first four years, followed by an increase to 12.5%. Uber went public at a valuation of $77.5 billion in May 2019, which was 89% greater than the valuation at issuance of the private convertible, so the IPO provided a worthwhile IRR for the convertible.

We have created a hypothetical example that resembles the Uber convertible but lacks the complexity of the actual issue. The hypothetical company issues a private convertible note paying an 8% coupon that steps up by 2 percentage points per year after the fourth year and a discount to the future IPO stock price of 12.5% that steps up 2.5 percentage points per year until the IPO.

A basic approach to visualizing the potential return and IRR of our hypothetical convertible is to create a matrix of cash flows based on the time to IPO and the change in the underlying valuation, starting with a zero future valuation (bankruptcy) and an assumed recovery rate. Table 14.2 has a column of dates starting with the initial cash-flow date and a value that represents the investors' initial cash outflow of −100%. Subsequent rows have incremental coupon dates and hypothetical IPO dates. The value represents the annual coupon rate and the amount earned by the discount on IPO, with the value increasing across the columns.

A matrix of potential IRRs can be created using the XIRR function in Excel, as in Table 14.3. If in one year the company completes an IPO or goes bankrupt, the IRRs range from +39.3% on a 250% leap in valuation to a loss of −46.0% in bankruptcy. If the company has an IPO or goes bankrupt in the sixth year, the IRRs range from +15.7% on a 250% advance in valuation to a loss of −0.4% in bankruptcy. The matrix of IRRs can be multiplied by a similarly sized matrix of probabilities representing the expected appreciation of the company valuation and the expected time to IPO to produce an *expected* IRR. The expected IRR is 9.65% inclusive of the bankruptcy scenario and 14.52% exclusive of the bankruptcy scenario.

Table 14.2 Potential Cash Flows by Year and Change in Valuation

Yrs to IPO	Coupon Ladder	Discount Ladder	-100% (50% Recovery)	IPO Valuation (as % of Valuation at Issuance)									
				-50%	0%	50%	100%	125%	150%	175%	200%	225%	250%
1	8.0%	12.5%		-6.3%	0.0%	6.3%	12.5%	15.6%	18.8%	21.9%	25.0%	28.1%	31.3%
2	8.0%	15.0%		-7.5%	0.0%	7.5%	15.0%	18.8%	22.5%	26.3%	30.0%	33.8%	37.5%
3	8.0%	17.5%		-8.8%	0.0%	8.8%	17.5%	21.9%	26.3%	30.6%	35.0%	39.4%	43.8%
4	8.0%	20.0%		-10.0%	0.0%	10.0%	20.0%	25.0%	30.0%	35.0%	40.0%	45.0%	50.0%
5	10.0%	22.5%		-11.3%	0.0%	11.3%	22.5%	28.1%	33.8%	39.4%	45.0%	50.6%	56.3%
6	12.0%	25.0%		-12.5%	0.0%	12.5%	25.0%	31.3%	37.5%	43.8%	50.0%	56.3%	62.5%
7	14.0%	27.5%		-13.8%	0.0%	13.8%	27.5%	34.4%	41.3%	48.1%	55.0%	61.9%	68.8%
8	16.0%	30.0%		-15.0%	0.0%	15.0%	30.0%	37.5%	45.0%	52.5%	60.0%	67.5%	75.0%
1 Year													
12/31/2020	-100%		-100%	-100%	-100%	-100%	-100%	-100%	-100%	-100%	-100%	-100%	-100%
12/31/2021	108.0%		54%	108.0%	108.0%	114.3%	120.5%	123.6%	126.8%	129.9%	133.0%	136.1%	139.3%
2 Years													
12/31/2020	-100%		-100%	-100%	-100%	-100%	-100%	-100%	-100%	-100%	-100%	-100%	-100%
12/31/2021	8.0%		8%	8.0%	8.0%	8.0%	8.0%	8.0%	8.0%	8.0%	8.0%	8.0%	8.0%
12/31/2022	108.0%		54%	108.0%	108.0%	115.5%	123.0%	126.8%	130.5%	134.3%	138.0%	141.8%	145.5%
3 Years													
12/31/2020	-100%		-100%	-100%	-100%	-100%	-100%	-100%	-100%	-100%	-100%	-100%	-100%

(Continued)

Table 14.2 Potential Cash Flows by Year and Change in Valuation (Cont.)

Yrs to IPO	Coupon Ladder	Discount Ladder	-100% (50% Recovery)	IPO Valuation (as % of Valuation at Issuance)									
				-50%	0%	50%	100%	125%	150%	175%	200%	225%	250%
12/31/2021	8.0%	8.0%	8%	8.0%	8.0%	8.0%	8.0%	8.0%	8.0%	8.0%	8.0%	8.0%	8.0%
12/31/2022	8.0%	8.0%	8%	8%	8.0%	8.0%	8.0%	8.0%	8.0%	8.0%	8.0%	8.0%	8.0%
12/31/2023	108.0%	108.0%	54%	108.0%	108.0%	116.8%	125.5%	129.9%	134.3%	138.6%	143.0%	147.4%	151.8%
4 Years													
12/31/2020	-100%	-100%	-100%	-100%	-100%	-100%	-100%	-100%	-100%	-100%	-100%	-100%	-100%
12/31/2021	8.0%	8%	8%	8.0%	8.0%	8.0%	8.0%	8.0%	8.0%	8.0%	8.0%	8.0%	8.0%
12/31/2022	8.0%	8%	8%	8.0%	8.0%	8.0%	8.0%	8.0%	8.0%	8.0%	8.0%	8.0%	8.0%
12/31/2023	8.0%	8%	8%	8.0%	8.0%	8.0%	8.0%	8.0%	8.0%	8.0%	8.0%	8.0%	8.0%
12/31/2024	108.0%	54%	54%	108.0%	108.0%	118.0%	128.0%	133.0%	138.0%	143.0%	148.0%	153.0%	158.0%
5 Years													
12/31/2020	-100%	-100%	-100%	-100%	-100%	-100%	-100%	-100%	-100%	-100%	-100%	-100%	-100%
12/31/2021	8.0%	8%	8%	8.0%	8.0%	8.0%	8.0%	8.0%	8.0%	8.0%	8.0%	8.0%	8.0%
12/31/2022	8.0%	8%	8%	8.0%	8.0%	8.0%	8.0%	8.0%	8.0%	8.0%	8.0%	8.0%	8.0%
12/31/2023	8.0%	8%	8%	8.0%	8.0%	8.0%	8.0%	8.0%	8.0%	8.0%	8.0%	8.0%	8.0%
12/31/2024	8.0%	8%	8%	8.0%	8.0%	8.0%	8.0%	8.0%	8.0%	8.0%	8.0%	8.0%	8.0%

Table 14.2 Potential Cash Flows by Year and Change in Valuation (Cont.)

Yrs to IPO	Coupon Ladder	Discount Ladder	−100% (50% Recovery)	IPO Valuation (as % of Valuation at Issuance)									
				−50%	0%	50%	100%	125%	150%	175%	200%	225%	250%
12/31/2025	110.0%		55%	110.0%	110.0%	121.3%	132.5%	138.1%	143.8%	149.4%	155.0%	160.6%	166.3%
6 Years													
12/31/2020	−100%		−100%	−100%	−100%	−100%	−100%	−100%	−100%	−100%	−100%	−100%	−100%
12/31/2021	8.0%		8%	8.0%	8.0%	8.0%	8.0%	8.0%	8.0%	8.0%	8.0%	8.0%	8.0%
12/31/2022	8.0%		8%	8.0%	8.0%	8.0%	8.0%	8.0%	8.0%	8.0%	8.0%	8.0%	8.0%
12/31/2023	8.0%		8%	8.0%	8.0%	8.0%	8.0%	8.0%	8.0%	8.0%	8.0%	8.0%	8.0%
12/31/2024	8.0%		8%	8.0%	8.0%	8.0%	8.0%	8.0%	8.0%	8.0%	8.0%	8.0%	8.0%
12/31/2025	10.0%		10%	10.0%	10.0%	10.0%	10.0%	10.0%	10.0%	10.0%	10.0%	10.0%	10.0%
12/31/2026	112.0%		56%	112.0%	112.0%	124.5%	137.0%	143.3%	149.5%	155.8%	162.0%	168.3%	174.5%

Source: Advent Capital Management estimates.

Table 14.3   IRR by Year of IPO and Change in Valuation

of XIRR -100% (50% Recovery)	-50%	0%	50%	75%	100%	125%	150%	175%	200%	225%	250%
1	-46.0%	8.0%	8.0%	14.3%	14.3%	20.5%	23.6%	26.8%	29.9%	33.0%	36.1%	39.3%
2	-22.4%	8.0%	8.0%	11.5%	11.5%	15.0%	16.7%	18.3%	19.9%	21.5%	23.1%	24.7%
3	-12.4%	8.0%	8.0%	10.6%	10.6%	13.1%	14.3%	15.5%	16.7%	17.8%	18.9%	20.0%
4	-7.0%	8.0%	8.0%	10.1%	10.1%	12.2%	13.1%	14.1%	15.0%	15.9%	16.8%	17.6%
5	-3.3%	8.3%	8.3%	10.2%	10.2%	11.9%	12.7%	13.5%	14.2%	15.0%	15.7%	16.4%
6	-0.4%	8.8%	8.8%	10.4%	10.4%	11.9%	12.6%	13.2%	13.9%	14.5%	15.1%	15.7%

Source: Advent Capital Management estimates.

Although the cumulative return increases the longer it takes for a private company to complete an IPO—especially when the coupon steps up annually, as illustrated in Figure 14.1—IRRs often *decline* over time. As shown in the figure, the IRR of a four-year IPO is significantly lower than the IRR of a two-year IPO, and the IRR of a six-year IPO lags that of a four-year IPO as the valuation increases.

14.7 CONCLUSION

Private capital markets have grown substantially and represent an important source of capital for companies, and a valuable source of returns for investors. This growth is largely due to the flexibility offered to both parties in structuring appropriate investment vehicles. Convertibles and convertible-like features are an integral part of this market. Investors familiar with the mechanics and value of private convertibles have the tools necessary to benefit from this growing financial market. The expansion of the SPAC market in 2020 and 2021 is only the most visible aspect of this growth. Both SPAC and non-SPAC PIPEs, as well as pre-IPO convertibles, and private convertibles in private companies are being used to finance some of the most innovative new businesses and spin-offs.

Figure 14.1   Cumulative return as a function of years to IPO and change in valuation

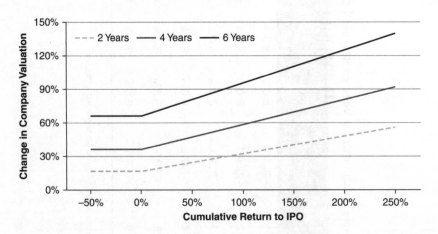

Source: Advent Capital Management estimates.

ENDNOTES

1. Buttonwood, "Up to Speed," *The Economist*, May 1, 2021, p. 61.

2. Global Private Capital Markets, Weekly Newsletter, October 1, 2021, JP Morgan Chase & Co., New York, p. 2.

3. Ibid., p. 13.

4. Ibid., p. 15.

5. https://www.investopedia.com/terms/a/accreditedinvestor.asp.

6. https://www.investopedia.com/terms/q/qib.asp.

7. "Stacked and Whacked," *The Economist*, April 11, 2020, p. 57.

8. https://www.startupgrind.com/blog/the-ultimate-guide-to-understanding-convertible-debt/.

9. https://www.brainyquote.com/quotes/warren_buffett_129835.

10. https://www.nytimes.com/2011/07/20/opinion/20iht-edstiglitz20.html.

11. https://dealbook.nytimes.com/2011/08/25/buffett-to-invest-5-billion-in-bank-of-america/.

12. http://investor.bankofamerica.com/news-releases/news-release-details/berkshire-hathaway-invest-5-billion-bank-america.

13. Bank of America data from *The Value Line Investment Survey*, February 5, 2021.

14. https://thestartuplawblog.com/warrants-the-tax-story/.

15. https://www.thestreet.com/investing/occidental-will-pay-200-million-dividend-to-berkshire-in-cash.

16. https://www.bloomberg.com/news/articles/2015-01-21/uber-said-to-raise-1-6-billion-in-convertible-debt-to-expand.

17. https://fortune.com/2015/01/22/uber-raises-another-1-6-billion-with-convertible-debt-sale/.

18. https://support.carta.com/s/article/convertible-terms-and-definitionshttps://www.sec.gov/Archives/edgar/data/1543151/000119312519103850/d647752dex47.htm.

19. https://www.startupgrind.com/blog/the-ultimate-guide-to-understanding-convertible-debt/.

20. https://www.investopedia.com/terms/a/accreditedinvestor.asp.

21. https://www.dwt.com/blogs/startup-law-blog/2020/07/what-is-a-valuation-cap#print.

22. https://carta.com/blog/non-debt-convertible-securities/.

23. https://support.carta.com/s/article/convertible-terms-and-definitions.

24. https://www.cooleygo.com/frequently-asked-questions-convertible-debt/.

25. https://www.legal500.com/firms/50229-cooley-llp/52803-san-francisco-usa/.

26. "Stacked and Whacked," *The Economist*, April 11, 2020, p. 57.

27. Bank of America Merrill Lynch, "Non-bank vs. Bank Commercial Lending: Structural Shift, but Watch the Cycle," Cross Asset Strategy, October 11, 2018.

28. https://www.preqin.com/insights/global-reports/2021-preqin-global-private-debt-report.

29. https://www.investopedia.com/terms/s/spac.asp.

30. Andrew Ross, "'144A's': A Large but Often Misunderstood Segment of the High Yield Bond Market," *DDJ Capital Management* 2018;5(4), https://www.ddjcap.com/wp-content/uploads/DDJ-Thought-Piece-144As-A-Large-But-Often-Misunderstood-Segment-of-the-High-Yield-Bond-Market.pdf.

31. https://www.cambridgeassociates.com/insight/private-credit-strategies-introduction/.

32. "Chinese Tech Unicorns Try a Different Approach to Raising Cash," *Wall Street Journal*, May 22, 2018.

33. https://www.bloomberg.com/news/articles/2015-01-21/uber-said-to-raise-1-6-billion-in-convertible-debt-to-expand.

34. https://fortune.com/2015/01/22/uber-raises-another-1-6-billion-with-convertible-debt-sale/.

35. https://support.carta.com/s/article/convertible-terms-and-definitionshttps://www.sec.gov/Archives/edgar/data/1543151/000119312519103850/d647752dex47.htm.

CHAPTER 15

Optimizing Corporate Capital Structures with Convertibles

Optimum: Greatest degree attained or attainable under implied or specified conditions.

— *Merriam-Webster Dictionary*

15.1 INTRODUCTION

A primary goal of the chief financial officer (CFO) of a corporation is to optimize the capital structure to maximize long-term returns for stockholders. Aside from accumulating retained earnings, capital can be raised in the form of equity or debt. Convertible securities merit consideration as a source of financing but are typically ignored. This chapter considers convertibles exclusively from the perspective of the issuer.

The equity portion of the capital structure of a public company can include common stock, preferred stock (including convertible preferreds), warrants (long-term stock options that create new shares when exercised—nearly extinct until a comeback through issuance in conjunction with Special Purpose Acquisition Company (SPAC) initial public offerings [IPOs]), and rights offerings (newly issued common stock that is first offered to currrent equity investors—rare in the United States). On the debt side, there are bank loans, straight (non-convertible) bonds, and convertible bonds. Features of debt include seniority in the capital structure, securing with assets, fixed or variable rates, calls or puts, maturities, and make-whole provisions for convertible bonds.

Business managers have faced choices in financing for centuries, yet, formal theory of optimal financing did not appear until the mid–twentieth century, and convertibles are absent from nearly all published work on optimal capital structures. We will evaluate the use of convertibles in the context of past models and then consider two new models that demonstrate that convertibles belong in the optimal corporate capital structure (see Section 15.5).

15.2 EFFECTS OF CAPITAL STRUCTURE ON THE EQUITY PRICE PROCESS

While most financial theory involving the stock price process is based on Louis Bachelier's finding in 1900 that stock prices tend to be log-normally distributed and that stock price returns tend to be normally distributed, management decisions can distort the shape of what might otherwise be a bell-shaped curve. The choice of financing vehicles is one of the primary causes of distortions.

15.2.1 Turbos and Brakes

Management and investors usually desire to speed up the advancement of the stock price and also to restrain any pullbacks in the stock price. Financing with convertibles effectively adds a turbo boost to the upside and brakes to the downside that alter the probability distribution of future stock prices. While this effect has not been incorporated into any of the standard pricing models, a modified distribution could be substituted for the normal distribution in the Monte Carlo model. (Greater detail is available on our website www.AdventCap.com/Book/SupplementaryMaterial) as well as in the capital structure optimization models in this chapter.

We can visualize deviations away from a normal distribution by considering the outcomes of the children's board game Chutes and Ladders (or Snakes and Ladders in British Commonwealth countries). A player advances on the game board according to the number rolled on a single die. The outcome of multiple rolls has a normal distribution. Consider the distribution of possible outcomes in the first three rolls.

Without any distortions, the maximum forward movement on three rolls would be 18 spaces on the game board (three rolls of 6), the minimum would be 3 (three rolls of 1), and the mean would be 10.5. But the board

Figure 15.1   Normal and distorted distributions of player position after three turns

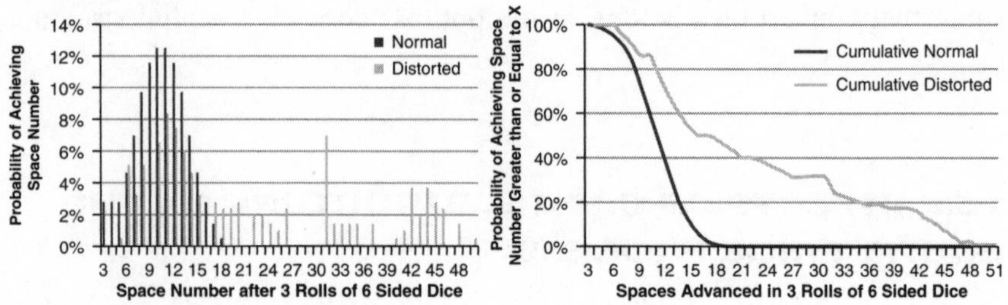

Source: Advent Capital Management.

distorts the outcomes. The first 18 spaces on the American board include three spaces with ladders of different heights and one space with a chute. If any of the three rolls of the die lands on space 1, 4, or 9, the player encounters a ladder and climbs to position 38, 14, or 31, respectively. If a die lands on space 16, the player slides down the chute to position 6. The normal and distorted probability distributions are charted in Figure 15.1.

There is a similar effect on the distribution of future stock price returns when a company issues convertible bonds. Between the stock price at the time of issue and the conversion price, there is no *economic* dilution from the stock price. Yet, the company is paying a lower interest rate on the convertible than on a non-convertible bond which means EPS is higher when financing is obtained with convertible debt. Moreover, part of the proceeds from the issuance of a convertible bond is usually used to purchase a call spread, which effectively raises the conversion price and thereby further reduces dilution (see Chapter 16 for details of accounting and call spreads). Consider the three funding alternatives in Figure 15.2.

Figure 15.2 illustrates how the shape of the earnings per share (EPS) probability distribution can vary depending on the source of financing. Both stock and high-yield (HY) bond issuances result in normal distributions of EPS, although HY results in a wider base (greater variance) because the earnings become more highly levered. The shape of the probability distribution for convertibles is more heavily weighted to the right side of the chart, that is, toward the upside. This is because the reduced levels of dilution and interest expense allow EPS to rise faster on the upside (EPS of 0.8–1.1) than if either HY bonds or common stock had been issued. Similarly, convertibles have the lowest probability of moderately low EPS (0.3–0.6).

Figure 15.2   Probability histogram of earnings per share (EPS) and EPS as a function of earnings before interest and taxes: a comparison of three funding choices

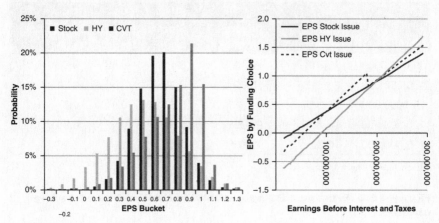

Source: Advent Capital Management.

Table 15.1 illustrates the relationship between earnings before interest and taxes (EBIT) and EPS for a hypothetical firm that is considering three possible sources of funding. The scenario depicted is for a $1.5 billion market-capitalization company with an 8% marginal cost of nonconvertible debt and a need to raise $750 million of capital. Median future earnings are expected to be $150 million with a $50 million standard deviation. The model uses a 25,000-iteration Monte Carlo process that causes the lines on the chart to be slightly wavy. The assumptions for the convertible are that it could be issued at a 3% coupon with a 40% conversion premium and that it could fund a call spread that extends dilution protection to the equivalent of an 80% conversion premium. Table 15.1 and Figure 15.3 summarize expected EPS for the three funding options at different levels of EBIT and cumulative probability.

In all but the most extreme tail scenarios, convertible funding results in the highest EPS. Until the stock price exceeds the dilution protection of the convertible conversion premium plus the additional call spread protection, there is no dilution of earnings. Even when the dilution kicks in, the stock has been sold at a higher price than when the funding was first required, which means that the number of shares is lower than if the company had issued common stock. Higher EPS from issuing a convertible rather than a straight bond is also due to the reduced interest expense, which boosts the bottom line relative to an HY issuance in all scenarios. This interest savings

Table 15.1 Comparison of EPS Given Levels of EBIT and Funding Choices

EBIT	Cum. Probability	1-Cum. Probability	EPS Stock Issue	EPS HY Issue	EPS Convertible Issue
50,000,000	99.81%	0.19%	0.1	–0.32	–0.02
100,000,000	91.81%	8.19%	0.38	0.09	**0.39**
150,000,000	50.52%	49.48%	0.65	0.51	**0.8**
200,000,000	8.71%	91.29%	0.91	0.92	**0.95**
250,000,000	0.32%	99.68%	1.18	1.33	1.27

Source: Advent Capital Management.

Figure 15.3 Average EPS by probability decile—three funding choices

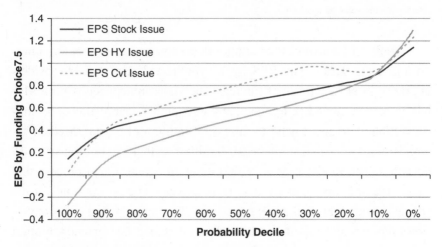

Source: Advent Capital Management

from issuing a convertible rather than straight debt may be affected by the US cap on deductibility of interest as a percentage of Internal Revenue Service–defined *adjusted taxable interest* (akin to earnings before interest, taxes, depreciation, and amortization [EBITDA]; see Section 15.3.2 for further discussion). Depending on the range of potential future earnings relative to the interest expense of HY bonds, convertibles may provide a greater amount of capital without breaching the interest deductibility cap. It is only in the event of much higher than expected EBIT that HY would have been the best choice, and it is only in the event of much lower than expected EBIT that stock issuance would have been the best choice.

Note that *dilution* per our calculations is a function of the *economics* of whether the share price has exceeded dilution protection. See Chapter 16 for explanations of convertible accounting.

15.3 EVOLUTION OF CORPORATE FINANCE THEORY

The theory of capital structure has evolved to provide investors and corporate executives with better tools for understanding the consequences of different capital structures. Although an entire book could be devoted to this topic, our purpose is to provide sufficient insight into the historical models to understand the value of our Monte Carlo–based approach.

15.3.1 Indifference to Leverage: Modigliani-Miller (M&M) Model A

In 1958, Professors Franco Modigliani and Merton Miller at Carnegie Mellon University—who were awarded the Nobel Prize for their contributions to economics and finance—theorized that the value of a firm is independent of its capital structure and is purely a function of its future earnings and assets.[1] According to the M&M Model A, there is no benefit from optimizing the capital structure because the capital structure bears no relevance to the value of a firm. This view of the enterprise value of a company is akin to the way houses are valued—independent of the size of the mortgage—as we discussed in Section 2.4.1. Anyone who has owned a residence—or has contemplated such ownership—should readily understand the basics of leverage.

The theory reasons that an investment in an unlevered firm (without debt) can be levered by an investor borrowing to finance the position. Similarly, an investment in a firm that is partly debt levered can effectively be delevered by owning a smaller number of common shares together with risk-free assets. Investors should be unwilling to pay a premium or accept a discount for shares of a company on the basis of leverage. The theory rests on the hypothesis of perfect capital markets (i.e., no transaction costs, an equivalent borrowing rate for both individuals and companies—and no taxes).

The M&M Model A theory is based on two basic propositions:

Proposition 1: The value of an unlevered firm is equal to the value of an otherwise identical levered firm. This is written mathematically as $V_U = V_L$

Proposition 2: The expected return on equity of a levered firm is equal to the expected return on equity of an unlevered firm plus the debt-to-equity ratio times the difference between the cost of equity of the unlevered firm and the cost of debt of the levered firm, written mathematically as:

$$R_{E(L)} = R_{E(U)} + \frac{D}{E} \times \left(R_{E(U)} - R_{D(L)} \right) \qquad (15.1)$$

15.3.2 Recognition of the Interest-Expense Tax Shield: M&M Model B

Modigliani and Miller recognized that taxes and financing costs invalidated Model A, so they published an updated Model B in 1963,[2] which incorporates the value of the tax deduction of interest, and has two propositions:

Proposition 1: The value of a levered firm is equal to the value of an otherwise identical unlevered firm plus the tax rate times the total debt of the levered firm, assuming that the debt is perpetual or will be rolled repeatedly at a constant interest rate. This is written mathematically as

$$V_L = V_U + T \times D \qquad (15.2)$$

This formula seems to be missing an important consideration: the interest rate. However it can be shown that rate cancels out, as is illustrated in the following formulas:

Dollars of interest = total debt D × annual interest rate I

Annual tax shield = dollars of interest × tax rate T

Perpetual value of tax shield

$$= \frac{\text{annual tax shield}}{\text{interest rate}} = D \times I \times \frac{T}{I} = D \times T \tag{15.3}$$

Proposition 2: The expected return on equity of a levered firm is equal to the expected return on equity of an unlevered firm plus the debt-to-equity ratio times the difference between the cost of equity of the unlevered firm and the cost of debt of the levered firm times one minus the tax rate. This is written mathematically as

$$R_{E(L)} = R_{E(U)} + \frac{D}{E} \times R_{E(U)} - R_{D(L)}) \times (1-T) \tag{15.4}$$

Model B demonstrates that different types of capital have different costs based on the value of the tax shield. The higher the tax rate, the lower is the cost of debt relative to the cost of equity because the value of the tax shield is proportional to the tax rate. This gives rise to two questions: What is a company's total cost of capital? And can its cost of capital be reduced?

Model B includes the *weighted-average cost of capital* (WACC), which is the percent equity capital times the cost of equity plus the percent debt capital times the cost of debt. The cost of equity is the required rate of return on equity given the beta of the stock and the index equity risk premium. The cost of debt is typically the market yield on the outstanding debt.

Because convertibles are a hybrid of debt and equity, calculating the cost of capital is complicated when the capital structure includes a convertible. The coupon on a convertible bond is usually the lowest interest of all debt in the capital structure, and the yield to maturity can be negative. Yet, a convertible bond has an equity component—and equity is usually the highest-cost capital.

For convertibles, the all-in yield (discussed in Chapter 12), adjusted for the tax shield, is the correct cost for the WACC calculation because it reflects the equity risk premium and the likelihood of conversion into stock in addition to the bond-like components of the convertible bond that determine the yield and the likelihood of maturing at par. In prior decades, higher interest rates and higher tax rates made the deduction of interest on debt much more valuable. Co-author Dan Partlow owned an 18% obligation of Ford Motor Company in 1980, when the corporate tax rate was 46%. The tax deduction on 18% interest had a value of 8.28%. If we assume a

2020 investment-grade coupon of 3% and a corporate tax rate of 21%, the value of the tax deduction is only 0.63%.

The Tax Reform Act of 2017 added a cap of 30% of adjusted taxable income to the deductibility of interest. The cap was temporarily raised to 50% during the COVID-19 pandemic. About 40% of HY issuers in 2018 had interest costs above the cap.[3] Although interest rates on HY bonds subsequently declined, issuance increased, so the cap on the tax shield may have become more significant. The cap should make convertible issuance more attractive to highly levered companies because convertibles have lower coupons, and therefore, convertibles enable more capital to be raised without exceeding the deductibility cap. The uncertainties surrounding the cap on interest deductibility demand up-to-date research for clarification.

The cost of capital and optimal capital structure should be based on expected interest and tax rates as well as current rates. Some models assume that borrowing rates and taxes are constant in perpetuity, but history suggests perpetual change is the only constant. A forward rate curve that can be derived from bond prices will provide an unbiased view of expected future interest rates. Furthermore, the process of planning the capital structure should account for discrete changes in internal funding needs.

The M&M Model B (tax shield), if taken to its logical extreme, suggests that a firm can maximize its value by creating a capital structure that is nearly entirely debt. The validity of a model is not only its prescriptive strength but also its descriptive strength; the fact that few firms have extremely high leverage levels has fueled criticism of Model B.

In their 1978 paper, "Corporate Income Taxes, Valuation, and the Problem of Optimal Capital Structure," Michael Brennan and Eduardo Schwartz observed that "the analysis appears to lead to the conclusion that an optimal capital structure will consist almost entirely of debt. This conclusion leads to the inconsistency between the premise that managements act so as to maximize the wealth of stockholders and the empirical observation that most firms eschew highly levered capital structures."[4]

15.3.3 Other Advanced Models

Since 1963, several models have been proposed, including the *bank-ruptcy cost trade-off theory* (Kraus-Litzenberger), the *pecking order theory*

(Meyers), the *agency cost trade-off theory* (Jensen-Meckling), and the *market timing theory* (Baker-Wurgler), which make intuitive hypotheses about offsets to the attractiveness or availability of debt financing. There are also more recent models relating to the optimal maturity of debt financing, such as the Leland-Toft model. While these models are useful for developing a robust understanding of optimal capital structure, none of them considers convertibles directly. For a thorough review of these models and how they might be broadened to incorporate convertibles, please visit www.AdventCap.com/Book/SupplementaryMaterial.

15.3.4 Flotation Cost and Capital Structure

The previously discussed models ignore the flotation costs of issuance, which are especially high for equity capital: reaching 7% to 8% for IPOs and slightly less for secondary offerings. Straight bond issuance can also be expensive when incorporating the cost of obtaining agency ratings. Although there is little published literature on the relative cost of issuing various asset classes, there is anecdotal evidence that suggests that issuing convertibles is a relative bargain, which may explain why issuers are often willing to issue convertibles below their theoretical value. Not only are companies saving hundreds of basis points on the coupon, they are also realizing a substantial savings on the cost of issuing equity if it is converted at expiration—at a substantial premium to the price at issuance no less.

US convertible issuers usually avoid the time, expense, and possible disagreements involved in obtaining credit ratings because US investors in convertibles rarely require credit ratings. Moreover, most new US convertible bonds are issued overnight and are exempt from registration under SEC Rule 144A, which further reduces the time and cost of issuance. Of course, US convertible issuers typically incur cash outlays for call spreads that minimize dilution, as explained in Section 16.2.6.

There are two approaches to incorporating the cost of flotation in the cost of capital. The first is to multiply the cost of capital divisor by one minus the flotation cost as a percent of the issue size. This effectively adjusts future returns for the cost of issuance. The second approach, based on the 1976 publication by John Ezzell and Burr Porter, is to add the flotation cost to the initial investment and then generate an internal rate of return based on that larger initial investment and unadjusted returns.[5]

15.3.5 Economic Capital Adjustments

Picking a security type on the basis of its cost of capital, while intuitively attractive, does have certain problems. The primary problem is that some capital has a low cost because of its position in the capital structure and the encumbrance of assets. Debt that is relatively low cost but encumbers all the assets of the firm may be less attractive than debt that costs a little more but leaves all assets free of restrictive covenants and encumbrances.

An adjusted cost of capital can be calculated based on the encumbrance of assets. A small low-coupon debt issue that is secured by all firm assets would have a much higher adjusted cost of capital than a higher-coupon unsecured bond. The value of the capital usage can be calculated as the difference between the yield of the encumbered liability and the yield of a similar unsecured liability. If a suitable unsecured liability does not exist, one may take the longest unsecured bond in the capital structure and adjust for the difference in term premium and position in the debt hierarchy.

The least-encumbered capital is common equity. A convertible is more encumbering than equity if it matures at par but is only as encumbering as unsecured debt, and it is unencumbered if it expires in the money. Therefore, the encumbrance charge applied to convertibles should be based on the likelihood of maturing at par, which is one minus the delta. New convertibles are issued with a delta of approximately 50%; therefore, the encumbrance charge should be roughly 50% that of unsecured debt.

The economic collapse of some businesses due to the COVID-19 pandemic in early 2020 demonstrated that extraordinary circumstances can bring profitable but moderately levered firms to the brink of insolvency. Airlines, hotels, cruise ships, restaurants, department stores, car rental agencies, ride shares, ticket agencies, oil field services, and exploration and production all saw revenues plunge in a matter of days. Markets initially penalized companies that had turned cash-flow negative. The HY market remained effectively closed through mid-May 2020, leaving many companies in need of liquidity to the lowest form of capital in their pecking order—equity—even as shares traded at distressed levels. The convertible market reopened in April, and many companies turned to the convertibles market for rescue liquidity—effectively a deferred equity issuance at a price substantially above market levels.

15.4 CAPITAL STRUCTURE OPTIMIZATION

The most widely published theories of capital structure have been the Modigliani–Miller and pecking order models.

The pecking order model simply concluded that CFOs should pick the source of funding that has the lowest cost of capital, which is retained earnings (if sufficient), followed by debt (unless finances are such that additional debt cannot be issued), followed by equity. Both the Miller–Modigliani and pecking order models ignore several important factors:

1. Interest in excess of adjusted taxable income is not tax deductible.
2. Variability in the cost of funding due to
   a. Changes in interest rates (floating-rate debt)
   b. Changes in stock price (convertible bonds)
3. Loss of financing flexibility due to covenants or the pledge of collateral
4. Internal information about expected changes in earnings growth, volatility, or the path of expected changes in EBIT
5. Niche funding sources such as municipal industrial-development financing, asset-backed securitization, non-dollar securities

The lack of a widely understood and comprehensive capital structure model causes CFOs to rely on the guidance of investment banks that charge advisory fees to help them optimize their balance sheets. This chapter is intended to provide the understanding of how to build a capital structure optimization and how to interpret the results.

Today there are many special financing options. Some companies are able to take advantage of state or municipally offered business incentives such as industrial revenue bonds, which make the interest on the bonds tax deductible, thereby lowering the interest rate that must be offered to float the bond. Some issuers choose to pay a third party to guarantee or insure the bonds, which also can reduce the interest rate. Some CFOs have the alternative of leasing rather than buying assets. Some assets can be monetized through securitization as mortgage-backed securities (MBS) or as asset-backed securities (ABS) or via sale to private investors. Subsidiaries may be spun off partially or completely via an IPO, and shares of a prior partial spin-off may be sold or used to issue an exchangeable convertible.

All of these possibilities have a different cost of capital and may be optimal or suboptimal in different settings. Such a wide variety of financing methods is difficult to evaluate using a simple formula or rule of thumb. To deal with these challenges, we will turn to Monte Carlo modeling. A Monte Carlo model is well suited for capital financing optimization because the flexibility of the methodology allows it to simultaneously evaluate many different funding options. Its nature allows it to incorporate the inherent uncertainty of business results. In Section 15.5 we present two Monte Carlo models that use prospective operating results as their primary factor for evaluating financing options. But first we need to discuss what is being optimized or, in other words, what are the goals of management when it decides how to finance the company?

Corporate executives have often considered their mandate to be solely to maximize shareholder returns. Contemporary companies have mandates to serve stakeholders, who may include bondholders, lenders, employees, customers, suppliers, the general public, and the environment—typically characterized as *environmental, social, governance (ESG) factors* (discussed in Chapter 16).

We will confine our analysis in this chapter to using the capital structure to optimize returns within the constraints of reasonable risk parameters. On this basis, stock return, or return metrics that incorporate risk-adjusted returns as measured by Sharpe or Sortino ratios, are important measures of management performance.

When designing an optimization model, one must first decide which metric to try to optimize and over what time frame. While stock-price return is an easily understood metric, it actually contains little information about the risk taken to achieve that return. Therefore, one of the four risk-adjusted metrics is preferable because the optimization model will try to achieve the best return relative to the amount of risk taken. There are pros and cons to each risk metric. Here are four possible risk adjusted return metrics which may be used as the optimized value:

$$\text{Volatility-adjusted return} = \text{stock return} \times \frac{\text{benchmark volatility}}{\text{stock volatility}}$$

$$\text{Beta-adjusted return} = \text{stock return} \times \frac{\text{benchmark beta}}{\text{stock beta}}$$

$$\text{Sharpe ratio} = \frac{(\text{return stock} - \text{risk free rate})}{\text{stock volatility}}$$

$$\text{Sortino ratio} = \frac{(\text{return stock return} - \text{rate risk-free rate})}{\text{downside stock volatility}}$$

Risk-adjusted return is described in the Modigliani & Miller model as the return of an asset times the ratio of the risk of the benchmark to the risk of the asset. For example, risk-adjusted return could be calculated as the return of Western Digital Corp. stock (ticker WDC) times the volatility of the S&P 500 divided by the volatility of WDC. Alternatively, other risk metrics could be used such as beta. Because the beta of the S&P 500 is always 1, the formula would simplify to the return of a stock divided by the beta of the stock.

A basic criticism of these metrics is that "you can't eat risk-adjusted returns." In other words, a risk adjusted return that is higher than actual return doesn't actually deliver an investor a higher return. That said, "risk" or volatility does result in lower returns for some investors depending on their investment horizon. If management's goal is to maximize returns over five years, but the stock swings wildly in the meantime, investors with a shorter horizon that must make scheduled redemptions, could be worse off with a volatile stock and high long-term returns than with a stock that appreciates more steadily, even if the long-term return is lower. Hence, managements often seek the highest *and* steadiest stock return possible.

For example, a risk-adjusted return of 15% can be obtained by earning a return of 30% with twice the volatility of the benchmark, 15% with the same volatility as the benchmark, or a return of 1.5% with one-tenth the volatility of the benchmark. As for choosing between Sharpe and Sortino, many investors prefer the Sortino ratio because it only penalizes the metric for downside volatility, whereas the Sharpe ratio penalizes both upside and downside volatility. The advantage of the Sharpe ratio is that total volatility contains more information about the potential for future volatility than just downside volatility.

For example, a stock that has had tremendous upside volatility with almost no downside volatility may have become unsustainably overvalued. The risk of a correction in its valuation might be more obvious in the context of total upside and downside volatility rather than downside volatility alone.

If the optimization involves a Monte Carlo process with thousands of iterations and multiple time steps to a future horizon within each iteration, then each iteration movement is based on the full volatility of the stock, not just downside volatility—so there is no loss of information in creating the range of potential future outcomes. Therefore, the iteration can be independently evaluated at the horizon date on a pro-forma ex post basis. In other words, because each hypothetical iteration was derived from a complete picture of volatility, there is no loss of information in determining prospective movement, so the risk/return ratio of each iteration at its horizon date can either include or exclude an upside volatility penalty in its excess risk/return ratio without the problem of having a metric that ignores the risk of overvalued straight-up stock situations.

Efficient financing incurs the lowest possible cost of capital net of the tax benefits of deductible interest expense. The cost-of-capital calculation historically presented in textbooks is a simple formula that classifies all capital as either debt or equity and generally avoids the difficulty of nuanced tax codes by using a single coefficient for the effective tax rate of a company. We will start with the historical approach and then show the refinements necessary to accurately capture the effects of the 2017 tax reform act as well as the nuances of convertibles. It is important to recognize the fact that the tax benefit of interest expense is of no value to companies that lack taxable earnings. Bankruptcy is a possible outcome for some companies.

Financing debt with a lower-coupon convertible that incurs potential future equity dilution may not seem attractive to CFOs who might be relying on overly optimistic business plans and sales forecasts, but the savings in interest expense may keep the company solvent in bleaker situations should exogenous events, such as pandemic or economic contraction, or endogenous events leading to underperformance occur. Therefore, optimization of the capital structure should consider many potential future earnings scenarios and identify the best capital structure based on a Monte Carlo evaluation of this stochastic process.

15.5 OUR MONTE CARLO MULTIPERIOD MODELS

We have built two separate models to solve for the optimal funding structure of a potential investment project. Both models use a Monte Carlo process to estimate how the average expected share price of a company changes based on what kind of security the company issues to raise capital. Although the models seek to answer the same question, they differ in inputs and underlying processes and can be summarized as a *balance sheet-based model* and an *earnings-based model*.

15.5.1 Balance Sheet–Based Model

The balance sheet–based model requires information on the firm's current capital structure, the beta of its stock, and details on its earnings power. The model uses this information in a two-step process to estimate the fair value of the company's shares in thousands of possible iterations.

The first step is to use a normal probability distribution to create a possible terminal EBIT for each iteration. To calculate preconversion EPS, the model uses another normal distribution to generate the three-month London Interbank Offered Rate (LIBOR) and Treasury rate for the purposes of determining the cost of any bank loans and whether or not there is an opportunity to refinance any debt (assuming that the call feature is enabled). The preconversion EPS is then applied to an assumed price/earnings (P/E) ratio, which is based on the initial P/E ratio of the firm adjusted for the change in the EPS growth rate implied by each iteration to project a future share price. The estimated share price is used to determine whether a convertible bond would convert as well as the debt-to-equity ratio of the firm at the end of the time period.

The second step uses the current beta of the company's shares and the forecasted debt-to-equity ratio of the firm to calculate a forecasted cost of equity. The cost of equity allows the model to estimate the fair value of the equity position using post-dilution EPS. This is then discounted back to the start of the investment case for an output that gives the average present value of the 5,000 iterations—the assumption being that the funding option that maximizes average expected present value is the optimal funding solution.

15.5.2 Earnings-Based Model

The earnings-based requires the earnings power of the firm as well as details on available financing options. The earnings-based model uses a Monte Carlo process with a large number of iterations to simulate EBIT in each individual year of the analysis. This differs meaningfully from the balance sheet–based approach, which only simulates the final year's earnings. The earnings-based model can use a more diverse set of earnings paths and can handle scenarios with very low or negative earnings. The model uses forecasted EBIT along with the same interest-rate modeling process as the balance sheet–based model to simulate the firm's EPS in each year. It then applies each iteration's EPS to an assumed P/E ratio. The P/E ratio is modeled as a separate stochastic process that is a function of the iteration's stochastically derived EBIT growth observation. This gives the model a market price for the stock, which determines whether a conversion event has occurred in each of the iterations. The model then uses the EPS and share count after any potential conversions to recalculate EPS and final market price. The average of the final share prices grouped by financing vehicle is the final output of the model.

15.5.3 The Two Models—and the Results Are Similar

Both models use Monte Carlo analysis to project future earnings and then use those projections to determine the likelihood of conversion. Yet, there are important differences between the two processes.

The earnings-based model forecasts earnings and share price in each individual year, but the model assumes that the term of any investment financing is five years. The benefit of this simplifying assumption is that it allows the spreadsheet to model each year on its own, but it also places a term restriction on the model's analysis.

The balance sheet-based model, in contrast, can handle any investment horizon but is more limited on the paths that earnings growth can take. The other major difference is that the balance sheet-based model uses a multiple-based approach for the initial share price estimate, but once the model has decided whether a conversion has occurred, it switches to using the forecasted cost of equity to discount the firm's future cash flows. In comparison, the earning-based approach uses earnings multiples for determining whether a conversion event will occur as well as for the final valuation of the shares.

Despite these differences, the two models generally produce similar results when given comparable inputs.

Table 15.2 shows the calculations behind a single iteration using the balance sheet–based model for a hypothetical semiconductor company with $2.5 billion in EBIT that is planning to supplement its expected 10% growth rate with a $2.5 billion project that should generate a 20% annual return before interest and taxes. The firm decides to finance this project through the issuance of a five-year convertible bond with a 2% coupon and a 35% premium. The firm already has $10 billion in preexisting debt that costs 5% per year, and it has 300 million shares outstanding at $60 per share.

This particular iteration projects a world in which EBIT has only grown by about 20%. Taking into account the extra $50 million per year in interest expense and the firm's 21% marginal tax rate, this leads to an EPS of $6.55. After using the expected P/E ratio and applying a (very small in this case) risk discount based on the coverage ratio, we are left with a projected share price of $74.60 at the end of the five years. Because the convertible bond had a conversion price of $81 per share, this is not enough to cause any conversion to occur, so the number of shares outstanding does not increase.

The projected share count and share price are used to find the market value of the firm's equity, which is used to calculate the firm's debt-to-equity ratio. The debt-to-equity ratio can be used to find the levered beta of 1.56, which leads to a cost of equity of 10.30%. From there it is fairly simple to use a growing perpetuity formula to find the fair value of the firm's shares in year five and then discount that back to the present giving us the final output of $47.94 per share.

It is important to remember that this is not the final result of the balance sheet–based model using these inputs. The $47.94 per share is the result of one out of thousands of iterations that the model would generate. The final result of the model is the average expected value that comes from the results of these iterations. *In this hypothetical case, using the aforementioned convertible instead of a traditional bond resulted in a roughly 2% higher expected fair value.*

Table 15.2 Balance Sheet Model - Formula Example

$EBIT_{Y5} = (EBIT_{Y1} + StD\,EBIT) * (1 + g_{firm})^t$ $+ EBIT_{project} * StD\,EBIT_{project}$	$3,037,913,473.70
$I = Interest_{initial} + Incremental\ Interest$	$550,000,000.00
$Coverage\ Ratio = \dfrac{EBIT}{Interest}$	5.523
$EPS_{5y} = \dfrac{(EBIT\,5y - I) * (1 - tax\ rate)}{Initial\ Share\ Count}$	$6.55
$Implied\ Market\ Price_{Y5} = EPS_{Y5} * Implied\ PE$	$74.62
Risk Adjustment $= .7096 * e^{\wedge}(-1.45 * Coverage\ Ratio)$	0.0237%
Adjusted Implied Market Price$_{Y5}$ = Implied Market Price$_{Y5}$ * (1 − Risk Adjustment)	$74.60
If Implied Market Price$_{Y5}$ > Conversion Price a conversion event occurs	No conversion
Share Count = Initial Share count + Equity Issuance + Converted shares	300,000,000
E = Share count * Implied Market Price$_{Y5}$	$22,380,000,000
D = Initial debt + Issued debt	$12,500,000,000
Levered Beta $= Unlevered\ Beta * \left(1 + (1 - tax) * \dfrac{D}{E}\right)$	1.560737202
Cost of Equity $= R_f + ERP * Firm\ Beta$	10.30%
$FV = \dfrac{EPS}{(CoE - long\ term\ growth\ rate)} - Accumulated\ Interest$	$78.26
$PV = FV / (1 + CoE)^t$	$47.94

Source: Advent Capital Management.

15.6 CASE STUDY: DELTA AIRLINES AND SOUTHWEST AIRLINES

A combination of travel restrictions and consumer fear linked to COVID-19 pandemic outbreak caused airline revenue to fall as far as 95% in April 2020. Both Delta and Southwest turned to the capital markets for funding. But the two companies took different approaches to structure their capital raises. Delta decided to issue a $3.5 billion HY bond, whereas Southwest issued $2 billion of equity and $2 billion in convertible debt. Both our capital optimization models identified the size of the initial revenue decline and the pace of recovery as the key variables in determining the most efficient method of raising new funds for the two companies. These assumptions suggest that the different decisions of the two airlines reflect different levels of confidence in the strength and speed of a recovery.

Using the earnings-based optimization model, we designed three separate scenarios for each airline, with each scenario representing a different path to recovery over the next five years. The first scenario assumes a V-shaped recovery with both firms returning to a 2019 level of operating earnings by 2022. From that point, we assumed that each would enjoy a comfortable level of earnings. The second scenario involves a slow recovery that sees Southwest and Delta not returning to 2019 levels of profitability until 2024. The third scenario envisions permanent impairment as a combination of new regulations and reduced demand keep 2024 operating earnings more than 15% below the prepandemic level of 2019.

Tables 15.3 and 15.4 show the projected share prices in 2024 under our model using the final deal terms and share prices. A call spread is assumed

Table 15.3 Southwest Airlines Recovery Scenarios

	SCENARIO 1 - V Recovery	SCENARIO 2 - Slow Recovery	SCENARIO 3 - Long-Term Impairment
Bond	**$53.22**	$43.88	$34.02
Convertible	$46.03	$38.40	**$37.18**
Convert with Call Spread	$46.88	**$46.94**	$37.08
Stock	$43.18	$36.13	$28.69

Source: Advent Capital Management.

Table 15.4 Delta Airlines Recovery Scenarios

	SCENARIO 1 - V Recovery	SCENARIO 2 - Slow Recovery	SCENARIO 3 - Long-Term Impairment
Bond	$62.37	$53.76	$42.94
Convertible	$54.80	$46.68	$37.50
Convertible with Call Spread	$55.68	$47.34	$44.09
Stock	$51.50	$44.64	$36.01

Source: Advent Capital Management.

to cost 10% of a convertible's proceeds and to effectively add an additional 30 percentage points to the conversion premium.

Our models show the role that recovery assumptions play when determining optimal funding options. Convertibles are especially cost effective for the issuer if the convertible feature is not triggered. Hence, the issuance of convertibles mitigates the damage done if the optimistic scenario fails to materialize. Our results also seem to support the actual decisions made by the management teams of the two companies. For Southwest, convertibles are the strongest option in both the worst-case and slow-recover scenarios. Issuing a bond only outperforms in the most optimistic scenario. In contrast, Delta's choice to issue a bond (despite incurring higher interest rates than Southwest) is also supported by our model. A bond remains the top choice for Delta in all but the worst-case scenario.

The difference between the two airlines likely reflects the severity of Delta's decline relative to Southwest. Delta does far more international business than Southwest and also was more heavily leveraged heading into the crisis, with roughly six times the liabilities of Southwest. Delta's credit was downgraded below investment grade in March 2020, which contributed to a sharper decline in its share price. Hence, assuming that the same conversion premium on a hypothetical convertible offering will lead to a lower strike price relative to its pre-crisis highs, it takes a smaller recovery to trigger a conversion event.

Yet, the model cannot recognize the hidden costs associated with the loss of financial flexibility that comes from issuing straight debt. Delta's situation was exacerbated by past decisions to issue debt. Southwest's use of both equity and convertible financing leaves its balance sheet less encumbered than if it had issued traditional bonds. Given Southwest's history of less aggressive capital policy prior to the pandemic, it's not surprising that management chose the conservative route of using equity and convertible debt for its capital raise.

15.7 BROADER MODEL RESULTS

In order to better understand the factors that determine the capital optimization process, it is helpful to use a broader array of potential inputs into the model and see the effects. We will use the same hypothetical semiconductor company from Section 15.5, but instead of assuming a 10% average growth rate and $60 share price, we will adjust these metrics and see the effects on the relative attractiveness of financing the project through a traditional bond with a 5% coupon, a stock offering, or a convertible bond with a 2% coupon and a 35% premium. Tables 15.5 and 15.6 show the different average present values that result from the different capital raises.

When we change the expected growth rate in aggregate, the magnitude of growth realized in any individual iteration within the model can vary from the expected quite sharply. But the average of all the realized growth rates will be the same as the expected growth rate. From these results we can see how important long-term earnings growth is when evaluating different financing options. Table 15.6 shows that the convertible financing option is anywhere from 3.78 percentage points worse to 2.81 percentage points better than a straight bond issuance depending on growth expectations (assuming an initial share price of $60). Projected earnings growth is important because, in the absence of a change in earnings multiple, future earnings determine future share prices, which, in turn, determines whether conversion occurs. When the expected growth rate is set to 2%, a conversion event only occurs in 5% of the iterations, assuming that all other assumptions are unchanged. Convertibles are very cost-effective compared with straight bonds when conversion probability is low because an unconverted convertible bond is functionally equivalent to a non-convertible bond with a lower coupon. Convertibles also benefit from higher initial share prices because the conversion price is based on

Table 15.5 Relative Value of Convertible Versus Stock Issuance

Initial share price	Growth rate								
	2%	4%	6%	8%	10%	12%	14%	16%	18%
50	-3.84%	-1.67%	-0.11%	0.82%	1.38%	1.72%	1.96%	2.14%	2.29%
55	-3.59%	-1.59%	-0.16%	0.70%	1.22%	1.54%	1.77%	1.93%	2.07%
60	-3.38%	-1.54%	-0.21%	0.59%	1.08%	1.38%	1.60%	1.75%	1.88%
65	-3.22%	-1.50%	-0.25%	0.50%	0.96%	1.24%	1.44%	1.59%	1.72%
70	-3.08%	-1.46%	-0.30%	0.41%	0.84%	1.11%	1.31%	1.45%	1.57%
75	-2.97%	-1.44%	-0.34%	0.33%	0.74%	1.00%	1.18%	1.32%	1.44%

Source: Advent Capital Management.

Table 15.6 Relative Value of Convertible Versus Traditional Straight Bond

Initial share price	Growth rate								
	2%	4%	6%	8%	10%	12%	14%	16%	18%
50	2.56%	3.11%	3.29%	2.88%	2.01%	0.74%	-0.82%	-2.65%	-4.71%
55	2.68%	3.20%	3.35%	2.94%	2.10%	0.90%	-0.57%	-2.31%	-4.24%
60	2.81%	3.28%	3.41%	3.02%	2.21%	1.06%	-0.33%	-1.97%	-3.78%
65	2.94%	3.37%	3.48%	3.10%	2.33%	1.23%	-0.09%	-1.64%	-3.36%
70	3.05%	3.46%	3.56%	3.18%	2.44%	1.39%	0.13%	-1.34%	-2.96%
75	3.16%	3.55%	3.63%	3.27%	2.56%	1.55%	0.35%	-1.05%	-2.59%

Source: Advent Capital Management.

a premium over the share price at issuance of the convertible. A higher conversion price decreases the chance of a conversion event occurring.

Beyond the probability of conversion, the *cost* of equity dilution is a function of the price at which the new equity is issued and how well the stock performs during the life of the convertible. When earnings growth is high and the stock does well, the effective cost of dilution increases. When the company does poorly, equity issuance becomes advantageous first because the firm is issuing overvalued shares and second because the firm risks becoming overleveraged as the value of its equity shrinks relative to its existing debt load (spiking its cost of capital in the process). Table 15.5 shows that convertibles are more cost-effective than equity issuance when growth is high and less cost-effective when growth is low. The relative advantage of convertibles over equity issuance in high-growth cases persists even when the probability of conversion approaches 100% because of the conversion premium. It's always better to issue shares at $72 than at $60 after all.

Beyond earnings growth, another important determinant of financing optimization is the volatility of the underlying business, as shown in Table 15.7.

Assuming a constant coupon and conversion premium, convertibles are more cost-effective when earnings volatility is low (or declines after issuance) than when earnings volatility is high (or increases after issuance). This makes sense given the structure of convertible bonds. We project share price as a function of projected earnings, so volatility of earnings feeds directly into stock volatility. From the perspective of an investor, buying a convertible is comparable to buying a bond plus a call option on the underlying shares. Therefore, the firm can be seen as *writing* a call option on its own stock. Options gain value as stock price volatility rises, which increases the cost of the firm's *short* option position,

Table 15.7 Volatility of the Underlying Business

Volatility of Earnings	12.00%	16.00%	20.00%	24.00%	28.00%	40.00%
Convertible vs. Stock	1.32%	1.22%	1.08%	0.93%	0.78%	0.61%
Convertible vs. Bond	1.88%	1.72%	1.51%	1.28%	1.02%	0.38%

Source: Advent Capital Management estimates.

reducing the attractiveness of a convertible issuance. A more volatile firm should be able to get better terms on a convertible issue to compensate the issuer for the higher option value. This means a higher conversion premium or lower coupon.

Another way to understand the relationship between convertible issuance and volatility is to consider what happens in extreme outcomes. If earnings quadruple over the course of five years, the share price will soar, and a bond issuance will have strongly outperformed equity or a convertible as the cost associated with dilution becomes prohibitive. In contrast, if earnings collapse 50%, an equity issuance (or mandatory convertible) retroactively turns out to have been optimal. These extreme outcomes become less likely when earnings volatility decreases, which increases the relative attractiveness of convertibles from the perspective of the issuer.

15.8 CONCLUSION

Our models conclude that while a convertible bond issue is not always the best choice for raising capital, it is almost never the worst choice. Convertibles constitute a middle ground between equity and traditional bonds, and convertibles limit the cost if the issuer overestimates growth in its projections. COVID-19 demonstrated that left tail risk to earnings is exogenous and significant. Funding with convertibles is supportive of EPS when growth turns out to be less than expected.

ENDNOTES

1. F. Modigliani and M. Miller, "The Cost of Capital, Corporation Finance and the Theory of Investment," *American Economic Review* 1958;48(3):261–297.

2. F. Modigliani and M. Miller, "Corporate Income Taxes and the Cost of Capital: A Correction," *American Economic Review* 1963;53(3):433.

3. https://www.guggenheiminvestments.com/perspectives/sector-views/q1-2018-high-yield-and-bank-loan-outlook.

4. Michael Brennan and Eduardo S. Schwartz, "Corporate Income Taxes, Valuation, and the Problem of Optimal Capital Structure," *Journal of Business* 1978;51(1):103–114.

5. John R. Ezzell and R. Burr Porter, "Flotation Costs and the Weighted Average Cost of Capital," *Journal of Financial and Quantitative Analysis,* Vol. 11, No. 3 (Sept. 1976), pp. 403–413, Cambridge University Press.

CHAPTER 16

Convertible Accounting, Taxation, Regulation, ESG Standards, and Execution

Managers thinking about accounting issues should never forget one of Abraham Lincoln's favorite riddles: "How many legs does a dog have if you call its tail a leg?" The answer: "Four, because calling a tail a leg does not make it a leg."

—Warren Buffett[1]

16.1 CONVERTIBLE ACCOUNTING AND TAXATION PERSPECTIVE

Neither accounting nor taxation affects the inherent positive asymmetry of convertibles. Accounting is the *language* that explains (or disguises) the fundamentals of companies. Because American companies are the largest issuers of convertibles globally and American investors dominate investing in convertibles, our focus is on US accounting and taxation.

Complications in accounting for convertibles have often arisen because issuers of convertibles seek accounting interpretations that minimize reported dilution. We found accounting background information in "A Roadmap to the Issuer's Accounting for Convertible Debt," by Magnus Orell and Ashley Carpenter, published by Deloitte in April 2019—a comprehensive report that required 247 pages.[2] We also found useful information on convertible accounting in "Demystifying Modern Convertible Notes," a detailed 38-page report from the law firm of Latham & Watkins in August 2019.[3] The prospect of simplified accounting may have been a factor in encouraging both issuers and investors to take advantage of opportunities in the convertible market in 2020, when new issuance in the United States surged to a record high of $116.5 billion according to Refinitiv.

16.2.1 Simpler Accounting

The Financial Accounting Standards Board (FASB) addressed complexities and inconsistencies in convertible accounting in August 2020 via an Accounting Standards Update (ASU 2020-06) that is subtitled, "Accounting for Convertible Instruments and Contracts in an Entity's Own Entity."[4] It is important to be familiar with convertible accounting prior to the new ASU partly because some issuers of convertible securities will retain the old accounting rules for a time and also because the classic "if converted" method of calculating diluted earnings has been restored to ubiquity by the new ASU.

Large public companies must implement the ASU for fiscal years beginning after December 15, 2021, including interim periods. "Smaller reporting companies"[5] and non-public companies must implement ASU 2020-06 for fiscal years including interim periods that begin after December 15, 2023.[6] Early adoption is permitted for fiscal years including interim periods that began after December 15, 2020.[7]

The new ASU essentially eliminates bifurcation (as we further explain in Section 16.2.4) of net-share-settled convertible bonds (i.e., bonds that can settle the principal for cash on conversion). The complexity of bifurcation increases the reporting burden on the issuing companies and has frequently resulted in restatements.[8] For companies outside the United States, international financial reporting standards will continue to require bifurcation. American investors have generally disliked bifurcation, as co-author Barry Nelson confirmed when he served on the User Advisory Council of the FASB in the early 2000s. (Bifurcation as a theoretical concept is essential in quantitatively evaluating convertibles. See Section 8.4.1 for details.)

16.2.2 Earnings Dilution

The historically rewarding total returns from convertible securities suggest that the inherent dilution from issuance of convertibles does not inhibit the performance of convertibles relative to equities. Yet, most public companies seek to minimize reported dilution from convertible securities. Top management bonuses often are based on reported earnings per share, and managers often have incentive stock options that may lose market value if reported earnings are reduced by dilution. Investors also tend to be pleased by avoidance of reported earnings dilution.

We emphasize the appellation *reported* earnings because a convertible security has the same effect on cash flow regardless of how earnings dilution is calculated, and cash flow is the ultimate measure of the value added by a company. Yet, some corporate managers may make different decisions in response to different accounting practices, which may affect cash flow. Issuance of a convertible is potentially dilutive because convertibles give their holders the right to convert into additional newly issued shares of the underlying common stock, and more shares outstanding means reduced earnings per share—assuming no increase in profitability from use of the proceeds of the convertible.

16.2.3 Simply "If Converted"

The simplest calculation of diluted earnings per share for a company with a traditional convertible bond (i.e., a coupon bond issued at par and fully convertible into common shares) is the *if-converted method*—which will apply to most convertibles under the new ASU 2020-06. For purposes of calculating diluted earnings, the if-converted method increases the fully diluted share count by the number of shares that would be issued if the convertible bond were converted. And the if-converted method ignores the interest expense on the convertible bond—as though the bond had been converted at the beginning of the reporting period.

This calculation usually reduces earnings per share, in which case generally accepted accounting principles (GAAP) require disclosure of diluted earnings. For companies with low or no earnings, however, the if-converted method may *raise* earnings or reduce the loss per share because the conversion assumption eliminates the interest on the convertible; in such cases, diluted earnings are prohibited by GAAP.

Over the years, investment banks and issuers have developed accounting interpretations and convertible structures that are intended to prevent or minimize the dilution of reported earnings as well as actually reduce dilution in an economic sense when a company issues a convertible. Such arrangements are generally received enthusiastically by issuers, underwriters, and investors.

16.2.4 Bifurcation Bye

A popular approach for reducing dilution is the issuance of convertible bonds with a *net share settlement* provision, which enables the issuing company to satisfy the principal of the bonds in *cash* on conversion. This method of calculating dilution dates to around 2005. In 2020, 75% of all new Rule 144A (i.e., domestic US) convertibles included net share settlement according to the *Prospect News Convertibles Daily*.[9] Settlement of the principal in cash significantly reduces the number of shares that must be issued on conversion; only the *excess* of the conversion value over par may be satisfied with shares or a combination of shares plus cash.

There are some odd *accounting* consequences of net share settlement, however. Under the pre-ASU GAAP, such convertibles had to be *bifurcated*, that is, accounted for as an original issue discount (OID) bond with an imputed market rate of interest equivalent to that of an otherwise similar non-convertible bond. The non-cash accretion of the resulting OID was added to the cash interest expense of the bond for accounting purposes (although not for tax purposes) to create a higher interest rate that was equivalent to the rate of a non-convertible bond. The balance sheet also was altered because the debt liability of the convertible was reduced to the accreted OID value, and the remaining portion of the face value of the convertible was added to *temporary* equity.

Under ASU 2020-06, if a bond gives the issuing company the *flexibility* to choose between conversion settlement in cash or shares, the calculation of diluted earnings per share for fiscal years beginning after December 15, 2021 (effectively beginning on January 1, 2022) can no longer assume cash settlement of the principal; hence, the dilution calculation *must* assume share settlement under the if-converted method, which increases the fully diluted share count.[10] This change means that the calculation of diluted earnings is the same as if there were no provision for the issuer to elect to settle in cash; that is, diluted earnings per share will be lower than under previous accounting rules that usually assumed cash settlement of the principal value of the bond, which permitted the *treasury method* to calculate the number of fully diluted shares.

The treasury method depends on the stock price because it assumes issuance of only the number of shares that would need to be added to the cash principal on conversion to equal conversion parity; that is, if conversion value were equal to $1,500 per bond, the bond would be converted into $1,000 cash principal plus only $500 worth of shares. The treasury method is still permitted for convertible bonds that *must* settle the principal amount in cash (as opposed to bonds that merely give the issuing company the *flexibility* to choose cash settlement). Without bifurcation, only the cash interest will be recognized, and calculation of fully diluted shares will be minimized by the treasury method. We assume that most new issues of convertible bonds with net share settlement will now *require* cash settlement of the principal on conversion in order to qualify for the treasury method of calculating dilution. A report from BofA Global Research in August 2020 discussed the potential effects on diluted earnings of the treasury method versus the if-converted method.[11]

Because bifurcation will effectively be eliminated, OID imputed interest expense will also be effectively eliminated under the new ASU.[12] Hence, reported interest expense will decrease, and income will increase slightly.[13] These changes may encourage issuance of convertibles by investment-grade companies,[14] which tend to be especially sensitive to the magnitude of interest expense. There will be no effect on cash flow because bifurcation was not used for tax reporting.[15]

In summary, under ASU 2020-06, diluted earnings will be calculated under the if-converted method if the convertible is settled in shares or if the company has the flexibility to settle in shares or cash. The treasury method will remain for bonds that *require* settlement of the principal in cash.

16.2.5 Calculations of Diluted Earnings

Assume that a hypothetical company with flexible settlement has $10 million in net income for the year and 10 million shares outstanding. Earnings per share without dilution would be $1.00. If we assume that the company has a $10 million convertible bond with a 2% coupon and a $10 conversion price (i.e., a conversion ratio of 100), then the diluted GAAP earnings of the company will be $0.927 under the if-converted method. (For simplicity, we have *not* adjusted the interest expense for tax deductibility.)

$$\frac{10+0.2}{10+(10/10)} = \frac{10.2}{11} = 0.927$$

Using the if-converted method, the numerator of the diluted EPS calculation is adjusted to add back the $0.2 million of interest on the convert-
ible that would disappear if the bond were converted, and the denominator
is adjusted to add the additional 1 million shares that would be issued if the
$10 million convertible bond were converted at a conversion price of $10.
If this bond provided that the principal *was required to be settled in cash*,
and the average share price was $11 for purposes of net share settlement,
then the diluted GAAP earnings of the company could be calculated under
the treasury method and would be $0.991—a trivial amount of dilution
relative to the $1.00 earnings per share without adjustment for dilution,
which demonstrates the advantage of cash settlement from the standpoint
of minimizing dilution of earnings.

The numerator is unchanged because the interest expense of the convertible is *not* added back under cash settlement of the principal. The denominator is increased by the excess conversion value (over par) of the
convertible divided by the average share price, which we have assumed to
be $11 for purposes of this example.

$$\frac{10}{10+(1/11)} = \frac{10}{10.09} = 0.991$$

16.2.6 Options Overlays

Most issuers of convertibles nowadays use private options to minimize
dilution—which has economic consequences. Buying options uses cash.
Selling options raises cash. The net cash outlay for creating a call spread
at issuance of a convertible reflects the cash outlay for buying a call option with a strike price equal to the conversion price net of the much lower
cash proceeds from selling an out-of-the-money call with a strike price
perhaps 50% to 100% to 150% above the conversion price. The two calls
effectively synthesize a much higher conversion price and therefore hedge
against dilution unless the bond is converted into common shares at a price
above the strike price of the short call.

The options are privately negotiated with the underwriters at the time
of the offering and may require cash outlays of 10% to 15% to 20% or more
of the face value of the bonds (depending on the magnitude of stock price
appreciation being hedged and the volatility of the stock). The net cash out-

lay for a call spread reduces the proceeds from a newly issued convertible bond but has no up-front effect on reported earnings. In our experience, the cash outlays for setting up a call spread are usually ignored by investors, but the hedge against dilution to the upper strike price is regarded as valuable.

16.3 TAXATION OF CONVERTIBLES

Some structures of convertible securities generate tax deductions. Most mandatory convertible preferreds and all convertible trust preferreds have embedded debt instruments, and the interest on the debt generates tax deductions for the issuing companies while creating equivalent taxable interest income for taxable investors (sometimes including taxable OID *phantom income* that exceeds the cash distributions).

Tax consequences are important for insurance companies that own convertibles in investment accounts (which are taxable—unlike pension accounts that are tax deferred). Aside from insurance investment accounts, few taxable accounts are concerned about the tax implications of individual convertible securities because the tax effects of a single convertible on an entire diversified portfolio are negligible. (And many hedge funds elect to be taxed under IRS Section 475(f) mark-to-market accounting, which lumps all gains and losses together as though they were ordinary income and ordinary losses—thereby eliminating the idiosyncratic tax consequences of individual securities as well as individual trades.)

16.3.1 Tax Consequences for Issuers

US issuers of convertibles often obtain a tax advantage from call spreads. An IRS ruling in 2007 permits tax-integrated call spreads to be treated for tax purposes as a single instrument having OID that reflects the issuer's straight (non-convertible) debt rate. The OID is computed by subtracting the full cash outlay for the lower call (with a strike price at the conversion price) from the proceeds of the bond. The proceeds from the sale of the upper call are not taxed because the transaction is treated as a sale of equity.

For tax purposes, the cash outlay for the lower call is amortized over the life of the bond. There is no reduction in reported income under GAAP. This hedge is particularly attractive to companies that pay significant cash taxes in the United States. The details of this structure are explained in an IRS legal document titled, "Integration of Convertible Notes with Hedges."[16]

Structures of convertible securities occasionally reflect tax considerations. Convertible trust preferreds generate tax-deductible interest expense for issuers, but trust preferreds are no longer issued (partly because of regulatory changes for banking companies). Some mandatory convertibles generate OID that is tax deductible for the issuer as it accretes. Exchangeable convertibles—in which the issuing company issues a convertible that is converted into common shares of another public company that the issuer *already owns*—provide a way to monetize a large minority investment while deferring taxes until the bond is converted. (This is akin to an investor taking a margin loan against appreciated securities, thereby raising cash without incurring capital gains tax.)

A recent nuance that may encourage issuance of convertibles by highly leveraged companies is the cap on deductibility of interest that was introduced as part of the Tax Cuts and Jobs Act (TCJA) of 2017. Under provisions of the TCJA, for tax years beginning in 2018, most businesses could deduct no more than 30% of the sum of business interest income plus 30% of adjusted taxable income (ATI), which approximates earnings before interest, taxes, depreciation, and amortization (EBITDA).[17] (Further details of ATI are beyond the scope of this book; see provisions of Internal Revenue Code Section 163(j).) Under the Coronavirus Aid, Relief and Economic Security Act (CARES Act) of 2020, however, the cap on deductible interest was temporarily raised to 50% of ATI for the two tax years beginning in 2019 and 2020.

The fact that convertible bonds have lower interest rates than nonconvertible bonds would seem to encourage highly levered companies to issue convertibles rather than higher-coupon non-convertible bonds in order to avoid exceeding the cap. Sophisticated tax information is readily available to prospective corporate issuers from the investment banks that underwrite convertible securities.

16.3.2 Tax Consequences for Investors

Many convertible securities are held in tax-deferred pension accounts as well as tax-favored endowments. The tax-deferred nature of pension accounts essentially equalizes the tax consequences of holding different types of convertible securities because it may be presumed that the distributions from tax-deferred retirement accounts (except distributions from Roth accounts) will eventually be fully taxed by the IRS as ordinary income.

Convertible securities are especially attractive for hedge funds because of the upside/downside asymmetry. The tax accounting consequences of the complicated and extremely active trading strategies of hedge funds are daunting, however. And hedge funds are popular with taxable investors. Hence, many hedge funds effectively override various tax consequences by electing to be taxed under Internal Revenue Code Section 475(f), which aggregates all net gains and losses into either ordinary income or ordinary losses based on mark to market at year-end. The simplicity of this tax provision is especially desirable in the context of the large number of trades and the multiple securities—including derivatives—that are characteristic of hedge funds. Section 475(f) reduces auditing fees because it obviates the need for identifying and calculating short- and long-term capital gains, wash sales, qualified dividend income (QDI), and so on. Moreover, simplification of hedge fund accounting reduces the odds that the fund will have to file an amended Form K-1 when auditing errors are discovered—and such amendments usually inspire client resentment by requiring the clients to subsequently file their own amended tax returns.

Although the ordinary income generated by a Section 475(f) election forgoes the reduced taxes on long-term capital gains and QDI, Section 475(f) losses are *ordinary* losses, which can be fully deducted against ordinary income *without limitation*—whereas individual investors face a capital loss limitation of $3,000 per year for purposes of deducting from ordinary income after capital losses have offset capital gains. Most Americans who are wealthy enough to meet the regulatory requirements to invest in hedge funds have significant ordinary income that can be offset by Section 475(f) losses if their hedge funds suffer a down year.

Ownership of traditional convertibles as a substitute for equities has the attraction that conversion into the underlying shares is not a taxable event. When a traditional convertible is converted, the cost basis of the convertible is carried over as the cost basis of the common shares received on conversion, thereby deferring capital gains until the shares are ultimately sold. Moreover, the purchase date of the convertible is used to calculate the holding period in order to qualify for the reduced tax rate on long-term capital gains. Contemporary convertible bonds that are settled for cash on conversion create a taxable event when converted. Conversion of a bond that is settled in shares remains free of tax consequences.

Convertible trades have occasionally been misidentified as *wash sales* by the computer programs of custodian banks in cases where an account sold one convertible (at a loss) and bought another convertible (or the common stock) *of the same issuer* within the wash sale period of 30 days prior to the sale and 30 days after the sale. The IRS wash sale rule is effective if the realized loss is in an account—or a closely related account—that buys a substantially identical security during the wash sale period. Different convertibles of the same issuer rarely run afoul of the substantially identical test in our experience—thanks to material differences in interest coupons, conversion premiums, maturities, and so on— but similar Committee on Uniform Securities Identification Procedures (CUSIP) numbers may confuse some computer programs.

Investors who lack experience in directly investing in to bonds in taxable accounts should be aware that if a bond is purchased at a market discount from par and the bond is eventually sold or redeemed at a higher price than the purchase price up to par value, the IRS treats the gain on the sale as ordinary income—rather than capital gain—unless the taxpayer has elected to recognize the accretion to par annually[18] (an unlikely election, in our view, except in rare instances when an account holder may be motivated to maximize current taxable income). The taxation of bonds purchased in the aftermarket constitutes a hornet's nest of potential tax stings that begs for professional advice and suggests that convertible bonds purchased at discounts should be placed in tax-deferred accounts. The contemporary convertible market has few OID bonds that have the disadvantage to taxable accounts of IRS taxation of imputed interest, that is, *phantom* interest with no associated cash payments.

Mandatory convertibles are essentially a type of preferred. Most mandatory securities nowadays are registered, and a few mandatory securities satisfy IRS QDI and dividends received deduction (DRD) requirements. The taxation of some mandatory preferreds may include phantom income, but again, professional advice may be necessary.

The few traditional (non-mandatory) convertible preferreds that remain typically generate QDI for individual investors (at the same reduced tax rate that applies to long-term capital gains) and qualify for the DRD for corporate holders. The few convertible trust preferreds are essentially subordinated debentures rather than equities and generate tax deductions for the corporate issuers and taxable interest income for investors.

16.3.3 Taxation Bottom Line

Traditional convertible bonds have obvious tax consequences for both issuers and investors. More complicated structures abound, however, and the tax consequences of different types of convertibles sometimes are obscure. Prospectuses are required to provide tax disclosures. Professional advice is often necessary and is always advisable.

16.4 REGULATION AND COMPLIANCE

Convertible securities are subject to the same regulations as other securities.

16.4.1 Hedges and Selling Short

The compliance challenge in hedged convertible strategies that involve being long the convertible and short the underlying stock. Convertible analysts and strategists at investment banks have repeatedly been constrained from recommending convertible hedges because of the seeming compliance contradiction between recommending that clients be both long one obligation and short another obligation *of the same company*.

Convertible hedges involve frequent adjustments to the short positions in the underlying common stocks; hence, money management firms that have strategies that use hedged convertibles must be careful to avoid inadvertently violating SEC Rule 105, which generally prohibits an investor from participating in a registered public secondary offering if the investor has shorted the stock within five business days prior to the pricing of the offering. A practical way to avoid violating Rule 105 is to implement electronic pretrade tests that prevent traders from inadvertently violating Rule 105 and other restrictions.

16.4.2 No Proxy for Convertibles

Institutional accounts that invest exclusively in convertibles are effectively exempt from the challenges of proxy voting because convertible securities cannot vote. In rare instances, of course, in-the-money convertibles (with miniscule conversion premiums) have been converted in order to obtain the underlying common shares and vote. (And some convertible preferreds become eligible to vote if the preferred dividends have been passed.)

16.4.3 Bonds Issued under SEC Rule 144A

Most convertible bonds are issued under SEC Rule 144A, which, technically, are private placements; hence, Rule 144A issues are restricted to QIBs: managers with at least $100 million under management or with other characteristics—some of which were liberalized in August 2020[19]—that satisfy QIB requirements. Rule 144A convertible bonds tend to be large and liquid obligations of mid-cap and larger companies that are actively traded among institutional investors. The expanded definition of QIBs in August 2020 may make the Rule 144A market even more liquid. The fact that Rule 144A issues are restricted securities can create a false impression that such issues are illiquid—which needs to be explained to clients. Smaller companies sometimes issue registered convertible bonds. The popular mandatory convertible preferred issues—which also tend to be obligations of larger companies—are mostly registered.

Rule 144A securities sometimes carry registration rights that permit participation by retail investors after the registration is effective. Rule 144A issues generally become *seasoned* or *free to trade* after six months, which technically permits trading by retail investors. Because of the tighter regulatory environment following the Great Financial Crisis, however, most broker-dealers and custodians have imposed a blanket retail restriction on bonds issued under Rule 144A regardless of seasoning, so few individual investors are able to directly tap this important segment of the convertible market. Hence, individuals typically participate in the convertible market via mutual funds or exchange-traded funds (ETFs).

16.4.4 Bonds Issued under SEC Regulation S

Numerous foreign convertibles are issued abroad under Regulation S, which essentially confines transactions to orders placed outside the United States and/or executed on exchanges outside the United States. Regulation S securities may settle into accounts located in the United States, however.

There are three common types of Regulation S issues: Categories 1, 2, and 3 and US accounts generally are prohibited from trading Category 2 and 3 securities until seasoning 40 days after the initial settlement of the issue. Category 1 securities have sometimes been issued concurrently with a Rule 144A tranche, in which case the Rule 144A tranche is exclusively for US QIB accounts, and the associated Category 1 issue is subject to the same 40-day restriction as a Category 2 or 3 issue. Key sources of online information including Bloomberg did not differentiate between categories as we went to press. Hence, US investors must confirm the category of new Regulation S issues through inquiries with underwriters, details in prospectuses, and so on. Fortunately, more than 80% of new issues of Regulation S convertibles in 2020 were in Category 1, and the percentage of Category 1 issues was rising as we went to press late in 2021.[20] We caution that the preceding discussion of Regulation S is a summary, and it applies only to debt securities—including convertible bonds. There are additional details that should be understood before transacting in securities that were issued under Regulation S.

Few individual investors have the necessary brokerage support to invest in Regulation S securities. Moreover, it has been difficult for US citizens to open (or even maintain) bank accounts in foreign countries since passage of the Foreign Account Tax Compliance Act (FATCA) in 2010 because banks in foreign countries resist the IRS data filings that are required for accounts of US citizens.

16.4.5 Bonds Are Credits

As we never tire of repeating, the primary rationale for investing in convertible securities is to obtain equity-like returns over time with less downside risk and lower volatility than outright investing in common stocks. Yet, convertibles are credit instruments (about 75% of the US convertible market is convertible bonds,[21] and the rest of the market is mandatory preferreds and a small number of traditional convertible preferreds). As credits, convertible securities in institutional accounts are subject to credit restrictions. This situation is confusing when convertibles are included in equity accounts because equity investments rarely, if ever, are subject to credit restrictions, yet equities clearly are *higher* risk than convertibles.

Money management firms must obtain clear credit definitions in the investment management agreements (IMAs) of accounts that utilize convertibles because 65% of US and global convertibles are non-rated (NR),[22] and almost all fixed-income accounts impose credit-rating criteria. Because significant investments in NR convertible bonds are essential in most diversified accounts, the IMAs must include provisions for the managers to assign estimated or implied credit ratings to individual convertible bonds. As convertible securities gain popularity with institutional investors, new account personnel who are unfamiliar with convertibles must be educated on the creditworthiness of convertible bonds (which tend to have low default rates and are inherently less risky than the underlying stocks).

16.5 ENVIRONMENTAL, SOCIAL, GOVERNANCE

Consideration of Environmental (E), Social (S), and Governance (G) factors accelerated in the institutional and retail investing realms into 2021. ESG importance, the sophistication of ESG research, the number of ESG data providers, and the attention paid to ESG by regulators have all increased. Investors who seek companies that satisfy ESG standards should be comfortable investing in convertible securities. The convertible securities market has always been dominated by growth companies that use the latest technologies, and this jibes nicely with the concept of avant-garde companies that intuitively seem more likely to embrace ESG standards.

ESG investing involves using one of more of the three topical areas in order to determine the appropriateness of a company or fund selection. As examples, ESG conscious investors can focus on climate change (emissions or waste) or natural resource sustainability within the environmental category, for social the focus can be on a company's effects on certain communities including workforce remuneration and diversity, and for governance can be on the structure of the board of directors, executive pay and disclosures. But these are hardly the only topics. Investors may also use a multitude of voluntary disclosures made by companies in corporate filings and may also rely on sustainability reports on corporate websites.

Technology is the largest sector in the convertible market, with 35% of US assets and 27% of the ICE BofA Global 300 Convertible Index. Healthcare and financials are each in low double digits.[23] Technology and financial companies should command above-average ESG scores. Healthcare companies have often been criticized, however, as explained in the FIERCE Pharma newsletter of April 15, 2021.[24]

Convertible securities are ideal for funding companies that will be involved in global ESG-friendly initiatives such as alternative energy and electric cars. Tesla is highly rated for ESG on the basis of its products,[25] and the company has funded its growth with multiple convertible bonds.

16.5.1 Green Convertible Bonds

An ESG concept that spread to the American convertible market in 2020 is *green* bonds, a self-declared appellation applied by corporate, supranational, and governmental issuers that is confined to environmental and climate effects[26] (i.e., the "E" in ESG, not necessarily the "S" or the "G"). The first of several green convertible bonds to be issued in the United States was the $200 million Plug Power convertible of 2025, which was issued in May 2020 with excellent terms: a conversion premium of 22.5% and three years of hard call protection followed by two years of 130% soft call protection. Three months after issuance, the bond had soared to more than double par after the stock skyrocketed when the hydrogen fuel cell manufacturer reported a smaller loss than had been estimated by analysts.[27]

Many green bonds have been issued by foreign governmental and non-governmental entities as well as by foreign companies. Europe has been leading in ESG investing through 2021. Green bonds have no clearly-accepted qualification. Many issuers and bankers use a Green Bond Principles (GBP)[28] framework issued by the International Capital Markets Association (ICMA) with a list of recommended pledges and disclosures ranging from use of proceeds to eligible sustainable or green projects to reporting to third-party external reviews that the terms meet the framework.

Green Bonds outstanding were more than $1.2 trillion in 2021.[29] Bloomberg provides a "green-bond tag and . . . related disclosures of issuers."[30]

16.5.2 ESG Performance

There are many uncertainties surrounding ESG. Institutions and individuals without the time or resources to analyze ESG can outsource to third-party ESG ranking services. Some services focus on one niche, such as the environmental work by CDP, the former Carbon Disclosure Project, and Bloomberg on governance with a Disclosure score. All three components of ESG are amalgamated by MSCI, Sustainalytics, and Standard & Poors and other services. The ratings can be traditional grading-style scores with a higher-is-better theme or risk-based (lower-is-better) scores that consider public reputational risks and other industry-specific risks. No two rating systems are the same, and companies and issuers often have differing ratings based on varying criteria or degrees of engagement with personnel at the ranking system. It is worth noting that the performance of strategies that incorporate ESG seems to have been superior, particularly during the market volatility in 2020, when most ESG indices and strategies appear to have outperformed conventional indices and strategies.[31] Funds may choose to apply ESG rankings, whether internal or third-party, as an essential element of the investment selection process or as an adjunct, add-on criterion such as utilizing the rankings as elimination criteria for poorly-scored issuers. With many institutional investors having strong desires to utilize ESG criteria—particularly public employee pensions and retirement plans—some money management firms take input from institutional clients as to criteria to use in evaluating prospective investments or in order to create custom exclusion lists that prevent investment in specific companies or industries. The prospect of continued outperformance from ESG investing suggests that ESG will continue to become a more important factor in investing.

16.5.3 Defining ESG

ESG has rapidly gained popularity since the late teens of the twenty-first century, although the concept is not new, having been coined in 2005 according to *Forbes*.[32] ESG means different things to different investors and to different asset classes. *The Economist* compared ESG scores in December 2019 from the two largest ESG rating agencies—RobecoSAM (acquired by S&P Global in January 2020) and Sustainalytics (acquired by Morningstar in July 2020)—and found low correlations between the ratings of the same companies by the two agencies. Moreover, the publication concluded that "it does not matter what firms are selling, as long as it is done sustainably. Tobacco and alcohol companies feature near the top of many ESG rankings."[33] Morningstar has introduced the Morningstar Sustainability Rating.[34] Research from investment banks has recently included ESG metrics. State Street has introduced a SPDR S&P 500 ESG ETF (ticker EFIV) that "is designed to . . . select S&P 500 firms meeting certain . . . criteria related to environmental, social and governance factors . . . while maintaining similar overall industry group weights as the S&P 500 Index."[35] Institutional money managers are adopting their own ESG standards and various benchmarks. Amid various ESG standards, active management seems advantageous.[36]

16.5.4 ESG Summary

ESG was summarized by a letter to the editor of the *Wall Street Journal* that argued that ESG embodies a "hierarchy of . . . customers and employees before stockholders. . . . A venerable business truth that long precedes . . . ESG investing: Shareholder profits are earned by catering to customers and rewarding employees."[37] The convertible market, with its tilt toward growth and cutting-edge technologies, should be an ideal hunting ground for ESG investors.

16.6 EXECUTION OF CONVERTIBLE TRADES

Convertibles tend to be more liquid than non-convertible corporate bonds because the conversion feature enables hedging that essentially transmits the liquidity of the underlying shares to the convertible. Yet, trading convertible bonds is complicated.

16.6.1 Information is Key

There is no continuous market for corporate bonds, but bond quotes are available on the Bloomberg Professional service, and there is free access to TRACE[38] prices on "eligible"[39] US dollar-denominated convertible bonds at Finra.org.[40] A single basic Bloomberg license is $24,000 a year.[41] Among institutional investors in fixed income, the Bloomberg Professional service is ubiquitous. As of 2021, there were more than 325,000 Bloomberg licenses globally.[42]

Convertible bond trading occurs over the counter (OTC) either by phone or via private online chats. There is potential for online trading to serve retail investors. Online trading of corporate bonds in general has been attempted since at least the 1990s, but it has evolved slowly. Such e-trading may be at an inflection point, as explained by Greenwich Associates in May 2020.[43]

A major challenge for retail investors is the absence of comprehensive information on the convertible market. Since closure of *The Value Line Convertibles Survey* in 2019, there is no longer any inexpensive way for retail investors to screen the convertible market and evaluate individual issues. Individuals may choose mutual funds, ETFs, or professionally managed separate accounts that hold convertibles. Institutional investors often buy licenses for sophisticated online convertible evaluation services provided by Kynex and Monis. The OVCV function on Bloomberg also provides evaluations of convertibles.

Retail investors not only need a Bloomberg license, but they also need relationships with brokers who trade convertibles in order to get quotes sent via Bloomberg. Moreover, they need to establish accounts with *multiple* brokers. Brokers dislike dealing with small trading sizes. Some financial advisors have access to professional convertible management firms, however; such managers are able to obtain good execution for retail clients by pooling orders for multiple accounts.

Institutional trading of convertibles tends to rely on information on Bloomberg. The first step for trading a convertible bond is typically a review of broker-dealers' bid-ask prices. Bloomberg's IMGR/MSG1 tool consolidates various indications of pricing and liquidity into a single report. Bid-ask prices that are published on IMGR/MSG1 always include a reference price per share for the underlying stock, which makes it possible to project changes in the bond price based on its delta. Banks that publish potentially actionable bid-ask quotes on Bloomberg include Bank of America, Barclays, BNP Paribas, Citigroup, Credit Suisse, Deutsche

Bank, Goldman Sachs, Jefferies, JP Morgan, Morgan Stanley, Nomura, UBS, and Wells Fargo.

Once a specific convertible bond is identified, the next step is to phone a knowledgeable broker and offer to buy (or sell) a specific number of bonds at a specific price, usually referencing a price for the underlying stock. Lots of fewer than 500 bonds often require the broker to contact an interdealer broker.[44]

16.6.2 Vernacular of Convertible Trading

We remind beginners that bond prices are quoted in bond points that actually are *percentage* points of par, although the percent sign is never used. That is, a bond trading at par value of $1,000 would be described as trading at 100. A classic joke among retail investors is that when they attempted their first bond trade, they placed orders to buy 10 times as many bonds as they intended because they mistook "100" to mean $100 rather than $1,000.

The most reliable quotes on Bloomberg tend to be found in one-liner messages that include *both* bid and ask prices transmitted in Bloomberg messages. Institutional investors expect that brokers publishing bid-ask prices for convertibles on Bloomberg will be willing to immediately execute *on the wire* at the quoted price for a minimum transaction size of $2.5 million—subject to sudden market fluctuations. We have found the most reliable bid-ask prices are in Bloomberg messages that include a preference for buying or selling and/or an indication of *big* or *small*. Bid-ask prices that include *color*—disclosing that the dealer was actively executing multiple orders for the convertible bond at the time that the bid-ask prices were published—tend to be reliable. A one-liner that includes a *TRADING* indication is often the most attractive and actionable bid-ask at a given moment. It is also positive when a dealer says *Traded*, which indicates that the bank has recently executed at least one order for the bond. ERUN on Bloomberg indicates that the broker-dealer has an *axe* in the bond, that is, a particular interest in buying or selling a given bond, or it is representing a client with such an interest, that is, a *natural* buyer or seller.

Published prices on inventories of bonds—labeled *INV* on *IMGR/ MSG1*—are rarely actionable unless a corresponding indication of size is included. Such prices are essentially *levels*, that is, indications of estimated prices. Prices shown on dealer runs—labeled *RUN* on IMGR/MSG1—that include available size tend to be prices at which the dealer is able to transact immediately.

A broker-dealer who says it *got hit* means that it bought bonds at its bid price; that is, a seller *hit the bid*. When a bond is sold at the ask price, the dealer was *lifted*. When a bond has been sold (presumably from inventory), a broker-dealer may also say *We lost the bonds* (possibly including the price at which the bonds were sold). *Better to buy* suggests that there is an imbalance of buyers relative to sellers of a bond, and *better to sell* suggests the reverse.

Natural is a widely used trading term not confined to bonds. The word *natural* is always followed by *buyer* or *seller*; that is, "We're a natural buyer of XXX" (or a natural seller), which means that the broker-dealer usually has a client who wants to buy (or sell) a specific bond. (In some cases, the dealer itself may have a need to buy or sell because of inventory considerations.) In natural situations, the broker-dealer is likely to be willing to buy or sell additional bonds without adjusting the price. (When a dealer is *not* natural, it presumably wants to earn a profit from its bid-ask spread, that is, *make* its spread; consequently, it will adjust its bid-ask prices after it is hit or lifted in order to maintain a profitable spread.)

Dealers typically provide market close quotes, and the next day these quotes can be adjusted by making delta-neutral assumptions that translate yesterday's closing price into a current bond price based on the latest price of the underlying stock. Delta neutral also has its own vernacular, including *nuking*. (See Chapters 7 and 13 for further details on convertible hedging.)

Market demand for a specific convertible bond may cause *richening* of the convertible price relative to the theoretical delta-neutral value. Conversely, *cheapening* may occur in the face of selling pressure.

A key consideration when attempting a trade is whether to *open up* with the dealer and reveal the amount of the trade and the price desired. The trader may give the dealer a *working order* inside the bid-ask spread. There is no guarantee that such an order will be executed, of course, and institutional investors often prefer quick execution on the wire, which avoids the market risk that occurs while an order is being worked. The dealers, of course, seek to limit their own market risk with delta-neutral hedges in the absence of a natural buyer or seller. A trader should ask what delta the dealer is using. Discount convertibles—often called *busted*—may trade more like non-convertible bonds if the delta is 20 or lower because hedging with the underlying stocks becomes uncertain.

When sizing bond positions, it is essential to remember that quoted bond prices *exclude* the accrued interest that must be paid when the trade settles. For example, a 4% convertible bond will pay 2% *coupons* twice a year. If one buys such a bond just before the coupon payment date, one will have to pay cash of nearly 2 bond points more than the stated price. The exact amount of accrued interest on specific bonds is calculated in online convertible evaluation models.

Details of execution aside, successful trading is an art.

ENDNOTES

1. https://25iq.com/quotations/warren-buffett/.

2. Magnus Orell and Ashley Carpenter, "A Roadmap to the Issuer's Accounting for Convertible Debt," Deloitte, London, April 29, 2019, https://www2.deloitte.com/content/dam/Deloitte/us/Documents/audit/ASC/Roadmaps/us-aers-a-roadmap-to-the-issuers-accounting-for-convertible-debt.pdf.

3. Gregory P. Rodgers and Arash Aminian Baghai, "Demystifying Modern Convertible Notes," Latham & Watkins, LLP, August 13, 2019, p. 13, https://www.lw.com/thoughtLeadership/Demystifying-Modern-Convertible-Notes.

4. https://www.fasb.org/cs/ContentServer?c=Document_C&cid=1176175020049&d=&pagename=FASB%2FDocument_C%2FDocumentPage.

5. https://www.sec.gov/smallbusiness/goingpublic/SRC.

6. https://frv.kpmg.us/reference-library/2020/convertible-debt-asu-2020-06.html.

7. https://www.fasb.org/cs/ContentServer?c=FASBContent_C&cid=1176175008979&d=&pagename=FASB%2FFASBContent_C%2FGeneralContentDisplay.

8. FASB Media Advisory 06-10-2020.

9. Courtesy of Abigail Adams, convertibles reporter, *Prospect News*, New York. Seventy-four percent of new convertibles in the United States in 2020 were issued under Rule 144A, and 26% were registered.

10. PriceWaterhousecoopers, "New Convertible Debt Accounting Guidance," https://www.pwc.com/us/en/services/audit-assurance/accounting-advisory/new-convertible-debt-accounting-guidance.html, p. 4.

11. Michael Youngworth, "CB Accounting Update: No Bifurcation a Win, but EPS Rule a Loss for Small-Caps," BofA Global Research, New York, August 7, 2020.

12. PriceWaterhousecoopers, "New Convertible Debt Accounting Guidance," https://www.pwc.com/us/en/services/audit-assurance/accounting-advisory/new-convertible-debt-accounting-guidance.html, p. 1.

13. *Ibid*.

14. Venu Krishna et al., "The Return of Zeros," Barclays Equity Research, London, March 18, 2021, p. 1.

15. https://www.withum.com/resources/tax-treatment-convertible-debt-and-safes/.

16. Office of Chief Counsel, Internal Revenue Service, Memorandum, "Integration of Convertible Notes with Hedges," IRS, Washington, DC, July 20, 2007, https://www.irs.gov/pub/irs-utl/am2007014.pdf.

17. Will and Emery McDermott, "The CARES Act's Changes to Section 163(j), p. 1, https://www.mwe.com/insights/cares-acts-changes-section-163j-partnership-international-us-state-tax-implications/.

18. James Chen, "Market Discount," Investopedia, August 9, 2020, https://www.investopedia.com/terms/m/market-discount.asp.

19. Cadwalader, Wickersham & Taft, LLP, "SEC Adopts Amendments Designed to Expand Access to Private Investment," August 27, 2020, https://www.cadwalader.com/resources/clients-friends-memos/sec-adopts-rule-amendments-designed-to-expand-access-to-private-investment-opportunities.

20. Based on counts of new Regulation S issues by the London office of Advent Capital Management.

21. Michael Youngworth, "Global Convertibles Primer," BofA Securities, New York, April 6, 2020, p. 28.

22. *Ibid.*, p. 30.

23. *Ibid.*, p. 31.

24. https://www.fiercepharma.com/marketing/esg-rise-pharma-grows-environmental-and-social-efforts-to-meet-new-expectations.

25. https://www.irishtimes.com/business/personal-finance/are-you-sure-you-re-investing-ethically-1.4104613.

26. Bloomberg, "How 'Green' Is Green?," New York, March 24, 2019, p. 1, https://www.bloomberg.com/news/articles/2019-03-24/what-are-green-bonds-and-how-green-is-green-quicktake?sref=vPbgZiuY.

27. "The Prospect News Convertibles Daily Early Update," August 6, 2020, p. 1.

28. https://www.icmagroup.org/News/news-in-brief/green-and-social-bond-principles-2021-edition-issued/; and https://www.icmagroup.org/sustainable-finance/the-principles-guidelines-and-handbooks/green-bond-principles-gbp/.

29. Jose Garcia-Zarate, "What Are Green Bonds?," June 17, 2021, p. 2, Morningstar, Chicago, https://www.morningstar.com/articles/1043249/what-are-green-bonds.

30. Bloomberg, "How 'Green' Is Green?," New York, March 24, 2019, p. 1, https://www.bloomberg.com/news/articles/2019-03-24/what-are-green-bonds-and-how-green-is-green-quicktake?sref=vPbgZiuY.

31. Casey Clark, "Five ESG Implications from COVID-19," Rockefeller Capital Management, New York, May 6, 2020, p. 1, https://www.wealthmanagement.com/etfs/five-esg-implications-covid-19.

32. Georg Kell, "The Remarkable Rise of ESG," July 31, 2018, https://www.forbes.com/sites/georgkell/2018/07/11/the-remarkable-rise-of-esg/.

33. "ESG Investing Poor Scores," *The Economist*, December 7, 2019, p. 67.

34. https://www.morningstar.com/company/esg-investing.

35. "EFIV: SPDR S&P 500 ESG ETF," State Street Global Advisors, Boston, https://www.ssga.com/us/en/individual/etfs/funds/spdr-sp-500-esg-etf-efiv (accessed October 8, 2020).

36. "Special Report: Asset Management," *The Economist*, November 14, 2020, p. 8, https://www.ssga.com/us/en/individual/etfs/funds/spdr-sp-500-esg-etf-efiv.

37. Lawrence A. Cunningham, Letter to the Editor: "What's New About Stakeholder Capitalism?," *Wall Street Journal*, August 15, 2020.

38. https://www.finra.org/investors/learn-to-invest/types-investments/bonds/types-of-bonds/corporate-bonds.

39. https://www.sec.gov/rules/sro/finra/2011/34-64084-ex5.pdf.

40. http://finra-markets.morningstar.com/BondCenter/Results.jsp.

41. https://en.wikipedia.org/wiki/Bloomberg_Terminal.

42. According to Bloomberg Radio advertising, April 2021.

43. https://www.tradeweb.com/newsroom/media-center/in-the-news/crossed-locked-and-loaded-trading-convertible-bonds/.

44. http://www.marketswiki.com/wiki/Interdealer_broker.

INDEX

Page references with *f, t,* and *n* indicate figures, tables, and notes.

Tracy V. Maitland has essentially devoted his entire career to convertible securities since he graduated from Columbia University in 1982. He is the President and Chief Investment Officer of Advent Capital Management, which he founded in 1995. The firm has grown to be one of the largest money management firms that emphasizes convertible securities. Prior to joining Advent, Tracy was a Director in the Convertible Securities Department at Merrill Lynch, where he was instrumental in introducing convertibles as an asset class to major institutional investors worldwide. The extensive investment knowledge that Tracy developed during his 13 years at Merrill Lynch (see Preface) inspired him to found Advent Capital Management. Aside from his leadership of Advent Capital Management, he has served on numerous boards, including the ASPCA, the Columbia College Board of Visitors, Columbia Grammar and Preparatory School (CGPS), Advisory Council for WCS (World Conservation Society), the Apollo Theater, the Managed Funds Association (MFA), and the Studio Museum of Harlem.

F. Barry Nelson, CFA,® has a broad background in investing dating to 1972. He is a Partner of Advent Capital Management, where he served as a portfolio manager for 17 years. He has served as a Senior Advisor to the firm since retirement in 2013. Previously, Barry was twice employed by Value Line, where he rose from analyst trainee to portfolio manager. He was Lead Manager of the Value Line Convertible Fund and the Value Line US Multinational Fund, President and portfolio manager of the Value Line US Government Securities Fund, and Research Director of the Value Line Convertibles Survey. Barry also served as a global equities analyst for seven years at three broker dealers. Prior to his investing roles, Barry served as an editor for *Datamation* and *Business Week*. He earned a BA in psychology from New York University and an MBA in finance from St. John's University.

Daniel G. Partlow has extensive experience in quantitative analysis. He is a Managing Director and the Chief Risk Officer of Advent Capital Management, responsible for overseeing market, credit, and operational risk management. Prior to joining Advent Capital Management in 2011, Daniel served as a Managing Director and the Chief Risk Officer of Stanfield Capital Partners, which focused on leveraged loans, collateralized loan obligations (CLOs), and tranche investment strategies. At Stanfield, he held responsibility for all risk management, quantitative analysis, and performance reporting. Previously, he also worked in risk management at MBIA and American International Group (AIG). He has also advised banks and multinational corporations as a risk management consultant. Daniel is a graduate of the University of Missouri. He earned an MBA in international finance from the Thunderbird Graduate School in 1993, where he taught risk management as a teaching assistant.